PAUPERS & PIG KILLERS

THE DIARY OF
WILLIAM HOLLAND

A Somerset Parson, 1799–1818

Paupers & Pig Killers

The Diary of William Holland

A Somerset Parson, 1799–1818

Edited by Jack Ayres

Alan Sutton Publishing Limited

First published by Alan Sutton Publishing 1984
Published with corrections by Penguin Books 1986
Reprinted by Alan Sutton Publishing Limited 1995

British Library Cataloguing in Publication Data

Holland, William
Paupers and pig killers.
1. Over Stowey (Somerset)—Social life
and customs
I. Title   II. Ayres, Jack
942.3'81   DA690.09

ISBN 0–86299–052–1

Typesetting and origination by
Alan Sutton Publishing Limited.
Printed in Great Britain by
The Guernsey Press Company Limited,
Guernsey, Channel Islands.

Contents

Publishers' Note

Originàl idiosyncracies of spelling and punctuation have been retained in this publication of the diaries. Editorial notes are grouped at the end, being listed by year and date. In some cases where these refer to a specific word or sentence an asterisk appears in the diary entry.

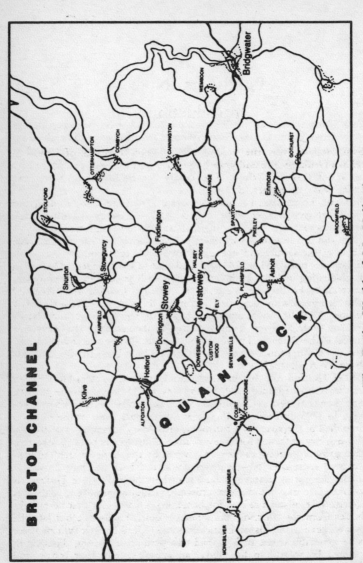

BRISTOL CHANNEL

QUANTOCK

The Daily World of Mr Holland

Introduction

William Holland was the second son of John Holland of Teyrdan, Llaneillian Denbighshire and grandson of Thomas Holland and Mary (nee Kinaston, of Ruyton, Salop). The family can be traced back to John Holland, Duke of Exeter, d. 1446.

The family home passed to his eldest brother John and to John's daughter Mary. A younger brother Jeffrey (1758–1833) was rector of Dolbenmaen with Penmorva from 1782 ('a man of no principle, unfortunate in his marriage and dissolute in his manners') is his brother's summing up. Even members of the family did not escape William's criticism.

William was born 9 May 1746 O.S. and entered Jesus College, Oxford in 1764, graduating in 1768. Following a short spell as curate at Cherington, Worcestershire he became curate of St. Mary's, Reading for Reverend Charles Sturgess who was also rector of St. Luke's, Chelsea. On 3 September 1779 he 'took quiet possession of the Vicarage and Parish Church of Over Stowey, being inducted in the same by the Reverend Nathaniel Blake-Brice Rector of Aisholt . . .' In 1786 he was inducted into the living of Monkton Farley, near Bath and held both livings until his death on 17 April 1819.

In 1792 Holland and his growing family moved to Monkton Farley where they remained until 1798, having Reverend Lewis as curate at Over Stowey. Lewis moved to Cannington when the Hollands returned to Over Stowey. In 1795 during an outbreak of scarlet fever, four of the Holland children died in the space of a fortnight, only Mary surviving, but then in 1797 'when my wife was forty-seven' little William was born. These two children grew up during the period covered by the diaries which Holland commenced soon after they were finally settled back at Over Stowey.

Initially there were ninety notebooks, each numbered by Mr. Holland as it was taken into use, but many are missing, including number 1, so there is no account of Holland's reason for becoming a diarist. At first he bought his books from the 'Bowing Mr. Francis Poole of Stowey', but later he appears to have made his own thicker books. Until his last two or three years he generally seems to have had two periods of writing. First thing after rising he went into his study, an unheated first floor room, and finished the entry for the previous day and started the current day with an

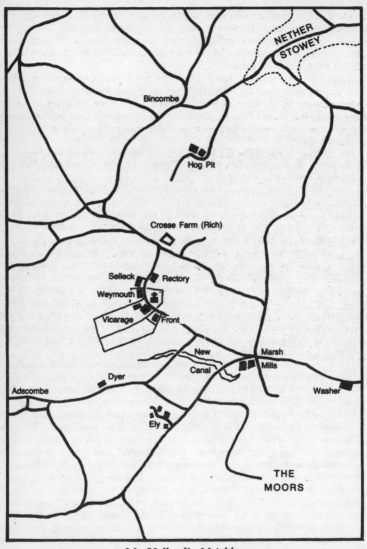

NETHER STOWEY

Bincombe

Hog Pit

Crosse Farm (Rich)

Selleck

Weymouth

Rectory

Vicarage

Front

New Canal

Marsh Mills

Dyer

Adscombe

Washer

Ely

THE MOORS

Mr Holland's Neighbours

account of the weather and state of the barometer and thermometer. The temperature readings in winter often fall to thirty degrees. During the evening he has his second spell of writing and brings the day's records up to date. Towards the end of his life he becomes lax and has to rely on memory for up to a week of entries.

It must be remembered that for much of the period the Napoleonic War was raging and that the French Revolution and the American War of Independence were récent events. Holland was a keen observer of world happenings but most of the purely historical recordings have been omitted. However enough remains to underline his intense patriotism and his loyalty to the monarch.

His writing is generally firm and legible although at times his pens need to be recut. His spelling is phonetic and variable, his punctuation almost completely absent and his use of capitals is random. Even his own parish varies from Over Stowey to OverStowey but is usually Overstowey. The neighbouring village is constant as Asholt, even though all contemporary records use Aisholt, probably he still retained a Welsh Accent. Ely, Ealy, Ealey and even Earley all refer to the present Aley.

His fierce comments on his friends, and others, together with his dislike or hatred of all Democrats, Methodists and Catholics shocked the vicar of Over Stowey at the turn of the century, but then Reverend Gordon Cuming was a friend of the octogenarian Miss Ward whose father appears as the partner of Mr. Tom Poole, the patron of Democrats and friend of Coleridge and Wordsworth. Now after the passage of almost two centuries one does not feel so inhibited but if Mr. Holland and I have rattled a few skeletons which time has pushed to the back of dark cupboards I am truly sorry, while my friend William would, I feel sure, present you with a few jugs of his Strong Beer or prescribe some Rhubarb and Ginger as a tonic.

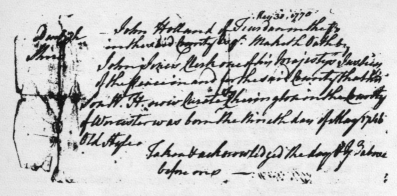

William Holland's Birth Statement

William Holland's Certificate of Birth

May 30 1770

Denbighshire John Holland of Tiurdan in the Parish of Llanellian in the said County, Esqr. maketh Oath before me John Jones Clerk one of his Majesty's Justices of the Peace in and for the said County that his son W.H. now Curate of Cherington in the Country of Worcester was born the Ninth day of May 1746 Old Style.

Taken and acknowledged the day and yr above before me.

This would have been necessary as proof that Holland was now 24 years old and so could be ordained Priest. Not long after this date he moved to St Mary's, Reading.

see it no more for this mean & Farthing
who is Churchwarden mean to entrap
me by some way or other & indeed there
is a diabolical scheme now on foot among
Methodists & the Dissenters to adopt the
Southcotonian scheme to harrass entrap
& to annoy the Clergy of the Established
Church by vexatious prosecutions
about tithes not for the good of Religion
but to gratify their spleen I return'd
after this to Dinner & so My daughter
& I spent the Evening at home they
winnow'd twenty six bushels of Barley to day

Thursday this morning rather doubtful & the Barometer falling Thermome
ter 44 sent dyer to Squire Creyk Heath
Fresh myself & Marrarel & went to
Dinner to the Allens met there the
Poole's of Murton & the Miss Price's
we were very long before Dinner again
& then it came every thing was Cold M[rs]
Allen manages very well & is a genteel
woman but she has got at present a lot
of Potatoe their Somersetshire Servant
that every thing was badly dress'd But
the Provisions were great & they eat
M[rs] Harris M[rs] Allen's mother is a
well bred Maiden Old Lady & talking

A page from the original diary

The Year 1799

Wednesday October 23 Went with my wife to Stowey and she bought a gown of Mr Frank Poole who smiled and bowed graciously. Saw that Democratic hoyden Mrs Coleridge* who looked so like a friskey girl or something worse that I was not surprised that a Democratic Libertine should choose her for a wife. The husband gone to London suddenly, no one here can tell why. Met the patron of democrats, Mr Thos Poole who smiled and chatted a little. He was on his gray mare, Satan himself cannot be more false and hypocritical. Called on the Overstowey Pooles – sad, solemn with many a sigh. Poor Nat I fear is dying but I would not ask questions, it only teases them.

Thursday October 24 My little boy cross this morning, wanted his breakfast. Margaret at her Musick. Tis almost nine and I must go and see what they are about downstairs and in the yard. Wm Frost brought me money from Bridgewater for my barley, a shrewd fellow and very proper to be employed in matters of this nature.

Friday October 25 This is my Wedding Day when we are to have something better than ordinary for dinner. We were married eighteen years to this day. The news from the Army under the Duke of York makes me sick, he has disgraced the Brtitish Arms.*

Saturday October 26 I hope to finish carrying the Tithe barley this day. I never remember such a year before. Barley sells for six shillings a bushell. Old May from Quantock House called and astonished me with the recovery of his wife. Her leg is perfectly well and the carbuncles over her body dried up. I gave him two more bottles of strong beer to strengthen her and told him that it would be right for her to come to Church to return thanks as soon as she was able.

Sunday October 27 I see no one moving about the Sunday School though it is almost nine o'clock. Only one newspaper, the Bath one not come, I do not understand this. At Church none of the Methodists. They are a little shy since I gave them a trimming Sermon about three weeks ago but it matters not for the rest of the Parish are well pleased. These gentry must be looked after for I fear that Democratic Orators are got amongst them for they are become now very disloyal.

Monday October 28   A great bustle – Wm Frost and Mr Amen* carrying apples to the cart for cyder. They are taken down to Hewlett's to be made through his hair cloths which is not the fashion of this county. Mr Amen thinks it is impossible for the cyder to be good as it is not made after the fashion of the county. I tell him he is a blockhead and that he knows nothing of the matter. 'Why Sir, I have made hundreds of hogsheads of cyder in my time.' 'Silence you Ass.'

Tuesday October 29   Mr Amen gone again to press out the water cyder. He was very desirous of having Robert to assist him for Frost does not come today but I would not permit it. Great wages and little work seems to be the general system of this place. The Somersetshire people are of a large size and strong but in my opinion very slow and lazy and discontented and humoursome and very much given to eating and drinking.

Wednesday October 30   Mr Frost and the Clerk gone to Hurley's to grind another hogshead of cyder. They will now have their favourite reed instead of the hair bags but things will not be better done. The French papers make much noise about the return of Bunoparte.

Thursday October 31   Mr Amen today about the water cyder. They were a little displeased yesterday that I did not permit my man Robert to idle away his time waiting on them. When I pay people well I expect some work, but the universal system in these parts is a great pay and little work. Mr Hurley is to send me a bag of red potatoes. Tho' an Anabaptist I do not dislike the man for he seems to be a fair dealer. I wish all Sectarians were like him for in general I have found them full of malice, ignorant, narrow minded and void of either candour or charity.

Friday November 1   The Clerk in the yard wheeling dung and Robert looking about him and moving like a snail. The Clerk cleared the liney and fetched three bushells more of pease for the sow. One of the Miss Chesters died yesterday, quite young, not ill above ten days. Poor girl her state of probation was soon over.

Saturday November 2   We had last night one of the greatest winds I remember. It rocked the house like a cradle and now in the morning it continues high. Alas the Fleet of Transports returning from Holland. Tho' engaged in the cause of God and Religion yet the very Elements seem to fight against us and to favour the French Atheists. Mr Frank Poole called on me and bowed and smiled and asked me whether I could undertake the Service of Aisholt Church as Mr Reeks has become absolutely incapable of performing the Duty. After some hesitation I agreed. Having wound up the clock I must go to bed.

Sunday November 3 I was up a little earlier than usual as I am preparing myself to go to serve Aisholt. Neither the Clerk or Ben Hunt have made their appearance at the Sunday School. I am afraid I must make use of spectacles for the Service as well as for preaching for I lost my verse in the Psalms and made a long pause to recover it at Aisholt which was owing to the unsteadyness of my sight without spectacles. Poor Reeks seems wonderfully bloated. We had a full Church here in the afternoon.

Monday November 4 I received another letter from the Duke of Somerset with another profile. The last he confesses was the head of a person I had given an opinion on before. I did not perceive this and yet he tells me that I have spoken of both profiles in the same terms. He endeavours to puzzle me as much as he can but I have had as yet the good fortune to come off with credit.

Tuesday November 5 Begins to rain again, a most horrible day, nothing but water to be seen beyond Bridgewater. Mr Woodhouse of Stowey has above forty acres of barley out.

Wednesday November 6 Rained hard last night and water everywhere. What will become of the Poor I know not, even barley above six shillings per bushell. Little Lewis the Apothecary came to me, rubbing his hands and moving his retreating chin in and out of his stock – attentive but rather avaricious, mean and trifling. Nathaniel Poole died last night, it was a consumption.

Thursday November 7 Still more rain, where will it end? The Poor, the Poor, how are they to live this winter? we must do all we can to assist and Providence will do the rest.

Friday November 8 Rain last night. The whole country looks so full of water that every little adds to the inundation.

Saturday November 9 Mr Robert has been wearing my spurs – now I have found out the method to get his horse on. Tis a difficult thing to get a servant worth anything. His slowness and laziness and want of method puts me out of patience. When the year is out he must go. Sent to the Pooles, very low, Nathaniel is not to be buried till next week at Cannington.

Sunday November 10 None of the Pooles at Church, poor Nathaniel is not buried. Went to Aisholt in the afternoon, found Ricks calm and composed but wonderfully bloated. I counted ten of my own Parishioners there. The farmers complained that they could not sow wheat.

Monday November 11 Rain last night too and the morning not very promising, tis surely dreadful weather. Briffet is here to kill the sow. A horrible looking fellow, his very countenance is sufficient to kill anything, a large hulky fellow, a face absolutely furrowed with the small pox (a very uncommon thing in these days of innoculations) two ferret eyes and a little turned up nose with a mouth as wide as a barn door and lips as thick and projecting they look like two rollers of raw beef bolstered up to guard against, as it were, the approach to his nasty ragged rotten teeth. However he is a good pig killer.

Tuesday November 12 Mr Amen in the barn and that horrible faced man Briffet is come to cut up the sow. I must now finish my letter to the Duke of Somerset to send it off by Briffet who is likewise a Postman as well as hogkiller. Mr. Barbay* dined here as usual and being busy with our pig we presented the Old Man with a few griskins.

Wednesday November 13 Mr Nathaniel Poole was this day carried to Cannington to be buried. He was born and lived and died in Overstowey Parish and I was pleased with the young man and he seemingly with me yet he was carried out of the Parish without the least notice or mark of respect paid to me, his legal and proper minister – twas unhandsome and unprovoked – a concealed dislike discovers itself. If so it originates in jealousy and envy. I love an open character, I hate a silent underhand man. Robert worked hard and well today, I hope he is going to turn a new leaf.

Thursday November 14 I hear my little Boy's merry feet padding along. Margaret at her Musick, Miss Dodwell* in bed and the Clerk in the barn. I am wrong in my conjectures about the Pooles for this morning a person brought me a very handsome sattin hatband and scarf, white, and two pairs of gloves, one for my wife as well as one for myself. – I expected a hatband but not a scarf and it is not the value of either I regard so much as the intimation of respect it conveys. Any neglect therefore on that head I should have considered as I have before intimated to be a mark of dislike or ill will which I am not conscious of having given cause for. I rode to Cannington this day and settled matters with Mr Lewis about his daughters' coming here next Tuesday to keep Margaret's Birthday.

Friday November 15 Briffet brought the newspaper and told me that he was going to Taunton and would bring me anything. I gave him a cloth for fish if reasonable. My wife and I called on Mrs Poole and family, they seem generally low to the loss of poor Nathaniel.

Sunday November 17 Went to Aisholt, not many besides Farmer Morle and family. Returned to my own Church which was tolerably full and a great appearance there of hatbands and all white, and my own sattin scarf white also (for poor Nathaniel) looked quite conspicuous. He was much loved I could perceive by the countenance of everyone. At Aisholt I said a good deal of Morality but here it was the third part of the explanation of the Parable of Pounds. The Family of Pooles not at Church. I prayed at both Churches this day for fair weather.

Monday November 18 Rich of Halsey Cross called here this morning and with wonderful civility offered me his Tithe potatoes in any way I thought proper. I have often observed and lay it down as a maxim that (among the lower orders of people) they who are very civil can be very much otherwise, and will be so if you are not cautious to disoblige them. This observation is verified in this man. He is a wonderfully fair speaker in general yet as full of tricks and as full of contention and impertinence if you cross his interest as a man can be. At one time he would pay me my Tithe by throwing out the tenth potatoe, which I refused and obliged him to pay his Tithe properly. At this time I had given it out before that I was aware that he was a litigious man and therefore was determined on the first provocation on his side to go to the Exchequer at once. This threat I suppose has come round and his abundant civility are the effects. Walls and Hedges have ears.

Tuesday November 19 The sun shines bright, quick and healthy. My family are all up. Miss Dodwell made a present t'other day to poor Betty Pierce of the Workhouse of a new stiff Petticoat and a new pair of stockings which the poor creature was very thankful for. She says she will go down on her knees to Madam to tell her that she will never wear it but on Sundays as long as a rag of it remains. The two Miss Lewises came here from Stowey to be present tomorrow to keep my daughter's Birthday.

Wednesday November 20 The young ones had a dance in the afternoon, minuets first and then the Steps and a Reel and I myself sung for them. Margaret dances a very good Minuet indeed. Miss Dodwell a most excellent dancer, so neat and nimble in her steps. Miss Lewis sung and played on the Harpsichord very prettily. Edward Selleck and his wife Esther supped here and they and the servants staid at the door to look on. Esther nursed Margaret and was delighted with the exhibition. The servants had a treat of rum and water in the kitchen. The youngsters were in good spirits, danced themselves quite fatigued and were glad at last to go to bed. Little William was not a little pleased with the sight, sometimes nothing can keep him from taking a turn with them.

Thursday November 21   A great Revolution once more in France, that rascal Beunoparte is returned from Egypt having stolen away from the Army and left 'em to Old Nick. Met two Miss Rolins from Stowgursey. They were dressed very smart yet trudging along in the dirty road with a servant maid attending. I never think young ladies appear to advantage along a dirty highroad and I would advise all ladies when obliged to pass thro' dirt not to draw their petticoats too high behind for I can assure them that they discover in so doing more than is to their advantage. The female leg never looks so well behind as before.

Friday November 22   Carried the newspaper to Mr Woodhouse. By and by came his Cara Espousa to call her beloved to dinner. Being not much endowed with Beauty she lived to the utmost extent of Old Maidenhood but at last laid hold of an Old Tuff Widower and thinks the Married State the happiest of all others.

Sunday November 24   I was not able to go to the Sunday School this day. A large Congregation at Aisholt. No Service at Stowey in the morning Mr Bradley* being suddenly taken ill, neither at Cannington for Mr Poole of Shurston sprained his leg. Reeks has been riotous and out of order last night.

Thursday November 28   Sent off a letter to Wm Tutton my Clerk at Monkton Farley and an old servant. He is to receive some Compositions for me on January First next. Had the new hogshead home by my cart. The Old Cooper a curious old man, hard of hearing and very deliberate of speech. He was in France at the destruction of the Bastille. Is a very good workman but they say both he and his wife drink and sometimes quarrel. Wheat sowing goes well I fancy.

Saturday November 30   I saw a boy lately apprenticed to Farmer White with his basket in his hand talking to another for a very long time. Indeed this is generally the way with apprentices, it seldom answers to take them for they scarce ever turn out well. At first they are great trouble and expense and when they come to earn anything they grudge their labour. The seeds of corruption and vice are generally sown before they leave their wicked parents, the Farmers have a bad foundation to work on. Met Mr Mackay and his invariable companion Mr Everett Poole with spaniels and two dogs with short tails which he dignifies with the name Greyhounds. Mackey they tell me swells the other's Guts every day with a bottle of good Madiera – Oh, brave – an Old Buck of Sixty and a young buck not thirty. Hum –.

Tuesday December 3 About dusk I put on my thick Bearskin coat and went to my neighbours Mr Riches,* found James in the yard. We went in – desired me to sit down. By and by in came Mr Thomas, who took out his pipe and smoaked, not forgetting to offer me one very civilly. I offered to take off my hat in the house. No, No says Master James, keep your hat on. So we all three sat down with our hats on before a roaring fire drinking brandy and water and talking politicks, another time of coursing and shooting, another time of Methodists and Religion, they are desperate toads. I was in good spirits, told many stories and cracked some jokes which made their sides shake and about nine o'clock returned home. Mr James and Mr Thos Rich are two old batchelors worth sixty or seventy thousand pounds tho' they live like substantial Farmers. Dine at the head of their table with the servants below, a cloth being laid on the upper end with a fowl or duck dressed in a better manner for my masters. They are loved and estimed by the servants. Mr James I believe has never been from home further than Bridgewater or Taunton. Mr Thomas has been a traveller, entered a Volunteer in the Militia and marched as far as Plymouth, for which reason he always comes to Church on Sunday in a tye wig well powdered, and has but lately left off his fine Scarlet Coat, the great and brilliant testimany of his Military Genius.

Thursday December 5 The madman in the Poorhouse outrageous. Farmer Morle's behaviour is absolutely scandalous but I'll make him know his duty e'er long. The man is chained and lies on straw, shocking situation. Alas poor human nature how many afflictions art thou liable to. It rained this evening. Wheat at 14 shillings per bushell and Barley from 6 to 7. We are all on short allowances. What will become of the poor at this rate.

Saturday December 7 Went to the Messrs Riches this evening about the man in the Workhouse, both determined to join in sending him to the Mad House in Bristol be the expence what it will. Says Master James 'Mr Holland I reckon it be a bad business, he is a very bad fellow, there is something more in it than madness.' Mr James thinks, in my opinion, that he is possessed by the Devil or bewitched.

Sunday December 8 A burial this morning but the Coroner first to have a sight of the corpse.* How this comes about or what suspicions there are I cannot tell. Went to Aisholt and found Reeks very bad, indeed quite insensible and little Master Lewis was there. He thinks Reeks cannot hold it. I called a Vestry about the madman, put off till tomorrow four o'clock.

Monday December 9 Were alarmed with an account of the madman in the Workhouse having got loose and threatening everyone around with destruction. We procured two men to sit up with him and secure him from doing mischief till morning. The Clerk and Robert winnowed twelve bushells of barley this morning.

Tuesday December 10 The madman was quiet during the night. I have written to two Phisicians about securing him in a mad house. We have at present made him sufficiently secure. I received a letter from the Duke of Somerset with a capital head to Lavatarise.*

Wednesday December 11 The madman in the Workhouse quiet.

Thursday December 12 The man in the Poorhouse raving. Mr Reeks of Aisholt died last night in the Horrors – A worthless little man and a disgrace to his profession. He killed himself by drinking. Was brought up to trade but did not succeed well in anything being idle and dissolute. Then he entered some Hall in Oxford, was there a few weeks but never wore a Gown all that time. Entered into Holy Orders, married a Miss Brice and had the Living at Aisholt with her even before the Father's death. Then gave himself up entirely to drinking and brought himself to the Grave in the prime of life. He did not want intellect but was very satirical, vulgar and even abusive in his language especially when he had got a little liquor. Mr Frost could not dispose of my barley at Bridgewater.

Saturday December 14 The madman in the Poorhouse silent. Mr Reeks to be buried Wednesday.

Sunday December 15 Two letters from Bristol about the madman in the Workhouse. Went to Aisholt, Mr Frank Poole was there bowing and Mr Blake, both executors of Mr Reeks. Twas late when I got back to this Church and so dark I could scarce do Duty. I called a Vestry and produced a letter from Dr Fox of Bristol relating to this madman. Farmer Morle is to call tomorrow and something is to be done.

Monday December 16 Went to Mr Ruscomb Poole at Marsh Mill to consult about the pauper in the Workhouse. Farmer Morle and Mr Lewis came in the evening and we went to the Poorhouse, examined the man, he had a fit at the time. We do not think him properly insane to be an object for a Madhouse. We shall try some other Methods.

Wednesday December 18 My Little Boy was measured for a suit of jacket and trousers which he is to put on Christmas Day next and to sing God Save the King. Took my dinner in haste and went to Aisholt to bury Mr Reeks. Bearers Mr John Poole, Mr Wm Poole and son, Mr Combs, Mr Lewis, Mr Thomas Poole. Mr Brice the future Rector was there. Lewis the Apothecary has seen the man at the Workhouse.

Saturday December 21 Tis late and so cold I cannot hold my pen. My wife and daughter walked to Plainsfield this morning, called on Mrs Rich a very civil well behaved woman with ten children which she and her husband struggle hard to maintain. Had three snipes for dinner this day, I have not tasted one before this season.

Monday December 23 Butter very scarce and Robert went out to seek some. Though it froze so hard that scarce any creature could stand yet forsooth he took the great horse and against my will too. He will rot with laziness by and by. The poor came for meat and corn this cold weather and against Christmas Season. Some very thankful and some almost saucy. If a man had not some object beyond the Gratitude of his fellow creatures he would never do a Charitable Act as long as he lived. A letter from the Duke of Somerset who compliments me with excelling Lavater in Physiognomy. It seems the Duke corresponds with that gentleman on the subject.

Tuesday December 24 Much harried by the Poor of the Parish who come for Christmas Gifts. Many persons rather in affluence came but this is not right because it takes from those who are real objects. The Lower Classes have no Pride of this kind among them, and the Somersetshire Lower Classes less of this Pride than any other. Tho' they have many good qualities yet I am not clear whether Falseness and Meanness be not the characteristick of the people. My little Boy had his jackett and trowsers on compleat this day for a trial. He cried not a little when taken off for tomorrow when he is to begin his career in them in earnest.

Wednesday December 25 Cold, clear and frosty. Christmas Day, Sacrament Day at my Church. Went to Aisholt in the afternoon, returned to a late dinner by myself on spratts and a fine woodcock. The kitchen was tolerably well lined with my poor neighbours, workmen &cc. Many of them staid till past ten o'clock and sang very melodiously. Sent half a crown to our Church Musicians who had serenaded the Family this cold morning at five o'clock.

The Year 1800

Wednesday January 29 Met Mr Forbes the surgeon going to kill a few patients. His horse has got the grease. Just as I was going to sit down to dinner a note came from Mrs Lewis of Cannington* desiring me to go and bury a corpse at Holford. Twas not a very pleasant request at that time but Mrs Lewis had tried all the Clergymen around and her husband, who was formerly my Curate, is always ready when able to help anyone. I therefore took a glass of wine and mounted my horse defended from the rain and sleet by my thick Beaver. I was there before the corpse was ready.

Thursday January 30 In many parts of the fields I remark very large and deep pits made use of for watering the cattle but that cannot have been the original intention for such pits. They were certainly Marle Pitts. Old Ben Hunt I perceive in the field beyond my Paddock crying 'Jubb along' while the boy is chaunting a somersetshire Recitation to the oxen. Jubb along I suppose is a corruption of Jump along.

Monday February 3 My wife up and gone in haste to bespeak a loaf of sugar as it is on the rise. Mr John Poole called this morning and we had a long talk on the Principles of Physiognomy. He admitted to the truth and certainty of the science but could not entirely admit of my Supposition of the vital principle, or Soul, formed the features according to the inherent energy given it by the Creator. Lavater thinks that the Soul and the Features mutually form each other, which in my opinion is nonsense.

Wednesday February 5 Went up to Mr Amen in the quarry. Found him with two savage kind of men, Old Ware and his son. They were both full of complaints against one Davies who came from Stowey to this Parish and has now informed against several persons for cutting Lord Egmont's wood. This Davies is the greatest Scoundrel and Rascal, pilferer and wood-cutter that comes into any Parish. I smiled at their complaints and said 'Well lads you have nothing to do but look sharp and I'll warrant you he may be caught at the same tricks then show the Scoundrel no Mercy but haul him to the Justice at once.' They vowed to watch him narrowly, nothing like setting a Thief to catch a Thief.

Saturday February 8 Mr Mathew, Rector of Kilve, called this day. He walked over. He seems a quick sensible intelligent gentlemanlike man, somewhat reserved I should suppose on the whole. I walked with him to the Poole's where he paid another visit. He had been, I believe, Mathematical Tutor to Mr John Poole when of Baliol College. Mr Poole is now Fellow of Oriel. I soon left them to carry my letter to Stowey. Returned in haste, spoke to Mr James Rich who seemed right glad that Porter from the Workhouse was gone for a soldier. James shook his head and said 'Master Holland I all the while said his fits were nothing. He is a bad fellow, depend upon it.' After dinner young Farmer Landsey came in saying 'Such a thing happened just now as never happened in all my life before.' 'Whats that?' cried I. 'Why that wench Carter, I caught her stealing potatoes in Charles Sellick's garden. Do ye, if your Honor be so good as to speak to her. She'll mind what you say.' 'Not the least' returned I, 'she is too hardened for me, has been often before a Justice already.' I went but a wench so ignorant, so savage and so stupid what I said could have but little influence. She is continually pilfering and I am afraid employed by others. Something must be done or we shall be overrun with Thieves.

Monday February 10 Hard frosty and clear morning, we all huddled downstairs to the fire. Margaret busy at her musick, the Little Boy busy in opening the cupboard for the sugar for tea. He has been somewhat cross this morning, not very well, I fancy, but calling him a Turkey Man stops his tears. The history of that business is as follows. A foolish fellow from Stowgurcy brought a turkey to sell and because we were not willing to take it at his price he began whimpering and crying and appeared so ridiculous that he has served for a bugbear ever since. Went to Stowey, paid Lewis the Apothecary for some Red Precipitate.

Tuesday February 11 Little news in the paper. The intended Union with the potato headed Irishmen does not go on well. Saw Mr Cruckshanks the elder at the gate. He gave me a receipt for the Paddocks and I gave him one for the Tithe of Quantock. He seems very civil and gets old and a little stupid. People who live full and well get heavy and stupid sooner than Abstemious men. Heard of Mrs Morris's death this day whom we formerly knew by the name of Baker. A young woman and left six children – sad news indeed – mysterious are the dispensations of Providence.

Thursday February 13 This is my Little Boy's Birthday and we are to have the Pooles here to tea and supper and rejoice a little on the occasion. We have reason to rejoice in particular for he was born after our great and sad calamity, the loss of four children within a fortnight, three boys and a girl.* Margaret my eldest was the only one who survived out of five, she had the fever too, a malignant Scarlet Fever. After all this boy was sent to comfort us when we were quite forlorn and had no expectation of any such thing. My wife was forty seven and he was born in the very same month when the others had been taken from me and on the very day when the first, Thomas, sickened.

Saturday February 15 Robert busy making a cucumber frame. This nick nackery business might do very well at leisure hours but I do not much approve his doing it to the neglect of other things, the stable is not over clean neither the bridles and saddles. Robert a sulky false fellow, in every body's interest rather than his Master's. I do not much like him. I settled with Mr Amen for the hedges. His charge was rather high.

Sunday February 16 Went to the Sunday School, most of the children there, no fire the weather so mild. The Church at Overstowey very full. Asholt Church in the afternoon was very full, more so than I remember. Christened a child and Churched a woman. The Parsonage House still looks dreery – they say Mr Blake is to come there.

Monday February 17 William has not been very good this day and was turned out in disgrace, however he returned at last and made his peace. Robert thinks there is too much work for him, I answered that his bloated carcase contradicted what he said. I went into the further Paddock to assist the overworked Robert to beat about the earth.

Friday February 21 Robert went off with the horse to be blooded, I must physick him. Wood the Musick Master again disappointed us. I do not much relish this unless he has the gout for his excuse.

Sunday February 23 The Clerk moving slowly towards the Sunday School. A little child I see is waiting for the halfpenny which I give to the first comer. I am shaved, with a clean shirt ready for my breakfast, the newspaper and Asholt. Did not go to the Sunday School this morning. Farmer Morle tells me how he has been summoned by the Palmers before Mr Barnard and Mr Ackland without real cause. The Law is too lenient to the Poor in this Kingdom. They summon the Overseers before the Magistrates for not complying with the unreasonable demands and tho' they do not always gain their ends yet it teases and harasses the Overseers and takes up their time which is a great hardship. They should be subject to Punishment if their complaints were found to be vexatious and without foundation. The Church was full this evening, some strangers with instruments of various kinds among the Singers. Poor Ben could not make it out this day being in the background with these youngsters. He is old Sternhold and Hopkins for ever in the plain old stile and cannot well comprehend this grunting and tooting.

Tuesday February 25 Old Scoundrel Ware and his son passed by. It is said they are going to burn the greater scoundrel Davies in effigy for informing against them for cutting wood, Lord Egmont's wood. Sing Tantararara Rogues All. Went to Asholt and married a couple, the lady did not appear very small about the waist. Saw a large party go up the Hill to burn Davies in effigy. They paraded first through Stowey and the Scoundrel Davies had the impudence to march before them all the time.

Wednesday February 26 Ash Wednesday and we have Prayers at Overstowey but I fear not at other Churches in the Country – Lukewarm, lukewarm, Religion declines yet I trust it will revive again as French Principles begin to be exploded. Our family, the Pooles, Mr James Rich and his maidservant were the whole congregation for Mr John Poole had no Prayers in his own Church. Dead – dead – Devotion is Dead. Sent Robert to Stowey but he could not get the Physick for my horse. That little insignificant chin-moving apothecary Lewis has nothing in readiness within his shop. One might clap him and all his medical goods in one's pocket and carry them all off without much inconvenience or fatigue.

Saturday March 1 This being the first of March and being a Welshman I must put a leek into my hat. The horse is bad in his heels. Mr John Brice came late to inform me that he wished me to induct him into Asholt Rectory tomorrow. It might easily be done today for now I must go there first and afterwards return to read Prayers at Overstowey. This is not pleasant, but we cannot pass through this life without some unpleasant things, yet I do not relish being hurried about my Duty. He drank tea and is to dine here tomorrow.

Sunday March 2 I was up early and Mr John Brice the Rector of Asholt breakfasted with me and I afterwards walked off to Asholt to put him in possession of the Church. Having inducted him I returned in good time for the Morning Service at my own Church. There was a tolerably full congregation and a vast number of Instrument Players among the Singers. Mr John Brice and Mr Blake dined with me, the latter expects to come to Asholt if Mr John Brice does not reside.

Thursday March 6 This is Bridgewater Fair Day and I see many of my neighbours in best attire moving off. Robert carried some stones from the Paddock to the road before the house. While I was standing by him he asked me if he was to go on for another year. I answered that I feared the work would be too hard for him and bring him down too much. He smiled and said he could do the work well enough. You can so if you so please returned I. It is to no purpose to change unless one can be assured to meeting with a better and if faults be not too glaring and of a bad nature we must overlook some few and he certainly has been very assiduous of late to please me. The night very keen, what will become of my cabbage plants I know not, they were two shillings per hundred at Bridgewater. Wheat is now 15 shillings per bushell, scarce any of the poor eat wheaten bread now. Hurley says that horses must not eat oats now, they want them for the poor.

Friday March 7   Mr John Poole shewed me the books of the Reading Society for the ensueing year. they are very judiciously chosen, the dinner is to be next Monday.

Saturday March 8   Master Webber past by just now, the Methodist, on a full trot for his zeal could not keep him warm. I believe his zeal has been not a little profitable to him, for by encouraging those good people to assemble at his house he gets rid of various articles in the shop, particularly breadcakes &cc. a cunning fellow. Brice of Porlock* called here this day and I went over to Asholt with him to induct him a second time into the Living, because the first was on a Sunday and therefore not valid. My wife received a letter from Mrs Benwell this day informing of the death of Mrs Taylor the wife of Dr Taylor of Reading. I remember her, a fine woman, always cheerful and liberal minded. She made a good wife and mother, was the widow of Dr Lyne when Dr Taylor married her.

Sunday March 9   Mr John Brice called before he went to Asholt to read in. returned here to dinner and is to sleep at Mrs Poole's. Went into the Sunday School, the children flocked into the fireplace in a disorderly manner which I objected to and desired the masters to keep good order otherwise it would not answer. The Church tolerably full considering the weather, the ground is covered with snow some inches deep. Read the Proclamation for a General Fast next Wednesday.

Monday March 10   A perfect thaw. Margaret at her Musick. I hear nothing of the Musick Master who is in Durance Vile still, I fear. I shall after breakfast send Robert down with some Club Books to the Globe, the Members are to dine there today and to sell by auction the books in reading to this time. i.e. the books of one year. Dined at Stowey, all Members of the Book Club there except Mr Davies. Mr Ackland full of wit and mirth, but at bottom he is a proud fellow, there is an insolence in his civilities. We all parted in good humour and supper at the young Widow Poole's Sung a song in high spirits and my wife and I returned home about one o'clock. Margaret staid this night at Mrs Richard Poole's.

Tuesday March 11   Raking does not agree with me! I drank very little yet sitting up late gave me rather an unpleasant feeling this morning.

Wednesday March 12   I went thro' the very long Service of this day and preached twice. In the morning at Overstowey. Then I went to Asholt and found more than I expected. It is the day for general fast on account of the War. At Asholt I had a child to Christen and a Woman to Church. I thought a Fast day not very proper for a Christening and observed as much, it being to them I supposed a Feast Day. Returned to a late dinner and rather faint with Duty.

Saturday March 15   Walked to Stowey under my umbrella though it rained hard. Margaret went to Miss Penelope Poole for some musick and a little instruction as Mr Wood the Musick Master is not yet out of Limbo.

Saturday March 22   Robert called me down rather early to see the horse's leg dressed. 'Tis a nasty wound quite to the bone. Robert has cleaned it and puts on a precipitate plaster. He wishes me to send for a farrier but I have no opinion of a country farrier, they always pretend a great deal of knowledge and know nothing about the matter. I am generally my own farrier by the aid of Bartlett and generally succeed. At Stowey met Mr Symes the Lawyer. He told me that Mrs Parrot had bought off her prosecutor. Alas, alas that money should be able to screen a person from Justice in this Kingdom so remarkable for good laws and uncorrupted Judges. She was accused of stealing lace out of a shop in Bath, is a person of considerable fortune and has a poor Jerry Sneak of a husband who adheres to her through all difficulties.

Monday March 24   Mr Amen has been with me and is gone off to invite the Farmers to dine with me on Monday next to pay their Tithe. The horse seems much better, and we shall, I believe bring him round. Weymouth's children have committed great depredations on my new hedges by drawing off the laid sticks. There is wood sufficient on the Hills and yet these wretches prefer damaging the hedges of their neighbours to fetching it. I must call them to account for this.

Tuesday March 25   Went to Stowey for Physick for the horse. Little Lewis, the monkey, could scarcely stand still for a moment while I was talking to him, rigling and jumping about as if he had St Vitus Dance. Sent Robert to fetch the physick, the illness of the horse is a fortunate circumstance for him as it will teach him the use of his limbs.

Thursday March 27   Frost gone on foot to Bridgewater. Old Weymouth our neighbour I called on to see his foot which is much swelled. I think it is the gout. I congratulated him on becoming a gentleman as the gout never attacks any but a gentleman. He shook his head and said he could not be a gentleman without money.

Mr Holland's diary for the rest of March and much of April is missing and when we rejoin the family they are in Bath, combining a holiday and shopping with his need to meet the farmers of Monkton Farley, his other Living, to collect their Tithes.

Thursday April 24   After dinner we all strolled out and as we passed along Bath Street I saw a man at a distance coming to meet us when Lo as he approached nearer we all cried out 'It is Mr Arthur Dodwell' my wife's brother. A very honest good-tempered man beloved by everyone. He came from Salisbury purposely to pay us a visit. He has one of the Churches at Salisbury and the Living of Bishops Canning, near Devizes, and he is Prebendary of Brecknock. We procured him a bed in our house and adjoining us so that we are one compleat party. He knows all the news of the country and tells his stories with great good humour and drolery without giving offence to anyone. My wife's niece staid with us till after supper and then she and her maid marched off to their own lodgings. My wife and daughter moved off soon after to bed and left Arthur and myself to chat a few minutes longer over a bottle of wine and then we likewise ascended towards Bedfordshire.

Saturday April 26   Old Mr Graves* called. He is author of the 'Spiritual Quixote' and several other things. He is a fine old man of eighty five and often walks to Bath from Claverton, a little thin hawk-nosed man, always in haste and on a run, inoffensive and very benevolent. Called at Mr Monkhouse's did not find him at home, his wife seemed a plain chatty woman. The farmers in general did not call today. Mr Cottle of Wick called and paid me, so did the farmer of Rush Mead. Mr Beak did not come tho' in town which I do not much approve of, neither did Mr Thomas Cottle. Their payments are considerable. Mr Farmer, a steward to the Duke of Somerset called. His Grace expected that very day, if so I think I shall see him. My new boot burnt by accident, a bad jobb, but it has been mended since.

Sunday April 27   Up early, a fine day. At nine o'clock the chaise came and my wife, daughter and self entered and drove for Monkton Farley. Beak, my tenant at the Rectorial House did not please me much by not calling yesterday and I had some thoughts of passing by him to the Clerk's house without calling. The Clerk and wife were both my servants and are now thriving industrious people. On second thoughts we got out of the chaise before we reached the village and walked down to the Parsonage thro' Innox, a Glebe field and from the Churchyard entered the Court before the House when Mr Beak came out to meet me. We shook hands and all passed off very well. He is a considerable farmer, a young looking man of sixty two, good tempered, talkative, a little boastful and vain but on the whole regular and a good character. The Old House smiled with joy on having the cobwebs brushed off and the walls so well scrubbed and clean. A glorious family, eleven children, seven sons and four daughters and all grown up, strong healthy, well clad and fit to serve His Majesty. But the most extraordinary person among them all is the Mother of this fine family, a jolly fat broad faced comely woman she is up at four o'clock in the morning in Summer I suppose and is fully employed all day, very religious, very industrious, very charitable, beloved by her husband, beloved by her children and beloved by all her neighbours. Went to Church from thence and in my Sermon I gave the followers of Methodists who run about with itching ears a Good Dressing. The Church was very damp. We dined at the Clerk's – we brought a loin of veal with us and Sally, our old cook, dressed it. Every one grinned and seemed pleased to see us and the poor seemed very respectful and did not make such dismal complaints of the times as I expected. We returned to Bath in good time through a land of curtesies and bows and greetings.

Tuesday April 29   We lay long in bed. My old acquaintance Mr Link came to cut and dress my hair for the Play. Mr Cottle from Farley came to pay his Tithe. He beat me down five shillings even against his own handwriting. However he dined with me and behaved very well and very civil. Mr Beak is to dine with me today and settle his accounts. We were much entertained at the Play. It was 'God speed the Plow'. The actors all did their parts exceedingly well. There was good morality in it and a proper sense of religion, but it was a mixture of Tragedy and Comedy, I think too much of the first and the Plot was horrible and shocking in itself:– Murder and Incest, repentance and reconcilliation. Eyre if I mistake not will rise to great perfection in acting, Ellison excells in comedy, Mrs Edwin performed her part with great good humour as usual, but for drollery Mr Cherry exceeded all conception. The Entertainment was 'The Babes in the Wood' founded on an old ballad but it is not exactly the same for the poor children are preserved at last which I was glad of and the Uncle killed. We returned late to our lodgings, had some negus and to bed.

Wednesday April 30   Slept till after six and got up a little after seven. Write this diary in my Chamber. After breakfast went about town in search of chairs, found six, very elegant, cheap. He being a workman who supplies great shops where we found them. This is a good method of procuring them because it prevents one profit on them. Called on Rosenburg, had Mr Poole's profile altered, paid for it. Mr Beak dined with me and instead of paying a large sum which I expected produced a counter account which eat it all up. I did not much approve of this and indeed was rather warm on the occasion. Fatigued myself much and so went to bed early.

Thursday May 1 Mrs Manningford remarkably civil on leaving her lodgings. At last we set off, the driver very civil and careful but one of our horses knocked up before we reached Wells. New chairs purchased by me for our best parlour, six in number, packed very neatly in matts rode very neatly behind and I am in hopes safe, a lucky thought this of my wife. Got to Mr Cobley's at Wells rather late but dinner being ready we had not time to brush ourselves up. Went to bed rather fatigued.

Saturday May 3 A fine morning to pursue our journey, apprehensive about our chairs. The Ostler proposed to place them on top of the chaise which I objected to as not having a good appearance – lashed behind. Reached Bridgewater in good time, drove to Mr Ruscomb Poole where we met Mr John Poole returned just from his tour to Oxford, London and Cambridge. We dined all together and set off for Overstowey taking Miss Charlotte Poole with us in the chaise while the two brothers, John and Ruscomb came home in their gig. We dropped Charlotte at Marsh Mill and drove over the Down to our own habitation where everything looked charming. The servants have done their duty in our absence which is a pleasant reflection. We took out the chairs and found them safe notwithstanding the forebodings.

Sunday May 4 Up early. My wife in bed but I have seen the Little Boy who is charming and well. The Church at Overstowey very full, a Vestry, Long list of poor, the isle full of them, times are very hard. I find on our return from Bath that our family has increased considerably, eleven fine duckling and nine chicken.

Monday May 5 A dreadful and uncommon storm of thunder and lightening about five o'clock, the thunder was in one continuous roar for above an hour with vivid flashes of lightening that shook the very windows and the rain came down like a torrent with large hail or rather squares of ice as large as the top of my finger. Three Miss Pooles called lateish and they sat and chatted some time, Margaret exhibited her new Bath dresses. Some argument with Mr John Poole on the nature of thunder and lightening. He asserts that the stroke of lightening sometimes ascends from the ground. I denied this and said it always came from above, from a cloud impregnated with electrical matter, that it always made its way to the earth as a common receiver but was often attracted from its course by some object or other but that finally it always reached the earth as its grand Attractor.

Thursday May 8 Finished my letter to my brother John in Wales and sent it off. My wife still in bed with her leg. Margaret made breakfast for me. Robert brushing my clothes in the sun. Unable to walk because my shoes pinch me – Price has worked for me about twenty years and yet serves me in this manner. After dinner my wife hobbled as far as the Pooles and by and by I hobbled after her to drink a dish of tea.

Friday May 9   Our neighbour Landsey seems a wary selfish man, turned off his Old Woman tother day, lives by himself and is watchful as an Argus over everything. Rode this day with Mr John Poole to call upon Mr Mathew at Kilve, found him at home. His wife big with child and another lady. we walked to the seaside and Mrs Mathew and the other lady would accompany us but a roaring bull near a farmer's yard as we passed along put an end to the peregrinations of the ladies. The seashore was very unpleasant, covered with large stones, muddy and craggy. Mr Mathew is a botanist and intelligent on any subject, his Physiognomy is Good. Overtook Davies of Stogurcy as we passed along. He is grown fat, pursey and unwieldy. He must take care of himself otherwise it will not do.

Sunday May 11   My Little Boy is up, loud and noisy but I have forbidden his drum being a Sunday. My wife takes Physick again, I hope it will do her good but think it relaxes too much. Few here at Church in the morning. At Asholt in the afternoon very full. In Country Parishes there are always more in the afternoon than in the morning. I saw a great number of people passing about dusk, I suppose it was from a Methodist Meeting at Hodges. These men do a great deal of harm, they pretend to great sanctity, but it is ostentation, not reality. They draw people from Established Church, infuse prejudices in them against their legal Pastors and of late they are all Democratic and favourers of French Principles and I suspect that some of the Philosophers get among them under the character of Celebrated Preachers and so poison their minds against the Established Church. Robert had leave to go to his Uncle but he did not return to Prayers which I do not much approve of, yet he returned soon after.

Monday May 12   There is a fire downstairs in the parlour which should not be at this time of year. Lent the great horse to the Clerk to bring some potatoes, this will not do, to keep a horse for the whole Parish. In going to bed I stepped into the brew house and found it full of faggots for washing. I grew very angry and insisted on some being thrown out lest they should set the house on fire.

Thursday May 15   We could not get any bread from our bakers here and were obliged to send to Stowey for a loaf. I never remember such a scarcity before.

Saturday May 17   My horse gone to Taunton to draw Mr James Rich's wood. I would not have lent him to any other person, neither do I like it much even now. It is very extraordinary that in all this large Parish there is scarce another drawing horse except Hurley's and they are but cats. Oxen are mostly employed this way. The wind has been very violent and blown down several large trees around us and one in the Paddock. The cabbages are almost blown out of the ground and some part of the tiling loosened. My horse has not yet returned from Taunton and it is now past ten o'clock. It will never do and I must never again trust him to such people.

Sunday May 18   A fine sunshiny morning after a most terrible night. The horse was sent home this morning, I do not much approve of this business and will be wiser in time to come.

Tuesday May 20   This is my Birthday in which I compleat my fifty fourth year. Oh Time how thou dost run on, yet alas what improvements in Virtue. What Services rendered to my fellow creatures. What exertions in my Profession. Some little I must have made good and yet not such improvements as might have been made. When I think of my God and how far short I come of what I might have been then am I staggered. I must endeavour to grow better and better as I advance in years. The family have been busy all morning in preparing dinner for the Pooles of Marsh Hill and the Widow Mrs Richard Poole of Stowey to dine with us.

Thursday May 22   A ship cargoes of potatoes brought to Bridgewater and Mr Jenkins the Mayor has bought them to be sold again in small quantities for the Poor. Mr Jenkins is a Clergyman, Vain, insolent and ostentatious but he has some good qualities. He makes a good Mayor but what business had he to serve the office. After dinner went with my wife to Mrs Poole's to drink tea. Mr John Poole and I had some discourse on passages of the Scripture and he shewed me what I had never heard before that the Lord's Prayer was collected from prayers in use among the Jews. I am afraid that Mr Jenkins buying up the cargos of potatoes at Bridgewater has served to keep up the price rather than lower it.

Friday May 23   Mr Lewis of Stowey came to see my poor wife's leg. Tis a bad business, obliged to use bandages. Robert went to Stowey to have a tooth drawn – if it was as obstinate as himself there must have been some work about it.

Saturday May 24   Mr Lewis called today, my wife's leg looks better. Robert cut the nettles in the Churchyard and howed the gravel walk. Edward Selleck in the afternoon brought me a trout of a pound weight and two eels which he caught in the Moors. They were a present but I gave him a shilling. times are hard. Wrote a good deal in my Study, part of a Sermon to be preached at the Club at Stowey next Thursday but I do not much approve of their conduct, a little Democratic.

Monday May 26 The cow being furious for a bull got out of the Churchyard and ran towards Mr Rich's. Robert went after her and I too marched down stairs in my nightcap, took down the lantern and lit the candle in it and so like another Quixote sally'd forth in quest of her. After hollowing some time I heard Robert's gruff voice. Soon bounce comes the cow in the narrow lane near the Workhouse. I ran before and at last with some difficulty turned her and the yearling into the Churchyard as the most secure place for her on account of the walls. Then we had to secure the lower gate which had not been properly fastened before, indeed the fence is altogether in a bad way. After this adventure I and Master Robert marched into the house and after putting all things to right moved up stairs. The cow very quiet this morning, so the fury is over. Little Lewis came this morning to dress my wife's leg. A trifling little man but very civil and attentive, it will go as far as great talents in the world.

Tuesday May 27 I went down to Stowey to dine with Mr Forbes, Mr Thos Poole, Mr Poole of Shurston and a Mr Thomas. Mr Bradley joined us after dinner. Poole of Shurston seems a Squire Buck Parson rather than a Divine, a man of some fortune but not much Religion, yet good tempered. Mr Thomas Poole in his usual insinuating way brought in some arguments about the mode of paying Tithe with vast professions of regard to the Church and feeling of Humanity with a good deal of Jacobinical Cant, but his arguments did not prevail. Mr Forbes snuffed in his nose every now and then and attempted a story or two but could hardly get through them and so he let them drop and pushed round the bottle. When I returned I met Miss and Miss Susan Poole here. About dusk we walked as far as the Down gate with them.

Thursday May 29 Walked down this morning with my daughter to Stowey where I preached the Club Sermon. They marched in great order and parade with Colours flying, drums beating and a band of Musick. After Church they returned in the same order and parade and we all dined at the Rose and Crown. An excellent dinner, a great many Loyal Toasts drunk after dinner and the musick played of God Save the King, and Rule Brittania. Stowey was very gay this day and I think shewed as many pretty faces, genteel and well dressed young Nymphs as any town of its size in the County. I drank tea with Mrs Richard Poole where my daughter was and in the meantime was entertained by a race of young girls for ribbons. Two heroes in their excess of gallantry to accompany them and remove all obstacles ran so violently against each other that both were struck down and rolled over and over within a yard or two of me. I thought it was high time for me to withdraw indoors. A little before dusk there was a large Cavalcade marching up Castle Hill for another race downwards. We stood on one side but this was so terrible a race, petticoats tucked up to the knees and stays open, or taken off, that I began to think it became almost indecent. I dont think I shall stand by to countenance such exhibitions in future for I hate to see the female character let down. Got home in good time, my wife and Little Boy had been at Marsh Mill drinking tea.

Saturday May 31 My little boy is not very well, has taken Rhubarb, he is cutting teeth. No potatoes to be got at Bridgewater, what will become of us. Robert went to William Hill and procured a few but he staid long, for which I gave him a jubation. He is, with all his surliness and taciturnity, at times as great a gossip as any old woman in the Parish.

Sunday June 1 A great many at the Sacrament this day. I had a Prayer of Thanksgiving for His Majesty's almost miraculous escape from Assassination sent me but I forgot taking it to Church. As soon as I got to the Reading Desk I recollected myself and sent Robert from Church into my Study to fetch it but the Blockhead could not find it, on which I whipped off my Surplice and got into the house and brought it in my hand and then began the Service. There were ten shillings and nine pence collected at the Sacrament which I distributed among the Poor that attended.

Wednesday June 4 We all of us lay long in bed this morning. William is tolerably well today about his teething. My wife's leg getting well fast. I have an inflamation in each toe, it is red and tender and I think it looks something like gout for it is very sore. Wm Frost viewed my pigs and says they are the finest he ever saw. Ben Hunt's son returned from Salisbury and brought my wife a letter from her brother Arthur and a capital watch for William from Betty his servant who has lived in the family of Dodwells for almost forty years. She is a very respectable woman and keeps Mr Arthur Dodwell's house in Salisbury with great Credit and Oeconomy. Wm Frost and the Clerk are to set about mowing the Paddock on Saturday next if the weather be tolerable.

Saturday June 7 The moon is full at eight o'clock, this very hour. If therefore it clears up I shall conclude that I shall have good haymaking. Margaret, tho'up, is not yet out of her bedchamber. I do not approve of this, she used to be a earlier riser. Robert is not well, boils breaking out – he seems full of humours. Wm Frost and the Clerk are at it mowing in the Paddocks. They were at it ever since three o'clock, there never was such a shear before. They cut by the acre and mowed three and a half in the day. I suppose there cannot be less than five tuns there. Mr Amen looked like a hunted hare by the end of the day, very stiff with eyes hollowed in to his head but they were well cheered by drink and some victuals, tho' the last not in the agreement.

Monday June 9   I must summon them to the hay for this will be a busy day. Robert as slow as usual. These Somerset people are very slow in their motions. Joe Hill brought me a couple of rakes which he asks eightpence a piece. I thought 'em high and rejected them but after agreed for them and gave him a shilling to change, but he changed his mind and said he would lose his custom if I did not give eighteen pence, on which I returned them and took back my money. Sally Hill, an old servant of ours (who alas is now in the Workhouse, and her husband in jail) trotted about and appeared to labour much but poor woman, understands little of the matter. Old Bishop in his eightysixth year came with his pick and rake. A shrewd, sly dog for while the others were busy at one end of the field he was busy in helping himself to a cup of beer from the keg and in order to deceive everyone as he thought, he turned his back to the company as if he was doing something against the wall of the garden. My wife very busy in preparing goose berries for bottling which kept her up longer than usual while I finished my history of this day before we both marched for bed.

Wednesday June 11   A very fine morning. Mr Amen busy about the staddle, the haymakers in the field. All up and breakfast over. We shall have plenty of haymakers to offer by and by but these are more eaters than workers. Got the hay in most excellent order and began to carry between eleven and twelve. They continued till almost nine in the evening. Wm Frost mounted the rick and made a handsome round cock of the best hay that ever was put together and the largest crop that the two Paddocks were ever known to give – above five tons from three acres and a half. The great horse performed gloriously this day in bringing in the hay but Robert was as crabbed and surly as an old sow. Mr Woodhouse directed everything but Robert swilled the beer handsomely. My wife, Margaret and Betty gathered and bottled off many gooseberries before night. The haymakers had a good hot supper with plenty of beer and so all ended well and joyfully. Old man Bishop got his quantum and marched off home before night.

Friday June 13   I intend to have my rick drawn and made up. It is now tolerably early, a little after seven and my Little Boy is now asking Blessing and saying his hymn to his Mama. He has just been in and said 'Tis Overstowey near Bridgewater in Somersetshire'. In London it is the practice to teach children to mention their name and the street they live in, which is a good method lest by some accident or other they should run out or be lost in the croud that pass along constantly. I cannot think what is become of the Duke of Somerset. His last letter to me mentions that he is to be married in six weeks time, that time is come and I hear of no marriage, neither is his name mentioned among the persons who have been to Court to congratulate the King on his escape from Assassination – I fear that he is ill.

Saturday June 14 My rick of hay does not heat much and is the first made, the best made and the best in quality and the best in quantity from the number of acres in the county. After his day's work Little Davy came to thatch my rick, it is now very handsome and very compleat. The newspaper came in the evening and the boy asked for a cup of drink besides his usual pay but I resisted the demand because it would make a considerable difference in the year.

Sunday June 15 Up rather early, a disagreeable cow running and roaring under our window disturbed us much. Our cow too makes a noise, she must be sent to the bull. Went into the Sunday School, not many children there but both Masters present. The fellow at the Poorhouse is beginning his mad pranks once more. Went to Asholt, found Mr and Mrs Blake there. He is come to live there. Mr Blake is one of the family of the famous Admiral Blake who was born at Plainsfield in my Parish. The Living of Asholt came to the Brice's by marriage with a Blake of Plainsfield. Mr Blake was bred an apothecary, was much respected in his profession. All of a sudden he went to Willington and set up a shop. This did not do and he is now come to Asholt, poor man somewhat flighty. Asked me to drink tea at Asholt but I returned to Overstowey.

Monday June 16 Robert has been down to Mr Wm Poole's at Stowey with the cow to the bull. Sent Robert to Farmer Morle for half a bushell of oats, price six shillings per bushell. Never did I pay so much for oats before, these are hard times indeed. We were alarmed just now by a great cry from the Poorhouse. The madman has his fit come on and has got his handcuffs off. I went out with a candle and lantern and Robert. The women were all upstairs and he below. None of the neighbours would get up to be with him. I said that it could not be expected that I should go to him and stay with him all night, but the Strait Waistcoat was the thing and that I told the Parish Officers before and they promised to have the straps of that in the Poorhouse repaired. But they have done nothing and I must go to a Justice of the Peace if matters go on thus.

Tuesday June 17 The man at the Poorhouse has been very tumultuous all night. Tis shameful that he should be turned loose among a parcel of women. I must look into the matter yet it is hard that I should have the plague and trouble of looking after a madman when it is the duty of the Parish Officers. Robert busy in the garden, he manages a cucumber bed for me and brings it on very slow and late like himself. As to myself I regard the cucumbers little and only eat them stewed, and the dung of the bed serves afterwards for the garden.

Thursday June 19 The Fish Woman is come from King Thorn, fine whiting, large, five pence a piece. Dear but everything is so and they are rather cheap in proportion. My Little Boy is saying his lesson to his Mama, he spells well and will soon read, not much above three years old, he is a quick child. The man at the Poorhouse begins to be troublesome again. After dinner drank tea with the Mackays. Mrs Mackay seems a very good tempered civil and obliging woman, a pleasing face with a very quick eye, dresses neatly and well and has been very pretty I think but is very shattered in constitution having lived for many years in the West Indies. Mr Mackay an Old Buck, sadly mawled by the gout, brought on probably by free living.

Sunday June 22 I met with a strange accident this day – mounted on my great horse I set off for Asholt, it being morning Service there but I had not gone further than the Watery Road hard by before my horse started at some heaps of stones placed on the causeway to mend the road. At this I beat him with my stick and drove him out of the mud and water to get on the causeway when he suddenly turned round so quick that Poor I was jerked out of the saddle upon his neck so far that I could not recover myself and finding myself in danger of being trampled under his feet in the mud I bounded sideways up and fell on my side into the mud and water, yet my right arm kept my head out of the water and I got up unhurt but sadly soused and loaded with mud, a most doleful sight indeed. My horse stood quietly enough until I drove him on and we marched back again almost side by side into the village. Clerk and Ben were alarmed. Mr Frost was alarmed. My wife was alarmed. Margaret, Betty and my Little Boy were alarmed but Robert cooly and without much emotion cooly laid hold of his bridle. I stripped myself of everything to my shirt and new-rigged myself from top to toe. Betty would have Mr Robert to mount the horse to pass the lane. No returned I, I can do what Robert can and therefore passed on afresh with a firm and tight rein and got on in a full canter, touched up my horse every now and then till my stick flew into splinters. On he went like a lion, whisking his long tail in the air like a meteor. When I got to Asholt I thought I must be late when Lo I found it was early with them, there clocks were slow I suppose so every thing passed off very well. Mrs Poole of Marsh Mill came in after Church and myself, Margaret and Betty witnessed a Will she had of her own handwriting. We walked back with her and what is not very common with us on Sunday drank tea there. Returned, had the servants in the parlour to Prayers, eat a crab and so to bed.

Monday June 23 I mounted my horse, posted up the Quantock, laced his fat sides and returned very safe. Wm Landsey called and I spoke to him about the keep of my horse. He very modestly asked four shillings for the Hill Ground which is all covered with furze and no better than the hill only that it is enclosed. He has borrowed my horse three times and then after all this who would have thought that he would ask such a price that was never heard of in these parts before and for such keeping. This man is a perfect Jew and a perfect Booby in every thing that does not relate to bargaining.

Thursday June 26   I called on the old woman Lovelace again but did not administer the Sacrament because we did not have persons to communicate with her. My wife was ready to go but the Old Woman's daughter was not quite clear in the head and there should be two beside the sick person and the Clergyman.

Friday June 27   Mrs Poole's cart busy in doing the Statute Labour. I hope we shall have the roads a little better. A great many stones I see have been carried and laid down in the middle of the road, the Somersetshire Boobies have strangely mended the road. After breakfast I mounted the great horse and rode to Cannington to see Mr Lewis. He is tolerable but has got the gout. The great horse was rather frisky but I sweated him and after this Robert took him to carry dung into the Paddock. My wife and I and Little William walked up to Mount Pleasant and as we passed Mr Rich's we perceived they were shearing sheep. The fields were covered with sheep and the outhouses were full of them and yet he pays me little Tithe. It is a shame and yet if I demand more I must quarrel with him, tis hard when a man does his duty to be defrauded of a great part of what the laws of his country has assigned him for his maintenance. The same law which secures to him his estate secures to me my Tithe likewise, yet if he was defrauded of his rents he would not much like it. This was altogether a fine day.

Sunday June 29   Went into the Sunday School, the children all there. The crazy fellow has kicked holes through the partition from the Poorhouse. Tis as easy to do a good action as a bad one says Ben, he knows what is wrong – cant think – but he might do better if he would. Few at Overstowey Church this morning, half the Parish had been sheep shearing Saturday and I really think were crop sick for I observed that the defection was among the sheep shearers.

Monday June 30   We shall breakfast in the Arbour this morning before the house. Took my horse this day from Jew Landsey's keeping into my own Paddock as I would not consent to his extravagant demand of four shillings per week for ground high on Quantock and covered with furze. The fish woman called and we bought thirteen pair of small souls, an eel and some shrimps for a shilling, a tolerable bargain. Just after came Ruscomb Poole's boy with part of a Salmon from Bridgewater, ten pence a pound. The woman from the White Horse came to offer their shearing of hay but I declined it. The woman is very tidy and industrious, they have a large family and some of them small and two crippled, hard times for such.

Received this day a letter from my old friend Dr Taylor a Physician at Reading and a very eminent one. He has lost his wife and is very much afflicted on the occasion, poor man.

Friday July 4 The Little Boy has quarrelled with Betty about washing his face and was somewhat peevish but he is now running about in high spirits. I walked to Stowey this morning and Christened a child for Mr Bradley the Curate, it was little Davy's the saddler's child.

Saturday July 5 Scrubbing and scouring the house as usual on Saturday morning. Drew this day on Messrs Newham Everett and Co, Bankers, London for my dividends from the Funds. The evening as usual except winding up the clock which is never omitted on this day. Tis somewhat mysterious that so much foreign corn should be brought into the Kingdom and yet the Markets continue to rise. The Farmers I fear are too eager to push the price still higher, too avaricious I fear, whereas they should all agree to bring the corn to market at a more moderate rate, reserving only to themselves sufficiency for their families. Where this will end I cannot guess. Wheat now one guinea per bushell.

Tuesday July 8 The family all up. Robert gone to Shurston Bar for coal, he returned by nine o'clock and is gone again, the horse bringing twelve bushells a time. Mr Barbay is just come to teach Margaret but I have not given up my Study to them this time nor do I intend in future as I intend to reserve it entirely to myself except when I chuse to permit the family to breakfast here now and then and sit with me in the evenings during the Summer Season. My wife and I and Margaret went to Mrs Poole's to drink tea and there we met Mr and Mrs and Miss Fanny Newton from Old Cleeve. Mr Newton is a sensible and respectable Clergyman, but very much affected by a paralytick seisure. Miss Poole is gone to Bristol with young Colston, I am afraid on a disagreable business, the confining of Mrs Coleston who is in a very bad way.

Thursday July 10 I mounted my horse and passed through Stowey, called on little Lewis for some Rhubarb. Then went on to the top of Quantock, saw the Turfman, he shewed me the turf cut. In the afternoon the Rascal called to ask me for the money and a cup of drink. What said I, before the turf is received, that is not the proper mode of proceding but he begged hard, said he had not eaten a bit of bread since yesterday and wanted the money to procure some. I gave it like a fool as I was, but the moment he turned his back all cried out that I should never get the turf now, so that I am laughed at by everybody. His name too is Trickey, as rascally faced fellow as ever I met with. Little Davy the bricklayer, or rather stonemason was hoisted up our Tower to Ruff-cast and whitewash it which is wanted much. I was obliged to exert myself much with the Churchwardens or it would not have been begun.

Friday July 11 Little Davy came towards evening and went on with his work merry. A comical little gentleman it is, very industrious working, drinking, a good tempered open hearted fellow and will fight like a Game Cock over his cups and shake hands the next moment. He has a house full of children, different broods, some his wife's and some his own and yet the dog bustles to maintain them. His situation and that of the man often perilous but they do not regard it – what custom and practice can do. – I saw a man stand on the iron cross on Salisbury Spire and waving his hat with one hand, but it is reported that a man stood on his head on the Ball in King Charles's time.

Sunday July 13 Not many at Church this morning tho' all the better sort were but most of the lower were, I suppose, in parties gathering hurtleberries on Quantock for I have often observed that the Church is more empty than usual at this season. In the evening Robert asked to go to his father's and Betty and Nanny walked to Asholt. Met the Methodist, William Hill, he squinted at me under his hat as we passed. How now said I, at neither Church this day. I have been elsewhere replied he. So much the worse returned I, the proper place is your own Parish Church. I overtook Farmer Dibble and his wife near Ely Green, he crept on very faintly. I asked him what the matter was. He said he had been poorly for the week past. I replied that I was sorry for it, that I thought he should have some Medical advice. I desired him to put out his tongue, he did and I thought it looked tolerable. I fear he is going off in a consumption. A little before dusk in came Mr Robert. These excursions on a Sunday evening must not be too frequent.

Monday July 14 The family all up and we have breakfasted in the Study. Little William singing loud and Margaret just by mending a shirt. I rode out this morning on the great horse and perceived a swelling on his shoulders, he must be blooded tomorrow for he is too full. My wife and I and Margaret walked out, called on the Woodhouse to deliver a china dish on which they sent me some strawberries. Hum – Heigh Ho. Tweedle Dum Tweedle Dee – Tis late, I must go to bed.

Tuesday July 15 The horse sent to be blooded, he is very full indeed. We marched up the Town, met Mrs Everett Poole and an elderly lady. Mrs Everett Poole is a very pretty lady and looks very young to be the mother of four children; pity such a woman could be thrown away on such a man. After dinner we went to Marsh Mill to drink tea with the Old Lady, Mr John Poole and Miss Susan. Mr John Poole, whom I always call the Divine because he turns his studies very much to Divinity, walked with me to the Moors where we saw that savage Rascal Dick Jones mowing bushes and grass. On our return we had a confam according to custom on points of Divinity.

Wednesday July 16 Little William as busy as a bee and says that he will get his book to say his lesson to Mama as soon as she has finished picking currants. Little Nanny gone up the Hill with Sally Frost to pick Hurtleberries I do not approve of such schemes for servants, it is not respectable and I'd have all my servants respectable and a pattern to all others. I tasted for dinner today a species of roast beef they call a Boss, or Buss, viz a young beast which has continued to suck the cow for a year or more. It was indeed very rich and tender. The Post Boy brought me a letter from the Duke of Somerset thanking me for my congratulations. He writes in a very friendly manner, and his young dutchess, tho unknown to either of us, desires her compliments. This looks well, as if Matrimony had not ruined him.

Sunday July 20 A very hot sultry day, breakfasted in the Study which we could scarce bear the sun being so very hot. Few at the Sunday School. Asholt Church tolerable full. I told Mr Castle the Churchwarden the Church must be white washed before the Visitation. He agreed. 'Tis Hurtleberry Sunday and when there was a Public House at Ealy Green there was a good deal of bustle on the accasion. Farmer Morle not at Church this morning or evening, a very uncommon thing for him but I understand he has got a complaint in his bowels.

Friday August 15 Mr Amen has disappointed me in coming to thresh out my new wheat. I have therefore ordered Robert to thresh out some bushells. He threshed out four bushells and puffed and sweated at it most marvellously. Several persons were taken ill in the fields lately, but they were mostly old people and one or two I believe drank cold water.

Saturday August 16 Robert has just carried off some of my new wheat to the Mill. It is very fine wheat, God be praised, I shall sell some bushells to the poor at an underprice. – Our flour brought from the Mill very fine indeed. I am offered twelve shillings per bushell for it by the miller but sell it to poor families for half a guinea. Wheat is risen at Taunton to fourteen shillings. I am sorry for it. In the evening the Clerk and Robert had to water the plants. However I stuffed the Clerk's guts at night and gave him eighteen pence a day besides, and every Sunday he takes his dinner with me so that Mr Amen is pretty well off. The celebrated Dr Langford, Cannon of Windsor and Rector of Nether Stowey popped in upon us from Mr Thomas Poole. He was tightly buckled up in his canonical wig and full of words, bows and civilities, a good tempered, vain, chattering man of good abilities but weak judgements and I think of too much levity in his manner for his station. In other respects I think him liberal and friendly. The evening concluded as all other Saturdays do, looking over Sermons, winding the clock, servants up and to bed.

Sunday August 17 Forgot to wind up the clock last night so set it right this morning. We did not move off the premises this afternoon, being Sunday. The evening as usual except reading to the servants which from various circumstances was omitted.

Wednesday August 20 The newspaper come. The boy owes us eightpence but had not the money to pay it. He took the money at Bridgewater for a false charge and spent it so that we must deduct it as we can. There is very little Honour or Honesty among the lower classes. This is Pout Shooting day and I can see several persons on the Hills, but I do not think it reasonable to give three guineas for my certificate and not be able perhaps to kill one bird afterwards. They brought four loads from Plainsfield this day of Tithe with my great horse, sometimes fifteen Stiches at a time, at others fourteen. After dinner I called on Mr Woodhouse and gave him a guinea to pay for a certificate for Armorial Bearings.

Friday August 22 Wm Frost's horse has been in the Churchyard all night, having I suppose pushed the gate open. I must speak to the Churchwardens once more, twill never do. Robert put down as I thought Brocolo, but when I came to look at them they were Savoys. About twelve I mounted my great horse and went to Cannington to see Poor Lewis and console him a little on coming into the possession of four hundred a year. I returned to bury a woman* about 7 but the person was not brought till very late so that she could not be carried to Church because I could not read it was so dark. The evening seems sour and tempestuous. Mr. John Poole sent me my next portion of the Society Books for reading and I too sent off those I had already read.

Saturday August 23 Mr Amen finished making the reed and two bushells of billy wheat. Mr Woodhouse brought my certificate for Armorial Bearings.

Sunday August 24 We had a fire in the parlour and breakfasted there, what a change from the twentieth of the month. Not many at Overstowey Church this morning. Great many persons at Asholt. There was a burying and a christening there. The father buried and his child christened on the same day, 'twas a melancholy circumstance. He has left nine children, many of them small.

Wednesday August 27 A showery morning going to the Visitation. Borrowed Mr Rich's horse and Robert to ride mine and to carry my Gown and Shoes and Stockings. Rode off to Bridgewater, Mr Walter and his son overtook me. He serves Crowcombe for his father, was going to enter a fine youth his son at Mr Jenkin's. Went to Church and heard a good Sermon well delivered by Mr Poole of Shurton. Dined and had some conversation with the Chancellor who gave a good account of his father the Bishop. We sat late and I drank some tea at Mr Ruscomb Poole's. Came home safe tho' late. Robert was with me on the great horse and very useful. Paid half a guines to Mr Poole of Shurton for the Clergymen's Widows. 7s 10d for Asholt and 4s for my own procurations.

Saturday August 30 Took a round with my wife and daughter to look for mushrooms, met Mr John Poole who had been to see Murry for Mr Bradley. Mr Bradley notwithstanding his fine preaching neglects his Parish much. I would not give twopence a dozen for such people who are instigated by vanity and not a true zeal for religion.

Sunday August 31 A great many at Overstowey Church, very full indeed, the Gallery and every other part. Before Church this evening in going to the bottom of the garden I perceived the plum tree moving and a person's head above the hedge. I called out and ran to the place but he was off, yet I secured the article of depredation, a strong hook, which he must have prepared for the purpose with some pains and care. It was a neighbour's son, Charles Sellick's son, a great looby from seventeen to eighteen years of age. It is hard to be plundered by ones neighbours who receive so many favours at our hands. I told the father of it.

Wednesday September 3 I walked over to Crook at the Mill, he was very ill indeed. He revived when I came in. I talked some time with him and prayed by him and gave directions for administering the Sacrament tomorrow. His wife expects the Apothecary. It was very warm and I returned to dinner and after my wife and I set out for Putsam. We found Mr and Mrs Mathew at home with Mrs Baget and dinner not long over. However we sat and chatted and my wife walked over the house. It is very elegantly furnished. Before tea we walked to the sea which was very full and looked sublime with the Islands and Promontaries around. On our return we drank tea then mounted our horses and got home by moonlight. The great horse carried my wife nobly and has gained great credit. Indeed he is a noble horse, handsome and useful.

Thursday September 4 Breakfast in the Study, Molly Selleck says that Ware's boy has been up my plumb tree, a sad Scoundrel. Molly Selleck is suddenly called off to her brother in law Crook who is dying, he was to receive the Sacrament today. I shall walk over to see what state he is in – I left him in a dying state. I could not Adminster the Sacrament to him he was so restless and often times insensible. I read the prayers of a person just departing out of my Father-in-Law's, Dr Dodwell's excellent Book of Prayers for the Visitation of the Sick. I returned to dinner and met Mr Amen and Robert going for some Tithe to Farmer Morle. This compleats the Harvest. Mr Amen supped at the Vicarage and had some strong beer and they tell me gave them a song or two. If his voice was as tremulous as when he cries Amen at Church there must have been many quavers and demiquavers in his tune.

Friday September 5   Robert's face swells very much, I fear that he has a gross habit of body. Robert took the great horse to haul out the dung in the further Paddock and I went to give him assistance. I and my wife and little William and his companion Charles began spreading the horse dung about and by and by came in Molly Weymouth while the wort she was brewing for us was cooling. She spread more than all of us together in a little time. I had a brace of partridges for dinner, they were a gift from Mr Macky and very good. I shall call tomorrow morning (if it pleases God) to thank him.

Sunday September 7   I see Ben and the Clerk, Wm Frost and another in deep conversation on the Stocks near the Churchyard wall. I suppose the subject is the rise of provisions. I think it is a shame after so good a harvest that it is a shame corn should be so high. I shall thresh out a few bushells and divide it into pecks at a low price. Poor Ben shakes his head in the Sunday School and takes off his spectacles and cries, 'Poor people must live, Sir.' Called at Crook's, very bad, his wife goes to Taunton tomorrow. Robert still has a swelled face and cannot come to wait at table. I am afraid it will turn out to be something of the Evil, if so it will disqualify him from my Service.

Sunday October 5   William somewhat cross this morning. The newspaper come. Malta has surrendered to the British Arms, Huzza. Mr Cruckshanks did not come to pay me Tithe for the Wood tho he dined at Farmer Dibble's being Court day. He says he will be happy to dine with me next week but he gives me unnecessary trouble, I do not like it. I rode out on the great horse. In coming down Quantock I met Miss Hale and her lover I believe, the Champion of England Mr Dymock and her father behind, Sir Philip Hales who spoke to me and I touched my hat and went on. After dinner the Pooles and Mrs and Miss Lewis came. They supped here and played cards. After they left we went to bed.

Thursday October 9   Robert in the garden. He seems to be clearing every thing that wants it least, a strange Wogheaded Blockhead.* Landsey gone to

Bridgewater. He would have done some business for us but he is not a good person at errands tho' he sells corn and can buy beasts well.

Saturday October 11 Just seen Margaret and her Mama is gone down stairs. Langford is in the barn, I must go down to see what they are about. It is highly necessary to show myself in order to quicken them. Farmer Morle dined with me and paid his small Tithes, his Great Tithe I take in kind. He is a careful industrious,open hearted, fair dealing man. It was the Tithe barley I took from him we were winnowing. They finished it very late. It was twenty seven and a half bushells. I must thresh some more to make it thirty. Paid Langford and the woman but the first is to come Monday again but he has been paid already for the day. The evening spent as we usually do on Saturday, poring over Sermons, winding the clock and so to bed.

Sunday October 12 I called in at the Sunday School. Poor Ben had a paralytick complaint in his hip, had not worked for some time, gave him two shillings from the Sacrament money for Ben always attends. Went to Asholt, few at Church and fewer at the Sacrament tho' I gave them a second Sermon on the subject. Mr Blake wondered how they could go out of Church after what they heard. There were only three besides Mr and Mrs Blake and the Clerk and myself. If I am to continue to serve the Church I must bring them into better order. In the afternoon my wife and Margaret and self walked down to Mrs Poole's and drank tea there which is not usual on Sunday. Mr Harford was there from Bristol, he has travelled all over Europe. Mr Anstis had brought some very great curiosities which had been dug out of a field near Bridgewater. They consisted of bracelets and torques, bits for bridles and other things curiously wrought in brass. The workmanship was very fine. We judged them to be Roman, Mr Harford is a great antiquarian. After tea we returned, had the servants in and to bed.

Monday October 13 After dinner there was a Vestry to fix on persons to serve the Office of Surveyors of the Highways. But the Poor of the Parish got intelligence of it and crouded upon us in such a manner that we scarce knew what to do. The Overseers are harrassed to death and summoned every day before a Justice, this will never do. Our Poor Rates are four times the sum they were two years ago. The Justices attend to every complaint, right or wrong, and every scoundrel in the Parish croud to make their complaints. Where it will end I cannot tell, the Justices if they are not more cautious will create the evil they meant to avoid. They plead the dearness of provisions and think by granting them all demands to make them quiet but it has a contrary effect. They expect to be kept in idleness or to be supported in extravagance and drunkenness. They do not trust to their own industry for support. They grow insolent. Subordination is lost and make their demands on other people's purses as if they were their own. I wish I could prevail on the Farmers to sell their wheat to the Parish at the rate of ten shillings a bushell and then keep the poor to their usual standard of allowance. Mr John Poole called on me and we examined Bundy's Roman History with Prints to see whether we could find anything like the brass antiquities found near Bridgewater but we could find nothing to answer our purpose.

Wednesday October 15 After dinner my wife and William went out to gather mushrooms and I was left in the Parlour in a kind of dozing way, when I was roused by a rumbling noise. I started up and ran to the door and found it was Mrs Southcomb,* my wife's sister, and Grace her maid. Poor woman she had a fit as soon as she was out of the carriage. She always has a fit when in the least hurried for which reason she came this day from Honiton in the Parish of South Molton without getting out of the Chaise, between forty and fifty miles and only changed horses, once, at Tiverton. They were in readiness as soon as she got there for had she got out of the chaise it would have brought on a fit. She has had these fits ever since the death of her husband eight or nine years ago. An extraordinary woman tho' so nervous and quivering on all occasions yet so determined that nothing can move her from her Resolutions. So very much attached to her Husband that she cultivates the Memory of him on every thing she does. She must live and die in the same house that he did, loves or hates every person that he did. In short the memory of her husband seems to be the primum mobile of her life. After her fit she cheered up and grew chatty and agreable. The driver and horses sleep here tonight by Mrs Southcomb's request as a reward for his merit and attention and great care in bringing her safe.

Thursday October 16 Mrs Southcomb did not come to breakfast. She brought no less than three hares with her and set no less than three packs of hounds ahunting for her in the neighbourhood of South Molton. Robert did a little work in the garden, he must be goaded sometimes to his work like an ox.

Saturday October 18 The family all up and I think I hear Mrs Southcomb below chatting with my wife. Little William is calling out loud that breakfast is ready, he calls Margaret Slug-a-Bed. After seeing Margaret dance and her writing I mounted my horse. He was a little frisky through idleness so I capered him a little up the hill. By and by I met Mrs. Woodhouse and Miss Beeston on the road. I spoke to the first but the other is a mysterious character, an elegant well dressed woman but I do not know what to make of it. She comes from London and some say — but we must not speak all we hear. Passed thro' Stowey and overtook Mr Errington who cocked his glass at me and walked along side my horse a little way. He is supposed to be a man of fortune yet often tapped on the shoulder.

Sometimes dashes away and at others lives like a mouse, a thoughtless good tempered man but somewhat defective in judgement.

Sunday October 19 Had a Wedding* but the Clerk did not give me notice the day before which made me angry. Sunday is a bad day for these things as it hurries me and I scarce get myself ready for Prayers. It seems the persons were but lately come to live into the Parish and they had lived together before and they brought a bouncing child to be Christened the very day of their Wedding. I gave them a good jubation and told them that had I known there were such people in my Parish I would not have suffered them to have remained long in that situation. This they were aware of and so came to be married. I had not much time in the Sunday School. The evening among ourselves. Mrs Southcomb continued her chat all the evening, till she went to bed. The little woman makes up for her solitary silence at home.

Wednesday October 22 Rode thro' Stowey, got some Physick for the great horse and some camomile flowers for myself as I have been troubled with bile more than usual of late. Trotted the horse up Quantock and down again. After dinner was called out to poor Ben Hunt. He was, poor man, in a sad condition, swelled testicles to a great degree. He seems apprehensive that he should die immediately but I do not think so, tho' perhaps he would not be able to work any more. He has a rupture also. I told him I knew not what was best to be done on the occasion as I had never seen such a thing before tho' I had heard. I told him I would make inquiry with some Physical Person. He had shewn it to several medical persons some years when he was attacked in the same way tho' not so bad, he seemed very disconsolate. I am to see him tomorrow. We spent the evening cheerfully, the little woman took the chattering department and performed surprizingly considering her nervous state. I had a letter from the Duke of Somerset this day.

Thursday October 23 I and little William walked to Stowey. I spoke to Mr Lewis about poor Ben Hunt. In returning Mr Thomas Poole overtook us and we walked into his field with him to see him plant wheat. There were both men and women. The women had a little stick tipped with iron and so made a hole with one hand and dropd the seed in with the other. The men had two short poles tipped with iron and so made holes two at a time with both hands and children followed with the corn. I liked the women's plan best. Lewis the Apothecary called and I walked with him to Ben Hunt. He examined him and said there was no danger of mortification, which revived Ben surprizingly. Little Lewis returned with me and he drank a jug of my beer which the chin-moving man seemed to relish very much. Mr Amen called and I gave him a receipt for Mr Cruckshanks for my Tithe, this is the second time I have been obliged to send. A trifling, shuffling man, I do not much like it.

Saturday October 25 Our Wedding Day, a fine morning but windy. I have been busy all day in writing, finished my Sermon. My wife has been cutting my hair. Mrs Southcomb came to dinner dressed out in a neat brown silk and a very neat cap and she looked really young but none but ourselves dined together. In the evening Mr John Poole, Mr Ruscomb, Old Mrs, Miss — and Miss Susan came to drink tea and sup with us. We played cards and were very merry and they all parted about ten.

Sunday November 9 A most tremendous morning, wind and rain to an uncommon degree. I mounted my horse and put on two greatcoats, one was the large bearskin coat, and so off I marched. The lane at Ruck's brook was quite full of water over the causeway. Knowing the bottom was level I ventured through and had a long continuation of water along the road to Dibble's. However I got safe to Mr Blake's and found the Clerk there who said they did not expect me, but I answered that I never neglected the Church if it was possible to get there. I could scarce get a Congregation, however two or three came at last. I returned to Over stowey but found the stream running towards Diddle very unpleasant. The wind and stream against me, every step the horse took brought water into my face. I did not go in to the Sunday School but I saw Ben Hunt in Church and he looked tolerable.

Wednesday November 12 Mrs Southcombe is to set out for Bath in the morning, poor woman she is very nervous and the thought of her journey distresses her. Two of the Pooles just come from Teignmouth called upon us in the afternoon, Miss Charlotte and Miss Penelope, they seemed well and in good spirits. Mrs Southcomb grows more alarmed as the time of her departure approaches. She has been up at 7 this morning and all day has been packing which has fatigued her. She intends to be absent from her home in Devonshire for some months, partly on account of her health and partly to see her friends and relations in Berkshire and London. She is subject to fits brought on by the loss of her Husband and afflictions of very various kinds. The Post rang the bell though so late, at half past ten, to let Mrs Southcomb know that there were no letters for her for which he received a sixpence.

Thursday November 13 Poor Mrs Southcomb with her servant Grace set off for Bath about 6 o'clock, rather somewhat after and Robert rode with the Chaise as far as the Turnpike. Robert tells me she was in tolerable spirits and I hope that she will get safe to Bath without fright or accident. I walked to Ealy Green Publick House, left a shilling there for Old Bishop, then walked to see Davy's potatoes and took a round by Mr Rich's house. We went to the Pooles in the evening and the young ones were very merry. Mr Clarke would set out for Monksilver when the party broke up about eleven. Robert lighted us home from the Poole's, it was very dark, bad for Mr Clarke but he was obstinate, foolish man.

Tuesday November 18 Wog headed Robert spreading the gravel in the yard, a work I desired him not to do till I was up. Busy this morning tunning the beer and baking, wheat of our own, God be Praised. The old Cooper here putting on hoops. We shall brew again this week as I have malt of my own. I took a walk in the morning and went into the field where little Davy was taking up his potatoes. He could not sell any for he had sold them before they were taken out of the ground. I shook my head and told him I did not like this, he ought to sell them in the Parish. Many were ready to take them. I went on and saw Phillip's wife. She was taking up potatoes and ready to sell them. I agreed for nine bags at five shillings pr bag. I cautioned her not to push them to a higher price as the crops were not bad and the price was high enough. She said she would observe what I said.

Monday November 24 Molly Weymouth has been brewing ever since one o'clock in the morning. My Malt turns out exceedingly well. At first the liquor looked too pale which is not the case now, I fancy the first brewing was made too soon after the malt was made. They finished brewing half a hogshead of beer and a hogshead of ale this day but they still complain the malt is pale. I bought some paper for to make new books for my diary.

Wednesday November 26 I rode out today, agreed with Phillips once more for nine bags of potatoes. He made me pay sixpence more for the red ones than I agreed for at first. I shook my head, however I agreed to give it for they sell dearer. We did not dine much before three and we had a cock and hen pye and some parts so tuff that I could make nothing of it either with knife or tooth. We killed these fowls because we had not corn to give them neither could obtain any for a moderate price. Strange times indeed are these.

Friday November 28 Walked to Stowey with my Little Boy, met my wife there. Went to conjuror Coles as they call him. He is a clockmaker and an extraordinary genius but a Democrat and from having too much Religion has now none at all. He made a wonderful clock for the Duke of Somerset that goes a twelve month without winding up. Edward Selleck brought us two immense fowls for half a crown.

Saturday November 29 I sent Robert to Philips with my horse and cart for potatoes and he brought them home in two loads and I have put them up very safe in one of my underground cellars. They are very fine potatoes and got cheap as times go, five shillings and five shillings and sixpence a bag. Robert after this brought in some water, both he and the horse did their duty today.

Sunday November 30   The newspaper come and a letter from the Duke of Somerset* dated London, inclosed a letter from Mr E King FRS a great antiquarian on the subject of a letter of mine describing some curious antiquities (Roman) found on Polden Hills near Bridgewater. This latter has been copied by Mr Ruscomb Poole and one copy sent to Mr Anstis who is now in London and another to Mr Harford near Bristol. I omitted writing my Diary before I went to bed, not having once thought of it which is no very common thing with me.

Thursday December 4   This morning before day I heard a noise at the kitchen window and jumped up to the window and threw up the sash and saw a man there and asked who it was. It was Robert's brother who wanted to speak to him. I told him it was an odd time to come and speak to him and rouse people in the night. The Post brought a letter from Mrs Southcomb. Robert borrowed my horse to go to his brother's Wedding. He is married to a Farmer's daughter which has turned poor Robert's head and he begins to think that both he and the family in a short time must rank with the principal men in the Kingdom. He is returned in good time and sober according to my instructions, which I am glad of. I walked to Stowey, bought a pencil and returned.

Saturday December 6   Writing my diary in the parlour for the first time, the weather being so cold I could not sit in the Study where there is no fireplace. We have not breakfasted yet owing to Saturday morning inundations. Robert made an impertinent answer to my wife this evening about carrying water on which I spoke to him and told him that he should go. He said he had no objection to stay if the well was made. Objection, said I good sir it is not a thing in your power, you shall not stay and so make no remarks on that head. To this he said nothing. I sent a sack of wheat to the Mill late in the evening and it is now brought back in flower by Mr Hurley, a civil man but an odd spoken one and an Anabaptist. His wife desired to be Churched by me. Yes returned I if you bring your child to be Christened, otherwise not. For why should a person be indulged with the Offices of the Church in one case who despises them in all other cases. However we agree very well on the whole. Mr Amen came in to be paid and I delivered to him a printed paper about bread to be stuck up on the Church Door. The evening closed in as usual and I looked over my Sermons and wound up the clock.

Tuesday December 9   Up late, the ground covered with snow and a hard frost. Walked with my wife to Stowey, called on Mr Francis Poole who bowed very graciously. We bought some cloth for a jacket for William. I bought likewise a pint jug for beer. A sad account this day in the paper of the rise of corn and commotions of the population.

Friday December 12 I served Asholt a whole year yesterday the eleventh. Mr Reeks having died that day. I served the Church indeed before but that was on another account. This year is for Mr Brice the present Rector. Little William said the first answer to the Catechism to his Mama without missing a word. He promises well and has a good Physiognomy. Staden the Taylor called to measure little William for a jacket and trowsers. He looked like Jerry Sneak with his little ragged lock of hair tied with pack thread behind, terribly henpecked, works hard and wifey spends all. But an honest man and a good taylor. I sent Robert with the sow to the boar at Doddington.

Monday December 15 Edward Selleck never came to the well as he promised, they never keep their word in Somersetshire. The common people have no notion of that kind of Honour and always think it sufficient to say I could not come, something prevented me tho they may have agreed to and appointed the time ever so solemnly. I could not move out much this day and was employed in writing a letter to William Tutton my old servant and now Clerk of Monkton Farley about receiving some Tithe due to me there the 6th of January 1801. The Clerk came to mend a hedge. Edward Selleck brought me a woodcock.

Saturday December 20 Family up and we are at Breakfast in Margaret's room that Betty may make a full display of her inundations down stairs. Mr Amen and Robert finished winnowing twelve bushells of wheat in the barn. Jones from Stowey came up and took half a score of bushells at twenty shillings. I said I was very sorry that it was so but I must sell it at that rate to be on a level with other articles of life. He would have given more I believe had I stood out but I did not attempt it. The afternoon passed in the same style with other Saturday afternoons, Sermons, winding the clock and to bed.

Monday December 22 Little William highly offended this morning by my giving him a little box on the ear instead of the box he asked for. He was not hurt but the indignity was great and he chewed the cud most great. Walked to Stowey with my wife, met a variety of the Stowey Poor going to beg or AChristmassing as they term it. The Singers I perceive have been to Church to prepare for Christmas Day and are now moving off. I finished a letter to my brother and another to Mr Brice of Porlock and sent both off.

Wednesday December 24 Newspaper come early with two letters, one from Mrs Kinaston pressing us to come to see her in May. She is a relative of mine, lives at Ryton near shrewsbury, my Grandmother was a Kinaston. A Vast number of the Poor of the Parish came for boiling pease which were distributed among them. Some persons came who ought not to, tis a shame picking the meat out of the mouths of real objects of Charity. Old Bishop passed by and I gave him a shilling and I went afterwards to Ealy Green, he had drunk up the money there except two pence. He is about eighty six years of age. Plaid at cards in the evening with the Miss Lewis and my daughter while Madam was making up her fine satin garter blew cloak for tomorrow with fur around so that she will be as stiff as Buckram. To bed in good time.

Thursday December 25   Christmas Day, a fine morning and pleasant with a few flying clouds. I gave this day a good dinner to the Sunday School children and had a great many to dine in the kitchen. I think that there were no less thirty nine that dined at my expence. A good many at Church and twenty eight persons at the Sacrament. Went to Asholt, a tolerable congregation. Returned to dinner. The guests bowed off between nine and ten in good order and thankful. Little Mouse Weymouth said not a word but sucked in the liquor very kindly. Poor Ben thanked me very kindly. I asked him whether he felt stronger, he believed he was. A good collection at the Sacrament, I gave most of it away immediately. I have four shillings remaining, I shall give Ben and the Clerk some of it they are both old men. Servants in, Prayers and to bed.

Sunday December 28   The family all up and William making a great noise downstairs with his whoop. I have spoken and he is quiet. That woman Tapp's horse in the Churchyard all night. I have no patience with her, I must pound him. Went to Asholt, few at the Sacrament. Returned, tolerable congregation. That fellow Cavill was at Church.

Wednesday December 31   The last day of the year. The ground is covered with snow. The sun shines clear and the horizon looks keen for frost. Thus concludes this year.

The Year 1801

Thursday January 1 Mr Amen called out of the barn to ring in the New Year, but the New Year has been *in* many hours ago. O Mr Amen, is this your method of proceding? Many things have been written in the newspapers pro and con the commencement of the New Century but nothing can be clearer to me than that the last century was all the preceding year in concluding. We were indeed in the year 1800 but that was not compleated before yesterday about twelve at night. The number ten being thus full and then we begin the number one of the New Century, but the year will not be compleated before 12 o'clock at night on 31 December next.

Saturday January 3 Mr Amen I believe is in the barn. The chimney was swept this morning but I had hard ringing to get Robert out of bed at 6 o'clock. A lazy dog yet he used to get up tolerably. Mr Errington called, terribly mawled with the gout. He dismounted and chatted with me for an hour or so. My wife and daughter walked over to Wm Hill's and they gave a sad account of their daughters who are at Winsley near my Living of Monkton Farley. There is a bad fever there, poor Nanney's child is ill and she ready to Lie In, and boarder in the house is ready to die of it and several persons around are dead already of this fever. Sally Hill who went from hence to nurse her sister is much alarmed about poor Nanney, now Mrs Goddin, was an old servant of mine. If she catches the fever in her condition it will run hard with her. They say that there is a bad fever at Stogursey. However God's Will be done. We must rely on His Providence and goodness for a terrible plague rages on the Continent. God Preserve this Island.

Sunday January 4 The Bath paper not come but in the London one there is an account of the King's Proclamation with regard to the Imperial Parliament. Little William went into the Sunday School with me, Gave a penny to the first commer. Not many at Church this morning, few of the Pooles but both the Richs were and all the better sort. Had a Christening and that Rascal Cavil and his wife stood Godfather and Godmother. That gentleman being brought to his penentials thinks he is got into favour again with me.

Tuesday January 6   In the afternoon Mr Clark of Monksilver called with young Newton. He informed me that his brother in law the Bishop of Chester had given him a Prebend in the Church of Chester and made him an Archdeacon and Rural Dean and in the Spring he is to have a good Living in the neighbourhood. A pretty good business at one time. Clark is a good tempered man does his Duty regularly, but is rather too fond of rural diversions. It is a good thing to be brother in law to a Bishop.

Friday January 9   Hard work to heave some of the timber lately cut down in the Paddock for sawing. I got together all the Scoundrels in the neighbourhood and gave them drink. Sarah Tutton came here with her child and brought me some cash from Monkton I rley. She and Wm Tutton my Clerk there lived once in my service and go on very well. She is gone to her father's at Asholt.

Sunday January 11   The Clerk taking off the shutter from the Sunday School but there are no children there yet. Went to Asholt in the morning. The newspaper came but little before I set out – spoke seriously to the boy about his delay in bringing it. Sally Hill and her child at Church. Had a burial and the Church full. Mr John Brice sent no message by young Blake from Porlock, I do not like this. He referred me to a person who had no money of his in hand. Margaret took a vomit this afternoon, has gone through it very well and is now fast asleep. She is under the direction of Dawe of Bridgewater and is to take a bolus in the morning and some pills afterwards.

Saturday January 17   Edward Selleck about the pump. Sad work all this day in drawing up the pump timber out of the well. There have been rascally doings about it, several stones put into the boxes. I am going to convert it into a well once more. Four or five fellows pumping the water out all day. Pump business is expensive for they drank gallons beside the pay for their work. The Post boy told me he would bring the paper this evening but he does not exceed in honour or veracity. Mr Ackland's man brought us a letter from Mr Wood the Musick Master who is now returned and discharged from the Army and now at Fairfield.

Monday January 19   Edward Selleck have been here and his myrmidons at work all day and a pretty jobb they have made of it. After bringing up the last piece of timber high above the surface the rope broke and down it fell breaking the ladder beneath to pieces, so that between eating and drinking they have made a good business of it. These fellows worked till late at night and after all their labour left things in a worse state than they found 'em. Men should know what they are about and be prepared withhall the instruments proper for the undertaking, but a Somersetshire man is a strange animal, ignorant yet conceited and wonderfully obstinate. He is always wrong in his notions yet thinks that no one understands anything but himself. 'I warrant I' is his usual phrase. The evening in the old method tho' I have not been in the best humour all day.

Tuesday January 20 Edward Selleck is here with his myrmidons. They have, by cutting the pump tree in two, brought the whole up and are now regaling themselves. The ladder has seven or eight wrongs in it broken but may I believe again be mended. Jane Tap's horse in the Churchyard this morning according to custom. She is a sad woman and keeps this craggy creature on the publick to carry her and what she pilfers.

Friday January 23 I walked to Stowey, met Price the shoemaker who is a great gardiner and shewed me some trees for sale. I liked them and believe I shall buy two or three. Met Mr John Poole who joined me and we took a circle together and examined Mr Thos Poole's wheat planted in the new manner, it looked very well. Farmer Morle brought me four hundred of bricks which I paid for and six shillings for carriage. I began reading my Diary to the family from its commencement and shall continue to do so as far as the last year goes.

Saturday January 24 Mr James Rich and Mr John Poole doing something in the Poor House, what I cannot tell. I suppose examining it, it is in sad repair and those two villains who dwell there tear everything to pieces. Mr Brice, the Rector of Asholt, paid me for serving the Church a twelve month's to December the 11 1800. Robert swept and cleared all this day.

Monday January 26 The family all up, it is late. Margaret calling that toast is in and breakfast ready. Robert went with a horse and dray to Dodding-ton, or rather to the Mine House, with a windlass and panniers which were borrowed for the well. I understand that there will be a bustle in the Poorhouse tomorrow as a Special Warrant has been issued against many of them. Indeed it is a sad set of thieves. Such people left to themselves will never do, they corrupt one another. Every Poorhouse ought to have a Governor to keep them in order.

Tuesday January 27 I find that the Constables have been at the Poorhouse and carried off three of them, viz. Porter the fellow who pretends to be seized with fits now and then when it serves his purpose, and Rich a woman of a very bad character in many respects and Bet Carter who turns Evidence and the worst of the lot. Another little woman, Bet Pierce, confirms the evidence of the former but that hardened villain William Hill as they call him stays behind and Porter's wife. The first is an old and experienced rogue and will not go out to plunder with the rest lest they should discover, and now he hugs himself in his Superior Sagacity. But I trust he will be found out when he least expects it as his haunts are pretty well known. My wife and I walked to the Poole's to chat about the Workhouse exploits while old Mr Barbay was left to teach my daughter French and by the time we returned we found Mr Wood the Musick Master. He has been discharged from the Marines among whom he inlisted in a mad prank, but however he is come to his senses and will I believe recover some of his scholars. The Workhouse rogues are sent to Jail I understand.

Saturday January 31   Met four of the Miss Pooles passing by just now as I returned from Hurley, who is an Anabaptist. The child has been very ill, I told them that I would privately Baptise the child on condition that thay would bring him to Church afterwards. We had a great deal of argument about it but I left them to their own feelings. At last they consented and they intimated that they would bring their other children to Church. I said I thought that was safer and without making any observations on the state they may be in if they died unbaptised yet certainly Baptism could be no injury to them, whereas the neglecting of it might be of infinite consequences. They seemed to be struck with this line of reasoning. The evening passed off in the usual way of Saturday.

Sunday February 1   I went into the Sunday School. There had been a bustle in the Poorhouse, Bet Carter and the others quarrelling. Some of them had beat down to partition and got into the Sunday School and stole some wood from thence. Poor Ben had got a black eye this morning. He says it came of its own accord, I cannot believe this. Little chin-moving Lewis sent in his bill today which I had often desired him to do, and a very extraordinary one it is. He absolutely makes two kinds of charges for the same thing. First for journeys, lotion and physick and then two guineas for the cure, in this manner making four at one stroke. A little rascally low lived fellow, he has adopted a curious mode to pick our pockets. I shall pay him and have nothing more to do with him.

Tuesday February 3   A terrible smoak in Margaret's room from the Parlour below. Mr Barbay came and dined as usual and drank tea, Wood the Musick Master came. Mr Parsons the Clergyman of Goathurst who is also a Justice of Peace sent a constable to deposit a fine in my hands to be given to the Poor for selling bean flour for wheat, its to be given away next Sunday. Called on Frost on the occasion, he is to give away the bread. I sent Robert for the paper a report having prevailed that Mr Pitt had resigned. This is not true but strong altercations in the Cabinet about Hanover. If Mr Pitt resigns we are ruined.

Wednesday February 4   I wrote a letter for Mr Beak of Monkton Farley for Sarah Tutton to take when she returns there. Robert went to Asholt with it but when he got there he found Mrs Tutton's father had just dropped down dead in the field. I intend to go there tomorrow.

Thursday February 5 Rode over to enquire about Farmer Castle who fell down dead in the field. Saw Mrs Tutton and her younger brother who both seem much affected. He left no will it is supposed tho' the eldest son has gone to Charters the Lawyer to know if anything was left there. It was a fortunate thing for Mrs Tutton to be at her father's, there is considerable property to be shared among them. He is to be buried at Bagborough, a sad swearing reprobate man and his end was awful, the last words he spoke were of that nature. Edward Selleck has finished the collar for the well and painted it.

There is now a gap in the story for four of the small books in which Mr Holland wrote have been lost. Whether he and his family went to Wales and visited his brother I do not know but it is certain that his man Robert left his service and was replaced by Morris. See also January 8 1802.

Thursday December 3 I did not stir out this day on account of the dose I had taken. Wm Frost brought home a pig for me this day but my blockhead Morris had carried the key of the back gate within his pocket, being sent on an errand. The pig was therefore driven through the garden round about into the back yard. I remonstrated with Morris in some anger and more so when he said it could not be helped. But he thought he had quite exculpated himself when he said the key was in his pocket upstairs, he could not perceive that (as long as we did not know it) twas all the same to us as if he had carried it along with him. I answered it should have been left on the nail in the kitchen. The evening was spent among ourselves.

Friday December 4 The Thatcher is here and so is the Clerk and Molly Weymouth is brewing. Mr John Poole called in and left with me some Society books, viz, The Kingdom of Ava, the History of. Moreover he informed me of a very disagreeable piece of intelligence, that he and his family must quit Marsh Mill next Michaelmas. I am truly sorry for it for they were very good neighbours. It is not a common thing to have such a clergyman as he is resident in ones Parish, a man of learning and Prudence with a solid religious turn of mind and the whole family are such as we are not likely to meet with again. I have known Mr John Poole from a boy and he has said his Catechism to me in this Church. Indeed they are all of an uncommon intellect with the best principles and liberal in their manners and sentiments.

Sunday December 6 A great deal of bustle this morning in getting me up, having the gout in my foot and a blister behind my ear which I hope will ease my gums. At last I ventured on my horse and had Morris with a couple of crutches walk beside my horse. I rode up to Church and summoned the sturdy little Clerk of Asholt to attend and so I got off my horse. It was late, but better late than never as the saying is, and it is not everyone would come in my state. So I hobbled to the Porch and left the crutches there and with some difficulty got to the Reading Desk. When there I did very well and got thro' the Service as if the heart was sound tho' the limbs were a little out of order. Farmer Morle came in after Church at Overstowey and drank a pitcher of beer and I paid him thirty shillings towards clothing an apprentice in my division. My foot grew fiery and painful towards evening, and I rather restless, yet on the whole I got through the day very well.

Monday December 7   I had a very restless night last night, my great toe very painful. We received many letters with the papers on Sunday which I should have noted yesterday. One from my brother Jeffrey, Rector of Penmorva and another from Dr Chapman near Bath. Jeffrey was bred to the sea and I wish he had continued thus for he is very unfit for a Clergyman, a man of no Principle, unfortunate in his marriage and dissolute and even desperate in his manners. He has wasted away considerable property and what will become of him at last I know not. My foot after a bad night is better this morning, my blister troublesome and teazing. We expect company today, the Mathews and the Pooles. They came, Mrs Mathew seems almost ready to lye in. We had prepared a bed for them here but they went to Marsh Mill being old acquaintances of the Pooles. I believe Mr Mathew had been Mathematical Tutor to Mr John Poole. Mathew is a very well behaved man, very placid, clear and accurate, very well informed, understands everything and is with all a perfect gentleman in his manners.

Wednesday December 16   From the eighth I have not been able to write my Diary having been afflicted with the gout. On Sunday Mr Eyton served my Churches for me, a savage looking man and very odd and peculiar. He has got a house and garden and two or three fields of his own and lives entirely by himself without man or maid and half starves himself to save money. He has no regular Curacy but is seldom unemployed and makes as much if not more of his services than a regular Curacy would bring in. I never employed him before, not much approving of his mode of doing Duty. They turned him out of the Curacy of Cannington on account of some connection with a widow Lady by whom he obtained the premises he now occupies, be that as it may the man is a strange fellow. He is a Welshman and a Denbyshire man and was at College the same time as I was. I remember him but had no acquaintance with him. However he did the Duty very well they tell me. Mr Forbes called yesterday and cut open a whitlow on my wife's finger, an operation she was unwilling to undergo. However it was soon over. Mr Holloway the Bridgewater Postmaster is turned out which I am not sorry for as he often withheld newspapers and made many blunders.

Thursday December 17 Snow this morning. My wife thinks her finger better. My gout still continues but my head is better having taken something to open my body gently. Breakfasted in bed which I do not approve of. My little Boy took Physick for the humour in his face. Mr John Poole called and shewed me a letter of thanks from the Antiquarian Society for some Roman Moulds* he sent them found on Edington Hill beyond Bridgewater.

Friday December 18 Mr John Poole called and buried a corpse for me. It was the man I visited at the beginning of my illness.

Sunday December 20 Sent off Morris with a note to Mr Blake at Asholt to inform him that Mr Eyton will do the Duty there. In the meantime I prepared myself for the Service at this Church. I was carried to Church in an armed chair. Mr Wm Frost with his broad back on one side and Mr Amen with his unsound leg on the other and Master Morris with his spruce Livery and spindle shanks behind. The shrivelled leg and spindle shanks had nearly given way, I called for assistance when Lo, a stout young Morle advanced and so I got safe to the Porch and walked into Church. I went thro' the Duty very well but few at Church the day very uncomfortable.

Wednesday December 23 A very wet nasty morning. We breakfasted tolerably early for invalids. My wife's finger somewhat easier but it is still in an unpleasant way. Margaret a little better. My gout considerably better. William running up and down stairs like a Buck. Sent the Clerk and Morris with the barley to the malster to be wetted tomorrow. Wrote a letter to Wm Tutton and received a facetious letter from the Duke of Somerset. The Poor of the Parish begin to come round for Christmas gifts.

Friday December 25 The Singers at the window tuned forth a most dismal ditty, half drunk too and with the most wretched voices. The day very rainy and uncommonly unpleasant. I got myself ready for Church and at last sallied forth with my feet well surrounded with flannel. I did the Duty very well and we had a Sacrament. I had a chair and carpet within the Rails being obliged to sit down often to rest my legs. After this I had Mr Woodhouse's horse and Morris rode the great horse and we sallied forth like Don Quixote and his man Sancho for Asholt. I got safe to Asholt and got out of my Gambadoes.* It was very wet from the Churchyard Gate to the Church and the Church itself quite wet with damp. The little Clerk was quite glad to see me. I asked whether I was not to have him to dine with me. He said he had ten children come to see him and he had them to dine with him. Ho said I thats another thing, indeed he seemed pretty well laden already. It rained on my return very hard but Morris had got an umbrella for me and so with my Gambadoes and two greatcoats I was a match for the weather where I found a full house, having no less than ten persons to dine in the kitchen. I trust and hope this day's business has not hurt me. A day of labour but I have got through it very well I think.

Monday December 28 Mr Morris seemed very brisk in his work this morning for I gave him leave to go home to suck his poor Mammy it being Christmas time. I hobbled this day to Marsh Mill and chatted some time with the Pooles. Mr John Poole told me, I was surprised to hear it, that he was to dine this day with his cousin Mr Tom Poole the Patron of Democrats and there to meet Coleridge and Wedgwood, hum, hum, Ho, Ho. Old Bishop I understand is dead, eighty seven.

Thursday December 31 The last day of the year which begun with the terrific preparations for War and the most ungenerous combination of all the Powers of Europe against Great Britain. Most of the Potentates of Europe had basely made their Peace with France and thus ingloriously given up the cause of Virtue and Religion. Great Britain alone stood the contest not only against France alone but in some degree against all the World beside. She not only stood but at last prevailed against them all and compelled France to a Peace which checked her aspiring spirit and at the same time secured to Great Britain the undoubted Empire of the Sea and a Superiority among the Nations of the Earth that I hope will never be taken from her. Nelson begun the Glorious Year by forcing the passage of the Sound and striking terror into all the false potentates of the north and Abercrombie first and Hutchinson last concluded the wonderful year by the capitulation of Alexandrian Egypt and the surrender of the French Army and the total expulsion from that part of the world which they had possessed themselves of in a most treacherous manner and all done by a body of British Troops far inferior in numbers to the French who were stiled the Conquerors of Italy and the Flower of the Gallic Army. After this the preliminaries to Peace were soon signed Glory be to God. Long live Great George our King. May French principles, Atheism and Irreligion vanish from the face of the Earth, Amen. A hard frost this morning, I rose early, Margaret poorly yet. I had a nice woodcock this day for dinner which I am very fond of. We dine at three and it soon grows dark afterwards. Little William read very prettily this evening. A person brought me a fine hare.

The Year 1802

Friday January 1 This is the beginning of a New Year. My gout is going off fast. Towards three o'clock we moved off to Marsh Mill to dinner and there we met my neighbour Mr James Rich with his round belly, a comely man of the rustic kind. Mr Robert Blake and his wife were there. A very handsome dinner. I still had my gouty shoes on but walked very well. In the evening we played at cards. We staid till after supper and parted late and I hobbled home over the Down Fields as well as I could. Mr Robert Blake mounted his horse and took his wife behind and jogged off and the night was dark and cold, I did not much envy him his ride.

Sunday January 3 The ground covered with snow and a hard frost. Some of the Pooles came to Church but very late, Mrs Richard Poole was there I went through the Duty well but had a burial,* Old Bishop who had he lived would have been eighty eight next May. He worked formerly with me and I allowed him a trifle ever since. I buried his wife who had, I fear, more religion than he had. There was too a Christening but when we come to the Font there were not two Godmothers, for it was a female child. This made sad delay and at last another came. I was half starved and as soon as I got to the house I was obliged to mount my horse for Asholt. It was slippery and unpromising and I took Morris with me. Few there, too few. Mr Blake at Church and a child or two. I hope I have caught no cold in walking through the snow to Church.

Wednesday January 6 Still snow, a vast quantity fell last night and now it continues to snow. Mr Amen snug at home tho' I have work for him in the barn. I see people moving about at the ends of long rusty guns, I fear mischief will be done. A brace of woodcocks and a goose brought me from Rich of Pepperill. I took the goose out of compassion for a large family but the woodcocks were immoderately dear, besides I have a woodcock and a hare and snipes in the house, and another to be brought today from another quarter. Master Morris put on boots that I gave him to walk in the snow. I told him I did not give them for that purpose, had they been old thick rusty boots, it would be another thing. What terrible weather this is for all kinds of birds, no food to be found anywhere and man, cruel man, adding to their calamity by hunting after their lives in every quarter, the whole region resounds with pops and explosions. Ann went off before dinner to her Father's, being Old Christmas Day when all the family are to meet, I like the plan very much and I find it very much practised among the lower orders in this country. Betty, under the direction of Margaret managed the dinner which was sent up very neatly and we enjoyed ourselves.

Friday January 8   Mr Amen has come today and he has all the appearance of having employed his time before in drinking. I paid him ten shillings which were due and told him I was glad I had not paid him before as they might possibly be gone by this time. Master Morris and I docked the great horse's tail, he holding it and I cutting with a large scissors. It is indeed very well done and the horse looks many pounds better. Hawkins brought in his bill for coal this day which I paid. I believe he has not charged for one load which I shall inquire into. He is a very civil, honest man. My bill was less than usual this year being almost half a year absent. Nothing further this evening but all past in the usual stile.

Sunday January 10   The snow comes on fast. Mr John Poole called, he was going to walk to Doddington, observed that it was very slippery. My horse was prepared so I mounted, Master Morris followed on foot. It was indeed a terrible morning, snowed to a great degree. The horse went steadily. I had an umbrella and was obliged frequently to shake off the snow and Morris every now and then shook the skirts of my coats. However we reached Asholt at last, no trace of footsteps to be seen. I rode up to the Church, set the bell a tolling, got off my horse and perceived a small congregation assembling. I went through the Service and gave them a Sermon. It snowed hard while at Church but stopped before I came out yet the tracks of the horse were covered. Returned very well and in good time. There was a dinner given by me to the Sunday School children who were all filled as tight as drums and my wife attended. To my surprise Mrs Poole and her daughters came to our Church, they were all well shoed and well stockinged and well clad and so they had need. There was a burial from Stowey, the Church was filled with strangers. My newspaper came while we were at Church. I was glad to get to dinner after all was over. Night soon came on and I did not stir from the fireside and the evening ended in the usual stile.

Thursday January 14   I sent off this day a keg of laver to the Duke of Somerset with directions on it and a letter to him and another to Mr Leighton. Wm Frost carried it himself and spoke to the man of the Inn where the Wagon put up. In the evening I sent my man on the great horse for malt. On his return he was attacked by snowballs by some children and Selleck's great girl just by. The horse took fright and down came Mr

Booby sack and all. He had in one hand a pitcher of yeast. The yeast he spilt but the pitcher he saved, but the man complained much of the fall and even cried. My wife was very much displeased and went out to speak to some of the neighbouring women. By and by I spoke to some of them and even threated them with an Action.

Friday January 15 Landsey of Stowey died last Wednesday. A singular man, honest but whimsical, obstinate and mulish. He sometimes would not speak even to his wife for weeks tho' she all the time waited upon him. He was full of infirmities and worth money and he and his wife kept seperate purses so I am told. Mr Woodhouse told me that my name is not down in the Income Tax which surprises me much for I left it entirely to him. I must look into the business.

Wednesday January 20 The Clerk in the barn. I have been busy after breakfast in the garden and made Mr Morris work a little, my son William was as busy as any of us. The news came and a letter from Mr Oldfield with two Bank Bills. After dinner Landsey's Corpse from Stowey was conveyed here and I had a Hatband. After this we sat down for the evening.

Sunday January 24 The family up and calling to breakfast. Off to Asholt. Mrs Blake gone to put her children to school near Taunton, she returned while we were going from Church. Few at Church, Mr Morle and his wife, the little Clerk kept beating time on his belly as he sung and raised his eyebrows in admiration. Returned, this Church very full and many from Stowey and sung a Funeral Anthem from Job. Farmer Morle came in after Church and drunk a few jugs of beer. Had the servants in and the evening concluded in the usual stile of Sundays. I hear the lasses below stairs and not gone to bed, I must not suffer this.

Monday January 25 Sent Morris with a letter from Mr Ruscomb Poole to put in the Post Office at Bridgewater. Went out and overlooked the Clerk in the Paddock and made Morris work a little in the garden. The Ladies walked out and I moved a little way with William, returned and found that Morris had sneaked in from the garden. Made him come out again. The Pooles came and staid supper and we played at cards. I lost every pool, however the evening passed off in a comfortable friendly manner. Miss Anna Maria Newton won one pool of Commerce and my wife the other.

Tuesday January 26 Sent off Morris to Dunster with my Statement of Income for Gale the Commissioner's Clerk. Mr James Rich and Jenkins his man called, the latter going to Crowcombe about the Taxes. My wife, daughter, Miss Newton and William walked to Stowey, met Mrs Richard Poole and William and Miss Elizabeth Poole began a great flurtation.

Morris returned from Dunster late, Found Gale drunk in bed after having sat up all night, a sad wretch and yet he leads all the Justices by the nose and particularly that booby Lutterel. We played a rubber and then decamped for Bedfordshire.

Wednesday January 27   The ladies at work but Margaret ready to dance and go through her steps as I think it necessary she should practice twice a week for her health and improvement. The Clerk and Wm Frost gone to Ealey Green, money and blankets being given away by Lord Egmont. He is very charitable and Cruckshanks his steward the distributor.

Saturday January 30   After dinner a man came for Asholt and desired me to bury his mother. James Bishop, seemingly drunk, came and claimed a reward for drawing up the bucket from the well. I was angry because I had paid the Clerk a few days before and moreover had my doubts whether he had not received something from me some time ago. He however, tho' drunk, was superabundantly civil. I looked over my Sermons in the evening, the rest as the usual stile of Saturday evening.

Sunday January 31   (originally February 1, crossed out and endorsed 'A Mistake') It is not a mistake and I was right again. I went into the Pulpit and perceived that the Clerk had looked out for the last day and not the first day of the month. My wife who is very accurate in general had persuaded me that it was the 1st day of the month and so I called the Clerk who insisted that it was the last day. Sent him to Farmer Morle and Mr Woodhouse and nodded to my wife as she was going into Church and she at last gave way. There were not many at Church this morning. Mr Ruscomb Poole borrowed the Registers to look for a Rich who was ancestor of a man in Cornwall of that name who hopes to gain some property. This Rich, I understand, was the brother to the famous Harlequin Rich some years ago who it seems came from Overstowey. Rode to Asholt. There was a burial, a relation of our Rich. The Church was very full, Mr and Mrs Blake at Church and several from Overstowey and some famous singing. The little Asholt Clerk had a seat by himself and lifted up his eyebrows and beat time like anything but poor man he could not be heard and if he was it was not worth hearing. I believe there are more coxcombs in singing than in any other art. If a man has any folly about him he is sure to show it when he sings or is in love. I went into the Sunday School this morning, few children there and they come late but they read well. I believe it does some good, at least it obliges them to come to Church and attend to the duties of Religion. Poor Ben is past his work now, says it is the Blast.

Tuesday February 2   On my return from Stowey where I got more plants I found William Tutton here, an old servant of mine and Clerk of Monkton

Farley and married to another old servant, Sarah Castle, by whom he has had two or three hundred pounds. In short he is now a considerable man, receives Tithe for me and is employed by the Dowager Duchess of Somerset in various matters. When I had the misfortune to lose four of my children at Monkton Farley of the Scarlet Fever in less than a forthnight's space this man who had then left my service came back to me of his own accord and gave me all the assistance he could under my uncommon calamity and at that time when every other person were afraid of coming near the house.

Wednesday February 3 Not over well this morning, tis nasty and rainy. It was late before I got up, breakfasted in bed which I cannot bear. Mr John Poole called, he has a slight soar throat. My wife not in a very good state. William is a perfect hero.

Thursday February 4 I am poorly and uncomfortable, took Physick this morning. Mr John Poole called this morning, he seems to've got over his soar throat. I have felt very unpleasant this morning yet was prevailed on to take a little of the soup of the beef and a slice of the breast of a chicken which agreed with me better than I supposed it would and so I ventured on a glass of wine and afterwards drunk some wine and water which agreed this better. I am in doubt whether there has not been too much lowering in the business. I found myself very tolerable in the evening and sat up chatting with my wife till eleven o'clock. William comes on very well in his reading and is a tolerably good boy but very noisy.

Friday February 5 I find myself better, my wife tolerable but alas her leg promises badly. Old Mrs Poole and her son the Divine called. Mrs Poole called and chatted a long while but the Divine went out for a walk. I should have been glad to have gone out too but my Physick the day before was still in an operating state. I eat a tolerable dinner and have been very well this afternoon. My wife is uneasy and so am I about her leg.

Saturday February 6 I find myself tolerably well. I put my head through the window and spoke to the thatcher passing by. He said he could not come immediately to my barn which he has begun and left a part uncovered and I have sent to him five or six weeks ago. I have represented all this to him and moreover that it rained into the barn and damaged it much. However he continued in the Somerset laconic come when convenient &cc. On which I told him that he was a Compleat Scoundrel and I would see whether I had not an action against him. I called after at Frost's where he was to pay him fourpence that was coming to him from his former work, observing to him that tho' he did not chuse to finish his work yet I chose to pay what was due. He then promised to come on Tuesday next. My wife's leg not very promising. Great difficulty to obtain a person to serve my Churches as we intend to visit Mrs Kinaston at Bath and then to go to Salisbury and Southampton. Mr Eyton is engaged.

Once again there is a gap in the record and so we are left to surmise that the Hollands went on their visits during the Spring. In Salisbury there was Reverend Arthur Dodwell, Mrs Holland's brother while one of her sisters, Mrs Ridley lived in Southampton.

Wednesday July 14   The family up and breakfast over. I went up with little William and Morris into the Tower to see the young Cuckow placed in a cage there. Quite alive and well, Morris shewed me the cleft in the inner part of the Tower where it was hatched. It was a white water wagtail's nest and this bird feeds him with the greatest care and attention. I have had the cuckow now brought down into the garden where the cage hangs under the bough of a tree and two water wagtails are continually feeding him. Morris is busy in the garden and has taken up fine potatoes and as fine carrots. The wagtails fed the cuckow all this day and Morris worked tolerable in the garden. After dinner and tea we sent Morris to Stowey for my greatcoat which he left at Mr Northey's and to carry boots to be stretched a little. My wife spoke to Sally Hill about sending her girl to School which she had neglected to do. Sat a while in the Study and then went to bed. Morris took care to bring in the cockow.

Thursday July 15   Alas! the poor cuckow with all its feeding is dead, perhaps overfed. Ann says that one Gookoo killed the other, meaning Morris. He is now gone for coals. Family all up, Margaret has received a letter from her cousin in Wales. Ann feeding the calf with milk in the Churchyard. Hill's wife brought to bed and a jug of caudle sent off.

Saturday July 17   The family up and breakfasted, Little William whipping his top in the passage for he must not stir out for he has taken Physick tho' it has not operated yet. I am to dine at Stowey to meet Mr Northey. We sat down to dinner before Mr Northey came, he had been at Bridgewater. It was a Clerical party but Mr King is a medical man of an independent fortune, a little nervous but intelligent and somewhat sceptical if not Democratic in his notions. Mr Northey was there and his son, young Ackland and Mr King's son, Mr John Poole, Poole of Shurston, Mr Davis and myself. The day went off pleasantly and we seperated in good time. Mr John Poole and I met three Miss Pooles in the street and we came homewards by Court House, the wind very high. I received a letter from the Secretary to the Society for Promoting Christian Knowledge and I am elected a Member. Saturday night in the usual stile.

Sunday July 18 I see no one about the Sunday School. We had some talk about Sunday Schools yesterday, Mr King thought that they did harm that plowmen were better without learning. I answered that I could not think that the teaching them of their duty could do them any harm, obliging children to go to Church, teaching them to read and say their Catechism, to give them some sense of Religion and due subordination to their superiors must be of some service in these times. Went to Asholt, few there but Mr Blake had his house full yet neither he nor his wife were there. That is bad business, I cannot see why strangers coming should prevent his going to Church, or if so then I would not receive my friends on a Sunday. I went into the Sunday School this morning and took my daughter with me and made the Clerk write down the names of all who came and if they continue for a month then they are to receive each a twopenny cake, for it seems they must be bribed into it or they will absent themselves tho' the whole scheme is calculated for their own benefit altogether and a great expence, so averse are people to instruction.

Monday July 19 I see my great horse leaped over to Farmer Landsey's field. He has not work enough, I must do something with him. The Duke of Somerset I have heard nothing of this very long time, I wrote to him last from Salisbury, tis strange, I cannot make it out. I fear he begins to be warped by the Philosophy of the times. If so I have done with him. Porter has been very ill in the Workhouse. I went into him, he was in a fit. I gave them some gin to put into his mouth, could not swallow. He came by and by to himself and they gave him all the gin. I called afterwards and he told me he was much better and that the gin relieved him much from the wind. He is very violent at times, but seemed very rational and tractable. Sat in the Study and soon to bed.

Thursday July 22 Morris is gone for coal. A Duty is taken off from the Parson's coal from Combage to Bridgewater, but it is paid at Shurston which will be a great detriment to poor Hawkins. It seems another young Cuckow has been found hatched in a house at Stowey in a sparrow's nest. These are strange things.

Sunday July 25 The family up and ready to go to Breakfast but I cannot go having cut myself shaving and it bleeds so plentifully that I know not how to stop it. I gave to Porter today a glass of gin as he apprehended a fit coming on. I have heard nothing of him since, perhaps it stopped it but giving gin is bad Physick. I shall have his fits coming on very frequently I fear. Had the servants to reading and to prayers and then supper and to bed.

Friday July 30 Mr Tom Ridding and his sister, my wife's nephew and niece from Southampton, up betimes and went off before I was up being to cross Brinon Hill towards South Molton. Charles Sellick I perceive finishing a coffin before his door. About eleven o'clock a terrible rain came on. Alas! My cousins *Tway*, On Brinon Hill they gang along and sadly trimmed are *They*. It did not clear up till evening. A servant came to offer for the cook's place. My Wife did not agree. Mrs Coles of Cannington passed by in a one horse chaise and a servant before her. She had been at Mr Rich's. Alas courting them for their fortune. She is no relation and yet she expects a great deal and they (poor fools bear coaxing and rubbing very well. Oh! Human Nature.

Sunday August 1 The family all up, Buller's horses about the road, this is wrong. The Clerk moving about the Sunday School. After breakfast I went in and saw a great many little people quite tight and clean. My daughter calls them over now every Sunday and if one is missing any one Sunday in four he is crossed out of the Roll and is not to have his twopenny cake for that month, next Sunday is the Cake Sunday. I went to Asholt and had a tolerable congregation for the morning, the seat was so full of musical gentry that the poor Clerk scarce had room to beat time according to custom. At last he found the shoulder of the man next to him and so tapped that and his own chin incessantly. I thanked Mr Blake for the fish he sent me but wished for the sport rather than the fish of drawing the pond. Returned and after dinner went to this Church. It was very full indeed, the Pooles here all except the Divine who has a Church of his own, and the Old Lady is gone to Wells for a few days.

Wednesday August 4 A very fine warm morning and a true Summer Day. Morris put the horse in the cart to carry out the dung before the heat of the day. Dressed myself before dinner and after that we all went to Marsh Mill to drink tea. Met Mrs and Miss Ward there who are lately come to Stowey. The brother is in the tanning line and in partnership with Tom Poole whom he admires and imitates. Miss Ward is rather pretty, had her hair oddly cut, very chatty and had not much diffidence about her. Two men, Chidgey and Weymouth, continued their jobb in the Paddock, making a pond and throwing up the ditches. Mr James Rich came down and viewed my calf and put a price on him, viz. four pounds ten shillings.

Thursday August 5 The family all up and early. Little William has read. Morris cleaning the windows, the outside with a ladder. Poor Frost wandering about in quest of his horse to go to Bridgwater. My wife received a latter from South Molton informing her that our cousins tway got as far as about Dulverton before the rain came on and then they dryed themselves and got very well to South Molton but from thence to Mrs Southcomb at Honiton House they wandered and missed the road and did not get there till nine o'clock in the evening. Morris had the horse shoed this day and he seized the opportunity of chatting a few hours at the blacksmith's. He is wonderfully fond of gossiping. Two men came in the evening to get on with their jobb work and Master Chidgey seemed to think it hard that poor people were obliged to work so hard and to fare so ill. I told him that they fared very well and I might as well complain that I was not a King, a Lord Egmont or a Bishop. The Rascal made one when the poor made a kind of insurrection last year.

Friday August 6 The family up early, the house scowerd and ready to receive our friends who are expected today from Bristol where they have been for some time to the number of eight persons in all so that we shall be tolerably full in the house for some time. About seven in the evening our friends came, first came Mr Dodwell over the Downfield, he walked and the chaises came afterwards, eight in number Mr and Mrs Dodwell, two sons and two daughters, a man and a maid. The Maid is Miss Dodwell's a daughter by another wife. William seemed all alive with his two cousins. By and by Mr John Poole called to see the young boys who are to have a bed there. The second Miss Dodwell is in a deep decline, poor girl. Mr Dodwell very chatty and full of action. Mrs Dodwell looked oldish. To bed all in good time.

Sunday August 8 A very warm day. The family all up, Mr Dodwell walking in the garden. Two children of Hester's at the Sunday School before the Masters. I called to them and said they should certainly have the halfpenny. The Pooles came in as usual, few at Church. Mr Dodwell preached and he spoke clear, distinct and well. I summoned a Vestry, observed to them that Porter had hung himself but was cut down by Frost. Sent for Frost who said he seemed quite dead when cut down. He must be removed from the Poorhouse for he is quite a nuisance. We dined and after dinner rode over to Asholt, a good many at Church. Spoke to Rich of Pepperel about Porter. He promises to move in the business. Came home, several parties of ladies pass through the village. Talked with Porter but he was soon after taken with a fitt. I gave him a dinner but that did not do. Had the servants in, read and supped and soon to bed.

Monday August 9 The family all up: Gave some Castor Oil to Porter, spoke to him and think worms are the foundations of his complaints. At breakfast a letter was brought me from the Duke of Somerset with a Ring and an account of the death of his Mother the late Dowager Dutchess of Somerset.* She was a good and religious woman, presided over the education of her children the present Duke and his brother Lord Webb. She instilled into their minds sound religious principles as well as adorned their understanding with all other instruction which has made them the ornaments of the present age. I some years ago on Easter Day administered the

Sacrament to the late Dutchess and her two sons the present Duke and Lord
Webb when the one was not above nineteen and the other eighteen. I could
not forbear mentioning to the Dutchess afterwards what pleasure the
circumstances gave me to see such persons so young and who were destined
to move in so high a circle in life to commence their career in so promising
a manner. Yess Mr Holland replied the Dutchess nor is this all for I can
assure you that it was from their own notion. So much the better returned
I. I finished a letter to the Duke of Somerset this day and shall send it off
tomorrow. Morris went off with the calf for Mr Blake of Asholt but the
calf broke loose and ran on and Morris after him, one calf after another till
they got to Asholt and Morris quite out of breath. To bed in good time.

Tuesday August 10 Up early, the morning warm. Miss Anna Dodwell up.
The horse caparison'd with a pillion and Master Henry Dodwell the father
fidgetting about with his boots. Alas! Just as she was about to mount a few
drops came, the horse ordered in and the pillion taken off. The rain
increases, comes on violently, puts a stop to everything for it rains very
hard. Morris went to the Hog Pit and then to the Blind Well for Stadle
Stones. Barbay dined here. He is going over to France by the twenty third
of this month, the day fixed on by Buonaparte, otherwise he is to be
forever excluded, but he says he will return. It rained so hard all this day
that there was no going to the Pooles so we staid at home. To bed in good
time.

Thursday August 12 Anna Dodwell, my wife's niece, does not ride. She is
very poorly a lost case in my opinion, weak and wan and with a tiny voice,
shrill and sharp. Ugly Briffet has brought the Bristol Water from
Bridgewater on his back, a heavy load. Morris has neglected everything I
gave him to do yesterday and I spoke to him very sharply. He certainly is a
very lazy fellow, quite an eye servant and has no thought or care about
anything. After dinner I took the young ones to see them putting fire to
some weeds. Saw Porter who told me he was much better. My wife spoke
to Ann about her extreme dirt and she was saucy, she is to go, however the
matter is made up for the present. No Riddings come yet and so we march
to bed.

Saturday August 14 The family up. Anna Dodwell seems better this
morning but alas it is a lost case. Ugly nosed Briffet brought some letters,
one from Mr Oldfield with a draft containing my dividends from the
Merionethshire estate, I have now answered his letter, Briffet waiting for it.
I have moved about this day in the garden and taken some apricots off the
tree. Mr Dodwell and his daughter Anna moved out on the great horse but
soon came back the day being too hot. Mr Tom Ridding and his sister came
here before dinner and after we went to drink tea with the Pooles. Returned

before night, sat a little after supper and seperated variously. Tom Ridding sleeps at Stowey.

Monday August 16 Mr Dodwell and his daughter gone out for a ride. Briffet brought a letter from Mr Dodwell. The family all up and assembled from all quarters, we had begun breakfast before Mr Dodwell returned. I walked down with Tom Ridding to Stowey, changed my N Wales Draft with Mr Poole. The fish woman came and we bought a great quantity of fish. After dinner Tom Ridding and his Sister went off for Salisbury and Southampton.

Tuesday August 17 Mr Budd my Curate from Monkton Farley came here today, he dined with us and has a bed at the Globe Inn at Stowey. I walked down with him after tea. Mr Barbay dined here, Mr Wood was here too to teach Margaret.

Wednesday August 18 Mr Budd came here from Stowey after breakfast. I walked with him through the middle of the Wood up to the top of Quantock, Little William and his cousin Edward Dodwell were with us. We got to a high hill beyond the limits of the Parish and saw part of the Vale of Taunton Dene and as far as Minehead Point, quite to the Channel. Mr Budd took his pencil out and took a sketch of that part. We then returned making a circuit into the Crocombe road and passed along over Quantock in a straight line along the Stowey road, the whole circuit we made about seven or eight miles. We were all tired by the time we were home but little William bore it as well as any of us. It was past three and dinner was ready. After dinner Mr Budd mounted his horse and rode to Piper's Inn where he is to lie this night.

Friday August 20 Morris's year is up and I have discharged him, he is an idle ignorant lazy fellow, let him go where he will. I walked with my Little Boy first to Marsh Mill and then to Stowey. When we came to Stowey we met the proud and pompous fellow Squire Ackland in an open carriage and three boys with him on pretty ponies. We called on Mr Barbay but he is gone for Bridgewater then to Southampton then to France. He is indeed much agitated on the occasion and it is doubtful to me whether he can come back. I bought a pair of gloves at the bowing tradesman Mr Francis Poole's.

Monday August 23 Up early, before six. Our friends are going off this morning. One post chaise came before six, this came from Bridgewater tho a Taunton chaise. The other came from Taunton soon after, quite a bustle. All busy in taking leave breakfast being over, now they are gone, eight in number so now I must look to my Tithe. My new man* is come and I employ him immediately. He and Mr Amen brought three loads from

Halsey Cross before dinner. After dinner sent Mr Amen to the barn and my
new man Charles to the garden, he carried dung and put down some pease.

Tuesday August 24   My man Charles in the garden seems to do very well.
As I was going to move out Mr Walters who lives at Crowcomb and his
wife came here, they said they were going on to Bridgewater, however
they dined here. He was well educated and is of a good family, the son of
Dr Walters, but he is a weak man and married a person below himself and
will have some fortune. She is really a good looking young woman and
conducts herself with great propriety, has much more understanding than
himself. He serves Crowcomb Church and has the whole of the Living
from his father who is the Rector. They went off after dinner for
Bridgewater. I did not carry any Tithe this day.

Friday August 27   The family up and William has read but we have not
breakfasted yet. Mr Northey called, he is going to Kent to marry his
Brother in Law to a great Fortune and wants a person to officiate at his
Church. I directed him where to go, a critical time for him to go while he is
taking his Tithe in kind and said he could not help it as he had promised.
Ann our servant left us this evening, her year being out, and we are left
without a cook and have only Betty who is a young girl. This is an
awkward time to get a servant and yet there will be many at our service at
Michaelmas.

Sunday August 29   The family up and my wife gathering kidney beans.
Wm Frost passing along and Porter from the Poor House looking like a
lazy sawney over the wall. Went to Asholt, few there in the morning.
Returned and found the family at dinner and Charles my new man waiting
and as it was his first time he seemed more expert than I expected.

Wednesday September 1   Charles and the Clerk gone for wheat. The
Thatcher here. The old Gardener from Crowcomb is come and I must walk
to Stowey for nails. Hot, Hot weather, walked with Little William to
Stowey and bought nails, a lock and curry comb. After dinner moved to
Plainsfield and spoke to Sally Hill to come here tomorrow to supply the
place of another servant till we can hire one. Mr Charles my man it seems
does not chuse to wear a Livery so he is to go at the month's end. They
brought forty stitches of wheat this day.

Friday September 3   No notice for Tithe yet which surprises me. Sally Hill
came this day to assist in the house, she has been our cook but is married to
a sad scoundrel. After dinner my wife and I and Margaret walked down to
Stowey. I was to bury young Coles. I marched up to Coles the stonemason, not necessary to walk before the corpse. Went down to the Church,

Little William walked with me and the rain came on very fast. After the burial called on Mrs Buller and Mrs Northey. Mrs Northey gave me a dish of tea. Got home, sat in the Study and soon to bed.

Monday September 6 Miss Penelope Poole mentioned a fact this night worth noting, – She said that her sister Charlotte this year purchased a bag of potatoes for sixteen pence for which very quantity the year before and in the same month she gave sixteen shillings. Wheat, the new wheat, they say sold at Taunton for six shillings and sixpence a bushell last week. About this time last year it sold at eighteen shillings and a little before that at twenty one, two, three and four shillings.

Thursday September 9 Charles and the Clerk are gone to Halsey Cross for barley They went afterwards to Plainsfield and brought four laods in all. My stomach was but poorly all this day. After dinner we walked to Stowey and drank tea with old Mr and Mrs Buller. He is past fourscore, a shrewd old Grazier of coarse vulgar manners. She is likewise a sharp spirited little woman and the sister of the present Bishop of Bath and Wells.

Friday September 10 There is a Parish Wedding.* Strange work, the couple come but not the Overseer and we cannot find the Clerk. At last they come just in time. They are marries, the man lives in my Parish, young Davies, but the woman in Nether Stowey. I do not like forced matches and so I questioned them much and they said they were willing and so now the jobb is done.

The year 1803

The winter and early Spring must remain a mystery for Mr Holland's manuscript is missing for the period mid September to mid March.

Thursday March 10 Young Morle came to be married this day in our Church to Miss Godfree, they have taken a house at Fiddington. Some snow this day which detained the new married couple at my house for a time but it soon cleared up. We walked to Marsh Mills to congratulate Mrs Poole on the victory at Bridgewater over the Democratic Party as her son Ruscomb had the chief management of the business, so Allen and Pocock are confirmed sitting Members for Bridgewater. By and by came Mr Mathew. He said with great good humour but dryly that they were all fighting at Bridgewater for that Pocock had but the majority of one and the other party would not believe it which provoked quarrels and battles. Met Rich of Ely Green carrying two parcels. Heigh day said I what are those fine things. They are for you said he. I looked, they were directed to Miss Holland, Shrewsbury Cakes and a fine Cymnel Cake with a box of the well known Shewsbury cakes either from Mrs Kinaston or Miss Kinaston but there is no letter. Carriage paid to Bath. After examining the contents we went on to Stowey, I paid Mr Poole for the carriage from Bath. Sent to Betty Bishop to come to brew as the frost is going off, she came at ten and brewed all night.

Friday March 11 Brewing all night, strong beer and ale, bad time for it. A man called about two persons dead at Quantock House, the shepherd and his wife. I would not suffer them to be brought in at Church time. They are to be buried at five o'clock on Sunday. The woman that looked after them is very ill and there are some suspicions that their fever being infectious. I called on the man of Ely Green but he had not seen the apothecary that attended them.

Sunday March 13 A fine dry morning. Barometer higher and temperature 34. Went to the Sunday School and told Ben, who is a great politician, that we were going to War again. Ben shrugged himself and cried that it was bad. The King has sent a message to Parliament that the French are arming.

Ah says Ben that Bonnypart will not leave us alone. Rode to Asholt in the afternoon and the Church full, met several persons from all parts going to the burial of the old shepherd which they thought would be in the morning. I returned and dined and then both of the corpses* were brought. Old Shepherd May from Quantock House and his wife and such a crowd before I never saw here. I had the Service at five in the afternoon purposely to prevent any infection spreading if there was any and to keep the people from being present but this alas was to little purpose. However I hope all is well. It is said there were no less than four hundred people at Church. After this business was over I retired but must observe that in Church there was best singing I ever heard. The Trumpet shall sound and the Dead be raised was quite sublime. We spent the evening at home according to custom. I had prayers twice, two Sermons, a Christening, Churching and Burying and was after all a little fatigued. Went to bed in good time.

Thursday March 17   Briffet brought the letters, a Welsh one from Mr Lewis and another from my niece Holland* addressed to Margaret. We were very anxious to know the contents. Mounted my horse and rode to Cannington to carry the letter to Margaret, she read it and told me that my eldest niece was certainly to be married to Mr Wynne of Coed Coch. I like the Mr Wynne very well as a gentleman of good principles and fortune but there is a madness in the family and that my niece, a young heiress of two thousand per annum should give herself, her name and Fortune to a man of the description is to me mortifying to a degree. Yet my brother and his wife approve of the Match very much. The name of Holland will be gone from Wales in a very short time. It was originally English. There is a place in Lancashire called Holland whence the name was originally taken. A branch of the family was made Duke of Exeter and two sons of the Duke of Exeter in troublesome times, about the time of Edward the Fourth, fled in to Wales. They were of the Lancastrian Party. They lived for some time in obscurity, till affairs bore a better aspect for their family and then they became known and one of them settled in Wales by marrying the heiress of Kymael from whence our family and the Hollands in Wales are descended. I have written a more full account of this matter on some of the white leaves in my large Family Bible. Returned from Canningon before dinner to their great surprise.

Sunday March 20   Very mild and the day turned out tolerable. Rode to Asholt, not many at Church, Came back, few at Church here in the afternoon. That Villain Porter had the impudence to come there, it disconcerted me much. His own daughter confesses herself to be with child by him. Oh Abominable Villain. I will punish him if there is any law to be had.

Monday March 21 I am rather poorly, something of the fashionable cold called Influenza. I did not move about except in the garden. Attended to William's schooling.

Tuesday March 22 My daughter is but poorly with the Influenza. My daughter grows worse and indeed is very poorly and has been on the bed a great part of the afternoon and now she is gone into bed and I hope she will be better tomorrow. Mrs Edith (the cook) has, or pretends to have, the Influenza. She is often ailing tho' she appears to be strong enough to knock down an ox and eat him up afterwards.

Wednesday March 23 Mrs Rich the Overseer's wife called. She made great complaints of some of the Poor, their impositions. That horrid woman Porter was brought to bed of a dead child this morning, by her own father. Oh Horrid Deed, and this circumstance I fear prevents our moving against him in a legal way for now we cannot compel the girl to swear to the father of the child. I hope there has been fair play. Charles does not seem to have done much this day, indeed I think he wants looking after. The Thatcher came yesterday as he pretends to finish his work and I understood he had done so. I paid him but to my great surprise this morning he had by no means compleated it and sneaked away and left me in a very unhandsome way and told direct lies on the occasion, for I sent to him to know whether he had finished and he said he had. He is a Methodist, a liar and a drunkard. The Faith without Work Gentry always act in this manner.

Monday March 28 The youngest cow has brought a fine heiffer calf. Mounted the great horse, Charles has so fed him that he is ungovernable. Called on Mrs Poole, Mr Woodhouse, Washer, Old Shawney and Old Becky, all very poorly of this reigning complaint. Old Becky had got some Apothecary's Stuff as she calls it, but I shant take any says she. Have you not returned I quickly, then you shall and so I made her take some immediately. They all smiled around her, however she had still some Pills to take which were never mentioned to me and this she told my wife soon after. Strange that old people should be so childish.

Wednesday March 30 Mr Rich called to see our calf and to value it. The old cow he said would not calve for some days. Breakfasted, came down from the Study and behold the other cow calved. Oh Mr Rich what wisdom. I mounted my horse and rode to Enmore wih Mr John Poole to see his new house which is going on very well. Ugly faced Briffet brought a letter with a draught from Mr Payne for the Interest on Maidenhead Bridge. There is talk of War and Mr Pitt coming in.

Friday April 1   No clock striking this morning. Little William jumped down from the staircase window, jarred the clock so much that the pandulum fell off and was bent so that we must have Mr Coles to it. After dinner Coles came to set the clock in order.

Monday April 4   Charles took a Tithe pig from Dick Jones but I gave the poor woman half a crown and sent them some excellent broth and veal stew. Jew Landsey in a great fright this day, he put fire to some furze in a field of his on the side of Quantock. It blazed very much and the wind blew it towards the Custom Wood on Quantock which he was afraid would take fire so he laboured to prevent it till the sweat ran down his face in torrents, poor Pilgarlic. Nothing further but Farmer Stone paid me for some barley and swigged my strong beer.

Tuesday April 5   James Rich passing by under the window, poor James walks very wide. He says it will rain. My man Charles is gone for coal. We called on the Pooles, they tell me that Symms the Lawyer from Bridgwater intends to bring an action against me for cutting wood in the Custom Wood which they are inclosing for Mr Balch. I am very well prepared for him having cut myself for above twenty years and I can prove the cutting out of the Custom Wood in lieu of Tithe for above a hundred years back. After dinner Blake from Stowey came about the Taxes on the very day they were due. I had but just paid one half year before. I fancy the money will lie in his hands for some time, this is not quite the thing. We passed this evening at home among ourselves.

Wednesday April 6   Charles in the garden putting down potatoes. I walked with Little William to Stowey, paid the malster for making the malt and grinding. Met two Miss Pooles at Mr Francis Pooles, bought some cakes and returned. The ladies walked out after dinner. While I was alone the servants uncommonly playful and gigling in the kitchen. I called to 'em and observed to Charles that he stayed within doors to play with the woman. Edith and he are like two elephants at gambols. Night drew on and we sat by a good fire, some to reading and others to writing and afterwards to bed.

Thursday April 7   Ugly faced Briffet brought a letter from Wm Tutton last night. We mean to go to Monkton Farley the week after Easter week. I walked down to Stowey and spoke to Coles once more about the clock, something he neglected. He is no better than a rascal with all his conjuration. When I returned I found Mr John Poole looking over Old Caradock Butler's* Book about the Privilege of cutting wood in the Custom Wood. It is mentioned in eight places. nothing decisive in the paper about war or peace. Our Ministers I fear are too languid or undecisive. To bed in good time.

Friday April 8   Good Friday. Most of the family up but I have seen nothing of Margaret. Sent Charles with the paper to Mr Rich. Betty gone for treacle to Hodge's. I see no one at work except Charles Sellick piddling in his garden. I suppose they will all be at Church. Not so, they continued there during the Service tho' I spoke to them more than once. That Charles Selleck under the character of a quiet good tempered man hides the extreme of meanness and a knavish dishonest disposition, his character is much mistaken. Few at Church but we had a grand Christening, Bristow's wife Churched. They chose an odd day for a Christening, to revel on a Good Friday, but these people know nothing of propriety. Rode over to Asholt, not many there. Came back and dined on eggs and bacon. I was rather faint with the Duty, I do not think fasting suits me. It does not make one more clear and collected for Religious Duties but rather disorders one – besides I always live temperate. Charles brother called, whether on the brother or Mrs Edith I do not know for our Somersetshire six foot high beauty seems to be very amourous, and fickle too. Betty's tooth ached and so Edith and she went off together and Mr Carlisle after them. Poor Betty had a miserable time of it. Master King broke and pummelled the poor girl's tooth to atoms and after all left a part behind and the poor girl fainted away several times and could scarce be brought to life. To bed in good time. No rain but the night looks suspicious and the glass does not rise.

Sunday April 10   Easter Sunday. The Family not up yet, I only. Stepped into the Study but am not shaved or dressed. After breakfast went into the Sunday School. Ben's grandchild received the halfpenny for coming first. A tolerable number at Church and four and twenty at the Sacrament, pretty well for a country place. After dinner I rode to Asholt. I never saw Asholt Church so full before they were continually thrusting one another and moving from place to place to find room. Got home and found Mrs Mackey here and Miss Wollen. Another little man asked me familiarly how I did and bowed. I even shook hands with him but could not make him out. When he was gone they told me it was young Axford from Bridgewater – the Puppy – had I known I should not have been so ready to take him by the hand.

Monday April 11   We were up before seven this morning. My wife and William are walked to Rich of Pepperel and not yet returned and all this before breakfast. We had few at Prayers. I was busy afterwards writing a case to be laid before the Council relating to the Custom Wood when Lo! Mr Symms, Mr Balch's Attorney called. He was civil, said he had no intention of hurting me and would do everything to my satisfaction. We parted amicably and I shewed him all the evidence I had. After dinner the Parishioners met. I represented the Altar in the Chancel and the Cloth that covered the Communion Table as shabby and rotten and proposed repairs and a new one. Farmer Morle agreed to rectify them at once, Mr James Rich objected with some warmth. I told him that I would present them, which fired him still more. I believe he had been drinking, however I gave him some strong replies and appointed Farmer Morle for my ChurchWarden and he partly declining for the other Church Warden, Farmer Dibble was chosen in his stead. After this I walked to the Poole's and found my family there. It is Mrs Poole's Birthday, being this day 70.

Thursday April 14 Sent Charles for Bridgewater for meat and fish if he can get any. Poor Weymouth I see crawling along, he has had the influenza and is scarce recovered. Charles returned with veal and fish but the fish is nothing extraordinary. I did not go out very far this day. For dinner we had some fish which is no very common thing now. I remember when fish used to be brought every other day. Salmon at Bridgewater at two shillings per pound, I remember it at fourpence and scarce ever above sixpence, tis strange this alteration in a few years.

Friday April 15 This is my Tithe day and what has never happened before two of my Farmers, Mr James Rich and Mr Buller are very poorly tho' they have brought the money and beg to be excused. Farmers White and Morle gone to South Molton. Mr Tom Poole gone to Bristol but he is to dine with me Monday. However a few came and very merry and well pleased they were and praised my beer beyond measure. Those that did not dine with me paid their money so all went off very well and they left before tea. A fire blazing tonight in the furze around Farmer Dyer's.

Sunday April 17 Briffet come, a letter from Mrs Kinaston, she is on her journey to Bath where we intend to give her the meeting next week. Mounted my horse and rode to Asholt. Not many there but there was a Burial and a Sacrament. I was obliged to finish the Burial Service before I went to the Sacrament. Returned to dinner. The Church here was very crouded indeed and very good singing. I am to ride to Bridgewater with Mr Ruscomb Poole before breakfast tomorrow as I want a Clergyman to do my Duty while I go to Bath and M Farley. It is very windy and there has been rain all this day.

Tuesday April 19 A blustery rainy morning. A great bustle above us, the masons about the roof of the house. I spoke to Verrier. Gave Charles last night a half guinea on account of wages. The chaise came at the time appointed soon off, called at Cannington, got to Bridgewater, started from Miss Charlotte Poole's door. The town full of Soldiers marching and countermarching. Off again, got to Wells, stopped at Mrs Richard Pooles, sat down to dinner, not expected. Mr Cobley* had been there the day before to say we should not come, Mrs Poole exceedingly hurt, a strange jumblement here. – Margaret slept at Mrs Poole's. my wife and I at Mr Cobley's.

Wednesday April 20   We all breakfasted at Mr Cobley's and were off about ten. Got very well to Bath, it rained very hard. We dined at Bath and then had a chaise to N Farley in the afternoon. We had tolerable accomodation at my old Servants William Tutton, and Miss Beak called and we drank tea there. Old Beak talked big as usual. Returned in the evening and soon to bed.

Thursday April 21   A tempestuous night and such rain this morning. Called on my new tennant Captain Burchell. He received me with great civility, is a little man of great spirit and vivacity, a good strong eye, a very tolerable forehead, bald the fore part of his head. He was Captain of a Line of Battle Ship at the Battle of Copenhagen. Captain Birchill agreed to meet the farmers with me but a Captain Mawd called on him, 2nd son of Lord Haywarden, so I left. He is an open hearted man but swears too much for me. The Farmers paid their money very well but Mr Beak attempted to shuffle a little.

Friday April 22   After breakfast our chaise arrived from Bath and we soon got in, Great rain, reached Bath however in safety. Go out for lodgings. First of all we drove to Mrs Manningford, none there. Found the streets barricaded and after wheeling backward and forward got to the White Lion Inn at last. Out again for lodgings, got some in George's Street, No 14. Dined at the Inn but no Mrs Kinaston come. We continued in our lodgings without stirring all evening.

Sunday April 24   A fine morning and after breakfast I took my new umbrella in my hand and walked to Claverton, called on old Graves author of the Spiritual Quixote, gone to Church. Then I crossed the ferry, asked young King how his father did. Dead replied he two months ago. Poor King he had travelled to east and West and was an honest worthy man. Marched up the steep hill and got to Monkton Farley at last. Stepped into Mr Birchill's then Wm Tutton's, sat there a while and then returned to Captain Birchill's to dinner. By and by came in a young gentleman, Mr Shute the Curate, Mr Budd having left us. A pleasing young man. By and by went to Church. Mr Shute reading Prayers and I preached. A corpse was brought to Church, poor Sweetland he was killed in a quarry on the downs, the stones falling on him. I did not drink tea at Monkton Farley, took leave of Captain Birchill, Beak etc. Walked with Mr Shute to Bathford, a corpse waiting for him. I left him and walked on. About the Turnpike as I was about to enter Bath a tremendous rain came on but I had an umbrella which protected me and so I got to Mrs Kinaston's much fatigued. Staid there and

about nine o'clock marched off with my wife, daughter and little William to
our lodgings over the way.

Friday April 29   Breakfasted at Mr Hume's, late Canon of Salisbury. We had
a very handsome breakfast and great civility was shewn us. An immense
Sally Lunn on the table, the first time I have seen one compleat. Mrs Hume
gave Margaret some presents, she is her Godmother. My wife and I enquired
about chairs at the coachmakers, none made at Bath. Moved about shopping.

Saturday April 30   Up very early, packed all things in readiness. Soon
appeared the chaise ordered from the White Lion. The people at our lodgings
were remarkably civil. We found that two of the servants were from M
Farley and Mrs Borinsale the Mistress of the House was a woman from
Bagborough and well acquainted with the Morles. We were soon off and got
to Wells without stay or hindrance. Called at Mr Cobley's and Mrs Poole's
but breakfasted at the Inn. Off again, reached Piper's Inn, the same chaise and
driver conveying us all the way from Bath. Here we left them and soon got to
Bridgewater. Stepp'd out, ordered another chaise, ran to Mr Ruscomb
Poole's, gave them a shake by the hand and soon entered our chaise and got
to Overstowey. The roof of the house finished, a compleat jobb notwithstanding the wind and rain. This pleased me much. Our servants have
conducted themselves with Prudence during our absense, Charles has
mowed the garden with a new scythe but he had mowed away the soil most
woefully, however on the whole matters were very well.

Sunday May 1   Not many at Church this morning. Old Mrs Poole came
who had not been for several Sundays. Dined, the rain came on, I robed
myself in two greatcoats and got to Asholt. The little Clerk was somewhat
impertinent, said Asholt ought to have been in the morning. I told him it was
no business of his but mine. This answer chilled him at once. Came back and
as I passed Ely Green I saw two or three going into the Publick House and
through the window I could perceive Farmer Dibble who drew back when
he caught my eye. I shall speak to the man of Ely Green. Came home and
spent the evening in the usual stile of Sunday.

Wednesday May 4   Margaret not up, the rest of the family are. Our great
maidservant fanceyed last night that she was not well but however she is very
well this morning. She, like Charles, if their finger ache are much alarmed yet
both so stout and large as seemingly to be able to knock down an ox and eat
him up. Edward Selleck did some jobbs in the Church and is to repair the
Altar in the Chancel at my insistence and representation to the Churchwardens. Mr Wood the Musick Master came here today to teach Margaret. Betty
went home to see her sister who is very ill.

Saturday May 7 Jenkins called about the Taxes, I delivered a schedule to him. Charles busy about the cucumbers, I joined him. Sowed some brocolo seeds. I mounted my horse and rode to Stowgursey to dine with Mr Davis. Met Miss Acland who asked me how I did and how my wife and daughter were. I told her I was glad to see her out. Reached Stow Gurcy, met Mr John and Mr Ruscomb Poole there, Mr Lewis and Mr Poole of Shurston. Spent an agreeable evening, returned in good time in company with Mr John and Ruscomb Poole. Found all well at home and went to bed in good time.

Monday May 9 Sent Charles to Stowey for malt and after sent him to the inclosed Custom Wood to see the Tithe properly set forth. By and by William and I marched after him, it was a hot day, great appearance of Whortleberries. Saw Charles and Davis, gave some of the men a shilling all goes on right. Returned to dinner rather fatigued. A letter from Mr Leighton, he is married to Miss Victoria Leighton a relation of his.

Tuesday May 10 Family up and have breakfasted. Margaret at the Harpsichord. William saying his Lesson to his Mama but he has been very unruly and I have been obliged to strap him. Mr Wood the Musick Master came to Margaret and brought her a musick book. I and my wife and William walked to Stowey payed Verrier a Bill for five pounds fifteen shillings and ninepence this day. I saw it crossed in the book and a memorandum entered with the day of the month. Got home and to dinner, the evening uncommonly cold and the wind chilling. We did not move much but had a good fire.

Wednesday May 11 I dressed myself and ordered Charles to get himself ready then I walked down to Mr John Poole and asked when the Book Society dined and was surprised to hear him say at four. I of course returned, sent Charles down with the books and before 4 I went myself. The members were all present, viz Mr Acland, Mr Archdeacon Clark, Reverend Mr Mathews, Reverend Mr John Poole, Mr Tom Poole, Mr Sealey, Reverend Mr Davis, Mr Ruscomb Poole, Mr Charles Poole and myself — Three vacancies and five candidates. Reverend Mr Northey, Reverend Mr Henry Poole of Shurston and Mr King chosen in. We spent a very agreable day and retired in good order. I bought a few of the Society's Books. Came home with Mr John Poole. Charles, who waited at dinner carrying my books. It was late when I got home. The newspaper came but nothing certain about Peace or War. Soon to bed.

Wednesday May 18 My wife and William up but I have not seen Margaret. Mr John Poole and Mr Brice called here and walked with me to Farmer Morle's. Spoke to Farmer Morle about Processioning on Thursday and the claims of Bagborough Parish. Returned, I walked lame my shoe pinching me. Mr Brice spoke to Farmer White about the state of the roads, he is going to indite them. Hurley called and has taken my Tithe wood on Quantock.

Thursday August 11 I found Mr Charles about the cucumbers this morning, not dead yet. I was called to him several times yesterday as Mrs Edith thought he was dying but I saw no signs of any such thing. I suppose he lived a little too well the day before when I gave him permission to go with the reapers to Farmer Landsey's wheat field. A poor creature good for nothing but bragging. I found too the Clerk had gone, he complained of a pain in his head. So, so, fine work if every one is to be ill or pretend to be so. Mr Charles has now got tooth ache, poor fellow he'll have toe ache next. A pity it is his broad back was not made to ache with a good stick. Sad work among them.

Friday August 12   My Lazy Scoundrel Charles I see is moving about, nothing but living a little too freely. Briffet come with the papers, there have been some alarms with the French. I rode out today to Stowey to enquire about papers to be filled up with the names of persons from the age of 17 to 55.

Saturday August 13 A great number of people in Mr Buller's field adjoining the Paddock reaping, and very noisy. Charles and the Clerk winnowed the wheat, it yields uncommonly well, almost thirty bushells to the acre. I did not ride out today but I had a good deal of talk about the enrollment and went down to Mr Hurley's and talked to him. The people in Buller's field became very drunk and riotous. I told Charles this day that I was aware of all his pranks and should certainly part with him when his year is up. Briffet brought the papers and a letter from the Duke of Somerset, he has not much acquaintance with any of the Governors of the Charter House as to get me a nomination for my Little Boy.

Tuesday August 16 Family up, the Clerk bringing in the horse to fetch Tithe. A very hot day indeed, every one busy in carrying. Charles and the Clerk brought me three loads from Plainsfield. The horse behaved incomparably well. I wrote down the list of Bincomb Tithings but did not stir from the premises. My teeth ache very much.

Wednesday August 17 Newspaper come, nothing material in it, Tobago taken by us. About one we all set out in the cart for Asholt and Charles to manage the horse. I did not like the jogging of the cart and so walked most part of the way. Got safe all of us and had a good day with Mr Blake. About dusk my daughter and Miss Lewis and little William took to the cart but my wife chose to walk and it was very pleasant. We all got home safe, supped and soon went to bed.

Thursday August 18   I had a blister put on my back last night to carry off the pain in my gums and it was very troublesome this morning and together with the heat of the weather made me very restless most of the night. however I am considerably relieved by it and can bear it very well now they have looked to it and I am up. Charles and the Clerk gone for wheat and barley. I did not stir from the premises, my blister running all day and I think it has done me good already. While we were at tea Mr John Poole came in and made me a present of Mr Harford's drawings of the Antiquities found on the Polden Hills where there are some observations made by Mr Harford and likewise a letter from Mr John Poole concerning some Roman Moulds found on Eddington Hill. Mr Hurley called and I delivered to him the list of the classes of men to be enrolled for Overstowey.

Saturday August 20   My blister ran prodigiously today. I hope it will do me good but the pain on the left side of my face is not gone. I have not stirred from the premises. In the afternoon young Landsey was brought to be buried, he died of a Frenzy Fever. A young man about 27 years old, had been married about half a year ago. A great many came to the burial. His wife, a young woman of some credit, was in agonies. A number of the most respectable neighbours attended. Charles went down to Stowey for some spirits for me but found none from Shidfield. Paid the Clerk and Saturday ended as usual.

Monday August 22   Poor Clark of Monksilver is returned from Windsor after having lost the Living of Monksilver by a sad mistake. A Clergyman of the name of Price called on me today, shabbily dressed. He was of Jesus College, Oxford, had been Usher to Mr Mant at Southampton. A good looking man and clever but seemed something wild about the eyes. I gave him half a guinea with which he seemed much pleased. I fancy there must be something wrong with him otherwise he would not be turned on the Publick in the manner he was. Mr Amen seems to get old and childish.

Friday August 26   The Clerk is here. I shall send for a load of wheat today. It came and now my wheat is all in. After dinner I mounted my horse and called on that Shocking Sinner Old Porter who is in a dying state. He has had a child by his own Wicked Daughter. He lay in a dozing state and did not seem to have much sense of guilt on his mind, but I spoke to him in Strong Terms. Told him that I had never visited a person before in so sad a state of sin and sincerely hoped I never should again.

Wednesday August 31 I rode out this day with little William behind. Called on Rascal Porter and he was gone out, he is a sad fellow. Went up on Quantock and saw many asses, had a mind to buy one for my Little Boy. Saw the paper and read an advertisement for the Clergy to attend at Wells in order to sign an Address to His Majesty.

Thursday September 1 I have just written a letter to the Bishop of Bath and Wells relating to an address to His Majesty and my wife and Little William are gone to Marsh Mills to give it to Mr John Poole to carry to Wells for he is going. My wife and I and Little William walked to Stowey, called on the Northey's. She had finished her Drawing Room in very good taste and not expensive. She teaches her daughter Musick and in an excellent stile. In short she is a clever little woman and highly accomplished, both useful and ornamental. Mr Northey came in and we had a long chat. I paid Price's bill and did some other little jobbs and then we returned home.

Sunday September 4 A fine pleasant morning, I must go and have one of these Military Papers stuck to the Church door. I preached a sermon on the present War which was much attended to. Went to Asholt and preached the same sermon and Wednesday next was appointed for the enrollment of Volunteers for both Parishes. I visited a sick person at Asholt and Church a woman and Christened a child at Overstowey. Poor Ben Hunt has not been at the Sunday School these two Sundays. He is not well, I must call on him

Monday September 5 Saw Mr Tom Poole and had long conversation and was sorry to hear that there are not a hundred Regulars in the County of Somerset and that the defence must be entrusted to the Volunteer Corps. Charles I found near the Workhouse quarrelling with Will Hill, he is often in some bustle or other, I do not like it but he shall not stay with me longer than his year. All that he said a few days ago about a Press Gang turns out to be a lie. He is always scouting about and under no control.

Friday September 9 Dressed myself and my wife and self and Margaret walked down to Stowey to dine with Mr Northey. We met there Mr Wollen* and old Mrs Northey, Mr Northey's mother, a fine old lady. After tea Charles came down with a lantern so off we set and got home before ten. The servants say that young Wollen came in our absense to play with William and he gathered fruit from the trees, this is a serious business as it teaches my boy bad tricks.

Saturday September 10 Charles went off early for Taunton to order a chaise for Monday when we are to go to South Molton. After breakfast I had a long conversation with William about the plunder of the garden. He told me everything honestly for he never tells a lie. I fear many nectarines and all the peaches off one tree are gone. I gave my boy two or three straps but as he told the truth and promised never to do the like again I did not chastise him further. In the evening of this day we walked down to Marsh Mill to drink tea and spend the evening for they will leave this Parish before I and my family return from S. Molton. The young ones were all born in the Parish and Mrs Poole lived here from her marriage and there is something Melancholy in their leaving this place. Mr John Poole is building a house at Enmore which will not be in a fit state to receive anyone this twelvemonths so that they must be put to their Shifts in a certain degree. I think it affects Mrs Poole very much.

Sunday September 11   Rode to Asholt, not many at Church. Returned to Overstowey and dined. A great many at Church, almost quite full. Porter again very troublesome, we found he had broken loose and all the Parish after him. They at last caught him and I went into the Poorhouse to see him. He looked shocking. I went after this into my own house, sat in the Study and in due time to bed.

Monday September 12   Up early preparing for our journey. Charles off before us on the great horse to Taunton. Edward Selleck here to put the lock on the Beaufet in the Common Parlour. The chaise came and we got safe to Taunton. After breakfast to Tiverton and arrived in good time. As I past by the School I was pleased to see the boys in such good order and in such numbers. Tiverton seems to be a smart town of some size yet I was surprised to see but one Church there. Soon after we left the place we pulled out our chicken and eggs and out salt and bread and bottle of cyder and we played away most heartily. This is the best method of dining for travellers, it is most expeditious and least expensive. I never enjoyed a dinner more. It was late when we got to Mrs Southcomb but for the first time for many years she had no fit on our first arrival. This is the house where Little William was born. Eat an enormous supper and marched to bed.

Wednesday September 14   Mrs Southcomb not down with us having a fit. Charles went off to Rose Ash to bring Miss Southcomb here to Margaret. Poor girl, she is the eldest of eleven and the father now in a deranged state and they are about to remove him from his family. We went to Chapel here and I read Prayers. It is a very neat Chapel, dedicated to the Trinity, and erected by Mr Southcomb the Grandfather of the present Mr Southcomb of Rose Ash and endowed handsomely on condition of Service being done there three times within the month and omitting the fourth. The Sundays were intended I am convinced but they have converted, or rather perverted it to one Sunday and Wednesday and Friday in the ensueing week. Mr Keats and Miss Keats came in after Prayers, an old gentleman formerly Headmaster of Tiverton School and now Rector of Kings Nympton. My jaws are still bad and I have got a cold. I must do something to get well for it will not do to go on in this manner.

Friday September 16   My face still rather painful and I went to bed rather poorly. I drank a little more wine than usual, perhaps that inflamed it.

Saturday September 17   My face is very painful, it is with difficulty that I can speak. I must get some relief else I shall not be able to feed at all. Went to bed in good time.

Sunday September 18   My face still bad and I was scarce able to speak and a good deal of phlegm. I have not been able to eat anything only drink some currant jelly and water which has cleared me up a great deal. It grieves me to pass away Sunday without doing Duty myself or going to Church. Mr Ling, Mr Bryant's Apprentice, came at last. We dined and after dinner I had leeches put to my cheek or rather lip under the nose. It is over after two or three hours and I seem easier and in spirits and made the company laugh and am to take Dover's Powder as I am to go to bed. Mr Ling is the Nephew of Mrs Southcomb's late Husband.

Monday September 19   I slept rather restless and felt little from Dover's Powder. My jaws seemingly better. After dinner we sat up as usual and went to bed as usual but my face does not appear much better from leeches or Dr Dover.

Wednesday September 21   I think my jaw is somewhat better today and I breakfasted with some comfort. Towards two o'clock I mounted on Mrs Southcomb's mare Ginger, and with Margaret behind Charles on the great horse went to South Molton to dine with Mr Stawell. Mr and Mrs Stawell live comfortably together his Church Preferment is not great but his fortune very considerable for a private Clergyman. We had present at dinner Mr and Mrs Riddiford, a medical man, but having married two women for their fortunes he left off business and commenced Gentleman and so squandered away most of their fortunes. He has lived freely and become an Old Man at 35. In other respects he is a sensible man. Captain and Mrs Law, the gentleman pleasant and handsome, the lady diminutive, affected and almost naked in her dress. It disgusts me much to see such conduct. We had a very good Handsome Dinner and spent a pleasant day.

Friday September 23   At the beginning of the long hill into Kings Nympton we met eight chaises full of ill-looking Frenchmen, prisoners moving (it seems) more inland from the sea coast on account of the threatened Invasion. There were no Soldiers to guard them and there were some on foot. I did not think it quite the thing. They are going to South Molton.

Had some conversation with a young Farmer about the French who seemed at first alarmed but when I told him they were prisoners his countenance brightened.

Monday September 26   An odd thing happened in South Molton tother day. Three Frenchmen took a bed in a Lodging House. It seems the bed had been engaged to and occupied by a Corporal of Marines. He returned unexpectedly and being told of the circumstances rushed up stairs with a candle in his hand In so doing his bayonet fell out of the sheath. He stopped to pick it up with one hand and with the other threw open the bed curtains which awoke the poor Frenchmen. While he was lifting up the naked bayonet one got out of the window into the street, seeing his red military dress and naked bayonet thought they were to be put to death. It caused some uproar, however at last things were set to rights.

Thursday September 29   I thank God the pain in my face has left me in great measure. Dined on a Michaelmas Goose, Mrs Southcomb did not join us, an apple fell on her head in the orchard which discomposed her much.

Friday September 30   Mr John Southcomb is still with his family at Rose Ash in a deranged state and his removal from thence is unaccountably delayed. Mrs Southcomb the wife and Mrs Southcomb my sister in law are writing letters backwards and forwards dayly and distressing each other beyond measure about it.

Saturday October 1   Up early to go Stag Hunting. I drank a glass of water, put a crust of bread in my pocket and had my horse saddled. Got to the Hounds, a vast concourse of Gentlemen. At last we moved on above three miles to Lord Fortescue's. He joined the Company which was very numerous, there was an Irish Lord, Lord Lisle, a Sir – Northcote, Mr Chichester and several of the First Gentlemen in Devonshire and several of the Clergy, in all about a hundred. A Mr North was Master of the Hounds though it is a kind of Subscription Hunt. They tried again and again but no deer to be found. I understand this is no uncommon thing which makes it not so amusing a sport as Fox Hunting or Hare Hunting. This Hunt and the wild deer is almost peculiar to Devonshire. It brings the Chief Gentry of Devonshire together, which is a glorious sight. Sometimes there are two or even three hundred horsemen together riding as hard as they can. I returned about dusk.

Monday October 3   Charles desired to go to a Burial at George Nympton. I desired him to be back by twelve. They have in this county a Funeral Sermon to every Corpse which I do not approve of much for it is bribing the Pulpit to give a good character of persons who may not deserve it. It is paying the Clergyman for supressing the notice of the bad qualities of the deceased and speaking only of the good. This is not properly holding him forth as an example to be followed, for his neighbours will recall what he really was and imagine they may go on as they please and still get a good name at their death. Both the people buried at George Nympton recently were drunkards, one was so when he fell into a pit and broke his neck, and often times he used to come home in this state and beat his wife and turn her out of doors. Now what could a Funeral Sermon say of such a man and yet he was whitewashed after his death. The best way is to be silent. He is in the Hands of his Creator and He knows best how he is to be treated. In sitting down after dinner wih old Keats we could not but remark on how common the tendency to Madness is among the Devonshire Families. There was not one around that had not the malady among them. The Physiognomy is very peculiar, a square flat forehead a nose rising gradually from it to the point, rather sharp chin and the arch of the head not very regularly formed, the complexion light and the face white and not often with colour. They are a perfectly different race from the Somersetshire and I have no doubt are descended from different people.

Wednesday October 5 Mr and Miss Keats could not come to dinner having had a serious Rumpus among the Servants. That tribe of beings are much altered of late years, no subordination among them. The Glorious Effects of the French Revolution.

Friday October 7 Up early, about five o'clock. The chaise came before we were ready. Off we went, horse's shoe loose, put on again at a blacksmith's, off again before we got to Tiverton. Tiverton a pleasant looking town, full of French Officers among whom is that villain General Boyer who says he gave orders for the Massacre at Jaffa. The people at the Inn very Civil to us, we made a hearty breakfast. Between Wellington and Taunton drew out our substantial Chicken Pye, stuffed with tongue, eggs and chicken. William eat like a dragon and I played a good part, then we all swigged the cyder. Got safe to Taunton and the Castle Inn very full and the Landlady not over civil. Charles had ordered a chaise and we got to Overstowey before dusk without any accident. Everything tight, clean and in good order. We had a comfortable supper and soon to bed being a little fatigued all of us.

Saturday October 8 More information about Edith's pranks – she is to go on Monday.

Sunday October 9 Mr Amen posting to inform the Parishioners that the Service will be in the afternoon at Overstowey. Rode to Asholt, a Sacrament and ten attended. Our Church very full indeed. Read a Proclamation for a Fast at both Churches. Edith forbid to sit in my seat Church. No news of importance in the paper except threats of the intended Invasion, tho' we are bombarding their towns on the coast at this time.

Monday October 10   Mrs Edith was this morning paid her wages and packed off, a most bold impudent woman. She behaved very ill during our absense at S. Molton and tho' we took every precaution against her. Sent Betty to her mother, took Charles with us and put the Old Clerk to sleep in the house yet she contrived to have her lover with her and revelled about in a very shameful manner. I see she is still at Frost's, Mrs Frost being from home.

Saturday October 15   Had Weymouth in to scour the house. Charles and the Clerk carrying dung into the further paddock. Rode with Mr Northey to call on Mr Yorke the new Rector of Spaxton. We got there and found things rather deshabeill, poor man he seemed a good deal flustered, a very plain vulgar kind of man and not over bright. He stared like a stuck pig and hardly knew what to make of us at first, however he grew better by and by and soon came in his dearly beloved in the same plain motherly stile which rather astonished Mr Northey and myself for they are people of considerable property, the Living of Spaxton is at least eight hundred per ann. and he has besides the Living of Fiddington and they are both his own. We walked about the premises and found he is making great alterations. A niece came in and handed out some cakes and wine. I suppose they may turn out to be good kind people but they have not been much in the world. Mr Northey and I staid some time and then rode off smiling at our reception.

Sunday October 16   Went to the Sunday School, it was cake day. A number of the little people were there. Edith whom I turned off goes about with a young fellow, Charles's brother at this very time, a sad woman.

Tuesday October 18   Charles went off at four to Bridgewater for coal. I have been employed most of this day in writing a Fast Sermon for Wednesday. A servant offered and is hired in place of Edith.

Wednesday October 19   This is the Publick Fast Day, I was up and had all things in readiness. A very full congregation at Overstowey this morning. I preached on the War and gave them a new Sermon as I always do on this occasion. Rode over to Asholt and had a very full congregation too at that place.

Saturday October 22   Dame Stone called with a roasting pig to sell for three shillings and sixpence, I bought it. I do not ever remember ever buying one before but I have sold many. Our new maid came just as we were sitting down to dinner, she had lost her road. I hear that Mr Tint after giving a great dinner to his Yeoman Cavalry at Stowey in driving himself home in a gig broke his leg which I am sorry for as he seems to be much liked and a spirited young man.

Sunday October 23   Newspaper come with a cargo of Pamphlets to be given to the Parishioners. Rode to Asholt, no Sunday School to be established there, the Master seeks for greater pay than is usually allowed. The Church here at two very full but Mr James Rich not at Church.

Monday October 24   Most of the Village coming to my well for water, never was such a scarcity before. Mr Parsons called, Rector of Gothurst and Wembdon. He is Rural Dean and examines Churches, I am to meet him again Monday.

Tuesday October 25   This is our Wedding Day, we have been married twenty two years to this day. Clerk came but he does not work, I suppose Cruckshanks gave him too much liquor yesterday. I wish he had sent me by him my money for Tithe Wood, this is the second time he put me off. I dont much approve of this mighty Steward of Lord Egmont. Mr Gravener came here before dinner, he is heir of Alfoxen, a good looking young man, sensible and decent in his manners.

The Year 1804*

Thursday March 15 After breakfast I mounted my horse and rode to Bridgewater and called on Mrs Lewis but did not stay long. Passed by Mr Eaton in his field and spoke to him. He is an extraordinary character. He is a native of Wales and was educated for the Church, I remember him a Batcler of Jesus College, Oxford. When he entered into Holy Orders he came down to Cannington and served the Curacy. But in a short time gave disgust to the Parishioners by an odd kind of connection which he made with a lady there who dyed and left him a house and two or three fields. These he has occupied and cultivated ever since living by himself without communications with any other person. A savage kind of life and penurious to a great degree, doing all kinds of offices for himself and suffering no other person to enter his house. Yet small as his premises are he has contrived by extreme penuriousness to save a great deal of money. He has no regular Curacy yet is often employed for pay to serve Churches in the neighbourhood. His manners are so rough and he dresses in so squalid a manner and does Duty in so irreligious and indecent a manner and with a strong Welsh accent that most persons object to his doing a Duty at all, and some say they would rather go without a Service than listen to him. He is very violent in temper and without Principle or Religion but he is generally civil towards me and wishes apparently to commend himself to my notice. But I always keep aloof but with a distant kind of civility. Got to Bridgewater, went to Mr Jenkins and saw William. I told him I understood Mr Jenkins had given him a sixpence for saying his lesson so well and I would give him another.

Friday March 16 I met Betty Bishop with parcels for me, two Cymnels from Mrs Kinaston, one for Margaret and one for little William. I think they are peculiar to the town of Shrewsbury, Large and deep, a thick crust with saffron in it and hard and filled inside with sweetmeat.

Friday March 23 After tea finished a letter to my old friend, school fellow, and Fellow Collegian Tom Hughes. He and I fought a most terrible battle in the Church of Lancilian when we were little boys, the school was kept in the Church. He is two years and a half older than I am but I got the battle then tho he is a much stronger man now than I am. News was brought that poor rat-tailed Staden died suddenly in half an hour's time. Poor Rat-tail the very picture of Virtue in Distress I did not think of Losing thee so soon. we played at cards this evening, abed in due time.

Saturday March 24 In the afternoon I walked out a little and went to Peter's Well to view the inclosure Jew Landsey had made. I observed to him that I thought the Well belonged to the Parish but he though it belonged to the farm. I have got an extract of the Grant of the Glebe by Hugh de Bonneville and St Peter's Well is mentioned as a distinct thing, besides it is clearly bounded out from the farm and open only to the road and the Village.

Monday March 26 After breakfast my new man William Willis, or Villis as they call 'em in these parts, came. Mr Amen shewed him the tools etc and I gave him some directions. And after dinner Miss Betty marched off to her father's. A brother and sister came for her, she wants a place but estimates her services too high. We do not intend to keep more than one maid servant now Little William is gone to School for by experiance we find that one servant will do as much as two. We spent the evening by ourselves at home for it snowed very hard, I sent my man to Stowey to excuse our drinking with Mrs Buller on account of the weather.

Wednesday March 28 William my servant gone for coal. A letter fom Mr Henry Dodwell stating that we cannot have our dividends from Maidenhead Bridge this fortnight on account of the Income Tax. This is rather hard to detain twenty five pounds because thirty shillings are demanded by the Government. After dinner I walked down to Washer's who said he wished us a purchaser for our calf. I did not understand the term at first but now I perceive that he meant he would recommend a customer.

Friday March 30 Good Friday Charles Selleck I see at work which I do not approve of, however if he comes to Church it will do. I gave them a Sermon at Overstowey, not many to hear it. Not many at Asholt Church. The little Clerk of Asholt after Service pushed a cake into my hand, I turned round and gave him half a crown for which he bowed. It being Fast Day we dined at four on salt fish, it neither agrees with me or my wife, however we are to mortify ourselves.

Sunday April 1 Easter Day The newspaper come, great news, Marquis Wellesley has defeated the Marattas in the Mysore and taken a French General prisoner. Not many at Church but a good many at the Sacrament, two or three and twenty. The Church at Asholt very full indeed. I received three children into the Church first and then I read the Baptism over again for another child, the eldest of the first three was ten years old.* The Duty of this day almost fatigued me, I had prayers twice, a Sacrament, two Sermons, two Christenings, and a Churching and so I went into Mr Blake's and they gave me a glass of mead and I drank tea there.

Monday April 9 After breakfast my Little Boy tightened up in greatcoat and handkerchief round his neck went off like a Hero to School and my man with a new great coat and hat and band, on the great horse accompanied him so they cut a fine figure and indeed William went off in manly stile and like a sensible boy to the admiration of our neighbours. I took a walk round by the Chapel and gave the Clerk's daughter a shilling of the Sacrament money. After dinner young Morle came in for the Poor Rates which I paid him. I think it hard that my money on Maidenhead Bridge (I mean the Interest) should still be detained on account of the Income Tax because Government are not prepared to give to proper receipts so that in fact when I am required to pay for my Income Tax that very Income itself which enables me to pay it is kept from me. This is an unjustifiable stretch of Power somewhere.

Sunday April 15 A tolerable number at Church at Asholt considering the weather. A disagreeable fellow was playing his fiddle in the Church when I came in, without tune or harmony, intending I presume to accompany the Psalm Singers. I however ordered him to stop his noise which he would hardly do and then he began trying his discordant hautboy. I had a good mind to order him to be turned out.

Monday April 16 I met the great Mr Tom Poole and young Ridoubt from London in our village. Well said I, I thought you were in London. Why returned he with an assumed degree of greatness, I received letters that my presence was not necessary for a few days. They were going to see Honiball who has been ill so long, for among his ather pretentions Mr Tom Poole fancys he understands Physick because his brother who is now dead was brought up an Apothecary. He is in fact an Universal Pretender, not an Universal Genius as he wishes to be thought. I sent in the evening my man to Charles Sellick with the horse for some oats. The horse was frightened and kicked him in the stomach. We were somewhat alarmed and he rubbed the place with Spirit of Wine.

Wednesday April 18 William has turned the horse into the Churchyard and the young heifer but it will not do for the latter is very discontent the Churchyard is in a terrible litter. I walked to Stowey and changed a draft from Maidenhead with Mr Frank Poole who gave us all in cash which was very handsome at this time when there is nothing but paper to be had anywhere. They deducted my Income Tax from it.

Wednesday April 25 The Farmers are to dine with me today to pay their Tithe. The Bincomb butcher called with an Oxford Bill which I refused to change, great scarcity of cash for everyone keeps it up and does not pass it into circulation, the butcher however did not dine with me. The rest of the Farmers came and paid very well and were cheerful. Some of them at the other end of the table helped themselves to the strong beer rather too plentiously and Bristow I was obliged to check once or twice for swearing and he spat on the floor every word he spoke, a vulgar dirty dog. However they left me very tolerable, Old Charles Selleck who is seventy seven in high glee, Mr Rich and our part of the table were sound as Rocks. Mr Buller staid to drink a dish of tea with me, he is the nephew of the Bishop of the Diocese. We went into the next room to drink tea.

Saturday April 28 I heard the Cuckow for the first time this year on this very day.

Thursday May 3 I and William put down some kidney beans in circles. Had sad work with some sheep of William Hill. They got in to the Churchyard and were turned out several times. At last I sent William with them to William Hill's and to tell him that if I found them there again I would pound them. After dinner Mr and Mrs Blake and their little boy came to drink tea here. Mr Blake looked savage wih a long beard. Poor man he is in a state of mind not far from desperate derangement.

Monday May 7 Sent William to the Brook with the cart to have washed for we are all to go to Asholt in it. William digged some ground and planted some dwarf peas today. We all went to Asholt after this, my wife and I walked but Mrs Lewis, her daughters and mine rode in the cart, William conducting the horse. William shewed some ingenuity in contriving the sheaves of reed of each side so that they could sit with ease. There was no gentleman with Mr Blake but myself and we sat a short time after dinner and then took a short walk on the slope opposite the house. On our way home we encountered an adventure at Ely Green, a great noise and two fighting, Jack Hunt and John Palmer. I spoke to them and they were seperated but I believe fell to again. I ordered a Constable to be sent for which I believe was done. The man of Ely Green spoke to me and said he could not prevent it and said that he had turned them out of his house. A man better dressed than usual followed us and spoke in favour of the Landlord and very civilly wished us a good night, but who he was I cannot tell.

Wednesday May 9 Mr John Poole called and we both walked down to Stowey, went to Mr Northey's and found Archdeacon Clark there, Then we all went to the Globe where we dined, being members of the Book

Society. There were present Mr Northey, Mr Archdeacon Clark, Mr Mathew, Mr John Poole, Mr Henry Poole, Mr Ruscomb Poole, Mr Charles Poole, Mr Sealey from Bridgewater and myself. We spent a very agreeable evening together, had a good dinner and sold our books and entered into fresh subscriptions. We all staid till dusk and then I walked home with William who brought me a greatcoat and I had an umbrella. It rained much this evening.

Friday May 11 Farmer Stone brought his fourteenth child to be Christened this day and she was Churched at the same time and looked very well and strong. We walked over to William Hills to buy some potatoes. Very dear, eight and sixpence a bag, however we were obliged to buy some ours being quite out. One Rich, I see, who was transported is returned and means to fix himself upon this Parish. Mr Parsons, Rector of Gothurst and Wembdon called on me, talked about this man for he is a Justice of the Peace.

Sunday May 13 A sad accident happened today during Divine Service, Mr Thomas Rich fell down motionless in the seat, his brother James and Farmer Morle being close to him. I stopped the Service, it made a great commotion. He was carried out and soon recovered as to be able to walk home leaning upon Jenkin's arm. I preached a Sermon very appropos to the occasion by accident which was something extraordinary as I could not have forseen the accident. This has happed to me on several times. Once when Walford murdered his wife when I came to live at Overstowey the year after and having prepared a Sermon for the purpose of preaching it was continually put off by some accident or other till the very morning on which a twelvemonth before the murder was committed, and when I preached the Sermon I was told that that was the day, the very day, which astonished me as I knew nothing of it before.

Wednesday May 16 Newspaper come, the new Ministry formed and Bunoparte declared Emperor of France. William digged ground in the garden for peas and like a true Somersetshire man he neither took the distance of the rows planted before, neither did he take the right measure of the stick he proposed to form them by. None but a Somersetshire Booby could make so many blunders in one simple action. Went to bed early for we are to brew tomorrow. I thought of sending William for coal tomorrow but shall not I think.

Thursday May 17 Sent William for coal and Molly Weymouth is here to brew. After dinner Mr Northey and his Lady came to drink tea with us and they staid till dusk. Molly Weymouth finished her brewing.

Friday May 18   I walked to Plainsfield this morning, saw Farmer Rich out and told him I was glad to see him able to go to work, but he was but poorly. Returned and no sooner had we dined but a Post Chaise drove up to the gate. It was Mrs Southcomb and her servant Grace. She had a fit as usual.

Monday November 26   Sold my barley to Mr Tom Poole for seven shillings per bushell, a very high price indeed and malt sells for 11 shillings pr bushell. Called on Coles, the clockmaker about the Jack. I wrote some things at night which brought on a violent headache which continued a long time after I went to bed.

Wednesday November 28   My wife tells me she will go with me to the Assembly at Stowey. After dinner we walked down with a candle and lantern, dry walking, got safe to Mr Northey's. There were both he and she ready dressed and prepared. Mrs Northey looked quite smart and pretty and her being far gone with child shewed her off to advantage. With a lantern we set off and were at the Assembly Room at the Rose and Crown early and before the company were collected. It was a card assembly and we made two whist tables and a round table. All the First People of the celebrated town of Stowey were present. Mr Northey, Mr Tom Poole, Miss Bennet and Mrs Francis Poole played at one table. Mrs Northey, my wife, Mr King and myself played at the other table and there was a large party at the round game of the young ones but Margaret was not with us, we think it not right to go to Stowey merely to play at cards, neither was she at all ambitious of going as she is not over fond of mixing with the young people of Stowey. I went as I had subscribed and out of compliment to the Northeys and besides I do not chuse altogether to appear to keep aloof from my neighbours. Before ten we returned with the Northeys to their Vicarage House, warmed ourselves and my wife eat a little cold meat and then we set off with our candle and lantern. Found Margaret at home with a good fire, warmed ourselves and so to bed.

Thursday November 29   The waters in the adjoining field of Mr Buller's very troublesome to me. About dusk young Farmer White called and I paid him my Income Tax. He sat some time, a rather decent young man, has a brother at Demerarey making a fortune.

Monday December 3   Charles Selleck pulling down the pigstye adjoining the road which I have so often complained about. Clerk in the barn threshing barley. I walked down to Stowey, called on philosopher Coles and paid for some little articles. He shewed me a curious clock of his invention which was carried to London and exhibited before the Society of Arts and then raffled for and won again by the philosopher. He is certainly a wonderful man.

Wednesday December 5   It rained very much and the floods are up. Took the Clerk to see the water in Mr Buller's mead and to rectify some matters. Then I walked down to Widow Jones, shewed her the water that flowed over the road from the water course to her Mill which was broken. Set the son to work immediately and promised him a shilling for that and other jobbs.

Friday December 7   A very dark misty morning. The paper came very late this morning and I was very angry with the girl. The Romney, man of War, lost on the coast of Holland and the crew made prisoner, used kindly by the Dutch but ill used by the French. A grandchild of William Hill fell into a vessel of hot mead and scalded himself very much. My wife and I walked to see him. There were blisters on his arms and on his breast and he was feverish and wanted to drink very much. The mother lived with us at Monkton Farley when that horrid calamity befell us viz.– the loss of four children, three boys and a girl by the Scarlet Fever. Atkins the butcher called about the Property Tax and we talked a great deal and made nothing of it, the little man was at his wit's end.

Saturday December 8   I met Mr Tom Poole just by Landsey's and another gentleman wth him with guns and dogs and Mr Michael, Mr Rich's man, with a gun likewise. I do not relish the idea of such gentry carrying guns, indeed the new Taxes on game has made every poacher a gentleman and restrained gentlemen or qualified men from shooting at all. This is not right, the Country Gentlemen should not be constrained in their diversions otherwise they will desert the countryside as a place not fit for a gentleman to live in. I stepped on to find young Jones to give him a shilling for what he did for the road, but he was not to be found so I returned without paying him.

Sunday December 9   I had a severe attack in my face this morning and doubted whether I could go through the Duty. Just before I entered the Church I was seized by a spasm in my face which pained me and alarmed my wife much, yet I went in and went thro the Duty tolerably. Rode to Asholt, Mr Blake thought I'd better go to Bath for the pain in my face and that first I had better take cinnabar and bark and offered a prescription to shew Dr Dunning. I got through the Duty very well and the Church was full for bread was given to the poor this day.

Monday December 10   Clerk gone with the barley to Stowey, twenty bushells at 7s–6d pr bushell, an immense price and last year I could scarce sell the barley at three shillings. A chandler from Spaxton called from whom we took some candles.

Thursday December 13 About 4 o'clock a chaise came from Bridgwater and my wife and I with Margaret and the two Miss Lewis went off. We reached Mr Jenkin's School some time before the play begun. There was a good deal of bustle getting the young actors ready. The play was Othello or the Moor of Venice, Mr Gill's Writing Room was the theatre and very well fitted out it was. The speeches begun first among the younger ones. In popped my little boy William who was the youngest of them all but spoke as well as any of them and was much clapped. Then the play begun. Young Blake did the part of Othello, the two Stradlings acted Desdemona and Amelia and two prettier girls I scarce ever saw insomuch that some said it was a pity they should be boys. One Giles acted the part of Iago, a tall awkward looking young man. All the dresses were very proper and Desdemona's head was covered with diamonds. The room was very hot and all was conducted very regularly. A boy dressed like an Orange Girl came with a basket to take the tickets and most gave half a crown, I gave half a guinea. We had a very pleasant and satisfactory jaunt and we got into bed before two in the morning.

Monday December 17 A hard frost. The Clerk busy putting dung to the plants and planting raspberries. Wm Frost cutting up the pig killed on Saturday. Sad complaints from the Workhouse, that Scoundrel Porter plunders the whole neighbourhood and threatens the lives of those that live in the Poorhouse. I called on Mr Rich to talk the matter over. Captain Davis called this day informing us of coal at Combych.

Wednesday December 19 Clerk gone for coals again. Newspaper come very late, nothing in it but a pompous and fulsome account of Buonaparte's Coronation, they make a kind of God of him.

Thursday December 20 The frost is very hard. I and William took a walk to Stowey where he bought a whip and top, came home by Marsh Mill. I sent the Clerk with a written notice to Charles Selleck about the roads for I am Surveyor. I have spoken to him several times about the litter he makes but he never minds it so now I'll make him. My wife is taken rather ill with the wind, but now somewhat better.

Monday December 24 I felt myself very poorly in the night and did not get up before breakfast which I took in bed, which is not usual. They have been very busy this morning in giving wheat to the poor, several bushells. Farmers Morle and Dibble called here about Landsey's Charity but the Poor Book not being brought we could do nothing effectually. I stirred very little out being fearful of wetting my feet and increasing the pain in my face. William wrote his copy, a firm bold hand.

Tuesday December 25 Snow still on the ground and it is very slippery. Clerk here to prepare things for Church. Not many at Church nor at the Sacrament. I walked to Asholt and some of them came in very late. As I passed Rich of Peperell's I heard musick. It was the Overstowey Band so I gave them half a crown for they serenaded us in the morning. We had twelve of our neighbours to dine in the kitchen today, Ben Hunt and Mr Amen, Robert Brewer an old servant of ours, and the Sellecks and the Weymouths. They dined about one and I hope enjoyed themselves for this is the day of Joy and Enjoyment in a decent way.

Friday December 28 I went to Farmer Stone who fell from his rick and twisted the sinews under his knee. I found him by the fire and better than he had been but still very lame. He has a large family but he is very industrious. He was very thankful for the visit. From him I went to William Hill's to see their little grandson who was scalded in the mead. He was running about and quite recovered. After this I came home but had an unpleasant fall on the ice, indeed I scarce remember it so slippery everywhere as it is today, for yesterday it thawed and today it glazed over so that the paths are become one continued ice.

Sunday December 30 A very hard keen frost and very slippery. Ugly faced Briffet came very late this morning and I was very angry and obliged to go to Asholt without reading the paper. I walked there with difficulty and administered the Sacrament to a tolerable number for Asholt. After the Service I walked back again and was rather late for afternoon Service.

Monday December 31 The last day of the year 1804, the snow still on the ground. My wife is mending my gaiters so that I may go out. I had two letters today, one from my old Friend and Patron Mr Sturges, Rector of Chelsea, he expects to see us, the other to my wife from her niece at Maidenhead where they are all in high expectation to see us, – we must go if it please God. William expects some friends to play with him today, young Buller and Poole and Blake and Master Northey. I walked with Mr Northey to Halsey Cross and shewed him what a short space of the Turnpike belonged to our Parish but there is above two miles of Turnpike Road in the Parish of Stowey. About dusk a boy came from Stowey for the Stowey young ones but Blake staid with us and slept with William, he was very quiet. After this we all went to bed in due time. Here ends the year 1804.

The year 1805

Tuesday January 1 Now here we are at the beginning of a New Year. I do not find myself in point of health or strength much on the decline tho' I have had some time pains in my face and the back parts of my head and jaws. Dr Dunning makes but light of it and says it is a flowing of the blood too rapidly to the head and that it will leave me if I have but patience to bear with it. Blake thinks it is a degree of decline of the nervous system, others call it Rheumatism. Possibly it may be some alteration in my constitution, we must all get older However I have followed the directions of my friend Dr Dunning and hope in time to be perfectly relieved. Be that as it may I hope and trust that there neither is nor will be any decline in my moral conduct and attention to Duty and that I need not concern myself about other matters. They did not ring in the New Year which surprised me much.

Thursday January 3 Jew Landsey and Wm Frost walked to Bridgewater to market but found it very slabby and disagreable on their return for a thaw set in very quickly. Wm Frost did some errands for me and got home a sad pickle. Mr Amen has been very indifferent today and I gave him a dose of Rhubarb in a glass of gin which seemed to comfort him and he went home.

Sunday January 6 Newspaper came and I paid Briffet for the carriage for one year to Christmas last. Went into the Sunday School and found Ben and the rest of them huddled into the fire. Few at Church. Rode to Asholt and the horse more on the start and alarm than usually not having been rode lately.

It is now Monday the 14 and from the 7 to this day has been a dreadful time and I have not been at home scarce any time of it and therefore could not write in my diary and indeed my mind has been in such a state of agitation as not to admit of writing. We have long meditated a journey for two months to see our friends in Berkshire and London but I have found great difficulty in getting my Churches served. So on Tuesday the 8th I mounted my horse and took little William on the little horse I hired from Farmer Dibble and drew up the straps short for stirrups. We were to go to Enmore to Mr John Poole to see if we could settle matters about the Service of my Churches. We approached a small cluster of houses called Pikely when his little horse started all of a sudden into a gallop. It was a narrow road so I put my horse across to lay hold of the rains of William's horse but it was so low and closing his ears and lowering his head he darted down the hill. The poor child was soon off but not disengaged from the stirrup. The moment I saw this I flew from my horse crying 'He is gone, he is gone for ever.' He was dragged about fifty yards when his shoe came off and he dropped down motionless. A decent looking man took him up in his arms all bloody and apparently dead, and two women, decent looking persons, rushed out of one cottage and carried him in in an instant and one prepared a bed for him. While I was lamenting in my great agitation the man who had picked him up came up to me and asked whether he should go on that horse, pointing to mine, to fetch a surgeon. Yes, to Forbes at Stowey. The horse will shew from whom you came. In the meantime we washed the child and put him in a clean bed and he seemed clear and in his senses. Forbes examined his arms and legs, no bones broken. Then he examined the wounds on his head, the scull is sound. The scull is sound repeated I. Now a dreadful business was approaching, to open the affair to my wife, and company were engaged to dine with me that night. The people of the cottage were the most clean and decent people I ever met with. I left the child in their hands while I went off with Forbes to open the matter to my wife. At Radlett Common I met Mr Tom Poole. I told him in great agitation what happened. Never did a man shew more feeling on the occasion than he did, he cried like a child. At last I ventured to Overstowey. Mr Rich and the Blakes dined with us and dinner was just over. My wife screamed and started but I said he is alive. Margaret had a kind of fit. I repeated he is alive and no bones broken but in great danger. Blake who formerly practiced as a surgeon and apothecary asked where it was. In the meantime a gig was ordered from Stowey for my wife and I made her take Sally with her and leave her with the child but come home herself. Mr Blake soon came back saying he had taken a great quantity of blood from him but that the child was in great danger. After this my wife returned leaving Sally behind. The company took leave and we went to bed with heavy hearts.

The next day, the 9th, we heard that the child had been ill in the night. It seems that something ought to've been given during the night which was neglected by mistake, a violent vomitting came on and after that a cold chill. However the child got over it and proper things were administered and the child has not had a bad sympton since. Such enquiries as were made by Gentle and Simple people in the neighbourhood as was surprizing and assistance of every kind was offered. The Yorkes, the Clergyman of the Parish sent message after message to ask us all there with the child, but the child could not be moved. At last after receiving every assistance from everyone and being hospitably accommodated by Mr Yorke and Family, on Sunday last, being the 13th, he was safely conveyed home in a Sedan Chair by four men, he being at the same time in the arms of a young lady, Miss Poole of Twinnel, to keep him from jogging and who being young and slender was no great weight, but I fear the fatigue was very great for the young lady. Some of William's schoolfellows and some of the uppermost and best called on him and many of the Farmers' wives and daughters and messages were continually sent to Spaxton and Stowey and Bridgewater. He is now here safe I thank God. It being Monday the 14th and he has been downstairs and played cards with his Mama.

Tuesday January 15   William slept well and seems to be getting on apace. Mr Forbes did not call or dress him this day, Mrs Buller, Miss Harriet Poole, Miss Poole of Twynel and young Buller called. He played at cards and staid up late this evening and I think eat too hearty and when in bed was a long time before he slept.

Thursday January 17   William gets on charmingly, sleeps well and rises cheerfully but his poor head has been sadly mauled and is at present bound round with a handkerchief. No fire in his room this morning. Mr Amen held my horse while I trimmed him, then he planted some pease the mice having made sad havoc with the first crop. The Clerk put down the pease rather in a scurvy manner. This evening I begun a letter to my elder brother whom I have not written to this long while. He lives at the Family House called Tirdan, in Denbightshire, N. Wales. After this we went to bed.

Friday January 18   Little William slept well and Mr Forbes came to dress him His wounds and bruises heal fast and he seems to go on very well and to be in good spirits and I trust his cure will soon be perfect. I set a trap this evening for a mouse and Mr Amen greased the butter pot in the garden.

Saturday January 19   I walked into the garden and found a Robin Redbreast in my trap. I did not know before that they destroyed pease. I walked to Stowey and sent off a letter to my brother. In my return at Hog Pit there were two young beasts in my way in the narrow path fenced in between the orchards. I called a surly fellow from the barn to turn them out as there was no passing them and they might run against me, but he would scarce undertake the jobb, but I insisted that they had no right to block up the road. The night is very dark and Molly Selleck has borrowed our lantern to go to Stowey.

Sunday January 20   Went to the Sunday School, few there and those small tho' it is cake day. There were very few at Church yet the persons who live in the Cottages where poor William was carried to after his fall were at

Church and dined here today on a fine rump of beef and pudding and all kinds of garden stuff. There were four of them for the Cottage was a kind of double house and in each a man and his wife. They staid till dusk and two walked home and two rode and they seemed perfectly well pleased with their expedition. Mr Forbes came and dressed William who is getting well apace but was somewhat peevish and restless before we went to bed. He is to take Physick tomorrow which does not please. Indeed Forbes is a terrible man for Physick which I think there is no occasion for.

Monday January 21   Rode over to Mr Yorke at Spaxton and thanked him again for his great civility to me and my child and asked him and his family to dine with me but they could not. Passed through Pikeley where the child fell, spoke to Mrs Stiling where he was taken in. Rode on to Mr John Poole at Enmore. Met Mr Cruckshanks as I was going. Thanked him for his enquiries after my child.

Friday January 25   I met today young Mackay who is come to see his sick father. This young man is his son by a Negro Woman and has had from the father an excellent education and is in Orders and has two Livings and is in good circumstances. Pity that he should suffer his father to suffer distress in his later days, but he is so far from assisting him that in all his visits he is drawing money from him and plundering him and I fear that poor Mrs Mackay will be left without a shilling – I am not very partial to West Indians, especially to your Negro Half Blood people. The evening went of as usual, my little boy in high spirits playing cards with his Mama.

Saturday January 26   Mr Forbes dressed William and said that he would want one more dressing, little William's head without a white handkerchief. Nothing very material until a stranger appeared. It was Mr James from Monksilver who offered to serve my Churches while I am absent. He was sent by Mr George Trevilian on Mr Northey's letter. A genteel young man, very tall and slender. He left us about dusk. We spent the evening in the usual stile of Saturday only I did not remember to wind up the clock.

Monday January 28   A hard frost, Clerk here carrying ashes to the Moor. I walked over to Asholt after breakfast and married a couple, registered them at Mr Blake's. In the afternoon Edward Selleck brought a man to offer for a servant whom I hired and he is to come Lady Day.

Wednesday January 30   William took Physick this morning but he is playing about and whipping his top. I walked to Stowey, called at Mr Francis Poole's to buy some stockings. Edward Selleck brought a box for

William's books. About dusk came Staden with William's new Greatcoat to fit it, and some new gaiters for me. I was busy in adjusting Sermons for my journey and other matters.

Saturday February 2 William seems perfectly recovered and in high spirits and dancing about. I walked along the road to Halsey Cross and then into the Turnpike and observed that there was but one load of stones carried on the part of the Turnpike belonging to our Parish tho' all our ploughs were summoned, which the Surveyors of the Turnpike had no right to do.

Sunday February 3 Briffet came with many articles as well as the newspaper. Ben not at the Sunday School, few at Church. Many at Asholt. Great preparations for our journey tomorrow.

Monday February 4 A rainy morning. Up early and the chaise come from Bridgwater. Some bustle − got in − breakfast at Cannington with Mrs Lewis. Little William with us. Got to Bridgwater, carried him to Mr Jenkin's, they were glad to see him. We dined at the Poole's, little William with us. I paid Mr Jenkins for William's schooling. Called at Dr Dunning's. Dined at Ruscomb Poole's, and went to a card society with Miss Charlotte Poole. Lost ten shillings there, I had no business to go. Came back to Mrs Poole's, supped and went to bed.

Tuesday February 5 A tolerable fine morning, mild and pleasant. William safe at School. The chaise just arrived and we are going immediately. Got safe to Street, a tolerable house with civil people. (Street from Stratum, an old Roman Road.) We passed Piper's Inn without stopping. It rained very hard as we left Street. Passed thro' Wells and called on Mr Cobley, he was not at home but Mrs Cobley was. Could not stay so on we went to Old Down. Had a chaise there with good horses but they did not travel fast. Got to Bath to the White Lion, a great bustle there as the Harmonic Society were to dine there. Then off we went again but it grew dark before we reached Chippenham. A great bustle at the Inn here too. There is a Great Ball here but the Mistress of the House is uncommonly civil, we have good attendance and good accommodation and I like the House very much. We are to have beds removed from the noise of the Ball and I hope we shall sleep well and be up bytimes tomorrow.

Wednesday February 6 Up very early this morning tho' disturbed by the dancers and the coaches. We got out of Chippenham a little after daybreak, a very keen clear frost and very hard for one night. As we came along we saw a very beautiful White Horse* cut on the side of the hill and if I am not mistaken there is another on the other side of the hill seen from Monkton Farley. Malborough is a strange looking town, chiefly of one street on the

side of a sloping piece of ground. We were rather uncomfortable at the Inn
having no fire for a considerable time. At last we were warmed and eat a
most unmerciful breakfast. We next made our way to SpeenhamLand
where we arrived a little after one. Had a sandwich or two and then moved
off again and had sad work to get on. They gave us a jaded horse which
required whipping and cutting the second mile, and we had fifteen more to
go. It was a sad business, I expected him to fall down every moment. The
evening in other respects was very pleasant but I thought we would never
reach Thale. A last we got to Thale, there I discharged the battered horses
and got fresh ones which carried us safe to Maidenhead, tho' it was late
when we came there. Did not call on my old friend Dr Taylor when we
passed thro' Reading as we did not stop. Reading I perceive is wonderfully
improved since I lived there. When we got to my brother in law's Mr
Dodwell, they had not received my wife's letter but they were glad to see us
and we did eat all of us to an amazing degree, and after chatted having
travelled 68 miles.

Until February 25 the Hollands stayed with Mr and Mrs Dodwell, visiting
and being visited by friends and relations whom they had not seen for many
years. Other highlights of their visit included an expedition to Windsor
Castle where they saw the Queen –'The Queen and two of the Princesses
were going to Frogmore, a farm of the Queen's, no bustle, no parade, just
like a private family. But the Queen had got into her carriage before I could
approach to see her perfectly and there was a good tempered handsome
looking young Princess looking full at me from the carriage and she
perceived that I was rather disappointed and I saw that she intimated as
much to the Queen who immediately rose in the carriage and put her head
out, nodded first to me then to the company, turning her head round to
them. What Queen in Europe could or would do this with so much ease
and condescention as the Queen of England? The two Princesses were
lovely looking women. The Queen I thought looked old and I thought
larger featured than when I saw her many years ago.' On February 16 'We
were suddenly called out for the King who was out ahunting. Passed by the
Stag, and the hunters came over the bridge here. A large cavalcade came on
first and then some time afterwards the King came on slowly. I was the first
who took off my hat. The King bowd very graciously to our party and
General Manners who rode to one side he bowd too. I thought his Majesty
looked old and his face of a black red. They rode slowly thro' the town and
went towards the Thicket.' February 25 saw them leave the Dodwells and
Maidenhead:– 'We entered the Chaise before eleven. We had a fine day. We
went to London thro' Hyde Park and indeed I was struck wonderfully with
the appearance. So large a space of ground surrounded with houses yet with
trees and a green verdure and a clear air was uncommonly gratifying. The
road through was like a gravel walk. We soon got to Doughty Street

through noble Squares and streets broad and handsome. There is no appearance of town or bustle, the street uncommonly broad and we can look into the fields.' Until March 23 the Hollands were with one of their sisters in law, Mrs Dodwell and besides visiting their relatives and friends did a full round of sightseeing. Drury Lane Theatre was visited to see Kemble in 'To Marry or not to Marry', an Exhibition of Pictures in the New Road found '– one opposite the door of entrance gave me great offence. It was the representation of the Trinity in the Glory, God the Father and God the Son and the Pope with his Three crowned Tiara higher than any of them'. Holland went alone* to dine with his friends the Duke of Somerset and dined 'In stile on Plate and vast quantities of Plate and China around us.' The whole family spent a couple of days with Reverend Sturgess the Rector of Chelsea for whom Holland had been Curate at St. Mary's, Reading before he obtained the Living of Overstowey. They went with Mr Sturgess, in his Gown and Cassock, to Morning Service – 'the Church is old and too small for the Congregation.' While in Chelsea they went to the Military Asylum established by the Duke of York for the children of Soldiers. 'The Foundation is for 700 boys and 300 girls. They are kept clean, well fed and educated, learning to read and write and taught a trade.' On March 23 they returned to Maidenhead though 'the driving in London at first was troublesome.' After a short stay with the Dodwells they continued their homeward journey on March 29, staying wih Dr and Mrs Taylor in Reading until April 2.

Tuesday April 2   A fine morning, up very early. The Post Chaise come and we are off a little after six. Dr Taylor's servants all very attentive. We had provided gingerbread and apples and oranges, got very well to Speenhamland, breakfasted there, soldiers at exercises in the fields below. Off again to Malborough, off again to Chippenham changing the Chaise there, had some cold meat. They were keen on us, asked for sandwiches but they brought us cold veal and beef and charged us eighteen pence ahead. After this we got to Bath about dusk and got to the Greyhound.

Wednesday April 3   To Saturday the 13 April, all this to account for by memory so I shall speak only of the Principal facts. They did not wish us to continues at the Inn unlass we went to very great expence so we only had rooms there and were chiefly at Mrs Hume's during the daytime. Went to Monkton Farley but the payment was woeful, sixty nine pounds deficit at first. Little tidings that were pleasing of Captain Birchell and Beake shuffled unaccountably. He at last paid the money late Saturday, a sad fellow. I called on Mrs Sheldon to show my disapprobation of her husband's conduct, he uses her very ill. He is building a house in Essex and keeps a woman. On Monday we set off for Wells and got to Mrs Cobley at three. On Tuesday I rode with Mr Cobley to Cheddar to see his Living which he

was lately presented to. The House is very bad. The Church is handsome
and the Tower uncommonly fine and high. After this we rode up the pass
in the Cheddar Cliffs. It was sublime, a good road passed through and each
projection on one side had a corresponding cavity on the other. Thursday
the 11th we went to Bridgewater, called on Mr Jenkins, saw Dr Dunning.
Went on and got to Overstowey safe and sound, God be praised. Good
Friday the 12th I entered on the Duty of the place. I have a new man
servant, a steady person he seems to be. Sunday had a great deal of Duty.
Prayers and a Sacrament at Overstowey and had a Christening after the
Second Lesson during the Service. It was Hurley's child, an Annabaptist. I
have prevailed on him to bring most of his children to Church and tho' the
day was inconvenient on account of the great Duty yet I was unwilling to
let him escape. After this I rode to Asholt and did the Duty there, then came
home and the day concluded in the usual manner.

Thursday April 18   I intend from henceforward to get on more regularly in
my usual stile every day and to catch every occurrence as it passes. Sally
went to Strinxon to enquire about a servant. John very busy in the garden
putting down potatoes. Agreed with Jones about the hedge in the Moors,
five pence a rope.

Sunday April 21   A very fine morning, rode over to Asholt. Blake has left
the place and just moved off before Church. A good many at the
Sacrament. Returned to Overstowey and dined and had a great many at
Church here, quite crouded. After Church I went into the Sunday School
and heard the children say their Catechism, midling, I know not what to
do, I wish to hear them at Church but fear I cannot get sufficient numbers
to say their Catechism. This is deplorable, parents will not instruct them
and tho' a Sunday School is established for that purpose yet they will not
send their children. A sad decay of Religion and Discipline in the world.
After this I went to the House and the evening concluded in the usual stile.

Tuesday April 23   I was up early, a little after six. John gone for coal. Mr
James called and I paid him nine guineas for the Service of my Church
during my absence. He dined here and before dinner we walked out to
Mount Pleasant which charmed him much. We expected all this day Mrs
Ridding, my wife's sister, with her daughter but no one comes.

Wednesday April 24   My farmers dine here today, Mr Buller nor Mr Tom
Poole here. They left me in reasonable time. Afterwards who should come
in but Mrs Ridding and her daughter. They travelled all the way from
Salisbury and did not intend being here Tuesday. Looked tolerable Mrs
Ridding did, her daughter rather thin. After some salutations and some
chatting we all moved for bed.

Thursday April 25   Mr Buller came and paid me his Tithe, soon after came Mr Tom Poole who says he had actually forgot the day. Briffet brought a letter from Mrs Dodwell of Maidenhead and we sent several things by him to Little William at School at Bridgewater. We spent the evening at home, Miss Ridding painting and making many curious kind of toys to be sold for the poor.

Sunday April 28   Briffet brought the newspapers and a letter from Mr Jones of Loddington informing me of the death of my old friend Mr Sturgess whom I have lately visited at Chelsea of which place he was Rector. He died of an apoplexy at Loddington. He was very fat and the family were always apprehensive of such an end. He was an excellent Parish Priest and I had been his Curate at St Mary's Reading for eight years. He was very fat and bloated and there is no wonder that he died in the manner he has done. Yet die when he would he was well prepared being a good conscientious man. He has left a large family and a widow not in distress I hope as he had considerable property besides his preferment, but then one daughter is at present deranged and there has been much affliction in the family in many respects. We spent the evening in the usual stile of Sunday, Mrs Ridding talking without ceasing.

Wednesday May 1   I mounted my horse and rode to Stowgurcy and dined with Mr and Mrs Davis, but before dinner Mr Davis and I rode over to the Heights looking to the Bristol Channel and we saw the Welsh Coast very plain. We mounted Farrington Hill and called on Mr and Mrs Ridler. They had a very neat habitation there. Mrs Ridler looked very fresh and well but Mr Ridler looked somewhat dirty having been on his farm. Mrs Davis cooked us a good dinner in a trice. I staid tea, then mounted my horse again and got home by dusk.

Thursday May 2   John busy in the garden, he works very well and I believe we have at present a good set of servants. After dinner Mr Brice the Rector of Asholt came in and drank a glass of wine with me. After tea we brought down and looked over some letters on Physiognomy by the Duke of Somerset who corresponded with me on that head. He sent shades to me and I sent the characters back which he in general approved of. I found that of Pitt on which I had given an opinion which astonished him beyond measure as no other person he says could ever find any marks of great abilities in that shade.

Monday May 6   John turned out the cows into the higher grass of the Long Paddock which is very good so that I hope we shall have a plentiful increase of milk. I walked to Stowey. Spoke to the woman of the Globe about the Book Society Dinner, it is ordered. John this day cleared the weeds and couch grass out of the Herb Beds which has not been done for these many years. Margaret and her cousin walked out and after that they ! ave been making jellies for tomorrow.

Tuesday May 7 Mr and Mrs Davis are engaged to dine and take a bed here. I find they are come and we spent an agreeable day together. After tea I got Mr Davis into the Study and read my account of Antichrist to him, making that person clearly to mean Buonapart, which pleased and gratified him very much. Then I read to the ladies my Treatise on Physiognomy and this pleased still more. Then we supped and went to bed.

Wednesday May 8 Mr Davis and I walked down to Stowey under our umbrellas to dine at the Globe it being the Book Society dinner. More came than I expected. Mr Mathews did not come. Mr Sealey from Bridgewater was there and Mr John and Ruscomb Poole, Mr Tom Poole, Charles Poole Mr Davis and myself. We had a very good dinner. Mr Sealey who is a Banker and Merchant and many things at Bridgewater was very pompous. Great Tom Poole laid out seven pounds in books, I about a pound. About dusk we seperated, well pleased with each other. Mr Davis and I walked home together, John having been sent off before with the Books. We met the Ladies before a good fire, chatted a while and soon went to bed.

Friday May 10 Could not get the Gig from Stowey with the usual horse so took my own horse and John with me on Farmer Landsey's rode to the Visitation. Davis and I went to Church together, heard a Sermon from Mr Burt. A good Sermon the people say he is no great orator. The town of Bridgewater was full of soldiers, Colonel Pyne spoke to me and said the Brest Fleet was out and an embargo laid on all shipping in every port. We had a large company at dinner, the dinner not very extraordinary and the Landlord not over civil. My man John came in and waited very well. I called on my Little Boy and gave him a shilling.

Saturday May 11 My wife and I called on a young girl dying of a consumption, of the name Davis. She seemd wasted to the bone, of a most ingenuous and interesting countenance I ever saw. I asked her many questions about her notion of Religion and she answered with great meekness and often burst into tears. We were much affected by her, poor creature what little comfort has she had in life, so young and yet so near her end. Her parents are very bad, full of knavery and thieving, yet she, tho' bred among them seems to be a very different kind of being, Innocent, Ingenuous and Resigned.

Wednesday May 15 I and Miss Ridding and my daughter set out after breakfast to walk to Stowgurcy. We got there is very good time and had hours to spare before dinner. We found there Mrs Lewis and her two daughters. I took a walk with Mr Davis and soon after our return Mr and Mrs Yorke walked in from Fiddington where they slept the night before at their Tennants House who rents the Glebe and Tithe for Mr Yorke has the Living at Fiddington as well as Spaxton. We had a very full and bountiful dinner. Mrs Davis is a very clever woman that way, shining and active, very useful to the poor, a doctor and all kinds of things in short a Complete Parson's Wife. The Yorkes are a good kind of people too.

Saturday July 27 A fine warm morning. My wife is busy in making currant wine and jam. John trimming the hedges and the maids scouring the house. I did not move much this day. My wife I believe walked as far as the poor sick girl who is indeed in a most deplorable state. I am advised not to go into her as she is in a kind of Putrid State and indeed my wife, I believe does not go in but we send her something every day. Alas, Alas! the misery and wretched-ness of human nature. Poor Creature, I hope God will take her soon.

Monday July 29 After breakfast moved about the garden and trimmed the Arbour. While I was at work with a hook in my hand Little Cockney Shitfield the Brandy Merchant called. I desired him to walk in, I paid his bill but did not order more as what I had is not yet out. I made him give me a receipt this time which he used not to do before. He said it made a great difference to him but said I the Law requires it. It does so returned he, then he jumped up skipped on his horse and was off in a trice telling me that any time when my stock was out if I would but drop a line I should have it in a trice. But really they are become now so abominably dear that there is scarce any drinking of them and moreover at the Custom House one may have very good spirits for half the price he sells at. So Mr Cockney I think I shall be able to cater better in future.

Tuesday July 30 Mrs Ridding and her daughter arrived this evening. Mrs Ridding has got fatter since she has been in Devonshire, Bessie Anne not so much. I fear she is beginning to be consumptive. Mrs Ridding did not cease talking till she went to bed.

Wednesday July 31 Ugly-faced Briffet came early today with the newspaper and a letter from Mrs Dodwell with half a Bank Bill, my dividend from the Funds from Mr Wm Moore of the Commons. A note was sent me from Mr Frank Poole of the return of the Combined Fleet off Ferrol with a terrible engagement with Sir R Calder and the loss of a Flag Ship and another Line of Battle Ship to the Spaniards.

Friday August 2 We expect company to dinner. I wrote some little in the Study and bustled about in the garden. At last to my great surprize Mr and Mrs Mathew came on foot, I was really surprized, no less than five miles, his Gig is mending at Bridgewater. Then came the Pooles, John the Divine, Miss Susan, Penelope and the widow Mrs Richard Poole who is with them, from Wells. Mr Tom Poole was asked but he did not come till tea time. They had a good dinner and all went off very well and in good humour tho' very little wine was drunk. Mr John Poole drinkd none, I very little, the ladies indeed drank their glasses. After tea the Pooles had their Gig and were away and Mr and Mrs Mathew would go tho' we offered them a bed, several times. I was almost vexed about it. I and my daughter and Bessy Anne and Mr Tom Poole walked with them as far as Doddington Common. I then asked them to come back for the evening began to look unpleasant but they did not chuse to return. Then Mr Tom Poole left us and we returned and the rain came on but the ladies made use of my umbrella. However I was wetted pretty much and quite grieved about Mr and Mrs Mathew. I changed my coat when I got home and we all went to bed.

Saturday August 3 John gone for coal. I walked under an umbrella to Stowey, called on the Northeys. Had a great deal of talk about the Fleets and the news. He proposed to me to assist him in the Service of Stowey when I had given up Asholt, and I partly promised to undertake it, only once a day alternate with my own except when he goes to Residence at Windsor for three months when I am to undertake the whole, but I mean to pay for assistance. Mrs Ridding continues her discourse which never ceases from the moment she is up till she sinks to sleep and indeed she seems as well and in as good spirits and eats and drinks as well as anyone, yet she always requires a good deal of coddling and nursing and scarce ever walks out.

Tuesday August 6 Price the shoemaker promised to bring my new boots home yesterday but he has not done it. A Somersetshire man I have often observed never keeps his promise. In the afternoon I walked with my wife to the poor sick girl. She is greatly emaciated and in a lamentable state yet very sensible, very grateful for anything done and attentive to what is said and also resigned. In short she is the most interesting girl I ever attended. Her mother who takes care of her is a miserable object too. She has got a cancer come on in her breast so that she too will soon be in a sad state. The husband has most shocking health and they are all poor to the greatest degree. Alas the misery there is in this world, the ways of Providence are very mysterious. Indeed the family altogether have been a very thievish, pilfering and irreligious family except this one unfortunate girl who seems to be another kind of being from the others. Yet we do not find that the misery and suffering of this world bears a proportion to the Magnitude of

Man's Sins. In the case I am speaking of it is not so for the poor girl who is the greatest sufferer is infinitely the best of the family and she must be Innocent as well as religious. On the whole there is so much suffering in this world that I trust the next will be a world of happiness. After this we spent the day at home among ourselves.

Wednesday August 7 I went today to Church to marry Wm Hill's daughter to a man from Stapletone near Taunton by Licence and the bells are ringing. The man is a widower a good deal older than her but he is rich. The rain increases.

Friday August 9 I called on Jew Landsey to walk into the further Paddock to view our fattening cow. The Jew thought it would be murder to kill her before Christmas. I answered that I believe I shall commit murder in two or three weeks. It will be a sin quoth the Jew. None at all answered I for it will cost me five pounds to keep her till that time and beef is now at eight pence per pound and will be at Christmas at sixpence, so if the cow be not made so fat now yet she will bring me as much money as she would at Christmas and I shall save the feed in the bargain. The Jew could not comprehend my argument tho' he had nothing to oppose it, only crying shame, law she will be so fat by Christmas. So we parted, but the cow is very fat at this time.

Monday August 12 I walked down to Stowey and as I was walking down Castle Street I saw an infirm old woman rolling down the declivity on one side of the street. She struggled feebly but could not get up and there were several persons looking on but no one offered to assist her so I went down and gave her my hand and with some difficulty put her on her feet and rather upbraided some of the persons around in not flying to her assistance. I walked down to Mr Northey's and soon came Mrs O'Darty the wife of a Captn O'Darty from Ireland but niece to Mr Northey. She married the Captain against her father's consent who was Colonel of the Regiment. He has not yet received the husband but I believe has the daughter. She is reckoned very accomplished and Handsome but as yet she does not strike me much either way.

Saturday August 17 Dressed myself, mounted my horse and set out to dine at Mr Ackland's on a haunch of venison. I got there in good time, Mr and Mrs Everett from Hill were there and Mr Mathew came just before me. Mr and Mrs Everett were dressed very smart, Mr Everett seemd almost friblish. He is tall, slender and of a good figure but I do not much like his Physiognomy, the whole seems sharp and rapid, the arch of the head is tolerable but the forehead falls off too quickly, the eyebrows small and the Muscle of Thought neither large nor powerful. He talks a great deal, his eye has fire but no benevolence and I do not think his Principles are very good but rather Jacobinical. Mr and Mrs Northey came in last. Then came in Mr Ackland with great ease and address and shook us all around by the hand. We had a very good dinner, two courses. Fine fruit after dinner and then in came a large silver-gilt cup, very handsome. It was partly purchased by the money given by the East India Company to the Officers on board the Ships that engaged and defeated Lenois the French Admiral in the East Indies. Mr Peregrine Palmer Ackland was a midshipman on board one of the Indiamen. He received from the Company thirty pounds and Mr Ackland added to it fifty pounds which purchased this Glorious Cup. On the whole I drank rather more than I like. A droll accident happened on the way home by the Blind Well. I saw a light in a line across the road. It was very bright and broader in some places than others, my horse started and would not pass by so I thought it best to dismount and lead my horse. Looking about and perceiving no moon I recollected that an old rotted stump of a tree had been rolled from the hedge on the morning as I passed that way and knowing that rotting wood will give a luminous appearance in the night I did not doubt but that was the cause of the light I had seen. After this I got home and found the ladies safe and snug, chatted a while and went to bed.

Monday August 19   Young Arthur Ackland came here today with a note from Mrs Ackland to Margaret. A famous artist of the name of Singleton* was with him, he is a portrait painter and is come to take Mrs Ackland's Portrait. I shewed him the picture of Phaeton in the best parlour, he says it is a French Picture of Le Brune's or one of his Disciples, in the time of Lewis the Fourteenth of France. He admired it much. They eat some cold meat and soon left us. Mr Rich came in the evening and viewed the fat cow. He says I should not sell her under 20 guineas. The ladies, I believe, called on the sick girl.

Tuesday August 20   Called at Mr Price the Shoemaker and shopmaker when the lady rather ungraciously popped a Bill into my wife's hand that had not been a month's standing and the husband thrust in another for shoes, the principle article of which (my boots) I had not had a fortnight. The tradesmen at Stowey are wonderfully shabby and pitiful, they are very long in their executing any orders but as soon as done they are upon you with open claws. In general they are so poor they cannot wait a moment, yet these people tumble in riches and have taken so much of my money and I too am so very ready a Paymaster that I am astonished at their eagerness. However I paid it immediately and shall take care to have no bill with either of them in future for no two meaner and more greedy and shabby people I scarce ever met with. Bet Carter I understand is to be transported for seven years to Botany Bay but the Villain Peregrine Palmer is discharged. I wrote a letter to Mr Brice of Asholt about resigning the Curacy but have not sent it.

Thursday August 22 Washer sneaked into our field this morning to view the cow before I was up and then said she would not suit him. I gave him the offer since he is our butcher and he promised to meet me and view her yesterday like a man but he chose to break his promise and to sneak in by himself. A Somersetshire man never keeps his word and as to meanness they certainly cannot be exceeded in any county, I scarce ever met a liberal minded man amongst them. I shewed the cow to Buller but he turned off tho' he in particular thought her an uncommon beast. When we come to the point they all sneak off. The man at the Globe seems to have a great inclination to the cow in order to make her uncommonly fat but he, notwithstanding his prating keeps at an awful distance. Met Farmer Morle's daughter who wanted me to send my man to turn Tithe Pease. I said No as in that case I should be obliged to send a man to assist every Farmer in the Parish.

Saturday August 24 The man of the Globe came to me and said he wished to purchase the fattening cow. We talked a good deal together but could not agree. I walked with him to Halsey Cross and there met Mr Rich and so we all set the bargaining and at last I let her go for Seventeen pounds and he is to keep my calf till Michaelmass next. My grass is grown low and not fit for fattening and the butchers were combining to beat me down so I nicked them at once. He is to fetch her on Monday and pay the money. Mr Rich thought I had done well.

Sunday August 25 A woman from Overstowey brought her child to be Christened and herself Churched at Asholt Church. They had before sent to me at Overstowey to bring the child there but had disappointed me and now without any apology brought the child to Asholt. I was very angry and spoke to them roughly and told them to carry the child to Overstowey this afternoon, its proper Church. However the woman was so weak and poor and ignorant that I Churched her at last and Christened the child as she said that Overstowey Church was so much further away and she fainted away in coming to Asholt. I said there was no reason for the mother to come at all and that the child might very well be Baptised without her presence. Returned to Overstowey, our Church very full in the afternoon, a great many strangers. I buried a child after Church and Christened two. They were twins,* and Churched the mother so that I had a good deal of Duty this day. Farmer and Mrs Morle came in and I gave the Farmer three Jorums of strong beer and made his face shine.

Tuesday August 27 The Clerk in the barn threshing some pease to fatten the sow given us by Mr Northey, the most mischievious animal in the world. She breaks out and gets into the garden of all our neighbours which I cannot bear, one of the Chinese kind. She has been to the Boar but we have no pigs from her so die she must and Mr Northey has sent us another, a small one.

Friday August 30 Mrs Ridding did not come down to breakfast she having recollected that it was her late husband's Birthday. Now had it been the day of his Death the recollection might have produced some disagreeable sensations but the day of his Birth seems an unnecessary recollection. John and the Clerk brought only twenty five stitches of Tithe wheat this day. I walked to Ealy this morn and John and the Clerk were gone into the House of Ealy to amuse themselves I suppose with a pint of beer. I soon called them out and observed that the horse was under his load waiting for them. They made some shuffling excuse and went on.

Thursday September 5 I was up early, a little after six. Wrote a letter to Mr Jenkins that I shall send for my little boy on Saturday. Busy this morning in preparing for dinner as we are to have company. About one first came Mrs Yorke by herself, a double horse had let her down at Marsh Mill. By and by came Mr Yorke with his sister-in-law Mrs Draper behind. In a short time after came the Graveners from AllFoxen, four of them, Mr and Mrs Gravener and son and daughter. They were all on foot having been disappointed in the Stowey Conveyance. But they ought not to have been ashamed of disappointment being immensely rich, and it is said Mrs Gravener has no less than twenty thousand pounds left her on condition that she should keep a Chaise. They did have a Chaise, had a driver and horses but the Chaise was never used nor the horses. The young man will be next year in full possession of the Allfoxen Estates with House and Park so that something they ought to do. The Yorkes too are very rich. In his own right he has the Living of Spaxton and the Living of Fiddington. Spaxton they say is worth eight hundred pr Ann but I believe he does not make that of it. He has only one daughter and he has considerable property besides Ecclesiastical. They are very charitable and do a great deal of good in the Parish but indeed they ought to keep a carriage. I have had lately the pains in my face returned but was in high spirits all day and everyone seemed in good humour and about dusk we separated. I walked a little way with the Graveners to show the road by Bincomb.

Sunday September 8 Never remember to've seen so many wasps nest in so short a space before, no less than five or six on the road from Asholt to Overstowey. They were burnt out and smoking and the places startled the horse several times. They say the wasps are so numerous this year that they get into the beehives, destroy the bees and eat the honey. The Church this evening was uncommonly full. I Christened Honeyball's child and Churched the woman. They say the woman has not been at Church since her child was Christened before. I wish I had known this, I would have given them a lesson to be remembered. The evening among ourselves in Sunday Stile.

Monday September 9 Up very early, Mrs Ridding and her daughter are to return to Southampton. The Chaise came before six, they made a snap breakfast. I had some serious conversation with William about his ticking with the Pye woman and spending his money. However I paid his tick this time and gave him some money besides his allowance on condition that he is never to tick or borrow any more as I never will overlook it again as it is a bad habit and may lead into bad consequences. My wife and I called on the poor sick girl. I was shocked to see her, she is emaciated to a great degree and in great pain and her poor mother who waits on her has got a cancer alas. The poor girl was very attentive and the mother while I spoke of the comfort of a good conscience hung down her head as if she was agitated, I fear she has not been a good woman, neither has her husband much to boast of on that head.

Wednesday September 18 After breakfast moved off for Mr Ackland's to see the picture. Mr Singleton is now painting Portraits of Mr and Mrs Ackland which we wished to see. He was very busy and had taken most of the old pictures out of their frames to clean them. Mr and Mrs Ackland were not at home. Mr Singleton is an eminent man in his line, gained the Gold Medal about twelve years ago, which gave him the Privilege of travelling to Rome and four hundred a year to support him on his travels. Is very interested in his work, begins at six and ends at dusk. Got to Stowey in good time, it was Faire Time and a great crowd in the streets. My wife bought a pound of tea and some gingerbread for William. Got home before it was very dark and found Sally alone. Kitty did not come until nine o'clock Which her Mistress resented much as she had ordered her to be back from the Fair by six. John came a little after nine o'clock which was very well for him being a man, Kitty was at the Globe in Very Good Company as she says, however her Mistress did not think a Public House so proper for her and was angry and the girl inclined to be saucy but my wife does not mean to give way to her.

Monday October 28 A very wet morning, so thorough a rain as this has turned out to be I scarce recollect. I did not stir out the whole day except to the garden. My wife read a novel of Camilla to us all the day with little intermission so that we were all entertained much with that very affecting narration. My face still indifferent, I sent John to Mr Forbes for more boluses but he was not at home. A good deal of Barley sold to the Poor. Baston called in the evening with a new Mahagony Tray for supper china dishes. He executed the bussiness in a masterly fashion and cheap I think, so I paid him. He is an excellent workman and has worked in London.

Tuesday October 29 Sent off John with Sally on the great horse to Stowgursey to see a relation who is in a dangerous way having been a week in labour. My wife and I set out under our umbrellas to see the Poor Sick Girl which has been so long in that truly forlorn manner. We found the Girl in a miserable condition, the mother was ill above stairs in a wretched loft to which they had begun making new stairs instead of a paltry ladder for the poor woman to go up and down whenever she should be able to do so. Two other women were adjusting some matters for the Poor Unhappy Sick Girl and all around seemed wretchedness, poverty and misery, I almost shuddered at the sight. I read some Prayers by her and she seemed content. I asked whether she understood me. She answered she did. I then desired to know whether she had ever taken the Sacrament. No. Do you understand what it means? I believe I do. What then? Is taken by people at the Altar. I explained a little. She continued My dependence is on God Almighty. I talked a great deal on the subject and told her at last she seemed to be well disposed and I was inclined to administer the Sacrament to her. I received my bolusses from Mr Forbes for the pain in my face and took one as I went to bed.

Sunday November 3 A very numerous congregation at Overstowey Church, a great many new faces from other Parishes. The Singers begin to shine as Musicians and the two Hunts blow the flute capitally. I spoke very seriously to Farmers Morle and Stone about the Poor House and insisted that it be visited regularly once a month if not every fortnight. Notices were given at Church this day about the Highways.

Wednesday November 6 Newspaper come, full of Buonaparte's exaggereted boasting of success over the Austrians. My wife went out to Mrs Woodhouse's and returned with the important news of Lord Nelson's victory over the Combined Fleets of France and Spain off Cadiz. He took 19 ships of the Line and sunk one. The combined Fleets were 33 ships of the Line strong, Nelson 27. Four Flagships struck. Villeneuve the French Commander in Chief is on board one of our ships, a Prisoner. But what has struck a damp on the whole is the Death of the Gallant Nelson. He was killed by a shot from the mast of the Trinidad just as she was striking. They have since sunk her. I had several notes from Mr Northey, Mr Forbes and others of this News but no Gazette has yet appeared. I intended going to the Card Assembly at Stowey but a misley rain came on which prevented me so spent the evening at home with my family.

Saturday November 9 I stood by John in the garden directing him to dig about the gooseberry bushes and currant bushes and dunging the ground. He did indeed scratch the ground a little but scarce covered the dung. I took the spade from him to show him but still he pushes the soil from him so feebly that I scarce had patience with him. The Somersetshire people are certainly very slow and unenergetic, very large and strong but lazy and motionless, very ignorant yet very conceited, Mr Northey called this morning and produced extracts from the Gazette about the Victory of Nelson. It seems he decoyed the Enemy out of port and then fell upon them with a very much larger fleet than they expected. Nelson was killed from the Main Top Mast of the enemy by a Person put there to watch an opportunity and he was very conspicuous having all the Embellishments of Honour about him, the Aigrette from the Grand Seignior and many other things. He delivered his orders after he was shot with great composure and when he heard that the Enemy struck he expressed himself wonderfully gratified and died content.

Tuesday November 12 It has rained hard and incessantly all this day and I have kept within doors. My face still pains me and it is a sad complaint and I have doubts whether I shall ever get rid of it. My wife would have gone to see the Poor Sick Girl but the rain prevented so we sent Kitty with the limb of a goose from our table with Apple Sauce and Mashed Potatoes which, poor Creature, may give her some comfort in her great Distress and Misery.

Saturday November 16 Clerk here making wood into faggots. I have been busy writing my Song on the Victory of Lord Nelson, and I have sent one off to Mr Northey and one to Mr Ruscomb Poole. After dinner John and the Clerk begun winnowing barley and they winnowed 10 bushells. This made them late and Mr Amen supped here, then I paid him for his week.

Monday November 25 John is gone off for coal to Combych. Such a call that I can have but one load, Captain Davis going again immediately. White called about the Income Tax and left the Notices. I received a letter from Carnarvon from a Mr Poole for his client Pugh about the Merionethshire Estate. He said that Mr Oldfield knew that he was to write to me. There is scarce anything but plague about that Estate.

Thursday November 28 It was our intention to go today to administer the Sacrament to the Poor Sick Girl who was so long in that state but I could not get anyone but my wife to go with me. for the Rubrick says there should be two besides the Minister and such as had received it before were most proper for I did not suffer the parents to receive it with her now because they never had received before and have been very indifferent people heretofore but seem to be Penitent at present and I have ordered them to attend the Sacrament at Church at Christmas as they are able to come there, which is most proper and in the meantime they are to come to Church every Sunday. As we were disappointed in a third person today we put it off till Friday. So I mounted my horse and rode off to Fairfield, met Mr Davis. We walked together up to the house. Mr Acland was not at home, neither was Mrs Ackland, but I delivered up to the housekeeper Mrs Acland's prescription enclosed in a little paper with thanks for the use of them. We went in and looked at Mr Acland's picture, it is like but not a pleasant likeness. Mrs Acland's is a most beautiful picture and very like her but of a younger aspect. After this Mr Davis and I returned to Stowgurcy, saw Mrs Davis and chatted till two then mounted my horse and rode home in good time for dinner. Mrs Davis shewed me a very fine pig they are going to fat. Mine has been up these five weeks and is not so fat.

Friday November 29 The newspaper come with a better account of Lord Collingwood than expected. They have brought home four more of the Prizes after having sunk the rest and they have preserved their own ships without much damage during the tremendous storm. My wife and I and Mrs Frost went to administer the Sacrament to the Poor Sick Girl. All things were very clean about her and she looked in the face tolerable but was sadly emaciated in the arms and often in great pain. However I administered the Sacrament to her. Her mother did not partake, I sent her upstairs and she is to come to Church. After this my wife and I went to Stowey, I called on Atkins, being sadly plagued about the Income Tax. After this I have been in the house and busy writing a Sermon for Thanksgiving Day.

Saturday November 30 A man from Stowgurcy called with a paper for Property Tax, sadly plagued about papers which no one understands. I think Government should not plague us in this manner and every one goes to a Lawyer for Explanation and is obliged to pay for it, which adds to the Tax and this is not right, but a kind of oppression. I did not stir out this afternoon and continued writing my sermon almost till bedtime.

Wednesday December 4 John went off early for coal and returned about one o'clock. The newspaper come and gives no credit to the news that was afloat yesterday that the Archduke Charles was dead and the Emperor of Germany having made a Peace with Buonaparte. I sat down today and finished my Sermon and then went to Marsh Mill to acquaint Mr Blake of the doubt about the bad news. After dinner I read my Sermon to my family who approved it.

Thursday December 5 The weather very mild. On my getting up I found no Laurel had been got ready for this is the Thanksgiving Day for Lord Nelson's Glorious Victory. Out of thirty three Ships of the Line which the Combined Fleets of Spain and France consisted of only three can be made serviceable by the Enemy. I ordered Laurel to be put to the Gate and put a

sprig in my hat and gave other sprigs to the family. In a short time most of
the Parish had Laurel in their hats and the Church was adorned with Laurel.
I read the Prayers sent by Government. We had a tolerable full congregation, then I mounted the Pulpit and gave them the Sermon I had newly
made and which I believe gave great satisfaction for they all were very
attentive. The two Riches were at Church and Mrs Woodhouse and the
Blakes. After this I rode to Asholt and as on Thanksgiving Days there is no
printed Afternoon Service sent I converted the Morning Service to Afternoon to them. So it went off very well but the Apparitor had neglected
sending forms of Prayers to Asholt tho' they had taken the money. This is
sad business and must be complained of. Our Bells were ringing all this day
and Illuminations were ordered at this House and great doings at Stowey
and I subscribed to their Fund for the purpose. When I got to Stowey I
found great Preparations going forward. Mr Northey was preparing
curious transparencies on his wall next the Street. A Crown with an Arch of
Oak and Laurel about it and Victory underneath beautifully illuminated and
on each side Nelson and Collingwood elegantly done and a row of Candles
in oiled paper. We dined about five, Mrs O'Dogharty and Miss Taylor a
sister of Mrs Northey were of the party. Miss Taylor seems a well bred
young woman with an animated countenance but short in stature and not
very elegant in shape nor healthy but I should think from her countenance
Ingenious and Clever. I believe she had a good deal to do with the
Ornaments of the Day. After dinner we paraded Stowey Streets to see the
Illuminations at the Cross. There was indeed a very curious Device
exceedingly well done. It was a Crown over a large Anchor, a Trans-
parency on each side of the Crown with a G and R in capitals. On the body
of the Anchor was Trafalgar and above it – England expects Everyone to do
his Duty – in a circular Scroll. The Rope of the Achor was exceedingly well
done and the whole would have been admired even in London. Mr Price
was the executor but Miss Taylor designed it. The Town was very lively
and on top of Castle Hill was a Glorious Bonfire and Musick. They
attempted Squibs and Crackers in the Town but Old Mr Symes, to my
great surprise, ran after and collared one man and so put a stop to it but they
had a Cannon at the top of the Hill which they fired often. We all went up
but did not stay long as there were Squibs thrown about. After this we
conducted the Ladies safe home. Mr Northey and I and Mr Symes and Mr
Forbes went to the Globe and there we supped tho' I had not much relish
for eating and drinking. We had a good Handsome Supper, Mr Tom Poole
in the Chair, Mr Northey on one side and I on the other. Mr Blake the
young Clergyman, the Bishop's Nephew, next to Mr Northey and Old Mr
Symes next to me. At length a song was called for and Mr Northey blabbed
that I had prepared one. On this I was called on, I did not relish singing a
song of my own making and declined it much. At last I began and it took
very much indeed, several bursts of applause at every Stanza and when I had

finished they all rose up with Glasses in their Hands drinking my Health and clapping for some minutes so that I began to feel myself a little awkward.

Friday December 6   Awoke and found myself tolerable. There is Glorious News indeed. Archduke Charles is not dead but made a Masterly Retreat and is in Full March to succour Vienna. There is no Truth in the Emperor having concluded a Peace with Buonaparte. This was a Fabrication of that Author of All Lies and the Dutch Admiral was the Tool of Conveying the Falsehood to our Fleet. After breakfast I walked with Mr Northey to the Globe but could get no account of the Bill. By and By my wife and I trudged homewards and have been all this afternoon writing my Diary.

Saturday December 7   Sad misfortune in putting Ink into the Stand it spurted all over my Thanksgiving Day Sermon, however I believe it will do. I understand that Mr Amen has been at Ely Green drinking out the money they received for Ringing on Thanksgiving Day. Instead of ringing all the rejoicing Night they left off at five and divided the money and went to different places to drink it. This is not right and I must see to the matter. Drinking I fear is the great Failing of Mr Amen. The Poor Sick Girl that I used to visit and at last administered the Sacrament to, died yesterday. I do not think she eat anything since she received the Sacrament and I am glad that she received it and that now she is Delivered of all her pain and suffering, for her suffering has been very great. In the evening Mr Amen and Dick Jones came in to be paid for the road. I did not know they had been on the road and thought the Clerk had been at the Ale House which he confessed in part but this day he has been on the road.

Monday December 9   Walked to Stowey, met Mr Northey. They were collecting for the Widows and Children and the Sick and Wounded killed at the Battle of Trafalgar. I went to the Globe and paid my quota towards the Supper. Mr Amen went round this day to collect money for the High Roads but brought in very little.

Friday December 13   This evening we were very much alarmed with John who (they said) was dying. He roared like a bull and rolled on the floor, complaind of his chest and his side. We could not make out what was the matter, summoned our neighbours around, got him to bed and paid Molly Weymouth for sitting up with him. Made him white wine Whey, which he would not touch. It was past one o'clock before we could get to bed. We thought of sending for Forbes but it was too late so there we left him in bed, quiet and calm and went to bed ourselves.

Saturday December 14 John better a good deal. We sent for Blake, he saw John in bed, declared him quite well, nothing but a stricture on his chest in coming over the Great Down Field. Mr Amen came in to be paid for his work on the road but as I had not the Book downstairs to enter it he is to be paid Monday.

Sunday December 15 Newspaper came very late, nothing in it, but Lying Bulletins from the French Army. I walked to Asholt, went through the Duty bravely and then walked back again. Had some soup and then to Prayers at our Church. The Poor Sick Girl's Corpse that I attended so long was brought to Church and after Church I attended her to the Grave. Poor Creature, I hope she has met in another world that Ease and Happiness which she could not obtain in this. Farmer Morle said he would attend me to make a collection for the Sick and Wounded at the Battle of Trafalgar but I see he sneaks off. This is the way with Farmers, they have no Liberality of Mind. The evening at home in the usual stile of Sundays.

Monday December 16 I went round this day to collect money for the Relief of the Killed and Wounded at the Battle of Trafalgar but Farmer Morle the Churchwarden did not come near me though he promised to do so. These Farmers are sneaking fellows when put to the Push. Called on the two Richs, old batchelors, worth a hundred thousand pounds or more. With difficulty they gave me a guinea each. I put down a guinea myself and certainly as much as I can afford but as to them they scarce know what to do with their money. Met Mr Blake and his son he promised to give me something to the Subscription. Returned home with full resolution to call on all the Farmers one by one but have no time now. I wrote to William Tutton about receiving my Tithe on the first of January next.

Saturday December 21 A very misley foggy morning. I had to go to Asholt to bury a corpse. It rained most furious yet with two coats and an umbrella I pursued my course and got there without Harm or Accident. The Corpse was there before me. I soon deposited it in the ground, it was an old man of the name of Rich and a near relation of the Richs of Overstowey. After my return went to dinner.

Sunday December 22 A full Congregation and the Singers had their New Instruments from London for which I subscribed one guinea. I was very satisfied with the Instruments they had before but Mr Tom Poole introduced the Business and then subscribed only half a guinea. I do not approve of this mode of picking money out of my pocket.

Wednesday December 25   A very rainy day. I issued out this morning to go to Asholt but the rain soon came on in a torrent like manner and well it was for me that I had an umbrella. I got safe and administered the Sacrament to ten persons, pretty well for Asholt. Returned through great rain yet preserved by my umbrella. I found at home the persons who dwelt in the Cottages where William was taken when he fell from his horse, and there was a large party in the kitchen. Robert, an old servant and some of our neighbours. We went to Church first and I had a Christening afterwards and a Sacrament in the morning and two Sermons and heavy rain and uncomfortable weather. It was altogether fatiguing. After dinner we called in the wives of the Inhabitants of the Cottage who came to see William and made an additional present of half a Guinea each to them for their Care, Kindness and Humanity and invited them to dine here every Christmas Day in Future. They seemed much pleased with the notice taken of them. They went off before supper in a very tempestuous night and had some three miles to go. Some of the party staid later and some till after supper. Robert, an old servant of mine, and now a respectable chandler seemed growing fat apace. At last they all made their bow and we soon trippd off for bed.

Sunday December 29   The Church not very full this morning but a great many at the Sacrament. Davis and his wife were there and that Villain Porter who had a child by his only daughter attempted to stay but I gave him to understand that he must not. Indeed the man may repent and in that case forgiveness is promised to any offence, but I feel there is no real repentance in this man, neither does he see his crime in its true light, and moreover he should have come to me beforehand to talk to me before he presumed to come to the Sacrament. After Prayers I walked down to Stowey about two o'clock and John took my Gown with him. I did the Duty and entered this day on the Service of the Church alternately with my own as an assistant to Mr Northey. In the meantime Mr Poole of Shurston has taken to Asholt. There were two Burials and a Christening but Mr Northey would not permit me to officiate, saying he always took these when in Residence so homewards I trudged under my umbrella, John carrying my Gown before.

The Year 1806

Wednesday January 1   This is the First Day of the New Year. I sent John early to Stowey with twenty bushells of Barley to the Maltster to be made into malt and I have married a couple but the newspaper has not brought very pleasant news. It speaks of an Armistice between the Emperor of Germany and Buonaparte. The Ways of Providence are very Mysterious. That this Man, an enemy to all Religion, an Assassin and Murderer and everything that is bad should succeed in all his Enterprises in this extraordinary manner is beyond Conception. Besides his success must have so evindently a bad influence on the Moral World as to induce many to distrust the Providence of God and make them think that it will be to no purpose to cultivate Moral Goodness and Uprightness of Conduct. However I pray to God that this Year may yet unfold some matters which tend to forbode the downfall of this Wicked Usurper. Perhaps by no Power is he to fall but by the British alone for hitherto no other Nation has been able to struggle against this Bloody AntiChrist. The Battle of Trafalgar has brought Security to us with regard to invasion of this country and I trust that this will prove at last to be the Favoured Nation which is destined not only to withstand, but even to Annihilate his Power and to Convey the Pure Precepts of Christianity to future Ages in defiance of the Contagious Influences and Depravity of the French Revolution. Mr John Poole and his sisters Jane and Penelope came to us this day. Miss Lewis is still with us but she is so silent and placid that we scarce know whether she is with us or no. They are to continue with us.

Thursday January 2   After breakfast the Divine and I mounted our horses and set William on his little Nag and we rode over to Kilve to see Mr Mathew. Met young Gravener on the way, he had been on a Bridal Visit to his neighbour Mr Sweeten. We got to Mr Mathew's and found there the two young Harfords who are pupils of his. Mr Harford the father pays three hundred pounds pr ann for both and yet they are but young, the eldest exactly the age of my Boy. We got home in good stile, dressed ourselves for dinner and we had to dine with us Mr and Mrs Blake and young Blake who is just entered at Balliol College, Miss Betsy Blake and little John, Mr Tom Poole and Mr James Rich, all these made up a good round company.

Mr James Rich after dinner took to Brandy and water rather than wine. Mr Tom Poole came late, very grand and important, took out his French Gold Watch and affected much the travelled man, coxcomby and with all the appearance of greatness and liberality he is the most shabby dodging man to deal with I ever met with. Played at cards after tea and in due time seperated rather late. The Divine has recently published a Sermon which does him credit, which he is not a little sensible of. There is in all the Pooles a good deal of Pomp and Vanity.

Sunday January 5   I was up early and we all breakfasted in time. My Little Boy and I walked to Stowey, called on the Clerk and then on Mr Northey. I did the Duty and took William into the Reading Desk with me. The Church tolerably full, the Northey Family filling their seat. John carried my Gown. We returned to our own Church, the two Miss Pooles were glad to hear Service at a Church they were so accustomed to. After Service we dined and then before tea the Pooles left us to go to Stowey so took leave and now we have only Miss Lewis with us.

Tuesday January 7   John has been busy in the Paddock and making up the garden wall under the Quick hedge which had slided down during this very wet weather. My pease come up very well in the garden I must plant some beans. Took little William with me and we walked to Chapel House to enquire after the Clerk, but he was not at home. He has given himself a Holiday or two which he spends at the Publick House – the Old Man gets worse and worse. William said a Lesson today in Bayley's Exercises and wrote and has been a very good boy all day.

Wednesday January 8   Sent William to the Blakes at Marsh Mill, then we dressed ourselves and George's Gig came and I mounted the great horse and we all went off to Fairfield. We had a large party tho' only the Pooles besides ourselves and the Aclands. A very handsome dinner we had and all things were conducted in an elegant and magnificant stile. After dinner the Pooles of Shurston came. Fairfield is a large Mansion House built about the time of Queen Elizabeth, the rooms are large, high and spacious, the windows in the old stile, but the house is fitted out in a very superb manner. Mrs Acland has a great deal of Benevolence in her Countenance and has been a beautiful woman but is now very fat. Mr Acland is large and tall and very personable and certainly rather fat with amazing fat legs. He is a sensible well bred man but sometimes violent and always Proud. After tea we had cards and we played low. I neither won nor lost, my wife lost eight shillings and Mr John Poole at our table was a great loser. In due time we all moved off for Bedfordshire up various staircases in this extended House. Margaret slept in a Dressing Room adjoining to our Room.

Thursday January 9 It rained hard in the night. A most magnificent breakfast we had. Mr John Poole left before breakfast and soon our John came with a double horse and took off Margaret and soon my wife and I trudged on foot leaving the Miss Pooles behind. The road was very wet yet as my wife had pattens and I had boots we got on very well. I was rather fatigued and did not stir out much after I arrived home.

Saturday January 11 A very tempestuous night which took off some of the tiles from the House and damaged the Church and Chancel very much. Edward Selleck has been this day and made the House in the Garden somewhat more comfortable than it has been of late. As William was going to bed there was a great uproar for it rained into our room very fast. Sally looked aghast and John stared like a stuck pig but not one offered to do or suggest anything. At last I ordered Sally to bring a mop to take up the wet in our room and a large basin to take the droppings. I called John up stairs with me into the Garrett behind his and there we found out the whole grievance. Who'd have thought it cried John whereas if he had thought about it at all he must have guessed that the rain came from above. I got a large tub to lie over the place and put some of the loose tiling in better order and secured it for the present, and then we went quietly to bed without further apprehension.

Monday January 20 Verrier's man about the Church and Davy on the Chancel. Little Davy has lost his Honour much since he failed in the business he undertook about the Body of the Church. I thought him once to be an honest man, open hearted, a sturdy little fellow but he turns out to be a Rogue or rather a Knave. I have been busy this morning in nailing the Grape Tree and the Cherry tree which the wind shook much. John carried the remainder of the barley to Mr Ward, in all thirty bushells at five shillings pr bushell. The Clerk is in the barn threshing wheat now.

Friday January 24 I walked to Plainsfield and talked to Farmer Morle about the alterations going on in the Singing Gallery and wondered how he could think of attempting any new erection without consulting me. He seemed amazed and thought I knew of it, said it had been talked of but I was not consulted answered I. Then I shewed him the Law in Burns Ecliesiastic. He seemed concerned and said he meant no disrespect. I believe it returned I and now I shall not consent to what is done unless it is finished in my way and have the top Arch glazed altogether. He said he would see to it. After dinner Farmer Morle came in and we went to Church together and I shewed him how I'd have the window, to which he assented. He then came back with me and drank three jugs of strong beer which made the Farmer's cheeks wax red. Then he marched home and we spent the remainder of the day among ourselves.

Saturday January 25   I hear that Willis who lived a Servant with me has fallen from a horse of Mrs Marsh's with some sacks of Flower and broke his arm above the elbow. Mr Blake posted off I suppose to set it, he is very charitable in such things.

Friday January 31   The newspaper come. A Public Testimony of Approbation of Mr Pitts Conduct and Honour was proposd by Lascelles but opposed by Fox and his party. Windham Tho once an admirer of Pitt and in the same Administration with him for some time voted against the Mark of Esteem designed for him, for which he received the neatest and most severe rebuke from Mr Rider that ever was given by any man. However a Publick Burial and Monument were voted by a large majority and I believe his debts are to be discharged out of the Publick Purse.

Saturday February 1   My gout rather better, I cannot get a gouty shoe that will fit me, sent different ways. My wife went down to Mr Blake's to change a large Bank Bill but I did not take those Country Bank Bills he sent, the three Nymphs went to Stowey to change it. Farmer Stone's wife has been here about the Poor Woman with a sore breast, she does not think a nurse will be necessary at the expence of the Parish. However I sent her a new flannel waistcoat and gave her a shilling out of my own pocket and I made the Overseers give her another but I fear her husband is an idle fellow and half starves her, they have but one Child.

Sunday February 2   The Church was full but I made a woeful mistake for I read the Second Lesson twice. I have been much concerned with this as I think it proves that my Memory and recollection begin to fail me. The Clerk endeavoured to set me right but I thought he was wrong, in short I was totally lost. If these things happen again once or twice I shall give over doing Duty for I never used to make such blunders. I am quite shocked at it. My gout is not much better yet I am in good Spirits.

Friday February 7   My foot still getting better so I ventured my shoe on slip shod with a lettle flannel round the heel. Moved out a little round the garden. We did not breakfast before ten this morning – I do not like this.

Saturday February 8   I have drawn on my shoe today and my gout seems to've left me in a great measure but my legs feel cold. Mrs and the two Miss Lewis dined here and after dinner the Post Chaise came from Bridgewater and carried them off and we are now left to ourselves. John finished spreading the dung in the Paddock and cleaned up the premises in the usual stile of Saturday.

Sunday February 9   After breakfast I went to the Sunday School and gave away a penny. Not many at Church this morning, the two Riches and old Mudd Headed White. I had a Christening and a Churching. Eat some soup and rode down to Stowey. The Church tolerably full. Chatted with Mr Northey as I rode home and had a Funeral. Old Kibby was 83 and yet his sister cried and seemed half distressed. I could not forbear observing that she could not expect him to live for ever, and therefor she might moderate her grief. After this we spent the evening in our usual Sunday stile.

Tuesday February 11 It is my wife's Birthday and she seems tolerably well today, the erysypales in her arm being much abated. She is this day 56, being nearly four years younger than I am. Sent John into the garden to prepare ground for potatoes. Turned the great horse in to the Churchyard to stretch his limbs. Walked to Court House and got some seeds from Furse, he had pease and beans very fine and Early Peep potatoes. Rain came on after dinner so we could not plant any.

Wednesday February 12
A fine pleasant morning. My wife has taken Physick and so is confined. Margaret made breakfast. I put down my Early Peep potatoes and John planted carrot and onions. My John Poole called and wanted me to ride to Kilve with him. Mr Blake of Stowey called and chatted some time. I dined at Mr Northey's and about six we went to the Card Club. There were three tables, I played against Mr Northey and won a crown off him. About nine John came and I walked home with him and his lantern. It rained all the time but I had an umbrella.

Sunday February 16 The newspaper came late, nothing material in it but I do not much approve of some of Fox's Speeches. I do not like the man. He certainly will do mischief. I walked to Stowey this morning with my umbrella, John carrying my Gown. I called on Mr Northey and we walked to Church together, I read the Service and preached. Mr Tom Poole was at Church and Charles Poole and Mr Symes the Lawyer and several others. There was a Christening which Mr Northey took. Home I walked, had a little soup and went to Church at Overstowey, the Church very full with strangers from Ashol, Fiddington, Stowgurcy and Stowey. There was a famous singer in the Gallery, a tennant of the Riches, a very strong bas voice, above all the others and I thought grating on the ears. The little Clerk from Asholt was there and Hawkins and others. I read the Proclamation for the General Fast and told the Clerk of Asholt that I would preach the Fast Sermon there that day. There was a Christening after Prayers and a Churching. Betty dressed the dinner today by Margaret's instruction – Sally is gone over the Hill to see her father and mother and not to return till tomorrow evening.

Wednesday February 19   Set John to work in the garden then I mounted my horse and rode to Fairfield to call on Mr Acland. I found him seated in his Study in a wheeled chair before the fire and Mrs Acland at work by him. He has not been out since he visited me. One of the great cords in his leg seems to've been wrenched while he turned in his bed, he is a large man and his limbs uncommonly large. He read a letter from his son now in the East Indies with an account of an attack made upon them by Adml Linois in the Indian Seas. It was past three when I got home, so Margaret and I went to dinner, my wife being not yet come down stairs having taken Physick. This day is Ash Wednesday and we had no Prayers, the first time I have omitted since I came here and I am sorry but it is so difficult to get a Congregation in the country that I have been obliged to it. This evening sat by a good fire and with my family compared the Four Evangelists on the Resurrection, having Clerk's Paraphrase by me.

Thursday February 20   John went on still very well in the garden but he was called off rather soon to go with our little sow to the boar to Strinxon, little Farmer Landsey went with him.

Friday February 21   John went off on the great horse for the little sow and brought he newspapers and then he went to work in the garden. I joined him but the wind blew high and was unpleasant and troublesome. I could not stand it but went in and wrote a good deal of my Fast Sermon. Many dead at Stowey at this time, Old Coles, Mrs Conduit and young Verrier's wife and some others.

Sunday February 23   Prayers here in the morning, the Church not particularly full. After a little soup I marched on foot to Stowey, found Mr Northey at home by himself. He said that he found himself very fatigued in doing Duty this morning. I fear his lungs are weak. In returning met Mrs Mackay who had been at Church. She got me to walk in to see her snug little room at George Paddock's. She said she could spend three hundred a year there very well. I answered that it was much easier to spend that sum than to save it. She was as merry as a lark and is looking for another husband before she spends all. She really has been a very pretty woman and is tolerably so still. After this I walked home but had given John permission to go to Stowgurcy to see his Sweetheart. He came home by reading time.

Wednesday February 26   This is Fast Day. I went to Church but we had not as many there as I expected. The Service was long and I gave them a New Sermon which I always do on this Occasion. When a Person has taken some trouble one would wish to have a Congregation to hear it. Mrs Blake and her two daughters were at Church but Mr Blake was not, and I have observed once or twice before he has shurkd the Fast Sermon, but he is an odd man. After Prayers here I went to Asholt this day for Mr Henry Poole. Brice the Rector and his wife were there but he either was, or pretended to be ill. I went to Church and did the Duty then called after Prayers. I found him and wife above stairs in a room without paper and a bed without a curtain, a small wood fire and a paltry oak table with two sorry chairs. She has been in the house for a week and he for weeks at various times and I am astonished that they have not provided better accommodation for themselves. I soon left them, came home and went to dinner.

Thursday February 27 The Clerk of Asholt has lost his son in a most extraordinary manner. He was an apprentice to Hawkins the Joiner at Bridgewater and went out to drink a cup of cyder with a comrade and workman at the same place. They parted and shook hands as they left the Valient Soldier Publick House. The young men took different roads, the Clerk's son was to go over the Bridge to Hawkins his Master's and it is now supposed he tumbled in the river. However he has not yet been heard of and the poor little Clerk his father is almost distracted. It is not supposed he has gone off from his Master as his clothes and money were left behind. Molly Weymouth brought some sugar from Bridgewater and said she had seen little William in high spirits.

Saturday March 1 This is St David's Day and I have a few leeks washed clean and put in water – I have now got one in my hat being a Welshman and soon expect Mr and Mrs Davis here with leeks each of them. We passed the day in great Sociability, then playd cards and they left us about nine. It was a fine moonshining night. We had a dish of leeks for dinner and very good they were.

Thursday March 6 We expect some company today so my wife and Margaret are busy. Margaret takes very much to cooking dinners which I am glad of as it may be of use to her through life. John has been all the morning in the garden and now he is going to tighten himself up to wait at table at dinner. About four Mr Mathew came to dine and soon after Mr Northey and his niece Mrs O'Dogharty and after that Mrs Northey and Miss Taylor in the gig and a servant attending them. We had a good dinner and were very merry and comfortable. Mr Mathew was very pleasant and chatty, they staid till about ten. Had a tray for supper. Miss Taylor remains here. It was about twelve before we got to bed.

Friday March 7 Miss Taylor up and downstairs, an agreeable well behaved young woman. Has been much among people of Fashion, very mild and composed in her manners, but I do not think her equal to her sister Mrs Northey who is sharp and pretty and clever but delicate in constitution. Mrs Northey came in her gig to take her sister off about twelve. Mr

Northey is gone to Ramsbury to his son who is at school there where Scarlet Fever has got among the Scholars and dispersed many of them.

Tuesday March 11 We walked to Stowey. Paid Mr Francis Poole for the newspaper for half a year to the latter end of last December. Called on Mrs Northey who had a good account of her son at Mr Meyrick's, he has not yet had the Scarlet Fever and will probably escape it now. Mr Northey is to bring him to Bath and leave him with his Grandmother. I had a letter today from Mr Parsons to threaten our roads with an Indictment.

From this date through to the middle of December no record remains but from the numbering of the books of the Diary Holland must have kept up his recording.

Thursday December 18 Very rainy. Mr Hartwell called here and he is going to Bridgewater for Summonses for the Roads. I do not recollect much after this.

Friday December 19 The best day we have had for some time. Wrote a letter to Mrs Benwell to thank her for promoting my little Boy's interest with regard to the Charter House.

Sunday December 21 A very indifferent morning tho mild and warm yet rainy and muggy. Prayers here in the morning but the waters have been out so much and the rain continues in such a manner that few were able to come to Church. Farmer Morle offered some money which is to be distributed to the Second Poor of this Parish according to the Discretion of the Minister and Churchwardens on St Thomas's Day. After dinner I walked to Stowey by myself, the weather being but indifferent. The Church tolerably but not very full. It was so dark by the time I had got half over my Sermon that I scarce knew how to procede yet however I finished it. Properly speaking I have done with Stowey and shall in future take Dodington with Overstowey but as Mr Northey is not prepared with a successor I shall continue to give him my assistance a little longer. It was almost dark when I returned but as this is the shortest day we shall soon have a change.

Thursday December 25 Christmas Day yet still warm and muggy and rainy. No Market today at Bridgewater. I had a new Gown from Oxford which I put on today. Prince's Stuff and it cost me a fine sum, almost eight pounds. The Church filled slowly but did fill at last. We had a Sacrament and pretty well attended. After Church we had some company to dinner in the kitchen. I had no further Duty. The company in the kitchen left us in good time one after another. Mrs Stiling and Mrs Rich were both here who received my boy after the fall from the horse and they are to dine every Christmas Day here.

Sunday December 28 Walked to Stowey, very dirty. A good many at Church. Preached against Methodists and Enthusiasts, the text from 2 Epistle to Timothy. The time will come when they will not endure sound Doctrine but after their own Lusts shall heap unto themselves teachers having itching ears. Very attentive. Indeed Mr Northey when I came from the Pulpit caught me by the hand and thanked me, said it was a Most Excellent Sermon. He talked so loud and the congregation who staid for the Sacrament heard, which made me point to the door of the Vestry for it was open. I left him to administer the Sacrament, being obliged to hasten to my own Church which began at two. Got there and we had a good many at Church. Terrible work with the Instruments in the Singing Gallery. After Church we dined and the evening went on in the usual manner of Sunday.

Monday December 29 I walked with William part of the way to Stowey, he is to dine at Mr Tom Poole's. There is a little lady there, Mrs Richard Poole and daughter with whom William has constructed a friendship from their infancy and the mother seems to promote more than I wish as it is a foolish thing for a boy to go and visit a little Girl, but the mother begged that they might see each other so I let him go.

Wednesday December 31 The most incessant and determined rain I ever knew, yet strange to tell the glass rises to a great height. Easter's two children* were buried in the same grave, poor things. Easter was in great agonies. I had an umbrella but the rain was so cold and the wind blew under the umbrella and I felt it on my head as I read the Service very much. After this I soon scudded in and the Ringers are now beginning to Ring out the Old Year. My daughter and I were to go to Stowgurcy but the rain was so great that we sent an excuse in the afternoon.

The Year 1807

Thursday January 1   A very fine clear frosty morning. The frost coming so soon after the rain will I fear hurt the wheat. The Ringers begun so early this morning that our sleep has been much disturbed. Another Year has commenced and the old has not ended badly. I have had good news from Wales and have succeeded in some measure with regard to William in getting a Prospect for the Charter House. I am certainly getting older but my health is not impaired from what it was last year and indeed the Pain in my face is certainly less than it was the Autumn before last. I mounted my horse and rode to Stowgurcy first, then to Shurton to speak to Mr Poole about the Church of Holford as I mean to take to it now instead of Stowey. Mr Poole of Shurton was at home but not his wife. I found I could not get to Doddington on my return as I intended.

Friday January 2   I mounted my horse and rode to Doddington and spoke to Mr Farthing about the Service of the Church. After this returned and got myself ready to dine at Mr Blake's. There all of us went and we had a good dinner. Mr Brice and his two daughters were there and young Chubb, son of the Celebrated Chubb the Philosopher and Atheist from Bridgewater and I believe descended from an even more Celebrated Chubb, and they have all inherited the same Principles. We had cards and I sat down to Commerce, William latterly playing for me and the little dog was so sharp that he won the Pool. I gave him a shilling and Johnny Blake another. After this and supper we returned home over the Down Field but Mr Brice and his daughters had walked and the frost had turned to thaw they found it so dark and dirty they resolved to take beds at Mr Blake's.

Sunday January 4   Church here in the morning, I had a Christening. Before dinner I mounted my horse and trudged to Doddington for the first time and so entered on the Curacy. The Church seemed well filled but a small one and I could scarce get into the Pulpit and when there really found difficulty in putting my hand to my pocket to take out my Sermon. The Church is unsealed and the Reading Desk out of repair. I observed this to an ill natured consequential man who seemd to be a Churchwarden. He answered that it had stood many years. That is the very reason returned I that a new one is now wanted, but he did not relish this conversation. I soon came back to dinner for there was no singing at Doddington. The congregation was more decent than I expected. After dinner the evening went on in the usual stile of Sunday.

Monday January 5 I received an odd letter from Mr Sealy (the Rector) about the Stipend of Doddington. Mr Northey and son called after breakfast and I rode with them to Crowcomb and called on Mr Humphries the Curate to know if he would do Duty at Stowey. He could not undertake it. Called on Mr Barnard at the Great House but he could not give us an intelligence on that head.

Tuesday January 6 After breakfast Farmer White called for the Income Tax. Walked to Stowey and called on Mr Tom Poole and Mrs Richard Poole. The first has been taken suddenly with a pain in his head in lifting a weight and there is some apprehension that a blood vessel in the head burst. Mr Ward was with him so we could not stay till he came down stairs and therefor did not go up. Made some calls at other places and then came home. I sent off an answer to Mr Sealy's letter. The Clerk was here today carrying out dung tho not yesterday it being Old Christmas Day as he calls it and therefor a Holiday, that is after he had kept a week of Holiday for new Christmas Day. A new servant came to offer herself today and is I believe hired. Miss Hartwell called in the evening but did not stay tea. She is so deaf that there is scarce holding any conversation with her.

Thursday January 8 Botany Bay Rich and Scoundrel Cavil passd by to go up the Hill on the road. Cavil was apparently very civil and submissive with his hat off at every word. Called on Mr Tom Poole, he is better but not recovered. Mrs Richard Poole was there with him and her little girl whom they design for William it seems but I have no such design and think it ridiculous to put such notions in the minds of Children. Let them grow to full Maturity and then let them chuse themselves. This little girl is very clever and learns surprizingly and writes Latin letters but I should not like women any the better for understanding Latin and Greek. All pedantic learning of this kind makes them conceited. I do not approve of the manner of Boys in Peticoats.

Saturday January 10 Mr Northey called, he had settled with Mr Starkey for the Service of Stowey during his absence. I was somewhat surprized about his choice for Starky and his wife are exceptionable people. She is the daughter of Sir Edward Baynton a very vicious character and has already played pranks and her husband, good man, has taken her again.

Saturday January 17 The weather is uncommonly mild for the season. Yesterday the Bell tolled and startled me in the morning. It was for Old

Porter who (shocking to relate) had a child by his own daughter. I never heard of his illness before and I am sorry for this as I would certainly have called on him and spoken to him and prayed by him. He was ill once before and I attended him but he shocked me by his insensibility on speaking of the shocking crime he had been guilty of. He answered that he hoped God would forgive him. I replied that I hoped so too but that it was a crime of a most heinous Nature. There are others as bad as me he answered quick. I did not approve of his answers at all. Some time ago after the Common Service was over and some staying to Communicate I took notice that he staid among the rest. I was shocked and surprized and sent the Clerk to tell him he must not stay. I was not prepared for him neither were the congregation. He immediately took his hat and went out. I am sorry now that I have not seen him in his illness before he died. Yet if he is Truly Penitent, God who sees the Heart will, I hope, forgive him. Certainly he attended Church very regularly some time before his death.

Sunday January 18 Prayers here in the morning and Old Porter was brought to Church and buried and the Church was very full. The wind was exceedingly troublesome as I read the Service so that I was obliged to run into a kind of shelter under a projection of the Church Tower. After this and when I had taken a little soup I set off for Doddington. Found the Church very full, I gave them a Sermon on the subject of Keeping the Sabbeth Holy to which they were very attentive. After Service walked into Mr Farthing's House, he and Mrs Farthing were both at Church. He seemed a young man, younger than his wife, has three children and another coming.

Thursday January 22 We lay long in bed. The rain continues violently, everywhere flows with water. We are engaged to go to Stowgurcy to Mr Davis but fear this cannot be accomplished. However at last I hit upon a plan. I recollected a frame I had made for my cart to cover it in case the French invaded us. Therefor summoned Edward Sellick on the occasion and he placed it on the cart and had an old blanket thrown over it very neat and snug. We all moved off but my wife and I walked to Stowey and got in at the turning to Stowgurcy. The wind was uncommonly high, so much as to alarm us often with its violent gusts and there was some rain. We got there in good plight and all were pleased to see us.

Friday January 23 Mr and Mrs Davis prevailed on us to stay another night. The three young Aclands came in today. The second is just going another voyage to the East Indies. He appears to be the finest of the three. Tis strange that Mr Acland a man who will be, first or last, possessed of a Fortune of from seven to ten thousand pr Ann. should bring up his son on board an East Indiaman. It is not a Gentleman's Education or Profession –

Money, money, money is at the bottom of his heart and he thinks the obtaining of it is Everything.

Saturday January 24   When we returned to Overstowey we found Mr Ruscomb Poole in waiting for us. He had got the Declaration of Trespass for me by Mr Richard Symes of Bridgewater on my cutting wood on the common within my Parish which has been done by the Vicars of Overstowey time Immemoriable in lieue of Tithe. This is a dirty business of Richard Symes which puts money into his pocket and must take money from mine whether I gain the Cause or not. These Lawyers are bad animals in the community.

Tuesday January 27   My wife and I walked to Stowey and called on Mr and Mrs Northey to bid them a good journey, they are to reside at Windsor. I spoke to George about the Gig. Verrier and the glazier came here about the lead cistern and the water in the spouts. John went for coals again and brought a load by eleven. I had more examinations taken about the Custom Wood. The evening spend in reading and cards. William is to return to School Thursday.

Wednesday January 28   A man came to me yesterday of the name of Joseph Hill for a Certificate of his Marriage which I gave him. Poor fellow he had walked down from London for the purpose so we made a Collection for him. The first news brought me this day was that poor Old Ben Hunt was dead. I had heard that he was ill and missed him last Sunday from the Sunday School but never suspected he was so near Death for he had often been ailing. My wife indeed had sent some broth and I had intended calling there this very day and very much do I wonder that he never sent to me that he wished to see me, or that someone did not inform me that he was not likely to live. Poor Ben he will no longer grace the Sunday School with his Coal black hair and Venerable face. No more shall I hear his deep sighs on the Immorality of the World around and the Simplicity of his remarks on the Follies of Weak Mortals as he used to call them. Yet when he heard a word or two of good news for Old England he often shrugged himself and smiled and put his straight hair behind his large ear to attend more fully to what was said. Buonaparte he hated with a Deadly Hatred. Poor Mortal he used to say what use will all his grandeur be to him when he leaves this world, what will become of him? Ben in Truth was a Pious man but he loved money rather too much. He was certainly industrious but not poor tho he always pleaded poverty, a little given to Canting and would never refuse what was offered to him tho he did not in reality want it. In this Ben had too much worldly cunning, yet on the whole passed through life with as few faults and gave as little offence as anyone in his Sphere of Life. I trust God will have Mercy on his Soul. He was among the Communicants last

Christmas Day. Poor Ben I shall miss Thee. I called on Old Buller today at Stowey, he seemed clean and comfortable and taylor Stadden had been shaving him.

Thursday January 29   We went to Bridgwater to Ruscomb Poole's to make a Wedding Visit. There we found the Bride, a modest unassuming young woman, civil and obliging but not handsome. We dined at Mrs Lewis's and had a bed there. After dinner I saw Mr Jenkins and went home with him and paid him £17–s10–d6 for my Boy's Schooling for the last half a year. He gave me no receipt neither does he give anyone, but struck the Balance in his Book. This hardly satisfied me, however I suffered it to pass.

Saturday January 31   I was summoned down stairs this morning to a gentleman who waited for me. It was Mr Rayne the French Master at Mr Jenkins. He had a petition to make for a French Lady who plays the harp, the Pedal Harp, and so endeavours to gain her livelihood but who has run herself in debt and they are going to detain the harp. I fancy she has been rather imprudent if not extravagant but Mr Rayne wishes to get her out of the town. After breakfast my wife and I walked into Town, made some calls and then ordered a Chaise. The Chaise came about twelve and all went well till we came past Radlett Common when we met a loaded waggon in a narrow part of the road. The Waggoner did all he could to close the Waggon up to the hedge but when we drove on a little the Chaise driver began to doubt our being able to pass especially as there was an ugly ditch on our side. I called and told him it would be best to get out. You cannot returned he get out in this dirty place. Oh cannot we returned I, I'll warrant you. For I deemed it better to dirty our shoes and get wet than be overturned and get our limbs broken, so we got out. But it was with some trouble and danger that they were able to pass afterwards. After this we got to Overstowey safe without further obstructions.

Wednesday February 4   John carried William's box to Stowey for Briffet to carry to Bridgwater. Made John work in the garden and Paddock. He did it well and expeditiously but reluctantly. Charles Poole of Stowey called here today, he wishes to be married tomorrow at Stowey. I answered that as Mr Starkey had undertaken the Duty I could not marry him without his permission so off he went to Mr Starkey and I am to marry them tomorrow.

Thursday February 5   Made John put down some dwarf peas. Walked down to Stowey to marry a couple for Mr Starkey and more properly to oblige Mr Charles Poole the Bridegroom. The lady was Miss Score. There were few attendants and the Bridegroom presented me with two guineas which I sent off to Mr Starkey tho some blame me for it as the Bridegroom certainly meant to compliment me. However I had rather err on the side of Liberality and prefer losing a couple of guineas to doing a mean thing. After dinner I had the Melancholy Office of attending Poor Ben Hunt to the Grave and reading the Service for him. They brought him to the Churchyard and sung before him for both his sons are among the Band of Singers at Church. They gave us a very Solemn, Pathetic Anthem and young Morle distinguished himself by a voice uncommonly soft and melodious. Ben had been a Singer too in his time but now he can sing no more among the Living. After the Service I walked up to the Grave to view the coffin and saw his age – 72. So much for Poor Ben with all his wise sayings, tho an infirm man always I did not think to miss him so soon.

Sunday February 8 I rode over to Doddington this morning with two greatcoats and my face well garded by a network knitted by my wife. I walked into Mr Farthing's, I saw the wife and asked if I might leave my greatcoat. She said Yes, but the husband was fled, none of them at Church. We had some at Church in spite of the weather and I got, with difficulty, into the scant Pulpit. After Service I went again into Mr Farthing's and had Mr Amen in to help me on with my coat. They were all fled except a little boy, they seem to be an ignorant family so I left them. Got to Church at Overstowey and it was full but not many of the Chieftains. A great many of the Broom Squires as them call them were at Church. A wild set of people heretofore never coming near any place of Worship. I am glad they now come to Church and seem well dressed. They live on making Brooms and carry them to Taunton. Their brooms are made of heath.

Monday February 9 A very doubtful morning, the wind high and the night has been very tempestuous. Barometer rises and Thermometer 46. Tis wonderful throughout this winter it has not been as low as 30 and not often lower than 40. I went to the stables today to see what John was about and observing that the stable was dirty. He wished to speak to me and desired that I would look out for a Servant at Lady Day. I told him I would. He said he had done all he could to please me. I answered that he had not done what he had engaged to do, that he had some good qualities, cleanliness as to his own person but in his things he was not cleanly and tho he did some work yet that it was with the greatest difficulty I could get him to do that. And moreover that there were some dubious matters relating to the Beer he had drawn. He said he was very sorry for that he had drawn it. In short he has been a very false fellow. I rode to Stowey, called at Mr Francis Poole's and carried from thence three pairs of Welsh Stockings and ordered a pair of Breeches to be made by little Staden, son of Rat Tail.

Wednesday February 11 This is Ash Wednesday. John has been very busy and very good. Mr Mathew our neighbour observes that there are two pleasant months in the service of a Servant, – the first he comes to you and the last he stays. Phebe our new servant seems now inclined to go on for another year.

Sunday February 15   I went into the Sunday School and gave away a penny to the first comers. I miss Poor Ben there, his son Jack Hunt has taken his place, a savage looking man and not very good but whether he will suit the place is a matter of doubt. The young Hartwells called, Young Adonis I call him, being a compleat Fop, has not been at Church these two months, he has been fearful of wetting his feet poor man. His boots shone today like polished steel and his cravat, shirt &cc appeared fine, pure and captivatingly white. After Morning Service and a little soup my wife and I walked to Dodington. It was very full indeed but it is a small Church and it would seem as if the Pulpit was meant to suit the Church for it is so small that I can scarce get into it tho not a very large or fat man. As we trudged homeward we overtook a curious man who had indeed been loitering about till we came up. It was John Mog of the Castle of Comfort hard by, a kind of Pot House. A short man, broadshouldered, scarce any neck, tolerably well stocked with a red face and a large bottle nose as big as my fist and well warted. He soon told us his History. He had 15 children by his first wife and four by his present, as fine children as your Honour ever saw and indeed so for on this the Cubs came forth. By and by came up a girl. There Sir that is my eldest daughter, twelve years of age, she'll read with any in the county for a guinea and can write 'Where art Thee' in writing, 'lord Walter' in small hand and in accounts, Long Division, upon my word a fine girl. By this time we had come to the Castle and there we parted but it was rather late when we got to Overstowey.

Tuesday February 17   Walked to Stowey and saw the Reverend Mr Starkey driving along in a strange kind of carriage and he in a strange kind of a white coat, a coachman's coat but white. A strange dress for a Clergyman and in the very Parish he serves, viz Stowey, for Mr Northey. This Genius is my successor in the Curacy of Stowey, a Buck Parson and has the Living of Charlinge where he is building a house. In the meantime he has taken the farm of Padnolla, married the daughter of Sir Edward Baynton, a vicious family, and this daughter proves herself one of the family for she has eloped once already and he has received her back again. So Buck to Buck and so much for the white-coated Parson and his equipage. Called at Mr Symes at Stowey, thanked him for the note he sent me about my Law Suit with Symes of Bridgewater. He said he'd bet a shilling to a guinea on my side.

Sunday February 22   I rode over to Dodington, few at Church, not even John Mog with his red face. I met him as I was riding on towards Dodington with another and talking about a hedge near the Mines. Not one of the Farthings at Church except a child. I fear their religious conduct will not be worth a farthing. Returned and found the weather still unpleasant. Few at Church here. Notice given by Mr Hartwell for a rate for the Highway.

Monday February 23 John begged leave to go to offer his 'Services' as a servant to Mr John Jeffreys. He returned by dinner but has not succeeded. Rode over towards Plainsfield, called on old Colonel Landsey as they call him to enquire about the Custon Wood, then rode to Farmer Morle. He is got pure and well since I gave him a dose of Rhubarb. Called on Farmer White who was ill in bed. They seem to be alarmed about him and call it Dropsey, but his leg felt hard and shone a little tho it looked white and he answered with a voice like a Lion's. I think it is gout.

Friday February 27 After breakfast witnesses came in to give intelligence about the Custom Wood. Knight, Frost and old Landsey are all shrewd fellows but Mr Amen seemed all aghast. After examination Mr Davis, Mr Ruscomb Poole and I with Knight Frost and Amen sallied forth on Quantock to view the Custom Wood ground. Then we, Mr Ruscomb, self and Knight took the road to Stowey, spoke to Poole who seems timid and reluctant in his service, then Ruscomb and I went and spoke to old Sully of Stowey. Came home to dinner and enjoyed ourselves on a notable Turkey which we bought from Mr James Rich.

Sunday March 1 This is St David's Day but being a Sunday I do not wear a leek in my hat. The Church not over full but tolerable for the morning. I did intend walking to Dodington but when I came out here I perceived that the ground gave way and some rain began to fall to I mounted my horse and rode to Dodington. John Mogg's boy was sent to open the gate but I had no Halfpennies on which the boy looked blank. I went to Church and found it full and behold Mr and Mrs Farthing vouchsafed to come in the afternoon. After Church Dodington Amen lead my horse out, a poor looking Amen tho young, but a very obedient Clerk. At the gate I again found young Mogg so I told him that at his house I would change a sixpence and give him a penny, so I overtook old John with his large inflamed nose. I told him what I was about to do. He pretended to be very shy and modest but however if I was determined he said his girl should go and change a sixpence so off she went and I gave the boy a penny and the girl a Penny so I think they were pretty well off. Home I came and got safe and then the evening went off in the usual stile.

(Under this last entry there is a note running up the page which reads :— "Perusing the Book of Tythes of Caradock Butler Septbr 1782 to lay before Councils that a statement be prepared by Mr Loyd – Thursday September 1779.")

Sunday May 17   Whit Sunday. A Sacrament here, both the Riches and the Blakes attended. My wife walked with me in the afternoon to Dodington. The Clerk of Dodington is going to vote at Ilchester. Preparations made to go to the Visitation tomorrow.

Monday May 18   Rode over to the visitation, got there late, heard the Charge which dwelt on the dangers of the Catholick Bill brought forward in the House of Commons. Ten only dined with the Archdeacon, not to be wondered at as I never knew of a Visitation being on a Whit Monday. Great bustle in the town about the Election at Ilchester. Mr Davis and I slept at Mrs Lewis's. We were to go in a chaise to Ilchester the next day to vote in the Election but on enquiry found the chaises so shattered and the horses so worn out and the Drivers so drunk that we resolved to ride our own horses, there was no alternative. From Mrs Lewis's we were all to go to drink tea at Mr Symes's but I declined it. Mr Symes has brought an Action against me for cutting wood on Quantock which he has failed in and withdrawn yet no settlement has been made on the Occasion for which reason I cannot go to his House to drink tea. However he and his wife came over and begged and entreated me to come but I kept firm. We went to bed soon.

Tuesday May 19   Up very early, Miss Eliza Lewis roused herself to make breakfast before we went. At last on our horses we got, I on the great horse, Mr Davis on his nag, broken winded as he was. We arrived safe at Ilchester without taking refreshment on the road, put up our horses and gave them a feed of corn, then Voted. Mr Davis a Plumper for Dickenson, I for Lethbridge and Dickenson. We were introduced to Mr Dickenson whose countenance I do not relish too much, the appearance of Design and Art in it. Lethbridge's features were prominent, his eyes sharp but half shut, and altogether a great deal of Spirit in his appearance but I was not introduced to him. After this we mounted our horses without eating or drinking and got to Somerton on our return by two o'clock, thus riding from seven to eight and twenty miles before dinner. We were very quiet and made a good dinner each of us and fed our horses before we went off. We got to Bridgewater by dusk thus riding 44 miles at least. Mr Davis is a corpulent man of 66 on a broken winded horse and I at the age of 61 years compleat. My friend was more fatigued than I was and was glad to get to Bedfordshire and so in troth was I.

Friday May 22   We walked to Stowey and talked about the Election. It is very true that Gore Langton has given up the contest, indeed all parties has strained the utmost. There were not as many Freeholders as supposed and Lethbridge who had least of the Elected Members had seven hundred above Langton Gore, a number that could not be recovered. I never knew an Election before carried on with so much order and Regularity. No noise or tumult and little or no drunkenness and the Candidates walked and conversed together without any animosity. Poor Mrs Mackey who is now in Stowey in George's Lodgings came here to dinner. There is a great deal of sense and nonsense in her, an inoffensive woman but generous to excess. She is somewhat neglected here now her husband is dead, for my part I cannot bear to see a person deserted in her distressed estate by many who received favours from her in her affluence and glory so I take more notice of her than before.

Wednesday May 27 I called on Mr James Rich to talk with him about Jack Hunt who neglects the Sunday School. Poor Ben is gone and his scoundrel son does not do as well. After dinner Miss Lewis thrummed Margaret's old Harpsicord, it has been much neglected of late, Margaret gives up playing entirely.

Thursday May 28 Wm Frost here early to cut up the pig he killed yesterday. The women weeding in the garden. Thomas gone to have the horse shod. The weather has been so chilly that I have been obliged to have a fire in the Best Parlour and very comfortable it was too. We had a tolerable good dish of fish for dinner today which we seldom meet with nowadays tho formerly fish abounded in these parts and so near the sea too. Salmon is now so dear that there is no getting at it. I remember when it was never higher than sixpence and now it is from a shilling to two shillings a pound. Mrs Hartwell is considerably better but she was thrown into a sad way by some bad news which she kept to herself. Her son, the Sailor, has played sad pranks and is not gone abroad with his ship as he intended but has been spending his money in low and abandonded company.

Friday May 29 I went today to Farmer Dibble to chose a Tithe Lamb which I sold for eleven shillings. Today is Club Day at Stowey and I was invited to walk in the Procession but did not as I do not much relish the noise and tumultuous proceedings. Mr Starkey preached. Thomas is gone to view the bustle. Thomas broke his parole. He went to Stowey to see what was going on and staid there all night tho I ordered him to return in good time. Phoeby staid up till twelve o'clock but no Thomas appeared so as last to bed she went.

Saturday May 30 A very tempestuous night. At last Thomas came. He said he was at his Uncle Samuel Sully's and seems stubborn and hardly thinks he has done amiss. I spoke to Thomas sternly and remonstrated for his conduct. He had nothing to say in his defence but still did not seem sorrowful or ask pardon so I gave him Notice to Quit this place in a month's time. This is an inconvenient thing for me but what can one do. If servants are to do as they please there is no end to all subordination, indeed the tribe are come to a sad pass at this time of day. They have little sense of Honour or Morality and act the Masters rather than the Servants, they scarce ever do the Service they engage to do and if you speak to them they are highly affronted and make a Practice of Hiring themselves to this or that place and go from one to another by way of variety and Amusement. Nay they engage at many places at a time and pick and chuse where they will go and this without Scruple or Notice to the persons who are disappointed. There needs some effectual regulation among these Profligate and Unprincipled set of Beings. My wife and Margaret have been reading the History of Sir Walter Raleigh.

Sunday May 31　We had Prayers here in the morning, very few indeed at Church and no Singing for the Singing Gentlemen were all gone to Enmore and had taken half the Parish. It is a pity Jenkins had not contrived to go to other Churches to sing when we had no Service here, for as we buy the Instruments we have some right to the Musick. After we dined I rode over to Dodington, the Church was pretty full there. Two boys played at fives against the Church while the Bell was Tolling and I soon routed them off. A man decently dressed had his hat on while he stood by the singers. I called to him immediately to take it off which he did. Rode back and found the Ladies all seated round a good fire and then the day went on in the stile of Sunday.

Thursday June 4　All of our party, the Lewises and the Pooles moved off after dinner to our neighbours the Riches. There are nothing but Old Bachelors in the house, the two Mr Rich, Jenkins and Michael and two apprentice boys from the Parish and Mrs Batty a Compleat Old Maid is Housekeeper. Very chatty and communicative she is, tho her Office be to wait and get things ready yet she perceives the Visit is as much to her as to her Masters. Mrs Poole, Mrs Lewis and my wife moved off first. Then came Miss Susan Poole and Miss Lewis and I brought up the rear with Miss Eliza Lewis and my daughter. Mr Thomas Rich had not returned from his walk to Mount Pleasant and I am doubtful whether Mr James had got his best stockings on or shaved himself, but certainly he had got his best hat on. Of course there was some little degree of fluster, however we were ushered into the Little Parlour, not into the Best for alas the Best I fear has not been opened these twenty years and had we gone in we must have caught an Ague apiece. Mrs Batty had now got on her best Gown and Best Cap and an Apron as white and clear as new fallen snow. In came Mr James all spruced up and with his hat on. Oh Master Holland do keep your hat on. Not said I (rather unguardedly) before the Ladies. This threw poor James into a kind of quandary – Why Sir, we keep our Hats on! On this, starting up, he boldly claps his hat on a peg. Oh No, cried I. Oh No, cried the Ladies, that must not be. Then immediately I put my hat on. At last he was prevailed to take his hat down from the peg and, Put it on, cried everyone. No says Master James, not this one, I know better. So out he stepd and brings down a new handsome Hat. It seems James and his Virgin Housekeeper had had some deep and serious discourse about the Etiquette of the Tea Table. Madame thought it was her absolute Prerogative to make the tea for the Ladies, but James thought otherwise and so pushed the table towards one of the Nymphs who was seated in the window. Then in came all the old China and accoutrements and loads of bread and butter and cakes and Mrs Batty curtseying low and handing round and very gracious she was truly to everyone. By this time Mister Thomas had returned from his walk and had got his best wig with a Knocker behind, and best coat. As the tea went round Mr Thomas recollected himself and started up, I drinks no tea Ladies, excuse, I must go to the Kitchin to smoak a pipe, will be in again presently. All this time the company kept steady fixed countenances they bit their lips now and again but not a smile escaped, no more than if it had been a Funeral. After Mr Thomas finished his pipe he came to us once more. Though very rich, both of them yet they are near in disposition and that may be owing in great measure to Education and mode of Living. After tea the Ladies moved off and first took a turn in the garden for this the Old Bachelors keep in a good *clean* and formal stile. Then we got home and amused ourselves variously till bedtime.

Sunday June 15 Coming back from Dodington we thought we smelled some new hay and I looked every side of the way to see who in the Parish had cut hay as well as myself but perceived nothing but the smell increased. It continued to do so till I got to my own premises and then I found my new rick smoking like a furnace. I was quite alarmed and summoned persons around and we were obliged to cut a hole in the centre some depth for we were afraid every thing would be burnt around. Wm Frost and Porter worked hard at it.

Monday June 16 It promises to be a fine day to get the hay in order again. The hole in the centre was down to the bottom, a sheaf let down it and worked up with old hay to fill round and a layer of old hay was laid on the top with the new so we secured everything and without much injury tho the expence be greater. Had in two young pigs, one a Tithe and the other bought for company.

Thursday June 18 A very fine day. William and young Anstis from Mr Jenkins's School came in before I was up. He looks stout and well and in high spirits. I sent Thomas for William's box. The Blakes drank tea here. Tom Poole called here today to ask us to be at the Friendly Society for Females. I do not recollect more of this day.

Friday June 19 I walked down with my wife to Stowey to attend the Friendly Society and the Nymphs walked with us. They were gone to Church when we arrived but we saw them when they returned walking in due Procession and order and they really made a good impression and appearance. Mr Starkey preached. Then we joined them for tea drinking. All the Stowey Ladies were there, young and old. Miss Harriet Poole was the Lady President who assumes no small state on these occasions and her cousin, Tom Poole, according to custom was very eloquent. Mr Starkey is a Dasher. They all thanked him for his excellent Discourse and he gave a guinea to the Society besides his Sermon which was very Handsome. It was proposed that I should be one of the Trustees in whose names the concerns of the Society should be transacted but I rather declined it. After Subscriptions were paid and tea was over it was found that they had Fifty Pounds in Stock and the number of members amounted to forty five which is very well for the first year. Towards dusk we moved off. I had given William sixpence to be spent at Stowey and it came out accidentally that they went into the Rose and Crown to a kind of Coffee Room there for some cyder. This account startled us and we began to make some enquiries how it came about. Young Tom Poole, a school fellow of William's prevailed on the others to go. Little Blake joined them, then William, then Anstis. Tom Poole drank most of the cyder and the others thought it quite manly but they did not stay many minutes. We talked to them very seriously on the Business and made them thoroughly sensible to the impropriety of their conduct. Anstis had the tears in his eyes all the time and William gulped at it several times. I believe they are thoroughly ashamed of themselves.

Tuesday June 23 Thomas does little besides wait at table and is to go next Saturday as I could not pass his staying out all night with out his making any apology about it tho it will be a very inconvenient thing for me to be at this time without a servant and very difficult to get one to my wishes. While we were walking to Stowey yesterday a woman told us that a man of the name of Hurdle fell down dead while he was mowing, or more properly while he was whetting his scythe. He was in good health and spirits before and boasting that he could perform as well as any of the younger ones. He was about sixty years of age if not more, a sober man of good character. He never spoke after he was struck but died almost instantaneously.

Wednesday June 24 Much disappointed this morning in not having the newspaper. Parliament met Monday for the first time, an important circumstance and when things of great importance happen then we are often disappointed in not having the newspaper. This is a most scandalous imposition on us for we are disappointed at the very time we want the Paper. I suppose the Mail Coachmen sell them as they carry the papers down?

Thursday June 25   After breakfast Mr Amen and Thomas got ready the cart to go to the seaside with the boys. Thomas shewed very little ingenuity in the matter and indeed does very little at present since he had Notice to Go. However I took him with us. Some sheaves of straw were laid in the cart and a covering above and myself, Philip Hartwell, Anstis and William moved off in it, Thomas leading the horse. Near Stowgurcy we stopped and I walked with Anstis to call on Mr Davis. He was in his hay so we returned and got safe to the seaside. As we approached the shore descending from an Eminence there were three or four vessels in full sail passing before us and in full sail and near the shore. It was quite beautiful. When we got to the seaside we got out of our car and the boys ran to the seaside and began looking for periwinkles and limpets and some took off their shoes and stockings and were highly delighted. Master Thomas being resolved to enjoy himself as much as they did had joined the boys but left the horse tied to a stone and he at last broke loose and was walking off very deliberately so Master Thomas was obliged to stir himself to catch him. We placed our cart in a high position and we entered in and went to dinner on a fine lamb pye and many bottles of excellent cyder, Thomas waiting on us. We were very merry and eat most hearty. We could see Minehead and Minehead Point and the boys had frequent peeps thro the Glass. At last being thoroughly satisfied and pleased with our Excursion we put the horse to the cart and walked him back to Overstowey, then we had to clean ourselves and dress and soon came in Mr Wm Poole and two of the Miss Wollens and Miss Harriet Poole so we had a tolerable party. Mr Wm Poole was very wise and sagacious as usual and remembered many things of ancient times for he was born in the Parish and he informed me of the state of the Parsonage House in his time. He has risen in the world by grazing and farming and has brought up a large family, is a wary and cautious man. Miss Harriet Poole is the only unmarried daughter and keeps his house. They say he is worth a great deal of money.

Saturday June 27   This morning Thomas got his matters ready, delivered up his Livery and I paid him his wages and sent him off. I spoke a long time to him about his conduct, his lying out at night, his habit of swearing and his sauciness to me, and tho he did not seem greedy for liquor yet when he got a little he had no command of himself. He seemed sulky and showed little sign of Penitence.

Sunday June 28   A fine day. Not much news about the new Parliament. A good many at Church. A man from the Club buried at Stowey and vast number of people gathered together to see them. I permitted the boys here to go with Phoebe to see them. Scarce any congregation at Dodington, most of the Parish belong to the Club. John Mogg with his large red warty nose was at Church. I remained in the Church while the Clerk was going for the horse and turning round perceived a boy fast asleep and leaning on the Altar in the Chancel. I could not wake him till I had once or twice touched him with a small cane I had in hand and then he did not know all the Congregation were gone nor where he was. I gave him a lecture and then left him and came home. After tea I had a severe attack with Spasms in the face which continued very distressing and frequent till Bedtime. I took my usual recourse, some Milk of Sulphur as I went to bed and that at last composed me.

Saturday July 4   After tea we walked to Stowey. George Paddock had got a glut of fish which he bought his very morning from the south sea where he had been with Mr Mackey's goods. Two fine turbot and gurnets and brills in abundance. We bought a very fine turbot for four and sixpence, six pounds weight, fresh and very good. After this we returned in very high spirits.

Sunday July 5   Very few at Dodington Church this morning tho Mr Farthing was. My old friend John Mogg did not appear tho his son opened the gate for me. John makes his family go to Church tho he thinks he himself may stay at home now and then to sell beer and to make his own large nose, bottle nose, redder than it is. After dinner went to our own Church, very full and they sung Psalms most gallantly. Mrs Hurley brought another child to Church to be Baptized and she herself was Churched. They have a vast number of children and are Anabaptists and I made them bring four or five to be Christened at one time and they continue to bring them to Church but go generally to the Meeting House. However it is gaining something to be Baptized at our Church.

Tuesday July 7   We had salmon again for dinner today so that for a week past we'v had our fill of fish. The boys I took into the Study and made them say a lesson in Cornelius Nepos which they did pretty well, then I gave them a Distich each out of Martial to make into a verse after giving them the English and Latin in their Primitive Mood and Tenses. They did their business very well.

Friday July 10   The weather very Sultry indeed, very hot in the night. We set off, my wife and daughter in the Gig driven by George while I rode on the great horse, so fat that I scarce know what to do with him yet he scarce has anything to eat and he stands in the house all day. The worst grass I have is reserved for him yet he always makes himself fat. We went first to Alfoxen to call on St Albyn, I fighting with the flies all the way, I never was so overcome by the heat before. We met the Graveners and St Albyn at home, staid there a short time then moved off towards Shurton to Mr Henry Poole's. Mr St Albyn was engaged to dine there too and he and I

rode together, which I was glad of. We got to Mr Poole's in good time.
Soon after came Mrs Acland her son and last of all, after we were seated to
dinner came in Mr and Mrs Davis. There was a Miss Coles, there was a
young girl a relation of Mr Henry Poole and the Governess appeared after
dinner. A good dinner and all things handsome and well. When the Ladies
retired Mr Henry pushed the bottle a little and I observed St Albyn was
very moderate but young Acland did not flinch and seemed to attempt
being witty on Mr Davis. By the by he gave me a book on Physiognomy
which I have now by me. However in due time we moved off to the Ladies.
The Society of the Ladies does a great deal of good, it regulates and refines
the men and keeps them from drunkenness and makes them decent and
affable in their manners. I fancy a little liquor has a bad effect on Henry
Poole for I observed that he was rather ill tempered in his remarks and
displeased with many things. I do not much approve White Nankeen
Trowsers for a Clergyman. About eight o'clock my wife and daughter
mounted the Gig and I my horse and we got home in the cool of the
evening, very pleasant and there was something of a moon.

Sunday July 12   Very few at Church, I never remember so few. The Singers
except a few were gone to Lydiard to Sing and have a dinner given to them
and I fear carried many of the Congregation with them. Our Singers are
become famous in the Country, which makes them vain and fond of
Exhibiting themselves and I think they think more of their own Praise than
the Praise of God. As we of our own Parish subscribed for the Instruments I
observed that they should not forsake us in the time of our own Service, for
we did not buy the Instruments for the Amusement of other Churches. This
time however they apologised and hoped I would excuse as they were
strongly pressed to go and promised a dinner which was not to be resisted.
However we had tolerable singing notwithstanding. After Church and
dinner I rode to Dodington and there we had a full Congregation.

Friday October 16   We got home by Mr Mullins's. Mullins is an industrious
man of low extract, patronised by Lady Tint and has now acquired
considerable property by the Law for it is the Law now brings in Money
above all other Professions and Lawyers are becoming the Lords of the
Land and men of all kinds of abilities thrive in it. We called on Parsons the
Clergyman of Gothurst, not at home. Then soon after we arrived safe at the
Parsonage at Enmore. When I say safe I must notice that my horse made the
lowest stumble that I ever remember him to have made and he seemd
evidently ill and almost totally unable to keep himself on his legs. I did not
play cards but my wife did.

Sunday October 18   My face continues to be troublesome. Prayers at this
Church in the morning. Miss Hartwell and her brother called and the

young Hartwell pushed himself into the seat with my wife which I think was rather forward. If they wanted room Miss Hartwell should have begged permission and not a great boy. I went through the Duty tolerably tho I had a spasm before I entered Church. I know not where all this will end but it is surely very painful and distressing, God's Will be done. My general health is very good. Afternoon Service at Dodington, the Congregation much as usual.

Monday October 19   We had company to dine with us, Mr and Mrs Poole from Shurton and Mr Brice of Asholt. Mrs Brice was ill. We were disappointed in the Graveners and St Albyn. They staid till the moon was up and then went off to their respective homes.

Tuesday October 20   Went to Stowey and met Mr Sealey from Bridgewater and walked with him to the house that was his son in law's, Mr Best. He is repairing and cleaning it up to be let again. Walked on to Mr Northey's, found them at home, sat and chatted a while. They are going to leave Stowey and preparing their furniture for sale. Young Blake is going to Oxford. Mr Hartwell called and sat so long that I almost fell asleep, he had got his Sitting Breeches on. He has gained a victory over Farmer Morle and some others and returned a Surveyor of the Highways for the ensueing year. They had formed a strange Cabal but I stood his friend and overturned all their schemes. My horse has been very ill and was blooded this day and some nitre given him.

Wednesday October 21   Very busy in making cyder and killing a pig. Wm Frost at it with Mr Amen. Whenever there is eating or drinking William makes one a good workman. I ventured on my sick horse to Stowgurcy, poor Mr Davis has had a Paralytic Seisure, he looks poorly. Dr Dunning has seen him and sent Haviland today to look at him. Mr John Poole came to see him and we both dined with him. Difficulties about the cyder, no horse to bring it home. At Last Jew Lansdey lent his and at last Master appeared to the great joy of the Vicarage House. Betsy Selleck is going into Service and called to take leave. The Portuguese in great trouble about Buonaparte.

Saturday October 24   A bad rainy morning, the Glass very low and Thermometer under 50. Sadly distressed for yeast for baking and George dispatched to various places for some and the rain so hard that he was obliged to carry a sack over his shoulders. My face still bad and frequent Shootings and Spasms. Nothing relieves me but Milk of Sulphur and that does almost instantaneously.

Sunday October 25   A very rainy day and a great quantity fell last night. I ventured to Dodington and had a great cloak over my great coat and a woolen knit wrapper which covered the lower part of the face so that I bid defiance to the weather. Scarce any one there but the Clerk and Knight who Tolled the Bell. At last came George my Servant who had been at his Father's to inform him that he was not drawn this time for the Militia. This is joyful news for George as he saves Subscrition money and himself into the bargain for I believe George is no fighter. Mr Farthing came into the Church at last with his own or his wife's sister and two of the Huggins. Notice given that Prayers in the Winter Season would begin at two o'clock. Few at Church at Overstowey. No material news in the paper but a shocking account of a murder in Hartfordshire. We endeavoured to have a peep at the Comet but in vain.

Wednesday October 28 I had a message from Mr Cruckshanks, Lord Egmont's steward, that if I would send the Clerk he would be at home to pay me my Tithe. So I sent off Mr Amen but as it was rather late and I was afraid of trusting him with my horse alone I sent George with him who took Mr Amen behind for the Clerk is no jockey. However they returned both of 'em safe. I have got the money, all this is very well. My wife went to Stowey to change a note and sent off a letter to Margaret enclosing a five pound note that she might not want money at that distance tho she is among her friends and relations. My face altogether poorly. My wife now reads to me 'The Conquest of Mexico, by Cortes' which amuses till bedtime and we do not find the Winter Nights so very long and tedious.

Sunday November 1 My face still painful. The weather still mild. The newspaper came with a letter from William begging forgiveness for missing the day for writing, it had absolutely slipped his memory but he twice mentioned his fears of my being angry, poor fellow. I shall certainly forgive him but my aim is to make him punctual in his matters by fixing appointed times of writing. I had a letter from the Tax Office this morning exonerating my Living from the Land Tax which is a good thing. Indeed I have been on the whole a considerable benefactor to this Living. I have defended its Rights in two Lawsuits in which I have succeeded most Gloriously and secured beyond dispute great advantages to future Vicars. I had the Christening of two children and the Churching of two women. Eat a mouthful and mounted my horse for Dodington. I spoke to two children of John Mogg, he is very poorly. I called at his house and he came to the door with his great red nose but it is shrunk much. He said he was very poorly and indeed by what he said I should think so. I prescribed a few grains of Ginger and Rhubarb for him and he promised to follow my prescription. I returned and was no sooner seated to dinner but they said the Corpse was come. However I eat my dinner first and then buried the Corpse. After this I had some rest from my labours and the evening passed off in the usual stile of Sunday.

Monday November 2   After breakfast my wife and I walked down to Stowey Vicarage House to view Mr Northey's goods and the auction is to begin tomorrow. We met there Mr and Mrs Allan who are to take the house and enter on the Curacy. They seemed genteel and well behaved persons but he is, I understand, a horrible Orator. This has struck consternation into everyone. They keep a Footman and have three or four maids and come to the Curacy two hundred miles off from Hastings. A most excellent man but desperate bad utterance.

Tuesday November 3   Not many at the Sale of Mr Northey's goods yet things went off well. I purchased a tea table, they say cheap. Sir Thomas Wheat bought several things. Mr Allan bought many things. Mr and Mrs Mathew were there and Mr St Albyn. A letter from Mr Ruscomb Poole, I am to pay off my Evidences in the Wood Cause that I might join in an Affidavit to recover costs.

Friday November 6   George Paddock attended with his gig and I drove off in it to Bridgewater, called on Mr Ruscomb Poole and made my affidavit about the payments I made. Saw William, payd for a suit of clothes and ordered a new one. Saw Dr Dunning, spoke about my face and he ordered me to take Calomile Tea with a spoonful of Brandy in it for the Wind in my Stomach which causes the pain in my face. After this I made George Paddock drive me to Enmore where I dined and sent him home to Overstowey to inform my wife that I should take a bed at Enmore. Mr and Mrs Allan dined there and Mr and Mrs Parsons. Ruscombe Poole informed me that Mr Stone his father in law had got a prize in the lottery of twenty thousand pounds, a great thing indeed and will be chiefly for Ruscomb Poole's benefit for Mr Stone cannot want it and he has but two daughters and one of them is Ruscomb's wife. – The Poole Family are rising fast. Mr Allan is a sensible, modest, prudent and well behaved man, is the Receiver for the County. Mrs Allan has been a very pretty woman and indeed is so still. Parsons is full of jokes and makes many and is sure to laugh at his own. They left us before supper. Oh I forgot to say Mrs Northey came with the Allens, Mr Northey was not present being left at Bridgewater far from well. I was well taken care of here and slept well until the morning.

Sunday November 8   I think this Comomile and Brandy has been of service to me. I went off to Dodington and for some time saw no person but the Clerk and myself. At last a few came, among them John Mogg with his large Crimson nose shining like a Cock's Comb. After Service I asked him how he does. Purely quoth John by the Blessing of God. He said he had most exactly followed the Prescription I had given and got well presently. This day I paid Old Landsey, the Colonel as they call him, the remainder of the ten shillings he gained for his Evidence in the Wood Cause. He seemed discontented with the pay allotted to him and demanded a guinea a day. He said the Lawyer had told him so and this Lawyer was Master Waddon, the Bum Bailiff and then to prove the rectitude of his case he told me that Mr Ruscomb Poole had a Guinea a day. And do you, returned I presume to put yourself on a footing with a Lawyer. I said I was quite sorry to hear him talk in this manner, I paid him five shillings a day in addition to his meat and drink, a sum he never earned in his life and if he did not chuse to take that he might try what the Law would give him. So I left him. Mr Hartwell told me that his son Philip was going to Mr Goodenough the Apothecary at Bridgewater. I dined after the Service and got through the Service well though I had frequent symptoms of Spasms. The evening was spent at home in the usual manner.

Monday November 9   The Clerk in the barn and George gone for coal. We had a letter from Margaret, all very well in Wales, my brother wishes much to see me there. Mr and Mrs Wynne live in a most elegant and superb stile. My face I think somewhat better.

Tuesday November 10   The greatest rain I remember this long time yet George is gone for coal which gives me great concern. What will become of George and the cart I scarce know. The Paddock is all covered with water and the Clerk gone out to direct its course a little. While we were in this bustle and state all of a sudden we heard a carriage drive up to the gate. It was Mrs Dodwell and her daugher and Miss Moore from London. We by mistake expected them tomorrow, this caused a little confusion at first but we soon brought matters to rights and we sat down to dinner somewhat late. By and by towards four o'clock we saw George come with the cart and the horse had not fallen. I now recollect he came before we sat down to dinner, moreover dressed himself first and then waited at table. After this we got comfortable and in due time marched to our respective bed chamber for the Ladies were tired tho they came this day only from Minehead, having travelled from South Molton the day before.

Thursday November 12   A very hard frost, I must look to the asparagus beds. It was very late before I came down, the Ladies were down before me. My wife and I walked down to Stowey and called on the new Curate but he was not got into the Parsonage House. After some other errands we returned to spend the evening at home among ourselves and very merry we were. My niece Dodwell, or rather my wife's niece is a modest well behaved girl. Mrs Dodwell the mother is a sensible, agreeable cheerful little person for little she is to a great degree. Miss Moore who is the eldest sister is pitted with the Small Pox but has good features, tolerable height and she is a sensible, clever woman. Earthed up the artichoaks.

Sunday November 15 The snow gone and the morning tolerable. The newspaper came so late I was not able to read it before Church. Very few at Church, however some came at last. All the White's in mourning. Farmer White was buried yesterday, not in this Parish but over the Hill. He suffered a great deal for a great length of time and I think it was a Happy Release. After Church I found in the paper that the Portuguese had excluded the British from their Ports and had joined the rest of the Continent. I did not dine this day until the Duty was over. Hurryed to Dodington but found the Clerk not prepared for me. He said it was not two but that was not true, and that his wife was ill and in short he had the Books to take out and the Cushion to place on the Pulpit and everything to do while I stood in the Church. I grumbled a little. I am afraid he is a poor creature, smell of tobacco and gin and water always. A few came to Church at last but the great Mr Farthing was not there. I went through the Duty tolerably this day without Spasms or difficulty.

Tuesday November 17 George Paddock went off this day in his Gig for William who is to come home for a week to meet his relations. As evening came on we began to be apprehensive about William in the Gig as there is no moon early in the evening. About tea time he at length appeared and relieved all, he was then introduced to his relations. He looks tolerably well but has a severe cold or perhaps measles coming on as I hear they are at Mr Jenkins's School and it is doubtful whether he had them or no.

Thursday November 19 The ground covered with snow. We are all in Good Spirits before a good fire and I am at present upstairs with my boy who is saying a Lesson in Cornelius Nepos, and we have a good fire in my bedchamber for he sleeps in the Study. It rains incessantly and is very rainy and windy and is in short a terrible day. William in the evening grew worse and went to bed.

Friday November 20 Rain, snow and sleet. The Glass very low, indeed lower than I can sink the marker to. I enquired early about William and understood that he was not much better. My wife went down to Mr Blake in the meantime. I looked at him once more and declared that the Measles were come out upon him and called Phoebe. She said they were not the Measles but Mr Blake came soon after and said they were the Measles sure enough. So now the point is settled and tho I never had the measles myself yet I was the first person who found them out to be so. So now he is removed out of the Study into the Nursery where there is a fireplace. This is Margaret's Birthday when she is two and twenty and we drank her health at dinner, and so did Wiliam upstairs in the Nursery. Edward and Esther Selleck came here in the evening to keep Margaret's Birthday, Esther having nursed her formerly.

Monday November 23 A prodigious fall of snow, indeed deeper than I ever remember at this place. While I was about to get up my nose began bleeding and continued so for two or three hours so as to alarm us a little. Mr Blake called and desired me not to stop it. I afterwards got up and have been well and in good spirits all this day. William too has been on the recovery and his cough is better. Edward Selleck sent us in some snipes. Phoebe's Lover called in and she having been an assiduous servant he was asked to dine with us but we did not expect that we were to give him a bed, which is rather much. But he has left his place at Bridgewater and he complains of being ill used, but we have nothing to do with that. He must go tomorrow early and I hope he will behave well to her at last. William considerably better all this day.

Tuesday November 24 Pheby's Gentleman I believe has gone, but I still have my doubts. William goes on well.

Thursday November 26 We heard early in the morning a great rustling sound and thought it was the snow falling off the roof but in the morning I found it to be a fine large bird, a Redwing, come down the chimney. I caught it and gave it to Mrs Phoeby who killed it. The Chaise come for the Ladies, viz: Miss Moore, Mrs Dodwell and her daughter Anne. The Ladies went off after breakfast and George went with them to the Turnpike Road. William is up and in good spirits but his cough continues. I hope the Ladies will find the road to Bath Tolerable but there is still a good deal of snow lying. They made the time here very pleasant during William's illness as they were very domestick and accommodating. The weather being so bad it was difficult for any of our friends to come to us.

Friday November 27 William seems in high spirits and well but his cough remains but not in a great degree. We have a letter about the Charter House, there is a vacancy and Mr Wyndham is contriving to give him this turn consistant with his engagement to another person. I pray God he may be able to determine for him, for now he has had the measles he will be quite prepared for a Publick School. I went this day with my Certificates for Exoneration from the Land Tax to the Collector to exhibit them. Called on Farmer Stone, shewed them to him but he is not now a Collector. Called on Hurley but he was not at home, shewed the Certificate for Adiscomb to her. William took Calamel at night.

Saturday November 28 Little William's Physick went off very well and he is still in a sitting state and I hope his cough will leave him My wife had a letter from Margaret, a great fall of snow in Wales. She gives us a great deal of Welsh News.

Sunday November 29 I walked over to Dodington for afternoon Service. As I was going a decent looking man came up to me and told me that a man who courts my Maidservant had run away from his Service. I answered that I believe he had been with us one day but that he was not here now and that he was gone to Kilve and that I should not encourage him. Master George who kept close behind me till I found some difficulty in crossing water in Bincomb Comb stepped forward before me without either touching his hat, saying by your leave or offering any assistance. On which I called to him and told him that when he was near his Master his first business was to attend to Him before himself, that he must be very ignorant of his Duty and Station if he thought otherwise. That however he could go on as he could be of no use to me if he was so stupid. A good many came to Church, among others the Church Warden Mr Huggins. I shewed him the top of the Church again where the tiling was blown off. He said it could not be done this frosty weather. I said it must be done with reed or something for the present. John Mogg was not at Church with his red nose. I fear John is about another wife tho past seventy. There is a young girl in the house which I suspect by and by may become his third wife. This however is a surmise of my own. William came down stairs to dine with us for the first time after the measles. Phoeby returned in good time from Kilve. The Clerk was told to fodder the cows while George was waiting at table but he said he'd sooner go home than do so, on which I called on him to go without his dinner and off he went. Hah said I then he comes no more. But behold, unexpectedly back comes Mr Amen and went quietly to fodder the cows and his dinner. This is the way to deal with a Somersetshire man, for if you give way to him he becomes insolent and very tame if otherwise.

Monday November 30 A hard frost. Clerk in the barn and some wheat was winnowed. The wary, cunning Wm Frost bought 10 bushells. I dare say he has got a bargain otherwise he would not buy. Walked to Stowey and called on the Blacksmith. I said for convenience I must use Letherbridge in my own Parish, from no dislike of him as I thought him a very Honest man. He thanked me very much, said he was ready to serve me at any time and that it was proper for me to use my own Parishioners. So I came home to dinner and did not stir out afterwards.

Wednesday December 2 The thaugh continues. The Clerk in the barn and thrashing peas and a sad crop it is. Mr Blake and his daughter Elizabeth dined with us on a very fine goose. They staid tea and Mr Blake was very pleasant and chatty yet soon after tea started up and there was no stopping him any longer. William seems perfectly well yet Mr Blake thinks another dose of Physick will compleat him.

Friday December 4 William took Physick for the last time for measles. I walked to Stowey, saw Hartwell attending men working on the road. Tom Poole they say has cleared the gout by putting his foot in cold water. He was carried in an armed chair to the water by four men, immersed his foot, or feet and they say kept them there for nine hours, not at one time I presume. He had all the time Kinglake's Pamphlet by him and a thermometer by which he was to judge the heat and circulation of the blood, or something of that nature. Nothing material and certain in the Newspaper but something appears to be going on in Spain and Portugal. Sir Sidney Smith is on a Secret Expedition somewhere in those parts. William was somewhat poorly at one time but got better towards evening.

Sunday December 6 Mr Briffet was very long in bringing the paper so I set off without it. When I came to Dodington I found no one and after calling some time out came the Scrub Clerk. I fancy I must have been before my time and when I came home I found that my clock was too fast by half an hour. Indeed I was at one time unsure whether I should read Prayers. At last I saw John Mogg's red nose appear and by and by came the Huggins and Mr Farthing, so at last we got a Congregation. There are so many crevases and holes in the tiling of the Church that I felt it uncommonly cold in doing Duty and I complained much after the Service was over and desired Mrs Huggins would tell her husband so. He has often promised to get it done and never does. I believe I must present it at last. When I got back to Overstowey I found the paper contained a Ridiculous and senseless Declaration of War from the Russians against this Country.

Tuesday December 8 At Ely Publick House as we passed I saw Old Nanny Hill with spinning work in her hand for a Taunton Clothier. She seemd glad to see us and cried – Hard weather for Old people – She is fourscore, a neat tidy woman and industrious and constant at Church and the Sacrament. George and Mr Amen carried out all the ashes and some dung.

Wednesday December 9 Still a very great frost, barometer high and rising, thermometer 30. George preparing the horse to go with us to Gothurst where we are to dine with Mr Parsons and take a bed there. My wife and I set out on foot and George behind on the great horse with a pillion. At Farmer Bishop's I mounted the horse and took my wife behind and we rode on as far as the Entrance into Lord Egmont's Park then my wife and I got off and walked across the Park to Mr Poole's, George riding round with the double horse. At Enmore we found Mrs Poole and Mrs Anstis and all glad to see us. They were going to dine at Gothurst so the Divine and I and my wife walked across the fields, the other ladies went in the Gigs. At Gothurst we met Mr Mullins and his mother and the great and pompous Squire Cruckshanks, fac totem to Lord Egmont. He seemed however, notwithstanding his greatness and pomposity, somewhat stiff and embarrassed in his manners. We had a most excellent dinner, two courses, and Harry Parsons the Master of the House talked and laughed in his usual voice and manner which are not a little singular. They had prepared a bed for us at Mr Parsons's but our friends the Pooles whom we were more used to were so pressing that we returned and took a bed with them. Mrs Anstis's child is at Enmore, a very beautiful Infant.

Saturday December 12 My wife had a letter from Margaret from Teyndon where she was then and another from Mrs Dodwell in London where she had arrived safe. Nothing particular in the papers today but that all the World had Declared War against us. Alas Poor England, Thy Religion, Virtue and Spirited Independencey has made the World Thy Enemies – a Base and Wicked World. Yet if God be with Thee and go out with Thy Armies we need not fear the World with all its Terrors and Machinations. The Clerk is in the barn thrashing beans and a very poor crop it is. It is supposed that this year there will not be beans or pease enough to crop the ground.

Monday December 14 Walked down after my wife to Marsh Mill to Mr Blake's. There is a sale of his goods he being about to leave the place, having purchased a spot near Bristol. He is a restless Being and has changed places six times within the space of a few years. Little Weddon was the Auctioneer and there were several farmers there. They did not sell their best things but only some lumber. We bought nothing. Mr and Mrs Tanner were there and Mrs Brice.

Thursday December 17 I walked on the road beyond Marsh Mill to see how it was mended. There I met a strange animal, Poll Philips, half covered in dirt and in rags tho they have got a house and field of their own and some money. They have mended this road I see said I. It is still said she dirty enough. I made no reply but thought it was clean enough for such a draggle tailed creature as she was. I returned and joined my wife and we walked home together. I received this day a letter from Dr Chapman near Bath about the Curate of Monkton Farley.

Sunday December 20 Still a thick fog but no rain. George was sent early for the Newspaper but (I thank God) no account of the death of our Good King for which reason I think it but a wicked report raised by a Scoundrel Democrat. But with the Bath Paper there came a printed account of a Cutter arriving at Plymouth with the account of Sir Sidney Smith having succeeded in the Tagus and conducting out the Portuguese Fleet for the Brazils. When I got to Dodington I found there Huggins who asked me whether I had spoken to the Rural Dean about the Repairs of the Church. I answered that I had not spoken to the Rural Dean* but to the Rector, Mr Sealy. It seems that men have been sent to view it and Huggins received a letter on the occasion. I said that it came from my speaking but without view to any particular person, but only because I thought it my Duty to do so. To be sure, Sir it was Proper. I went on I certainly dined recently with the Rural Dean but to tell you the truth forgot it. I gave notice of a Sacrament for next Sunday.

Monday December 21 A letter from Wm Tutton with a melancholy account of a house of the Gaddings being burnt down. Poor Nanny Gaddings was a servant of ours and a very faithful one and reared William and she was with me when I lost four children in the Scarlet Fever in Monkton Farley. I went to Wm Hill the father and met him in the road, he had received the account by the same post. She is very near her time and has no house to lie in. I advised him to send a covered cart to fetch her and the children. At last it was agreed that a pound or two should be sent and she was to come by the Machine if able.

Wednesday December 23 The boys went off early to fetch the Newspaper, the news is rather good altogether. The Prince Regent of Portugal rather than fall into the Hellish fingers of Buonaparte has freight several ships with the whole wealth of Portugal and entered on board with many of his Principal Nobility and sailed off under the conduct of Sr Sidney Smith for the Brasils. Five Men of War and several Frigates and Portuguese Transports full of men and troops accompanying. It was a Glorious Determination rather than sacrifice his Ally Great Britain. Four British Ships of the Line conduct them there. There is too an answer to the Russian Declaration against this Country, very moderate yet sufficiently cutting and confuting the Russian Declaration. Besides that the Americans are by no means agreeing with their President Jefferson in their Malice against this Country. I have a very bad cold and cough which has fallen on my lungs and is very troublesome. It came very suddenly yesterday and I feel my breast very sore. Mr Amen is here and some barley has been winnowed.

Friday December 25 Christmas Day, a pleasant gentle thaugh. We had not so many at Church as I expected and fewer than I remember at the Sacrament. They were all women except Mr Thomas Rich, the Clerk and I being the necessary and Official Attendants at the Communion Table. I found not many at Dodington. We had twelve people to dine in the kitchen where they had Port, Beef and Plum Pudding and as good strong beer after dinner as ever was drunk. The Clerk of Dodington who dined here I presented with a good old black coat of mine, of which he stood in need for he is but a miserable wight and drinks up every thing and keeps himself as poor as a Church Mouse. He is so bad a stick that he is obliged to have his old mother look out the Lessons. However he was made desperate proud this day. William was called out of the kitchen this evening as the Company were strangers in a great degree. What I said put him in such Dudgeon that he sobbd and cried for an hour or two. It made me at last very angry and he was obliged to come and ask Pardon which I hope will be a lesson to him for the future.

Saturday December 26   George has been permitted to go with his father to visit his friends. I charged him to come home in good time but he has not made his appearance and it is past nine. Wm Frost had his son in law, wife and children come and see him this Christmastime and has a son in law wife and child besides in the house so that I cannot conceive where he can put them all yet it is pleasant to see families meet on Christmas.

Tuesday December 29   I walked over to Farmer Stone's, found him just rising from dinner. Talked to him about Parish Matters and settled the Poor Rate with him. Went with him to see the Clerk's daughter. She seems in a miserable state and the Parish she belongs to have taken from her what they allowed and say that we must send her to them, so now she is thrown on this Parish.

Thursday December 31   A parcel from London, from Mrs Dodwell, silk for a gown for my wife and a very handsome Court Calendar bound in Morocco, a present for me. Indeed it has in it twice what others have in general with the Peerage of England and Baronets and their respective incomes and supporters and various other articles. It has clasps and is as thick as a small Bible, in short a very capital present. I walked to Stowey and met Mr Baden Buller. Have you seen the paper lately? There was a Captain Buller mentioned and it was I fear my brother. Poor Fellow he had just been made Captain by Lord Cochrane and in going to England to have his Commission confirmed he was attacked by a superior force. He, in order to distinguish himself attempted to board the Enemy, was shot in the head and expired immediately. The Bells ring out the Old Year but the wind is so loud that we can scarce hear them. William is busy drawing. It is the Church and Steeple of Shotesbrook in Berkshire which belonged to Dr Dodwell formerly and consolidated with White Waltham there. The father, the Celebrated Henry Dodwell formerly lived and died and is buried there where there is a Monument erected to his memory. The wind not quite so loud as it has been so that possibly the year may expire gently at last.

The Year 1808

Friday January 1   A fine mild clear and pleasant morning. The Bells ringing from five o'clock. The Clerk is not here, pretends he is not well and has gone to Ely Green to cure himself. After dinner and as night drew on the boys were in high spirits being promised a high treat to go out with a candle and lantern and a net to catch birds. So off they went after it grew dark, Edward Selleck and Will Weymouth conducting them and George bringing up the rear. A little after nine the Heroes returned with a bag of birds tho not so many as they expected but they were highly delighted and tired and as they had wet feet we hurried them to bed and we followed in due time. Thus begun and ended the first day of this New Year. How the year will end only God knows and who may live to see the end. We are at present at War with the whole World and Buonaparte is at the Head of that World, who seeks, our destruction with a malice that is truly Diabolical, but I trust the God, the Great Ruler of the Universe who has permitted him to succeed hitherto will not suffer him to gain his end in this. For if he does Morality and Religion must soon be expelled from the face of the Earth. Tho not impaired much in my general health yet I do perceive that I am getting older and I am approaching my Grand Climacteric, yet if while I grow older I get better in Religious Principles and Moral Practices I shall be no loser in the end and that it may prove so I pray God.

Saturday January 2   I promised the boys a treat this day so soon after breakfast we all walked to Stowey and at Mr Wm Poole's Miss Harriet shewed us a most capital Work, A Botanical Book of Plants, part uncoloured and part coloured in a most masterly manner. I indeed never saw anything equal to them before. She got them by a Raffle and they cost about forty guineas, being taken in numbers by a Clergyman who parted with them in this manner. We were indeed all of us highly gratified. We have Wm Frost and his family this evening with us to take tea and supper as guests for Pheby and George and they are here at this very time regaling themselves.

Sunday January 3   I rode over to Dodington, some few there. Found a wind behind me that I scarce knew how to do Duty. I complained exceedingly and told Huggins that I must give over doing Duty. We found some pains of glass broke in Mr Farthing's seat and the tiling of the roof shattered in several places. Returned and my horse started which provoked me to give him a brisk trot. We had a Dumbling of the little birds for the boys but they did not value them much. I gave the Clerk a Jubation for deserting me Friday and Saturday under the pretense of illness but in truth to go to the Publick House. He is a sad Old Man. The evening spent in the usual stile.

Monday January 4 I received a letter from William Tutton from M Farley with a Bill in it for twenty Pounds and more is to follow during the course of the week. Captain Davis called about coals and George is to go tomorrow.

Tuesday January 5 Mr Amen begged for a Holiday for tomorrow, it being Old Christmas Day. A sad old man, he has had so many holidays and every holiday is a day of drunkenness. William has been this evening drawing a Landskip of the House and Premises and the Church and Churchyard. It is surprising how he does it considering he has had no instruction and scarce attempted such a thing before. We expect to hear from Margaret every day. In the evening George was taken ill and thought he was going to have the measles but takes not one symptom of them. However I sent him home.

Sunday January 10 There was no Prayers at Dodington this day, the roof of the Church being untiled. Not having Prayers at Dodington this morning we had the Servants in to Prayers and Reading in the morning as well as after noon. Mr Hartwell tells me the Churchwardens have refused to sign his Certificate for the payment of his Annuity, a most unjust and malicious thing. They avow it because he was put in an Overseer for the Highways and has done his duty. We generally say an Honest Farmer, but they are the most Selfish, Avaricious and Envious Persons in the Community. William did not say a Lesson yesterday for which reason I had a few words with him which brought tears to his eyes. He has remarkable quickness in learning but rather too great a reluctance in going to his books.

Monday January 11 It was a joyful day to me and this House for this very day I received an Appointment for William for the Charter House on the Foundation. He was nominated by Mr Windham* by the application of my good friend Mrs Benwell and Mrs Windham both which Ladies I was well acquainted with in my younger days and they have recollected their acquaintance at this distance of time. It is a Glorious Act and deserves to be recorded. This has settled the Education of my Son William for the time to come and I hope it will be the foundation of his future advancement in this life and the means of securing his expectations and happiness in the Life to come. I hope it will be the means of instilling into him sound Principles of Religion as well as other knowledge and then it will turn out to his real good and advancement and I pray God it may be so. William immediately hastened to Stowey to communicate the great intelligence to his School Fellows and brought Buller* up to dine here. The two boys enjoyed themselves till nine o'clock and then Buller left us.

Friday January 15   A hard frosty morning. After breakfast I and William and my wife walked to Stowgurcy to dine with Mr and Mrs Davis. They were glad to see us. Mrs Davis is still lame but Mr Davis looked tolerable. Mrs Davis is in morning for a Relation, Mrs Casa Major an old lady who lived to the age of ninety. She left Mrs Davis a handsome legacy. We slept at Stowgurcy and passed the evening very agreeably.

Saturday January 16   After breakfast Mr Davis and I walked to Shurton to speak to Mr Poole about the Service of Dodington. George our servant brought some letters and a Certificate of William's age from Devonshire where he was born. After this we all set out for Overstowey and Mr Davis accompanied us part of the way. Made some calls and then got home to dinner where we found all ready to receive us.

Sunday January 17   A very fine clear frosty morning, barometer very high indeed. Prayers here in the morning. I thought at first we should have no one at Church but they did come at last, the Singers very full. A message was brought to me that there would be no Prayers at Dodington, the Church has been stripd and wants great repairs and they say there will be no Services during my absence. After Church we spent the evening at home as William is going off tomorrow with us for Bridgwater and on to the Charter House. It was necessary to have some time for preparation and packing up. In other respects the day was spent in the usual stile of Sunday. Edward Selleck came in the evening and his family to sup and take leave of William.

Now we have another of the unfortunate gaps in the Diaries for three of Holland's books are missing, covering the period to December 9.* Where the Hollands went during the period of his Absence mentioned above or how Little William survived his first terms at the Charter House we do not know. It seems most likely that Holland went to Wales to visit his brother and other relations while his son had certainly settled down well by the time we can take up his story again.

Friday December 9   Margaret still getting better but wears something around her face. George brought in the newspaper but nothing material in it. Buonaparte is still publishing his lying Bulletins. In the evening Margaret and I played Domino. My Stomach is still very indifferent and brings on pains in my face which annoys me much.

Saturday December 10   Still a foggy unpleasant morning, I did not stir out. George has been very busy in cutting wood and placing it out of the rain he works a good deal with fair words. Phebe, tho a good servant, is continually scolding him, tis a pitty. This day ended as it usually does in cleaning and scouring. George and Phebe have been very busy in putting up the bacon up our Brew House Chimney to smoak and hope it will be well done, for this is the first in our own house as it must be done with wood fire and we burn coal except in the Brewhouse. Smoking bacon is not the practice in this county but my wife is a Berkshire woman.

Sunday December 11   I have been very poorly this morning with pains in my face and puffiness in my stomach. I ventured into Church and got thro the Service much better than I thought. There were few at Church but I had a Christening*. As soon as I was up in the morning we were somewhat alarmed by a note from my wife desiring Phebe to come to her to be taught how to bandage her leg, so we got the little pony William used to ride and off she went and she actually returned before we dined. Dodington Church was pretty full but indeed the Church is so small that one may almost put the Church and Congregation in one's pocket. Returning me thought I heard the note of a thrush so I called out Davis for it was at Bincomb and he said it was a thrush. He said last week a colly and a thrush were singing as if it was Spring. This is the eleventh of December, a most unusual time for such birds to sing.

Monday December 12   I have been poorly all this morning with Spasms in my face and at last determined to send for Mr Forbes. We resolved to try Dr Dunnings prescription for the stomach for their lies the complaint. I did not move out afterwards, was very poorly after dinner but having sent for the draughts I took one and was better by bedtime. Bathed my feet in warm water went to bed and slept tolerably till morning. John Radlett who formerly lived with me called in and so I desired him to walk in and dine. He was well dressed and lives with the same Master he went to when he left us. He was in himself cleanly but very slow at work and very false for I fear combined with the other Servants to leave us as they thought all together in order to distress us and I fear Edward Selleck was in the plot as well as his daughter who lived here. However their schemes were frustrated. I fancy he has a bed here which the Dibbles might have furnished him with where he lived many years and has now money in their hands But how he will get on from thence I know not for I have no very high opinion of those two brothers.

Wednesday December 14   My face better, Margaret pretty well. Dyer* is here, George and he winnowing barley which is very fine. I mounted my horse after breakfast and rode before Margaret to Asholt to call on the Brices. Mrs and the two Miss Brice at home but the Reverend gone to Bristol. I think the young ladies were languid and poorly but the mother in high spirits. In coming home I met Mrs White and my daughter ordered some ducks from her and butter. George Paddock came for more straw and I have ordered his Gig to go to Bridgewater on Saturday next to bring home my wife and my son from the Charter House.

Thursday December 15 I sent Molly Weymouth off to old Blind Chedsey to come here having received a paper from Christ's Hospital by signing which he is to receive ten pounds. The woman, his wife, came and I gave her the paper but did not sign it. I said I must, and would, see him first. She is not a good woman and uses the old man scurvily, perhaps she expects to receive it unknown to the old man if she could get me to sign it but I'll take care of that. They are to come tomorrow morning.

Friday December 16 George carried one and twenty bushells of barley to the maltster very fine barley indeed. The old blind man Chedsey came here with his wife and I signed the paper by which he has ten pounds paid him by Christ's Hospital. I walked to the Malsters and while I stood by the door someone knocked at the window of the house opposite – it was Dr Dunning. He came down and we had some chat together. Fisher is dangerously ill with the gout in his head and by and by Bennet came to Dr Dunning and I left them. Then I went to Mr Allan's and found my daughter. I paid Mr Cole the clockmaker a trifle this morning. We marched homeward and got home by dinner time. George winnowed some more barley, three bushells, after he'd carried the other and Phebe out of her great anxiety to get all things in order against Mrs and Master William's come home must needs go and assist him to worm, as they term it, these three bushell. I hope William is got by this time near Bridgewater and George Paddock is to go for his Mama and him tomorrow.

Saturday December 17 Dyer is here and threshing wheat to be given away to the poor at Christmas. George has been very busy all this morning in cleaning up and clearing the garden. I walked almost into the Turnpike Road beyond Halsey Cross. Near the Turnpike I met Mr Michael and another man of Mr Rich going to cut down an old rotten pollard tree and they threw it down across the road. I observed that I expected George Paddock's Gig with my wife and son. They answerd that they would soon cut it up and carry it off, which they did. I could stay no longer the weather was so cold tho I had my Gollosseas on my feet and my network on my face and a greatcoat on my back. Before I reached Washer's a severe storm of hail poured upon me. I put up my umbrella and in turning my head I saw Mr Paddock, my wife and son William. I went up to them and shook hands but they took shelter under a barn and onwards I went and got home before them. William is grown and looks well and my wife seems to've got stout again and I hope she will continue so.

Sunday December 18   A very hard frost. I walked to Dodington. My wife was ill in the night. I did not find a soul in the Church but at last got a scant congregation. I told William that another time I expected him to walk with me. Our Church very full, among the rest Mr Tom Poole with that disagreeable boy Phebin his brother's bastard. Tom came up to me after Church and we spoke, then we dined and the evening afterwards was spent among ourselves in the usual stile.

Tuesday December 20   A severe frost, barometer high and thermometer 30 and under. Dyer is still here, George carrying long dung into the garden to guard against the frost. William busy about his task, a translation from the Greek. We did not move out much this weather and kept close to a good fire.

Saturday December 24   A hard frosty morning and a good deal of snow on the ground. After breakfast the poor poured in for corn and my wife was very busy. Dyer is here carrying out dung, or rather ashes, to the Moors. Miss Hartwell dined here today and we had hare to dinner which we have not very often tho I am qualified to kill game and we have game around us, yet not having taken out a Licence I do not go out and no one sends me game, at least not often tho this hare was sent me by Mr St Albyn. I cannot think Government take such a very large sum by this Act and it is hard that qualified persons should not be allowed to have their amusement without restraint. As to the unqualified they in fact cannot in general afford to idle their time away in this manner.

Sunday December 25   This is Christmas Day and the frost very severe. Few at Church and few at the Sacrament. I had some bad spasms while doing Duty and with difficulty got through the Duty yet I persevered. We had several persons of our neighbours to dine in the kitchen. They left us about five o'clock and then the evening was spent in the usual way of Sundays.

Monday December 26   I read Prayers this morning. We had a few at Church and a Christening and a Churching. Gave George leave to keep a holiday, he is gone on a visit with his father. When I got out of Church I found young Southcomb here from Rose Ash in Devon. He is at Allen's of Bridgewater from Tiverton School, a nephew of Mrs Southcomb's Husband. A very plain young man and a madness in the family. William asked one of the young Hartwells to dine here and they have been firing lttle brass cannons all morning.

Tuesday December 27   Snow fell in the night. Both Margaret and William disappointed in not being able to go to the Ball in Bridgewater, nor even to Enmore as they intended, it being a hazy morning and the snow very high. George had a holiday yesterday but he came early in the morning and I have since sent him for coal as I concluded the roads must be beaten along the Turnpike and towards Combych. William has been all morning making a large snowball and has curiously hollowed the inside and placed a candle in it and got some black paper with eyes, nose and mouth cut in it which at night will look tremendous. When night came on it did appear somewhat strange and terrible.

Thursday December 29   This morning too very dismal and foggy, my face tho somewhat better. The frost is quite gone, even William's hollow ball in the garden is almost entirely vanished. About 2 o'clock a horse was brought from Mr Ling for Mr Southcomb who is to dine here today in his way to Stowgumber. He came, but not till half an hour after time. (A curious Genius I think). However he dined here and so did the servant but he's left his horse to be sent back to Bridgewater by the Post tomorrow and taken Mr Ling's horse to go to Stowgumber and the man not much pleased marches off on foot. After this my wife, self and William played at Five Card Loo.

Friday December 30   I have been very poorly with a nervous agitation and Spasms in my face. Dyer is here in the barn. I promised to go over with William to Enmore but feel myself almost unequal to the undertaking yet my wife seems to think a little society may do me good. So after a good deal of resolving and unresolving I, covered with two great coats and my faithful woolen network around my face, moved off and William on his little poney, neatly trimmed, with me. We had a good deal of rain and passed along that awful road at Pikeley where William fell, and in short got safe to Enmore where we found old Mrs Poole better a good deal than she has been. Margaret too I found well, and the Divine and his sister Charlotte. There we dined and there we staid the night. William was my bedfellow this night and now and then he moved about a little unpleasantly.

Saturday December 31   This is the last day of the year and a dull foggy dark misly day it is. William and I got up not very early yet before the breakfast was ready. I cannot boast much of myself nor indeed much of the day, indeed it grows worse and worse. The Divine I see has got on new black gaiters up to the knee so he is at last come into my fashion, which I observed to him and he smiling acquiesced for in general he will not confess that he follows anyone. Soon after breakfast William and I mounted our horses, my face was very nervous and my stomach very puffy and I at first could with difficulty bear the jogging of the horse but the rain poured down and I quickened my pace by degrees and home at last we got in safety tho in truth very handsomely soaked, but I had two greatcoats on and William changed his clothes. At home I found my wife and Mr Batchelor who is going to return to Monkton Farley. He dined here and paid me some money and left after dinner. I have taken some concentrated Ginger which I trust will do me good. Dyer is here and what he has done I scarce know. The Bells are merrily Ringing out the Old Year.

The Year 1809

Sunday January 1 A very foggy dark morning, I scarce ever remember before so many foggy days of this kind. My face very bad this morning and I have had several severe spasms. I scarce know what to do and how to venture to Dodington this morning yet did not chuse to give it up. Before I got to Dodington I had two or three spasms. I was long on the road and the fog was very disagreeable. Got through the Service and administered the Sacrament tho I was all the while very poorly. Crept slowly home and then I was obliged to hurry to Church again for I had been so long detained at Dodington. In preaching I was hard put to it for I begun the Service so late and the evenings now so short and the fog so thick and dark that I knew not how to make out my Sermon. I had two spectacles with me so I very deliberately put up one and took out the other, the one that magnified more and by that means got through. The Singers afterwards gave us a long Psalm so that it was very late and dark before we got out and I had not dined and felt myself empty, cold and poorly. Then at dinner I had one or two spasms so that this is a poor beginning of the New Year, I pray to God that it may end better. A heiffer too was this day thrown into the crib by the other cows but I dont find yet that she has been much injured.

Monday January 2 We are about to go to Stowgurcy but I am still poorly with my face. The fogg so very thick that you might almost cut it with a knife. Mr and Mrs Davis are both invalids and were expecting us. Mrs Davis had a nose bleeding a little before and Mr Bennett was there when we came in. She looks thin and yellow but she is in good spirits and Mr Davis looks better. My face is very indifferent and I had several spasms while at dinner.

Tuesday January 3 I had a very painful night and little sleep, much continued throbbing or rather spasmodic throbbing in my temples and my wife too complained of her leg so that we had but a bad night. At breakfast I could not masticate my food and had to be content with liquids. Miss West came to us in the afternoon, Miss West is a violent woman and of a bad temper but has some good qualities and she has taken lodgings in the house of another violent woman and ill tempered. They soon quarrelled and a good deal of ill natured tricks pass between them, in short Miss West has notice to Quit and no one will take her in. Bad as her temper is I pitied her and would do her a kindness, but at a distance. I believe she intends to throw herself on Mrs Lewis who indeed would gladly do anything but take her under her roof, a sad case. I went to bed somewhat better, Mrs Davis is an excellent nurse.

Wednesday January 4   It was very late before I could get downstairs. I felt myself exceedingly poorly and wanted to get home as fast as I could for though this is an excellent house to be ill in yet Home is better. My wife, to my great surprize is determined to walk to Overstowey, being more fearful of the horse than her legs, tis a bold undertaking not having done such a thing for this past half year. I, suspecting snow, borrowed an umbrella at Mrs Rollins and my wife Pattens and just as we got to Stowey the snow began to fall. I spread my umbrella and my wife was so resolute that she bid William and George make the best of their road home. We were right glad to find ourselves at home and all things clean to receive us and Dyer hard at work in the barn. The snow is already deep.

Thursday January 5   A very deep snow. Mister Forbes gave me something to take last night but it had not much effect. I am still unable to chew my food and live chiefly on eggs and liquids.

Sunday January 8   A very rainy foggy and unpleasant morning. I have been very poorly with my face, yet attempted to do the Duty and got through it with difficulty. Very few at Church owing to the badness of the weather, scarce any females on account of the great rains that made the brooks everywhere overflow. I was so poorly this day that I could not go to Dodington and so sent over George to acquaint them with this. I cannot eat yet anything but spoon meat.

Thursday January 12   I walked down to Stowey being somewhat better than I have been for some time with my face. I called on that venerable couple, old Sully and his wife. He is eighty six and the wife about eighty two and tho he said at first he was poorly yet on my talking to him he cheered up and spoke very sensibly on many occasions. My face has not been as bad as usual today which has put me in spirits.

Friday January 13   My wife preparing to go off to Bridgewater with William. In the meantime Dr Jenkins, his former Master of Bridgewater came in to see him. He now lives at Blackheath and takes 26 pupils. He is very fond of William and says he will have him over to him at Easter. Many people called about Taxes with their Assessments and confused me much, and altogether I have been nervous and poorly.

Saturday January 14 In coming down stairs some flecks of snow fell and more since has come down. I begin to be very uneasy about William, he is to go off in Fromont's Coach at three on Sunday morning and if a deep snow falls we shall be much alarmed. Yet he will be under God's Protection so why should I be alarmed. A poor idiotish girl Totterdale is to be buried today she absolutely killed herself by eating, her appetite was so voracious that she never knew when she had got enough.

Monday January 16 The snow still increasing. A note from my wife saying that William went off in the coach as at first intended and in good spirits. He breakfasted with the passengers who all spoke to him and the Coachman laughed at the dangers of the road. The man who slept at the Inn to see him off said he never in all his life saw a young gentleman behave better and go to School in better Spirits. I did not stir further than the garden. I felt so poorly that I sent for Forbes who however did not come till it was dark. Mister Forbes muddled and hummd and hawd, at last agreed to send me something and I was obliged at last to send for it in the night very late.

Tuesday January 17 Still deep in snow and a very hard frost. Mr Forbe's Physick has not, I thank God made me worse. Nay I slept tolerably and as I think somewhat better.

Wednesday January 18 Out came a little bit of history about William. He was ill used in going to School. I paid a man to sleep in the same room to see him off. He paid his fare and took his place in the Coach with the other Passengers when Lo another Passenger came and demanded his place in the Coach and in short turned William out and at last he was put in the Basket, the coldest morning this season and the snow falling fast, and thus he went on as far as Wells when the other passengers took him in. It was the most cruel and brutal act I ever heard off. The thing lies between the Book keeper and the Coachman. It was a shameful thing, they took his inside fare and then put him outside. However I have written to Fromont the proprietor of the Coach. His trunk had not arrived when he reached London, we are in great anxiety about him. I have called on Mr Anstiss and he says I have the Rheumatism and that he will send me some Guanicum Pills. My wife has seen Dr Dunning about her leg, nothing further can be done. She takes Bark and he has prescribed Brimstone twice a day.

Saturday January 21 I made a good dinner for the first time for these many days if not weeks. I eat some snipes for dinner and was able to eat them as usual. A letter from Wm Tutton containing some Bills.

Sunday January 22   A most deep and serious snow. My wife poorly and lies in bed. I sent to the Riches about the Service and they advised me not to ring the Bell. I sent to Frost and Farmer Landsey and they said they could not go to Church if there was a Service. Indeed the path is so high with snow that people must work hard to clear it, so it is resolved there will be no Prayers this Sunday. I never remember such a thing before and I have been Vicar of the place these thirty years.

Tuesday January 24   A most quick and remarkable thaw, the morning very misty and rainy. George went off to Bridgwater with letters. The most uncomfortable day I ever remember, everything moist and slutchy. I had that huge fellow Porter from the Workhouse to throw the snow from the gutters of the House. A poor miserable creature called Fortune Hill died yesterday by herself in a lonesome house tho there is a woman paid by the Parish to be with her. Little Betty Pierce in the Workhouse I have sent a flannel waistcoat to and currant wine. I must make some enquiries about the repair of the poor house and whether they have got blankets. My cold is considerably better and the pains in my face quite gone.

Wednesday January 25   We are disappointed in the quantity but not the quality of our corn. Sad news from Spain, our Army has retreated to Corunna, all Buonaparte's myrmidons pouring upon them to an immense number yet Moore says he offered them battle at Lugo which they declined but they attacked him as he was embarking at Corunna and they were repulsed with great loss, but General Moore himself was unfortunately killed by a ball on the breast and Sr David Baird lost an arm. I am sorry the Spaniards suffered Buonaparte to fall on their Noble Allies in this manner for he drew all his forces from every quarter to attack the English. The Spaniards should have harried his rear. This news of our Army has troubled me much. I received this day a letter from Windsor from Mr Northey. There has been a great fire at St James's and one life lost and many of the Royal Appartments burnt down.

Thursday January 26   In the evening I was called out to see two very bright stars very near each other. I viewed the stars through my telescope, they seemed very near each other and something similar in their faces tho one was brighter than the other. There seemd clearly and distinctly a black line round the surface of each with a luminous appearance beyond this ridge like a border and the middle had several black dots like writing in two or three lines across. They both had apparently some kind of dots or lines but the one was far more luminous than the other. My wife and I and all our people were out and I do not remember seeing such a thing before. I suppose our papers will be full of it by and by. After this my wife and I played a little Domino till bedtime. The waters out everywhere and have done much damage.

Friday January 27   The waters still out. I walked down to the Paddock with George and made him give vent to the waters. Mr Buller who rents a field of Lord Egmont's above me is a great nuisance to me for he turns the water out of its natural course to water his land and it falls on my hedge and has nearly undermined the whole. I have mentioned the thing often but can get no redress, tis hard to seek ones remedy by the Law. Mr St Albyn wants me to obtain some Prize Money for an Old Woman who lost a son at Monte Video. At night I could not see the two remarkable stars I saw the night before, indeed the sky was too much clouded for it.

Saturday January 28   The morning is very mild, open and pleasant. I mounted my horse and rode over to Mr Poole of Shurton to consult about the Church of Dodington if I should go to Bath. He was very friendly and said he would take it if I was driven hard. A poor miserable sister of Wm Hill's was buried this evening and tho Wm Hill neglected her in her lifetime he buried her handsomely. This evening I received a letter from Mr Fromont about his Coach and William being turned to the outside. He will be down at Bridgewater to investigate the matter. No mail this night nor expected till Monday morning.

Sunday January 29   I had not done Duty for three weeks past but ventured this day to Dodington through most rainy and tempestuous weather. Mr Farthing spoke to me marrying a couple tomorrow, his sister and another. I told him that it could not be unless resident 21 days before.

Monday January 30   Still very windy and rainy. Barometer so low that the marker will not follow it. This evening from five to nine o'clock had the most terrible wind I remember. It alarmed us while sitting in the parlour and had it continued we should have been lothe to venture into bed. We have seen no more of the strange stars, the sky has been too cloudy every night.

Tuesday January 31   A fine pleasant mild morning but the havock of the wind is everywhere. The Church is Stripped and so is my house in three parts and a branch split off the plumb tree. Verrier came here and says all the houses in Stowey have been damaged and many of the elm trees in the Churchyard of Stowey and the tiling of the Church. In short the damage has been general. Verrier and his man have been busy repairing for me with reed till we can get it compleated. George went for lime this day to repair the tiling and Verrier slackd it.

Thursday February 2   They have been up early for brewing. I ventured out up the hill with my umbrella but even the hills are full of water. With great difficulty I picked my way to Farmer Stone, not at home, gone to market. I did not chuse to go the same way back and by and by passed by Wm Hill, he was working just by but rather hid himself tho he saw me very well and so did his grandson who skulked and dodged about watching me, but I took no notice of either of 'em. He had got a child by his apprentice girl and keeps her and the child, in defiance of his wife, in the house, – an Old Fornicator.

Sunday February 5   Everyone has a rheumatic cold, my wife did not get up till late and did not go to Church which is unusual with her. A tolerable congregation and good singing. Went to Dodington in the afternoon and gave notice of a general Fast of Wednesday next. Returned to dinner and found my wife downstairs. Two snipes which I had kept for some time to make a present of with others I was obliged to use and found that I could not touch them, a disappointment to me who am fond of them but disappointments will happen sometimes and so I laid hold of some other things at table and made a good dinner.

Wednesday February 8   This is the General Fast, very cold and piercing and windy. I could scarce get any to Church but I went in at last, had a very small Congregation for a Fast. However I went thro the Intricate Service and gave them a Sermon. Mounted my horse and rode to Dodington and the snow came on very fast No Congregation to be found except two or three boys, at last came Mr Huggins and so I begun the Service and two or three came. Finished the Service and made some stony observations to Mr Huggins on the state of the Church. A torrent of rain poured in on one side so as to make one side quite black, one window half gone and pains of glass in abundance wanting and the roof full of holes that the sky was visible in many places. I told Huggins I could not do Duty in a Church in this state. Why Sir, replied he if next Sunday should be bad you need not come. You know the wind blows on me from all quarters answered I. Cant get a Glazier and Mason returned he, not immediately. Church Work said I must be done without delay. So we parted. Notwithstanding my umbrella the wind blew the snow under it and I had much ado to guard myself in any tolerable way and the skirts of my greatcoat was glazed with snow, yet home I got at last. Tho a Fast I did, now the Service was over, eat a little stoutly.

Thursday February 9   Wet, wet, wet. No probability of dry weather. The oldest man living does not remember such great floods and so much water. Everything beyond Bridgewater is like a sea. That Dirty Rascally Fellow, Buller's carter at Tryon is continually pouring the water over the Mead which come direct on our hedge and will certainly carry off the bank. I must not suffer this any longer and if Buller supports him I must defend myself against such an injurious encroachment. My wife still poorly that

Mr Forbes was called. He is the very Deuce of a man for Visits Physicks and Charges. I think I must put an end to this man's visits.

Friday February 10   Heavy rain, water everywhere. Bad as the weather was I ventured to Stowey under my umbrella. I called on Mr Allen, they were preparing to go to Plansfield. I called too on Mr Forbes. He snuffled out that he had made up some bottles for Mrs Holland which I might send for if she wanted them. We did send after but as I am alive the man sent five for my wife and two for Miss Holland – I never will submit to this long.

Friday September 22   Mr Crosse is come to his house which the Hartwell's inhabited. Was to have had a Peal of Bells about five o'clock this evening to celebrate the expiration of the Decimal Year and the beginning of another for he is a very Mathematical Genius. Old Mrs Poole is here, very cheerful and well considering her age.

Saturday September 23   Passed through Stowey and called on Conjuror Coles (as they call him). I asked why the Decimal Year was not rung out in our Parish as I had promised not to prevent it. He answered that they rang at Stowey and likewise in the morning. I rode on towards the Copper Mines and returned home by Bincombe. My poor wife's leg does not get better, I scarce know what to make of it. A proposal is made by Mrs Southcomb for my wife to come to her once more and place herself under Mr Bryant's care for some time but I know not what to say to it.

Tuesday September 26   I walked over to call on Mr Crosse this morning. I found him busy about his Astronomical Matters in a neat undress and I had a good deal of talk with him. He has a Decimal Thermometer, a decimal clock and all are to go by Decimals, and he spoke of a curious thing to tell which way the wind blew. He had indeed so many new things in his head that I asked him whether he had any particular horror about the Old Rules and Customs. He answered if there was no change there would be no improvement. True but the improvement should first be made evident before the changes took place. He breakfasts at 6 in the morning and is for going to bed at six. Why then said I you must live by yourself but man is formed for Society and must conform in some degree to the Society he dwells among, especially in things of little moment or he must be content to live by himself. Then I proposed that he should go and live on the top of Dowesbury and have a little hut and Observatory for himself. He laughed heartily at this. I then took my leave of him as his Decimal dinner was ready to which he often invited me and I as often declining, intimating that I had a dinner at three which if he could partake of after his Decimal dinner I should be glad to see him. He seems a pleasing good tempered man but somewhat enthusiastic on Mathematical matters. I know not what servants he has but I saw only one young girl and she without a cap which I did not much approve of. After this I returned home and we spent the evening before a good fire.

Friday September 29 Dyer is here and very bad with the toothache but is gone to Squire Cruckshanks for his composition for Tithe. I rode to Ely to see Tithe Apples taken, there is one bag for me. Rich was there and looked poorly, he complained of a swelling or fullness in his side, very painful at times. He has been a famous wrestler in his time, I suppose some of the wrenches and bruises he received in those times begin to trouble him as he gets old. Farmer Morle dined here and paid his Composition and so did farmer Landsey. They made each of them a good dinner and drank strong beer and Brandy and Gin till they were brim full and then they left me. I was afraid of pressing another glass of brandy and water on them lest it should prove too much, so we were left to ourselves.

Sunday October 8 Just as I was preparing to go to Dodington the Clerk came in saying that Palmer would marry the woman, the woman that had been asked out six times. I cannot do it today said I, I am going to Dodington, but recollecting that this was a slippery gentleman and only proposed the thing because he supposed I would not marry them I was determined to nick the gentleman and said I would marry them. So he came, but in his worst clothes and behaved so indifferently that I was obliged to reprimand him. After this I moved off to Dodington as fast as I could. There was to be a Sacrament there and to my great surprise only the Clerk staid with myself, a thing which never happened to me before tho I have been now forty years in Holy Orders. I told the Clerk I could not consider *two* as a Congregation and therefore must decline administring the Sacrament to the Great Shame of the Parish. But as I intended giving a shilling to the Poor I gave it to him. Mr Farthing was at Church but tho a Churchwarden he marched out like Goliath himself. I returned and we had a full Church at Overstowey in the afternoon and then the day past off in its usual stile.

Monday October 9 I was up early, before six, and taking a morsel of bread and port wine I mounted my horse and rode to Mr James Rich of Crosse and summoned him to come to Bridgewater to attend me tho he has been confined to home a day or two before. He is appointed one of the Commissioners to swear me to an Examination relating to the Merioneth-shire Estates. He and I had a good ride and arrived before nine o'clock. Mr Ruscomb Poole was not within being busy about the Local Militia who are this day to march to Taunton for Duty and he is a Captain. Being the other Commissioner he soon dispatched my Business, packed up the parcel, directed it and sent it off to London. We breakfasted together and Mr Rich and I left him soon after as the Military Heroes were collecting together. The Bridgewater Heroes were collecting from all parts and Drums beating. Mr Rich and I scudded among them as fast as we could and we were moving towards the Inn we met another Regiment, in White, the Langford Militia and the Colonel in the midst of them from whom I had a gracious bow, Colonel Pine. Then we got to our Inn and hurried on our horses as fast as we could as the Drums were coming upon us with Martial Ardour and Din and as soon as we were up trotted off pretty briskly being Right glad to escape from them as our horses did not much relish their Military Noise and Parade. Met Sr Philip Hales to whom I bowed and several of our Parishioners and among others Farmer Landsey who was quite astounded when he met us for it seems our wise Parishioners have got some deep schemes in agitation about the Roads and they verily thought we had been at Bridgewater to disconcert their schemes. But poor men, we never said a word about them for as Mr Rich said all nominated for Surveyors are like Addled Eggs, not one better than the other. I was glad the business relating to the Exchequer Cause was compleated and I hope soon we shall touch either the money or the Estate. In the afternoon I wrote a letter to William inclosing a one pound note to discharging newspaper deficiencies at the Charter House, and another letter to Mr Oldfield informing him of the parcel being arrived at Bridgewater and the Business being done.

Tuesday October 10   My wife went off behind George on the great horse and Dyer attended on another horse with a Portmanteau. So off they went and got well to Taunton for my wife to go in the Coach to her sister, Mrs Southcomb to make another trial about her leg under Mr Bryant's care. George and Dyer are returned. I pray God she may meet with the success she expects.

Thursday October 12   I am still poorly with my cold and did not stir further than the garden. Just as we were sitting down to dinner a Chaise drove up to the gate and out came my wife's Niece, Hatton Dodwell and her maid servant and she stays with us I hope some time. A very small person and most excellently proportioned and wellmaid. She is in better health than she used to be but her maid, a good kind of girl, is in a bad way. She made a good dinner but my daughter and I are both invalids with cold at present. I received a letter from Dr Stone, Charterhouse Square saying that he received a brace of pheasants in high perfection from me and that William was quite well but had had a complaint in his bowells which had kept him under the Matron's care only one night.

Saturday October 14   After breakfast Farmer Dibble called for the Poor Rate which I paid him. George went to Major, the Methodist, for Tithe apples which however he does not receive till he has been there three times. These

People wish to be very troublesome, indeed all Methodists are when they have it in their power. After this we went to Haste's but they had no apples, they too are shuffling people. I spoke to Wi Philips, she has potatoes to sell and I said I would take some at s3 6d a bag. I have not seen any swallows for four or five days past, I suppose they are gone tho I saw them later last year. I should think they were gone about the ninth or twelfth of this month. They do not as some suppose go to a day but much depends on the Season. The weather is now keen and frosty and that may be the reason for their departure this year.

Wednesday October 18   Three of our lasses, Margaret, Miss Symes and Miss Eliza Lewis walked to Asholt but Miss Dodwell staid at home, she never moves out much and when she does it is chiefly with her maidservant. I cant think but that she might move about more than she does, she coddles herself. I walked to Halsey Cross to see the potatoes I have bought.

Monday October 23   After breakfast I rode down to Stowgurcy, met Mr Davis. He looks poorly I think. Met Mr Coombs and Mr Dawes, they were going to order a bullock towards celebrating His Majesty's entering the Fiftieth Year of his Reign. They are making great preparations at Stowey for that purpose. Dibble's oxen have been in my Moor and made sad work. Fourteen beasts which have swept off the grass clean. These Dibbles are sad Depredators, that biggest fellow of the two it is said lets in cattle into People's grounds. They certainly knew of their cattle being in and never acquainted me with it. Mr Rich promised to go down to estimate the damage but did not.

Tuesday October 24   Mr Rich called on me after breakfast and we walked down to the Moor together. They were my bounds and they have broken through and have eat up all the grass entirely. After this I walked to Dame Selleck, she is dying. I prayed by her and am to administer the Sacrament to her on Thursday. Dyer and Wm Frost are making cyder for me, they finished a Hogshead this day.

Wednesday October 25   A very fine clear morning. Disappointed about a newspaper last night and I have written to the Printer about it. This is the King's Accession into the fiftieth year of his Reign and the Bells are ringing and we are to have Prayers. Few assembled. Farmer Morle after promising fairly last Sunday to provide cyder disappointed us all, a mean shabby fellow. Farmer Landsey though as rich as a Jew contributed nothing tho he was at Church but the other was not. However we had some few and the two Richs. I believe I gave them as good a Sermon and as well delivered as any they will hear this day in these parts (Tho I say it myself as the man observed.) and moreover it was my own composition, which will not be the case in general I presume. We are at a loss about the cyder to be purchased. We did not get cyder at last but they had a quantity of strong beer and the Bells rung merrily and a Bonfire on Quantock and Musick playing God Save the King. There was indeed some drunkenness, but they cannot rejoice without it, such people. The Plainsfield people behaved very shabby on this occasion, but we did very well without them. There were great doings at Stowey and much given away, they kept it up until ten. I sent George for the paper which was brought me.

Thursday October 26   I called on Mr Rich and settled about the expence of the beer yesterday. Called on Old Becky Selleck and administered the Sacrament to her. She is dying I think, tho not so old as her husband. When we were going to tea we were alarmed by a great noise at the gate, I thought all Stowey was come up to us, when Mr Coles, alias Conjuror Coles, presented his compts and said John Bull was come to visit and begged he might be admitted, which I granted. A large figure, as big as life was admitted. He stood on a kind of stage and was dressed in a red sattin waistcoat with stripes of Gold Lace or Tinsel and a great deal of gaudiness about his head. He had a full red face but I objected to his nose being broad and flat at the end. I told Mr Coles that John should have a better nose. John was a very honest, good tempered man but that he should have a predominand and rather aquiline nose for that John when aroused was of a Martial Spirit. They sang God Save the King and I gave Coles half a crown and some cyder to his Myrmidons. The paper was brought and contains little but what related to Peace between Austria and Buonaparte.

Monday October 30   The morning was very foggy but then it goes off and we have a warm day. Dyer is here in the barn. I have not been very well and this cough and cold hangs on me and really distresses me. George I made to work a little in the garden. Phebe has been very bad with her leg and has been obliged to go to Stowey once or twice but Bennet was too busy to attend to her. I continued in the garden pruning and planting but I fear it has increased my cold.

Wednesday November 1   A very foggy morning, I do not think my cold is much better. Dyer and George have been winnowing pease and Frost bought 4 bushells. Joseph Palmer, a savage looking fellow came here to pay Tithe as I had threatened him. He said before that he never had paid Tithe and never would. He grumbled at the sum. I observed to him that tho he never came to Church yet it was proper that he should pay Tithe. Then I asked him what he thought of another World. He answered that he was no Scholard. I do not presume you are but it is proper you should know that there are two places, there was one for the Good and another for the Bad. Then I talked to him seriously so that he began to wish himself out of hearing but I would not let him go. At last I told him that I did not value his Tithe and if he promised to come to Church I would take but one shilling from him instead of two. He smiled at this, God Bless you I can easily do this. Do so returned I and now before Clerk Dyer it is a bargain, if you come to Church I take one shilling but if you do not I will have *two*. So we parted. These Broom Squires as they call them have no Religion and I do not ever remember seeing this man at Church, so we shall see now what he will do.

Thursday November 2   About four o'clock this morning I found a shooting pain in the toe of my right foot and it continued and increased till morning. When I got up I found it swelled and red and now it is become a compleat gout. I cannot walk without crutches. However I ventured out on horseback with a gouty shoe. Our neighbour, Sally Stiling fell down in a fit and has been raving and violent ever since, her father, our Phebe, George and her mother can scarcely hold her. She seems to me to be in a Frenzy Fever, and the family are in great distress. Young Blake dined here and staid rather late and then went to Stowey. He is of Oxford and means to take Orders. At first he talked very well and seems very well disposed and Religious, seems much inclined to enter into the State of Matrimony but expects Fortune, Beauty and every thing else of the Lady's Side but has nothing to offer of his side but his precious self, and has no notion that self could meet a refusal from anyone. It is strange men should be so blind to their own defects. This man is one of the last I should think of were I a woman, nothing in person or manner, nothing in Fortune and not much either in Learning or Sense. His father is at this very time half mad and he himself is ready to get into the same way. In short he appears to me to have nothing but extreme Presumption on his side. He has a sister an idiot and another cracked and the other nothing extraordinary, and yet this young man speaks as if he was the perfection of Human Nature. I was indeed astonished at what he said but laughed and suffered him to run on.

Sunday November 5   I found myself so well this morning that I got up early and prepared myself for Church tho I had some forebodings about my face. Yet off I went and George with me. Poor Farmer Chedzey was buried today he died of a cancer, a most shocking death. The Church was very much crouded and I got through the Service very well tho I coughed hard.

Monday November 6   My gout is better but my cough and spasms not much mended. I rode to Stowey this day with my gouty foot wrapped up. I called on Mr Allen, sat a while and chatted and then mounted my horse again. Mr Allen mounted his horse and we turned back to back at his gate, he went in quest of a man who had been impudent to him in driving his cart on the High Road and he is determined to have him before a Justice if he does not make proper submission. I like this Spirit in Allen, he has made a man come to once before and there is no keeping due subordination without it. My newspaper came today instead of yesterday, I hope this will be rectified e'er long.

Monday November 13 Horses in abundance passing on to Bromfield Fair very early this morning. I rode out by Halsey Cross passing thro Stowey. By Long Cross a man called to me, said his goods were taken on account of Rent. I said I could not help it. They talked that they must come to the Parish and that they must pay his arrears of Rent. I answered that they had a right to immediate relief if wanted but no Justice could order them to pay the debts he had incurred. They were rather loud and saucy but I moved off. Called on Mr James Rich, he said the Parish could not pay his debts, there was the Workhouse for them but that he and his wife were young and had only two children. I came home and nothing material after this.

Tuesday November 14 A sad disturbance here about ringing. An Impudent Rascal of a fellow had the Impudence to come into the Garden before the house and demand the Key of the Belfry. The Clerk told him that it was with me. He replied that I had no right to keep it. I answered from the house that I could soon convince him of my right and bid him go about his business. He was very abusive. So out they went and got Farmer Landsey's Key to the Chancel and in they got. I sent to them to desist at their Peril, they stopped and soon began again. I sent out a second time, sent to Farmer Landsey for the Key and they were turned out a second time. There were one or two worthless fellows beside this Joe Hill and I think of making an example of them.

Thursday November 16 This day George brought home a dreadful account of a Murder, the most horrible that can be conceived. It was that poor woman was killed who formerly took up my little boy at Pikely and saved him so humanely and with so much attention. Her name was Styling. A lad taken into the house, of eighteen, watched the opportunity when she was alone and cleaved her skull with a hatchet. He mangled the poor woman most shockingly and left her dead before the fire. Then went upstairs and robbed the house of two Bank Notes of Ten Pounds each, picked her pockets of what she had, then carried off wearing apparel of various kinds, took a gun with him and powder and shot and mounted his Master's Horse and travelled off thus to Bristol. The husband did not come home till late, had he come sooner the Villain, it is thought would have shot him. They are now after him and, I trust God, will soon take him and that he will be hung up in Gibbets for a more barbarous murder was never heard of before in these parts tho indeed we have had a man murder his wife* in this Parish some years ago. There must be something Gloomy and Villainous in the people of these parts. I never heard of a murder in Wales when I lived there. This woman murdered was a pleasant good looking woman. The lad was a stranger, neither could find out where he came from, probably connected with a gang at Bristol and London. Canvassing briskly for the Chancellorship of Oxford. I hope Grenville will not come in who has deserted the Good Old King in the manner he has done.

Monday November 20   This is a fine day and after breakfast I mounted the great horse and rode before Margaret and George had Farmer Landsey's Poney and carried some clothes and so off we posted to Enmore and found them all at home (the Pooles) and they were glad to see us. Tho I had my Diary with me yet I did not write as there was something to catch my attention during my stay at this place and so I must pick my observations and occurrencies as well as I can recollect and get through to the 26th. Old Mrs Poole looks remarkably well and is now free from pain, she is seventy five and very shrewd and clear. Miss Poole and Miss Charlotte are the only daughters at home. Mr John Poole was at home of course for the house and Living are his. We had a good dinner and a great deal of chat.

Tuesday November 21   We assembled all at breakfast about nine and chatted pleasantly and cheerfully but the Old Lady does not come down to breakfast. After breakfast the Divine and I walked over to Mr Parson's, Rector of Gothurst who is the Commission of Peace. He had before him that Horrible Villain who murdered the poor woman Mrs Styling his Mistress. The very woman who so kindly saved my Little Boy when he fell from hs horse. He had handcuffs on and seated on one chair with his leg extended on another for he had a bad leg. Quite a boy and not very strong set and scarce the appearance adequate for the Horrid Deed he was taken up for. Mr Tynt came in and Mr Leeson a Welsh Gentleman. Mr Tynt joined in the examination, he is a man of large Fortune and lives at Heswell, just opposite Mr Parsons. A singular character a great horseman and Chariotteer and, like Jehu, always drives furiously. He has an odd Physiognomy, a good forehead but a prodigious sink from the nose to the forehead. The nose is rather short tho not broad. It is very strange that tho it is clear that this Boy must have committed the act yet he framed his tale so artfully that nothing pointed came out. A man swore to his being in the house and left with his Mistress alone half an hour before the murder could have been committed and he was found the day after thirty miles from the place and the horse was found grazing on a Common hardby without saddle and bridle and seemingly much driven. He yet said that he walked all the way, tho it was impossible he should have walked so far in the state his leg was in. He had driven the horse of Mrs Styling's Father so hard that he fell and hurt the boy's leg and the horse died and Mrs Styling was threatening him that he should be sent to Jail for it, so he artfully accounted for what happened by saying that two Ruffians broke into

the house whom he thought to be the men to take him to Jail and that he
fled and escaped and travelled home on foot, thus insinuating that these
Ruffians committed the Murder. All his answers were very guarded and he
never varied and by this means rendered what was thought a clear case
somewhat intricate. No other person either saw or heard of these two men,
nor is it probable if there had been any such that they would have driven the
horse the same way that he fled and have left the horse where he was. When
we returned to Enmore Mr Davis from Stowgurcy came there and staid all
the time that we remained there. Wednesday Mr John Poole and I walked
out and over a Farm of his Mother's which is to be his, a very pretty farm
and yields a considerable rent. Friday Mr Davis and I called on Mr Parsons –
he has committed the Lad to Jail.

Sunday November 26

I rode to Dodington in the afternoon and found the Church very full
indeed. Mr Farthing desired to have his child Baptised on Wednesday next.
I answered that this day was the proper one, however I consented to come.
I have during the past week been harrassd with the Spasms and a fullness in
my stomach but on following Mr John Poole's directions in taking
Magnesia and Rhubarb I find myself considerably better and I mean to
follow this regularly. Mr James Rich gave me a book to read, written by a
young man of this Parish, Solomon Rich, now Sergt. to the 28th
Regiment, giving an account of his campaigns and the movements of the
Armies at different places – Copenhagen, Spain and Flushing. Considering
his education, which he modestly apologises for, it is surprising what a
good account he gives.

Tuesday November 28

I walked out this day to Farmer Stone and had a good deal of talk with
him about his affairs. It seems the great man, Lord Egmont's Steward Mr
Cruckshanks, is going on very oppressively. Stone has brought up 14
children on a small farm with great credit and decency, and his father lived
there before. Now Cruckshanks is going to turn him out almost at a
moments notice tho he has three years to come on his lease. He has indeed
offered him another Farm but the old one is much preferred by the old
people. He will at this rate soon depopulate the Parish for he turns out all
the smaller tennants and the houses are going to decay and we shall soon
have nothing but labourers and beggars in the Parish. What Lord Egmont is
about I cannot tell for it must be detrimental to his Interest as well as to the
publick in general. I went to Mr Rich after this and had a good deal of talk
with him on the Subject. A letter from William – All well.

Wednesday November 29   Rode to Dodington, went into Farmer Farthing's
and there I met the most malicious man Mr Woodhouse of Stowey who

erected a Meeting House in opposition to the Church. I was surprized to see
him offer himself as Godfather to stand for the child. We had exchanged
some civilities before but I was staggard to see him there and observed, but
with mildness and a smile, that I thought it inconsistent for him who had
withdrawn from the Church and erected a Meeting House in opposition to
the Church, for him nevertheless to come here to answer for a child to be
brought up in the Principles of this Church. He said that he had Principles
of Religion. No doubt he had I returned but according to the present
Establishment was the point. He rambled something that he approved of
the Present Establishment. Very well said I and there are others to be
depended on and so I proceeded and there was no disturbance but when I
came out of Church towards the house he came to me and said he wondered
I should be so ignorant of my Duty, but he'd make me know my Duty, I
did not Catechise the Children. Certainly I do for we have a Sunday School
for that purpose at Overstowey. Then he went on crying that I did not knoe
my Duty. I wull make thee know thy duty, and this he expressed with such
Violence as to make him Ridiculous. He went in and I desired Mr Farthing
to come out to me. I asked him very calmly how he could bring that man to
insult me in the manner he had done. He answered that he did not know
there would be any objection to him. He certainly had left our Church and
how could he answer for a child to be brought up according to that Church
he despised. However I mounted my horse and left 'em. I shall give up the
Church of Dodington and serve it no more for this man Farthing who is
Churchwarden and this man mean to entrap me by some way or other.
Indeed there is a Diabolical Scheme now on foot among the Sectarians and
Dissenters to adopt the Southertonian Scheme to Harrass, entrap and annoy
the Clergy of the Established Church by vexatious prosecutions about
trifles, not for the good of Religion but to gratify their Spleen. They
winnowed 26 bushells of barley today.

Thursday November 30   Dressed myself and Margaret and I went to dinner
at the Allen's. Met there the Pooles of Shurton and the two Miss Brice.
We were very long before dinner came in and when it came everything
was cold. Mrs Allen manages very well and is a genteel woman but
she has got at present a set of Potatoe Headed Zomerzetshire servants
and everything was badly dressed, but the provisions were great and
elegant. I took some Rhubarb, Magnesia and Ginger before dinner for the
pains in my face but after dinner I worked me off very inconveniently.
Add to this it rained most terribly and I was obliged to march off with
a candle and lantern to find the House in the Garden, through lanes
and wet bushes that it was quite unpleasant. At last I found it with
some difficulty and while there my candle went almost quite out which
alarmed me to a great degree so that I hastened back and with great
poring ang groping, and running now and then into a wet bush I did

find my way back at last, and upon my word if my candle had gone out I know not how I should have got out of the Garden. I was obliged to undertake the same Expedition once or twice and to leave the company for that purpose, which made it quite disagreable for me tho indeed I was in other respects very well and hope it will do me good. When we went to tea we found Mr Bennet and his Bride, and Mr Ward with his spectacles dined with us. We had a large party but all the evening the rain came down in torrents. We supped there and when late I mounted the great horse double coated and Margaret well cloaked and muffled up mounted behind and Sancho with a lantern and candle before we sallied forth. Before we got to bed it was one o'clock.

Monday December 4 I rode out on Mr Landsey's horse and Margaret behind George on the great horse and in spight of the rain and the weather we got to Mr Lyng at Stowgumber. There we dined and sent George home and staid the night.

Tuesday December 5 This day too we were prevailed on to stay. I rode out with Mr Lyng as far as Monksilver to see Mr James while he was seeing some patients for he is in the Medical Line and getting on fast in business and has a pretty Fortune of his own. Mr James is lately married. A great Christening here among the Poole family of Wexford. They are branched into a great number of families and cover this part of the County and are very wealthy, the very top of the Yeomanry, good tempered, proud, noisy and extravagant. Poole of Shurton is one of the Tribe. In short there are no less than eight or nine families of them in the neighbourhood around.

Wednesday December 6 Mr Lyng was called out to a patient about twelve. George came with a horse so we mounted, I on the little horse and Margaret behind George. There was a misly fog all the way and the fog was very thick on the top of Quantock and had we not known our road very well we might have lost it. However we got home safe and dined and found ourselves comfortable.

Monday December 11 A very unpleasant misly morning. Ugly faced Briffet came here to kill a pig. I did not stir out much and nowhere without Goloshes. We sent George to meet Miss Lewis who came in the coach to Stowey.

Tuesday December 12 Ugly-faced Briffet came here to cut out our pig. He weighs thirteen score and three pounds, a larger and fatter pig than I ever remember being killed here as we do not admire them much larger. George is gone for coal and his jacket will be peppered with hail.

He does this business better than any servant I ever had. He came home in good time and without being wetted much. I walked to Stowey to see my malt. It does not grow very finely which surprised me as the barley is good. The walk was very dirty, so much rain having fallen of late.

Thursday December 14 We have been in the house very busy salting our pig. This evening proved a terrible one, the rain drives into all the front windows and forced itself under the sashes. My poor Boy is to set out from London this day so that he travels now throughout this terrible night. The wind is high beyond what I can remember, the bed shook under me. I did not sleep for hours and the rain dashed against the windows so violently that it sounded quite alarming. At last the wind grew less and I fell asleep.

Friday December 15 I have had my face bad again and my Bowels still continue in a disordered state tho I continue taking Rhubarb and Magnesia and I feel myself cold and chilly. I did not stir out far but moved about a little in the garden with my Goloshoes on. I and the two young ones spent the evening as we usually do, I reading and they working or chatting.

Saturday December 16 We dined early before two and my daughter and Miss Lewis went off soon after and George to carry their parcels. I am left alone and not in the best of health. They expect me to ride to Bridgewater on Monday but if it rains I shall not go and if it does not I do not think I shall go, such rides in the Winter do not suit me now. After the ladies left me I have been writing a letter to Mr Leighton and find that I can pass my time very well for when I do not read or write I can amuse myself with my own thoughts on various subjects for hours on end.

Wednesday December 20 Dyer is here and I had my cart patched up at the Blacksmith's. I called on Old Sellecks and found them downstairs and at their dinner, Charles eating and hearty and cheerful but the Old Woman sour and grumbling, however they were both glad to see me. I here now a sad story of the Old People that they beat a poor Base Child they have taken into their home almost to death in a most unmerciful manner. She is a child of their son William's taken out of the Workhouse and put to these Old People for protection. I must look to the matter. I sent afterwards George to meet my children who are to come by coach. They came about three and here we all are at last. William looks very well and healthy but Margaret has an inflamation in the eyes. They have both been at the Ball in Bridgewater. I am still uncomfortable in my Bowels and with pains in my face. Alas! how chequered is life with Joy and Sorrow. William sleeps with me now.

Friday December 22 Farmer Dible came in about Landsey's Charity to be paid to the Poor and Farmer Landsey paid down the money and I have been detained all the morning about it and am sick of the business. I do not much approve of the Commotions in London among the Livery, headed by that Democratic Rascal Waithman.

Saturday December 23 The Poor of the Parish came in all the morning and I gave away three bushells of wheat. Wheat is very dear at fifteen shillings pr bushell. I sent George on a Message to Mr Mathew today, he and his family are to come to us on Thursday next.

Monday December 25. Christmas Day We had prayers and a Sermon here in the morning and a Sacrament, about 17 besides myself attended. We used to have more when the Pooles lived here and the Blakes. Washer came to Church with four or five of his children in a very decent manner. He is a Butcher and always called here before he went to Market and sold excellent meat, but my wife it seems bought some of a Butcher that called once and this gave offence and he now does not call and of course we do not buy of him. This makes a coolness which I am sorry for but as I always pay ready money for my meat I cannot give up my Independence to him or anyone. I had twelve people to dine in the kitchen, Labourers and dependents. Went to Dodington where something of a disturbance happened. Before I begun Prayers people were very loud in the Porch and Churchyard. I sent someone to them to order silence, then I sent to order them into Church and after I begun Prayers I was quite interrupted. I then sent out to take their names. Old Hodder spoke and was going out then they ran away, but I have got their names. Two were servants of Mr Farthing. I spoke after Church and am determined to make them sensible of their impudence. Came home and dined by myself. The Clerk of Dodington came and made a hearty dinner and all went home very well satisfied. The Singers were up early this morning to serenade us with Musick and a Christmas Carol at 3 o'clock in the morning.

Friday December 29 We are to dine at Asholt with Mr Brice on a haunch of Venison, wild venison hunted down. We had no company to meet us tho Mr Rich was expected. We spent on the whole a rather agreable day, Mr Brice is better in a tete a tete than in mixed company when he Rhotomon-tades and Brags most Egragiously. The venison was very tender indeed but had no fat, however I made a hearty dinner of it. Played a rubber or two of whist and all slept at Mr Brice's.

Saturday December 30   Mr Brice was up early to look after his lambs for he
is a considerable Farmer and has a charming and extensive Glebe. About ten
we moved off tho much pressed to stay for dinner. I met the Botany Bay*
man who lived at the Workhouse. He has had another child by his Sister in
Law and in shoart they have lived together and the husband is in Botany
Bay. He asked me about marrying her but I said that she ran a risk if the
Husband should come home, besides she was by law his sister. But he said
such do marry and that it could not in the Sight of God be worse than it is
now. I was staggard but replied that I begged he would not ask me any
questions on that head as I could not consent to anything or advise anything
but what the Law directs. I would not marry him nor have anything to do
with him. He says it is his wish to live soberly and honestly and maintain
his family. I replied that it was what I could wish to do. He walked with me
and wished to know whether it was more sinful in the Eye of God than
living in the manner he did with her. I answered that he knew what the Law
was and that I could say no more. I asked him whether he had any sense of
Religion. He said he had and knew there was another World. In short he
spoke sensibly. It was a difficult case to determine but certainly marriage of
any kind is some sanction rather than to live together as they do without
any sanction in a Moral Sense. After this the day ended as Saturdays usually
do.

Sunday December 31   The last day of the year. I administered the Sacrament
at Dodington to only one person beside the Clerk and myself.

The Year 1810

Monday January 1   The Old Year was rung out and the New Year rang in tolerably early this morning. I begin to feel the approach of Age. I have felt myself more feeble and weak than I used to be and less exuberant in Spirits. My wife has been absent now in Devonshire for these twelve weeks past and I pray God she may return sound and well. My children are both with me, William in excellent health and Spirits but Margaret has had for some time an inflammation in her eyes.

Tuesday January 2   William and I moved off under our umbrellas to Stowgurcy to see Mr Davis and we dined there and took a bed. Mr Dawes and Mr Coombs a Restectable Gentleman Farmer gave us meeting. Mr Dawes the Curate, has a very uncouth manner with him and a good deal of the Westmorland Brogue. A tall raw-boned young man much pitted with the small pox, which is uncommon in these times, strait strong black hair with strong features and a sallow complexion. They staid supper and we had singing and William gave us a droll song which pleased everyone and I think he has some Humour. We made it late when Mr Dawes and Mr Coombs left us and William and I went to bed.

Thursday January 4   After breakfast I mounted my horse and with William behind rode to meet my wife who is expected this day from Devonshire. Just on the extremity of the Parish we met the Chaise coming up the hill near Asholt. My wife looks quite well and fat. She had Nurse Wychery in the chaise and William got in and we all got safe to Overstowey. After Nurse Wycherly had refreshed herself the Chaise returned to Taunton and then on to Devon. My wife is really better and her leg well and I pray God there may be no return of the complaint. William went out for an hour or two bird baiting and brought in a few sparrows but Frost and Dyer and others swilled themselves with cyder. Buonaparte is going to declare himself Emperor of the West and has divorced his Empress Josephine without asking the Consent of the Pope or anyone. Oh God how long is this wicked man to flourish and succeed in his enterprizes.

Thursday January 11 I am poorly in my Bowels and have been so, more or less, for some weeks past. I cannot think what the Reason of it is. My daughter has taken some Physick and is better considerably in her eyes. William amuses himself very much in drawing but I must not have him neglect the important matter of Greek and Latin. Sad rainy weather, everywhere full of water.

Tuesday January 16 My wife's leg goes on charmingly. After breakfast we walked towards Esther's. She went in but I went on, took a turn by Ely Green and came through the fields to Old Charles Selleck's where I found my wife. She had been giving a lecture to the Old Folks about a base child they had taken from the Workhouse of their son William, to work for them and wait on them and it is said they use her cruelly. I came in and found my wife by the fire with Old Becky who seems surprisingly recovered, she is 75 years of age. At the door we met Old Charles to, he is 80 but seems hearty. They denied beating the girl with a stick except once or twice. My wife and I after this walked home together. Received this day my Dividends from the Funds from Mr Wm Moore of the Commons.

Wednesday January 17 My wife continues well in her leg but I am not quite so well in my bowels, yet after breakfast I walked to Stowey. We dined on goose. Dyer brought a letter from Stowey from Mrs Dodwell containing the other half of a forty pound note from the Funds.

Thursday January 18 I went to Mr James Rich and changed my forty pound Bank Note into small ones. Sent a letter to Mrs Dodwell with two Bills of Ten Pounds each to pay the Charter House Bill and matters due to her relating to William.

Monday January 22 Farmer Landsey is somewhat better I think, yet still poorly. His blister did not rise and Bennet has sent him several Boluses. I went to Stowey and paid the Sadler half a crown for mending a horse collar and conjuror Coles three pence for mending a gold sleeve button. Returned to dine with my wife on a fine woodcock which we have not eat often this year as they are very scarce. Called at Paddocks and had letters to the amount of three shillings.

Saturday January 27 Called on Farmer Landsey, he seems much better. Dr Dunning said he has injured his constitution by drinking and soaking but he may be got round again if he will but take care afterwards. Finished my letter to Mr Northey, Canon of Windsor.

Sunday January 28 The most foggy, frosty dark morning I ever knew. Walked to Dodington and with difficulty made up a Congregation. I did not see my friend John Mogg which I lamented as his red nose might have warmed the Church. A full Church in the afternoon, Hugh Hill was buried and we had a Christening and a Churching. When I walked out to read the Burial Service I had a woolen network around my throat and an umbrella over my head. After this I dined and was glad to find myself before a good fire.

Thursday February 1 This day tolerable so we sent off my wife to Mr Mathew to Kilve where we are to dine and when he returned I rode there before Margaret and George walked to take back the horse. Mr John Poole and his sister Susan passed us in their Gig. We found Mr Mathew very placid and well as usual and there was Mr Harford and his two sons brought to remain under Mr Mathew's tutorage but none of the other young Gentlemen were come. Mr Harford a very generous man and overloads Mr Mathew with presents, being a man of very ample Fortune. Indeed so are all the persons who have their sons at Mr Mathew's for they pay a hundred and fifty pounds pr Ann each. Mr Mathew has been a day or two at Mr Tynt's who made a present to his son of an excellent Silver Watch worth eight guineas and young Heckwych and Phillips always bring presents with them so that Mr Mathew must make things answer very well. We had a very pleasant day here and we all had beds. After supper I gave 'em some Welsh Penillion and Mr Harford copied some things from my mouth for he is very curious and has a choice collection of many things. He took the etymology of Down Heigh Derry Down from the Welsh Druidical Chorus of Hai Down yr Derri Dano – Ho Come under the Oaken Trees.

Saturday February 3 This morning not very promising but it did get tolerable towards eleven when George came with the horses. My wife would not venture being afraid of the wet but Margaret mounted the pillion behind George and I jogged on before on Farmer Landsey's poney. But first I took leave of Mr Harford whom I found very busy with his two sons skinning a polecat. I wished them good morning but hoped they would excuse my shaking hands with them.

Sunday February 4 The day so pleasant and mild that I resolved to send George on a Sunday to bring home my wife who is very fearful of catching a cold on account of the Medicines applied to her leg and a fine day is a very uncertain thing at this season. So after we had gone to Church he set off and got to Kilve just as my wife came from Church.

Thursday February 8 Mr Davis staid with us and so we both mounted our horses and rode to Spaxton to see Mr Yorke. We found Mr Yorke at home and Mrs Yorke and Mrs Coombs a sister of Mrs Yorke. They prevailed on us to stay dinner and by and by Mr Brice the Rector of Asholt came and he stayed dinner too. He was very great and mighty, hand in glove with Mr Luttrel and Mr Barnard. Just now acting in the Commission of the Peace, he knows all law matters better than anyone, scarce anything to be done without him. After drinking a glass or two after dinner Mr Davis and I started again. Mr Yorke seemed pleased to see us, called it a friendly visit. He is going to farm more than he used to do and is about to sell his Living. They ask ten thousand pounds for it, for it is a very good Living. He has besides the Living of Fiddington. A good kind of man but a terrible stick in the Pulpit.

Saturday February 10   After breakfast I called on Farmer Landsey. He still complains of his head and calls it a cold, I think it is something worse. I found Mr James Rich with a servant boy beating about the mole hills. He and I had a little talk together. His was a very curious figure for a man of his Fortune. His beard an inch long, his breeches shining with grease and his coat not worth five shillings. He is very jealous and suspicious of the designs and circumstances of everyone. He shakes his head when he talks of anyone's expenditures but as to women ! He is an old batchelor and has not a very good opinion of them for, says he, I never knew one that could work or would work, for that is his idea of Excellence. After this I rode up the Hill and the prospects were very fine, the objects very distinct and a kind of light mist gave a softness to the Atmosphere as made things very pleasing.

Monday February 12   Dyer came here but he was soon called off to an important wedding. About eleven the company came in state, two by two, dressd very respectably for farmers. First Mr Batchelor and the Bride's Maid Miss White, then Mr Shepherd and Miss Moore the Bridegroom and Bride. Edward Morle the married brother and two of the sisters and another brother and so to Church we went and finished the Business and then we had them all to my house and gave them a Glass of Wine a piece and entered them in the Register and so off they all went well pleased. There is a Grand Dinner at Farmer Morle's where there will be no less than thirty people to dine, great doings for Overstowey. What surprised me much was their prevailing on Farmer Landsey to go with them who will do himself no good there. We have had ringing of Bells all day. After this I walked to Stowey and ordered a large cake to celebrate William's Birthday tomorrow and I endeavoured to purchase an umbrella but they were too small for me.

Thursday February 15   We were surprised this morning by seeing the snow very deep, indeed I never remember so great a fall in one night. My very handsome Arbutus tree in front of the door is splintered to pieces. Dyer says the apple trees at his father's are very much injured. They have been shaking the trees and making paths all this morning.

Saturday February 17   A worthless girl in the Poorhouse is in a sad state, she has begun to be in Labour but when it will end is a very melancholy consideration. She was brought home to the Parish by an Order with every kind of disease about her. The child they say is already dead. She at times suffers a great deal and has neither comfort nor a word of pity from any one around, but indeed Medical Assistance she has. Alas what a state is this for a Human Creature without any ease while she continues here and what prospects with regard to futurity.

Sunday February 18   The Sexton had some trouble to clear a passage to the Church. While I was at breakfast this day the sad young woman whom I spoke of the day before was brought to bed of a fine girl to the astonishment of everyone, for it was supposed the child was dead. It was brought to me to be Baptised and so I left breakfast and went to the Kitchen and poured water on its face and baptised the child, but the mother had the Itch and many other bad disorders that I did not care to handle it much. I ventured to walk to Dodington, I was very fearful as the snow is penetrating and beginning to thaw. However off I went and George like Sancho behind me. Where the path was beaten we did very well but on Dodington Common the snow got between my Goloshoes and Boot which gave me a cold feel. The Clerk had but just made a passage into the Church and several limbs of the large yew tree I perceived were splintered off. I scarce had a Congregation and those that came followed me from the Castle of Comfort. I read the Service, preached and read the Proclamation for a Fast and then moved homeward again with Sancho George behind. I found myself much fatigued having a greatcoat, boot and Goloshoes to drag through the snow. When I got home I was heartily glad to find a good fire and good dinner and down I sat endeavouring to recover myself from my fatigue which to a man almost 64 was no small business.

Saturday February 24   This morning very mild and the snow has gone off very fast. After breakfast we sent off George to buy a pig of Mrs Poole and bring him home in a cart. I moved about little this day the ground being so rotten after the snow. George did not return so soon as we expected but brought us at last a very fine pig, black and white of the Chinese kind. But poor thing, the pig that we have here already falls upon him and beats him unmercifully, for George has fatted this pig so as to make him very proud and insolent and does not care that another Pig should come into his territories and partake of his good cheer. This is the case with other Creatures, as they grow fat they grow insolent. Nothing material after this.

Sunday February 25   As I was going into Dodington Church I met my old friend John Mogg with his face and nose redder than ever. How are you Mr Mogg? Bless you Sir, I could not see you my eyes are cruel bad, I fancy Sir it must be old age. How old are you? 79 Sir. We must expect something or other to fail us at that time. Ay sure, very true Sir. John would have been even better had he not sipped some good ale and adorned his face and forehead with a few precious Carbuncles etc. The tiling in the roof of the Chancel was blown off and let in the air most uncomfortably to the back of my head. The Churchwarden careth for none of these things so he must be presented. We had the Church very full at Overstowey. I had a Christening after Church and a Churching and after that I buried the little child from the Workhouse and never did I perform the Service with greater difficulty before. I posted myself under the Tower and had an umbrella close to my head and Dyer on one side and George on the other hand yet for all this the wind almost blew the umbrella out of their hands and the Book out of my hands. No one could stand by the grave and poor Betty Price could not stand at all and I called out to someone to assist to carry her off. However I got through the Service at last and was glad to get home to a good dinner and good fire.

Monday February 26   After this I got to Stowgurcy and found Mr Davis at home and he prevailed on me to eat a bit of dinner with him on condition that he would eat with me on the First of March, being St David's Day, we being both Welshmen and each is to have a tremendous leek in his hat. They are at Stowgurcy taking down the Priory House and well is it that they are so doing for a little longer continuance would have brought it on the head of someone or other. It is a pity there are not proper persons under Government to inspect Publick Buildings before they get too ruinous. A Tower tumbled lately in Liverpool and killed forty people. The Parishioners will always push off things of this nature to the next generation and thus are neglected from time till they tumble down.

Wednesday February 28   This is the General Fast Day for success in the tremendous struggle we are engaged in with Buonaparte. Poor mouse Weymouth came here to me and begged that I would permit the thatcher to go on with his work today as his house is quite open and if it rained the poor Sexton might be drowned in his bed. I consented provided that he came to Church and did not work while the Service was performing. Made a poor dinner on Eggs, yet very well for a Fast Day.

Thursday March 1   This is St David's Day, the Tutelary Saint of Wales and a very fine day it is. I put a Leek in my hat after breakfast and rode to meet Mr Davis who is to dine with me, he is a Welshman from Carmarthenshire. I rode on to Stowgurcy when at last I saw Mr Davis just mounting his horse so we returned together, found Mr Coombs and Mr Dawes borrowed his horse and soon joined us and we all rode to Stowey. Mr Dawes was taken rather as Guard to Mr Davis who is grown old and feeble than as a

Welshman for he is from West Morland, adjoining Cumberland, which was the Country of Lowarchthen and the Land of the Cimbri. Dyer is here today and dined here on account of St David and they all wear Leeks. We had a good dinner and cakes and wine etc. We wished Mr Davis to take a bed here but Mr Dawes being with him to take care of him he chose to go.

Wednesday March 7 This is Ash Wednesday and I have ordered Prayers but am doubtful whether any will come. A very few did come at last after much tolling, the two Mr Richs and Betty Pierce from the Workhouse and Joanny Knight and Charles Selleck and two children which with my own family made up the Congregation. In country Villages there is no keeping up the Service of Weekly Days, they cannot leave their respective Labours. Indeed they have dropped these Prayers entirely at Stowey which is a Market Town, I remember it otherwise tho they could never assemble above two or three people to attend. I think the fault lies in the People and not in the Clergy for dropping the weekly Services and Saints Days for to read at bare walls must be tiresome at all times.

Friday March 9 I sent for Mr Rich's horse to make our visit to St Albyn. It grew brighter and brighter as we went on and got safe to Alfoxton. We found the young Married Couple at Home in a most superb room, lately built and furnished. The young lady is tall thin and handsome, has good eyes and light pretty hair. The nose I do not approve of quite so well. Miss Gravener was there and looked, as I told her, better than I ever saw her. There is something very formal in young St Albyn and tho he does not seem to want sense yet one cannot get much out of him. In short I never could find out what he was particularly fond of except money. His wife brings him a large Fortune, but she is young and did not understand yet much of doing the Hostess, the Honours of the House. We, after staying the greater part of an hour mounted our horses and got home in very good time for dinner at four o'clock. I saw Farmer Landsey today, he is very poorly and talks of making his Will. I encouraged him to do it but to remember Justice in the Distribution of his effects.

Tuesday March 13 The masons are here and a terrible bustle it is. Verrier has taken possession of the Parlour and is busy in preparing for the stone to be laid and George is gone with the cart for it. My wife and I had fire and breakfasted in a bedchamber upstairs, we live there now leaving the Myrmidon Masons to range the lower house at large. My wife and I set out to Stowey but while we were ascending the hill we saw a very handsome carriage coming to meet us. It was Mr and Mrs St Albyn returning from their Bridal Visit. We were in a terrible Dishabille and apologised much for the Pickle we were in and were in hopes it would have been over before they honoured us with a visit. However they were shown into the

unoccupied parlour and in a short time after they left us. Miss Gravener, Mr
St Albyn's sister was with them. He took the name St Albyn with the
estate.

Thursday March 15   There is a Fair at Bridgwater today but poor Farmer
Landsey could not go, still poorly. Tucker from the Globe came to me
yesterday to buy my large cow for fattening but we could not agree. Some
of the Idle, Lazy Masons came to work but said they could not stand, yet
Verrier the Master having housework staid with us all day, and the thatcher
finished. (God be Praised.) These are people we must submit to have about
us at times but they are expensive idle and very troublesome. Met a man
making a fence out of Bullock's horns and he told me it was very strong and
excellent fence against sheep.

Sunday March 18   We were awakened about two o'clock this morning by
Phebe informing us that Farmer Landsey was dead and she was called to see
him. This shocked us much tho we did not think he would recover yet
certainly we did not expect his death so soon. He went off very easily
without a sigh or groan. I fear he shortened his days by soaking Gin and fat
ale. There was not much harm in him and some good, he rather laboured
after wealth too much but attended Church constantly.

Tuesday March 20   Mr Rich and I after breakfast took an account of Farmer
Landsey's cash and Securities in the house with the Executors or Administrators. We found two hundred and forty guineas in gold there besides Bills
and Securities to the amount of £1800 or thereabouts. Tis strange the man
should keep so much money in the house. John Landsey and Charles
Selleck carried all to Ruscomb Poole and they lodged it all or nearly in
Woodlands Bank. I fear there will be some quarrels among the brothers and
sisters about the property. Farmer Landsey went to Bridgewater last
Monday Sevennight to make his Will and a rough draft was left in the hands
of Mr Ruscomb Poole but it was never executed. It was never the intention
of the Farmer to make his sisters equal to his brother in the distribution of
his property which will be the case now.

Saturday March 24   Dry but very cold. George and I have been busy in the
garden. Farmer Landsey is to be buried today. About four o'clock I walked
down to Farmer Landsey's and there I found a large company, the two
Riches, two Starkeys, a Mr Lee and various others. The Funeral was rather
magnificent, Hatbands in abundance, and too great a profusion of wine and
Mr Rich's Betty dotting and pushing the wine to everyone and chattering. I
should not wonder if she had taken a little too much herself. Our Phebe was
there but did not make herself quite so ridiculous. Poor Farmer Landsey
was committed to the ground with great solemnity and decency and there

ends his History. He had been at pains to heep up some money but he died at last without a Will and the distribution of his property was very different from what was intended by him. He was an odd man but not a bad man tho he had one serious vice – Drinking, which brought him to his grave. May God grant Rest to his Soul.

Tuesday March 27
Our ringers were ordered to ring the Bells for Mr Crosse who has taken the Park Cottage (as they call it) and brought his wife home, a niece of Jones the landlord of the Inn at Minehead., a sad connection for a young man of family and fortune. His sister married a servantman in the family, Mr Porter, and they were both with him and certainly countenanced the whole business and the aunt from Minehead saw the dinner well dressed and a pretty society of them sat down to it alas ! He is a young man of some abilities but his head is cracked. The sister has a very good estate which she bestows on this manservant, a pretty hotch potch indeed. George came home by two with very good coal.

Friday March 30 My horse sent to be shod as he is tomorrow to carry my daughter to Bridgewater to set off for London on Monday with Miss Symes. All this day Margaret is busy packing up. We hear nothing of the new married couple in Park Cottage.

Saturday March 31 About eleven o'clock Margaret mounted behind George to Bridgewater. She is to stay some time in London. William at the Charter House will be delighted to see her and she brings him good news for I received a letter this morning informing me that Dr Hall the Dean of Christchurch, Oxford, will with pleasure appoint him to be a Student of his College if he brings a good character for Learning and Morals from the Charterhouse about four years hence. So with the Exhibition from Charter House and his Studentship of Christchurch with all the Patronage of these Foundations before him I think if he lives and behaves well he stands a good chance to rise in the world whether I live to assist him or not. God be Praised. Had a letter from my Brother in Law Henry Dodwell with interest money from the Maidenhead Bridge.

Sunday April 1 Prayers here in the morning and Mr and Mrs Porter, Mr Crosse's sister and brother in law made their appearance at Church but no Mr Crosse nor his new Bride. They behaved well at Church and tho the lady has so very good a fortune and was a Gentlewoman yet he who was but a servant appeared full as well as she did. The singers in the Gallery showd off today for Mr Porter, they say, is a famous man at the Baseviol. Rode to Dodington, did not preach but read the Swearing Act.

Monday A;ril 2   Dyer is gone to cut wood on Quantock and George is to follow about twelve o'clock. Dyer cut half a hundred of the finest wood I ever saw and George brought it home in the cart. It was a great load for one horse and they first had to carry it on their backs and afterwards the horse drew as far as the road in two divisions and then it was put together and carried home, a great undertaking indeed for men and horse. By this means I get the wood very cheap, not above three shillings pr hundred and it is worth a guinea a hundred and moreover it exercises my right on Quantock. My wife and I walked to Stowey, stopped some time at the Sealey's but he is a bragging pompous man. I do not much like him.

Wednesday April 4   There has been a great hubbub at the late Farmer Landsey's house, the husband of one of the sisters is come down with her and made a great hubbub. He has entered the house and lives there and tapped the beer and swears and curses and threatens in such a manner as alarms everyone and that mean fellow Charles Selleck and his drunken wife and the drunken and lying Widow Crook, another sister, all fall upon poor John Landsey and they had nearly come to blows. This is sad work and I think Mr Ruscomb Poole is to blame in not being more explicit in the business as something should be done without delay as one cannot tell what may be the consequences. I rode to Stogurcy to ask Mr Davis to come to dine with me but he is to dine with Mrs Silk. He formerly boarded with Mr Silk when he first came from Wales. Silk is a vulgar, purseproud man and very cunning, married his maidservant who was with child by him before he married her and this was the lady dining with Mr Davis.

Saturday April 7   This morning not very pleasant. Farmer Landsey's affairs are still in an unsettled state. The Judges have been at Taunton all this week. It is reported that the lad who murdered the woman who took up my boy at Pikeley is condemned to be hanged, which I am glad of and I walked to Mr Rich for information. On my return I met Mr Sweeten of Putsham who said that he is just come from Taunton and that the boy was to be hanged on Monday next and it is said that he made a confession of it to Mr Acland. So much the better as this satisfies everyone and it would have been a sad thing to have let this Villain loose on the Publick, and some people talked of the husband having murdered his wife, but this was without the least foundation and probably came from the boy's friends originally.

Sunday April 8   I went to Dodington, very few at Church as there is an innoculation for the Small Pox which shuts up Mr Farthing and one or two families more. But now the Cow Pox is so much approved of and so much safer I do not think it right in Mr Bennet recommending innoculations for the Small Pox which is infectious and if one family begins it obliges others to adopt the same measures, whether they approve of it or not.

Tuesday April 10   We have had full confirmation from persons present that the boy who murdered Stiling was hanged. They say he gave some information where some of the things stolen from the house were hid. He charged persons with being accomplices but made nothing of it and it apeared more Malice and Revenge than any sign of Repentence or wish to satisfy the Publick. Mr Score called this morning and took Taxes from me to the amount of nine pounds and more. Income Tax for one Tithing was included in this, thus I have paid the Income Tax of three years in the space of one year. There has been assuredly something very wrong in the management of this business.

Sunday April 15   The Clerk of Dodington was, I fear, rather tipsy this afternoon for he was asleep when I expected him to say —Amen. I stopped and looked round for some time till some one jogged him. Poor miserable wretch with a large family and what he earns he drinks. After this all went on as usual on a Sunday.

Monday April 23 (Easter)   I had offered George a Holiday today which he declined at first but towards Dusk he surprised me with asking to go to Dodington to see Wrestling and shooting at a mark. I said that he might go but observed that he must be back by nine and I wondered that he had not taken more time for his pastimes when I had offered him. He returned very well and in good time.

Tuesday April 24   We are very busy preparing a dinner as we are to have Mr and Mrs St Albyn and others to dine here. About four they came Mr and Mrs St Albyn in their Chariot and two servants in great pomp and state. Mr and Mrs Allen and Mr and Mrs Poole of Shurton in their Domestic with a thumping great servant too so that the house was filled with menservants. We had a good and agreable Party and we talked, drank tea and chatted till dusk when they all passed off as there was no moon unfortunately. They had hard work making St Albyn's horses move, they danced about all the time on the same spot. I should not relish such horses.

Wednesday April 25   This is my Tithe Day and accordingly they assembled to dinner. Mr Thos Poole came not knowing the day, thinking it was to be Friday on which day he was engaged to another place, but when he found it was to be this day, being St Mark's he staid to dinner. Mr Buller did not dine with us, he too having made a mistake. We were all very merry, aspecially the Farmers when the strong beer began to warm them a little.

Farmer Dibble who seems a very poor Honey at other times now began to open his mouth and oratorise most wonderfully and poor Old Charles Selleck, who seems sunk very much since last year, at last began to display his usual keenness and was wonderfully animated. He is now 82 years of age. Farmer Stone was very deaf, heavy and dull tho when he had his hearing was as shrewd as any of them. William Hill talked a little at last with his scabby nose, but he has been in disgrace for some time past about a Bastard* Child by his girl Apprentice so I could not notice him much. Rich of Pepperil has something mild and modest in his character. Mr Rich and Tom Poole stuck to the Brandy and water and they staid tea after the rest were gone. I was not quite in the High Spirits I am generally in, having an unpleasant headache with a rash coming out over me. They all left us in good order and Spirits and without Drunkenness.

Saturday April 28   Farmer White of Staplegrove called early to inform me that his sister was to be married today if I would perform the Duties. So here they all came and I got myself ready to go to Church. Poor Miss White seems much distressed and she is to part from her mother and a very moving scene they tell me it was. A genteel young woman, Miss Staple accompanied her, and two brothers. So they were married. The husband was a person from Box* near my Living of Monkton Farley, a widower, but full young enough for the woman. We had them in and gave them a glass of wine apiece, then they went off in a Gig to Bridgewater and they go no further than Glastonbury tonight. She would have no ring till she was out of the Parish which was complied with. She is a well behaved young woman and I hope her husband will treat her well. The Executors and Administrators of Farmer Landsey are in a sad state of discontent and animosity owing to this Will which one Party intend to establish and the other to oppose. We have a large Oozle Thrush in the fork of one of the trees sitting on its nest and I can see its head from the steps of my doors and we have had such a bird making the nest annually ever since I came to the Living.

Saturday May 5   Phebe came up from the cellar in a fright and said some wine had been stolen and begged I would go down to see. I found the wooden steps down to the cellar some day or two ago to be loose and Charles Selleck being much engaged of late about Landsey's Will. I employed his son who is now with him and a Deserter from one of His Majesty's Ships. He came here and was the whole day and got out several bottles and carried them off in a bag he brought for the purpose under the pretence of taking away chips. The man was charged with the thing and came over but had little to say for himself, only denying the fact. He was charged with being drunk on the day which he owned, saying little would do it, and that he had some liquor from the Parsonage, the late Farmer

Landsey's. However he was dismissed and he shall never come into this house again. He has the look of a Villain and I am sorry to see the whole family are addicted to stealing and brought up to it.

Monday May 7 After breakfast I mounted my horse and took George with me to the Visitation at Bridgwater leaving my wife in bed poorly. We got in late. There was no Sermon at Church and a very bad dinner at the Inn and badly served. The Archdeacon is old and feeble and hardly fit to go about on such Offices. It rained hard after we sat down and soon after we were obliged to adjourn to another room that the Officers of the Local Militia might dine in ours. I do not relish such maneuvres. The Clergy as a body of people are surely the most respectable and ought not to be turned out of their rooms backward and forward to serve the conveniency of any other body of men whatsoever. But the Times, the Times are sad and very little veneration is held for Religion or the Ministry of it at this day. Starky, tho a young man, seems quite worn out with gout already. Kinglake the Archdeacon's Registrar seems a sensible gentleman like man. Poor Mr Yorke would sit by himself on the other side of the table notwithstanding everyones attempt to remove him. Mr Allen and I drank tea at Mr Sealey's and then we had two Post Chaises to carry us home. George had two horses to lead which was a miserable business and we were home before him.

Wednesday May 9 This is the day of our Book Society dinner and sale of our books. I walked down to Mr Allen, sat some time and then came Mr Brice. From thence we went to the Globe and members dropped in one by one. We had a good dinner and good wine and the sale of books went on very well. Mr Henry Poole of Shurton withdrew his name and Mr Allen of Stowey was elected a new member. Mr Bennet was proposed but he had but two votes. Neither Mr Acland nor Mr Henry Poole was there, the first had just buried a son. Mr Sealey was not as pompous as he used to be, Mr Davis seemed very infirm. I had a bed ready for him at our house but he said he must go home and when I said he ought not to go be himself he was most offended. Orator Tom Poole and his shadow Mr Ward launched forth in admiration of the Decimal Yard of Mr Crosse. Now Mr Mathew is a man of real Mathematical Knowledge and abilities. They endeavoured to explain things, Mathew asked some question as to this or that, they explained again, Mathew stared, they explained again til Mathew at last spoke in a louder tone – Gentlemen, I do not understand you. I do not know what you are about. In the meantime I was drinking my tea and smiling and enjoying the dialogue to a great degree. At last we seperated and Mr Brice and I rode homeward together.

Friday May 11 The morning cold and sharp and we have a fire still in the Parlour. All the parties seem ready to come into my proposal about Farmer Landsey's Will except Chamberlayne and he is haughty imperious and overbearing as if everything belonged to him alone tho he only acts in Right of his Wife. He had not a shirt to his back when he came down and now he carries himself so pompously as if he could be the First Man in the Kingdom, so true is the old Adage – Set a beggar on Horseback and he will ride to the Devil. His own wife thro whom he claims is for acceding to the brother's proposal and yet they permit this man before their faces to domineer in their brother's house and make use of the property. I had intended to ride out this day but I was obliged to have the horse shod. John Landsey is come here from Taunton where he has been today and there is sad work at the Parsonage House where his brother lived. All the brothers and sisters are agreed yet this Rascal Chamberlayne will come to no agreement and will run the risk of losing all by his perverseness.

Tuesday May 15   The second day of the sale of Farmer Landsey's Stock and Goods. Baste the worst Auctioneer ever known. They had not finished and he had intended to go on for another day but they prevailed on him at last to go on during the night when they finished.

Friday May 18   We are preparing to go to Enmore to a Christening of Mrs Anstis's child from Shropshire. We had a pleasant ride and the day turned out well. To the Church we went, Mr Ruscomb Poole carried me in his Gig Mrs Anstis was there and her husband but Mr John Poole and his brother stood Godfathers and Mrs Anstis Godmother, (Mrs Wm Anstis) He was only received into the Church for he had been privately baptised at Madeley in Shropshire. We had a large company at dinner, all of one family except myself and my wife. We had a very handsome dinner and we spent a very agreeable day there. Mr Robert Anstis the Custom House Officer is a very intelligent and superior man. After tea we had a game of Commerce and some of the company left us. My wife and I slept there.

Sunday May 20   This is my Birthday and a fine morning tho cold. This day I compleat my 64th year and am at this time on the whole very well and much better than I have been heretofore for the last has been a trying year. Yet it is an awful period of my life and I must look down the descent of the Hill towards the Grave which closes all our earthly views. No. that shall not close my view for I must look even beyond that to much brighter scenes and I trust I can look that way with some degree of Hope and Comfort through a Crucified Saviour. O God do Thou enable me to go on and improve and persevere in that Hope which Thou hast given me till it be realised in actual enjoyment. The Church was very full and good Singing. Mr and Mrs Porter were at Church and I bowed to them and I think I spoke to Mrs Porter. But neither Mr Cross nor his wife have been to Church since they were married, a strange couple indeed. He, I fear, has no Religion for he has not been at Church since he took the house he is in. I shall not call upon unless he comes to Church. At Dodington a wind came from behind me from the crevices of the tiling which rendered it very unpleasant to me. A letter from Margaret and William this morning, they are both well and William is to go into the Shell but he speaks a good deal of Fagging from the Upper Boys, it being the last year they are to be fagged in for the next Form (the Fourth) they neither Fag or are fagged. William hopes Dr Raynes will find out as it prevents their doing their Exercises.

Tuesday May 29   The Bells rang merrily in the morning being the 29 May and I have an Oaken Bow before my house. I was to have gone down to Stowey and have walked in the Procession for it is their Club Meeting. Mr Tom Poole wrote a note to me but I excused myself for the noise of the dinner is intolerable. Dyer was not here today for he attended the Club with his Musick.

Thursday May 31   I have been writing a good deal this day, sent off an appointment to the Curacy of Monkton Farley to a Mr Hickes. The Rascally Masons never came this day but have left me in the lurch and tomorrow they must not come as we are to brew. I walked down to Stowey, called on Verrier but he was not at home. Walked down the town, saw the Masons at work at Mr Tom Poole's, enquired for Verrier. He was not there they said, I believe he was but kept out of sight. I then said I would send to another person to finish the work if he did not come Saturday Morning.

Tuesday June 5   I mounted my horse after breakfast and rode forth to Mrs White about ducks which we want for Thursday. They are very dear 4 shillings a couple, when I first came to this Living they were, full grown, only 14 pence a couple. Meat from three pence to fourpence a pound, now it is from eightpence to nine pence. Corn at 6 or 7 shillings a bushell, now from 16 to 17 shillings. Yet with all this alteration to the state of things men live more luxuriously than ever tho we hear complaints of the times from every quarter. Mr Wyndham is still most dangerously ill. Alas this will be a great loss to the Publick if he dies.

Thursday June 7   Mr Tom Poole informed me that Mr Wyndham had died on Monday last about one o'clock. This indeed was bad news to me and a great loss to the Publick, a great Statesman of first rate capabilities and incorruptable integrity, an excellent man at Bottom and a good Christian. He died as great as he lived for he submitted to a most painful surgical operation with a fortitude that few can boast of. First he received the Sacrament at the Charter House Chapel, settled his Will and domestic affairs and sat down to the Operation with an undaunted resolution, his hands were not bound. He uttered not so much as a groan but it was too much for him and a putrid fever came on and it carried him off. He was a good friend to me in appointing William to the Charter House. God Rest his Soul. He brought on his indisposition by an over exertion at a fire at Lord North's. A schinous swelling formed in the loins. There is a great Character of him in some of the Papers but the Rascally Paper I take in now did not do him Justice tho it spoke highly of him which it could not avoid doing.

Friday June 8 I mounted my horse to ride to Plainsfield to speak to young Morle, the Churchwarden, about cleaning our Brazen Chandelier as Coles of Stowey has disappointed them. He is as keen to have the Chandelier cleaned while they are whitewashing the Church as I am and will send immediately to Stowgurcy for another man. I have been hastening them all this day to clean and finish the Church. Mrs Ware, Old Savage Ware's wife, came here about burying her child on Sunday next. She has kept the child already above a week. This very sultry weather I told her that I insisted on bringing the child immediately. She answered she would bring it tomorrow. I told her she had no right to keep the child so long, to keep the dead to destroy the Living. John Landsey called on me and tells me that Mr Beadon and Mr Ruscomb Poole and Mr Symes are to meet at Stowey on Tuesday next and settle the dispute about Farmer Landsey's Will.

Tuesday June 12 I called on Mr Ruscomb Poole in Bridgewater and paid him £39 15 0 being the remainder of my Law Bill for my Rights on Quantock. Tho I gained my cause and the Adversary paid Costs yet I am a considerable loser, yet what I lost in pocket I gained in Credit and Reputation. The Object was trifling to me but it will be of moment to those that come after me. The Polden Hills Militia were arranged in Castle Street and the Military Bands were playing.

Thursday June 14 Drank tea at Mr Sealey's, Rector of Dodington. He is a very peculiar old man, twisting and bending himself, so argumentative and particular but on the whole a well meaning man. His wife is a good deal younger than himself but deaf. Mr and Mrs Sealey the brother took me to see his Brick Kilns and garden. He deals large in various ways, has many ships and is with his two sons in the Banking Way. Vain and Pompous and full of Money. He has many houses on the Brick Grounds and a whole company of people there, seemingly in a comfortable way. In the evening it was pleasant to walk up and down Castle Street.

Sunday June 17 After dinner a very full Congregation. Rich of Pepperil his wife and the whole family were there, his daughter Avis just married was there with her husband too, a good looking man and in good circumstances. A Butcher, kills two or three bullocks a week and lives in a house of his own. I congratulated Rich on the occasion She is a pretty, modest young woman and sharp and keen and will make an excellent wife. It is remarkable that the three Principal Farmers in Plainsfield married off their daughters this year, and married them well and the women are likely to turn out very good wives. Mr Porter was at Church this afternoon but not his wife.

Sunday June 24 Before I went to Church I was called upstairs to see that Savage Rascal Chamberlayne who now occupies the late Farmer Landsey's house. He was hard at work in his shirt and common dress shovelling up a passage for water to run from the well just as the Parishioners were passing by to go to Church and the Bell tolling. When Church was over I called to the Churchwarden, young Simon Morle, and told him to go to Chamberlayne and tell him he was seen at work while the Bell was tolling for Church and inform him that if he was seen again to do so he would be prosecuted according to the Law. The Message was delivered. He answered that he should not ask Mr Holland what he was to do on Sunday. On Mrs Porter remarking what a pretty place mine was my wife asked them in and they walked about and admired the place very much. Mrs Porter said her mother in law used to speak of the place very much, she was to'v been married to Mr Milward* a predecessor of mine but he died before the Match took place. Mr Porter was a kind of Steward to Mr Crosse when the sister cast her eye upon him and is I believe a Relation of the family. They have been for some time at Mr Crosse's the brother who married the Bar Maid at Minehead. But they have not been at Church so I cannot call, a sad degradation of a respectable family.

Thursday June 28 This is a fine day too and I up early having a disagreable business in hand. It was to Summon a Methodistical fellow, Farmer Major, for Tithe of land he purchased in Overstowey Parish and now occupied by his son. The father had it in hand but would pay only what he thought proper for it. He is a Methodistical fellow as well as the son who never comes to my Church and therefore cares not how or in what manner he tricks the Parson out of his Dues. However I made him pay more than he wished to do and the Costs into the bargain tho it is hard to be obliged thus, but there is no dealing with these people without it. Mr Allen was there and Mr Wollen as Justices and behaved very civilly to me. I was asked by Mr Ruscomb Poole to dine with him but was engaged with Mr Wollen. We had a good dinner at Mr Wollen's. We had a Tete au Tete after dinner, he talked a good deal of his complaints and produced many boxes of Pills as good for one thing or other. He is an odd tempered man but a tolerable good Justice, a poor stick at Church and not a very accomodating Parish Priest. Dyer was with me at Bridgewater and a good Evidence.

Saturday June 30 This too is a very warm fine day. People are busy at their hay which is very scanty everywhere and speculators are even now ready to give from seven to ten pounds a tun for it. I have however as much as usual which is a good thing. George has been very busy in watering the strawberries and other articles in the garden.

Monday July 2 A sad fracas has taken place between Phebe and George and she informed my wife that she could not live any longer with him and at last she made some very heavy charges against him. At first I was very unwilling to discharge him at this critical time when we expected company and when I was going to take in my Tithe. But when it came out what she charged him with I was Shocked to the Greatest Degree and so was my wife too, and she slept little all night. The Charge was no less than Bestiality which she affirms she detected him some time ago but concealed it because she did not know how to open the affair with me and was afraid to be called on as evidence against him to prove it. Thus it rested this evening.

Tuesday July 3 After breakfast I consulted with my wife about George and it was determined I should turn him off immediately, tho it would at this time be attended with great inconvenience to me but under such a charge as this there is no bearing of the man in the house and it would be inconsistent with my character to bear it as soon as I was informed of it. I therefore sent for William Frost to be a witness of what I was going to do and then I spoke to George before him, first in the Brewhouse. He understood immediately what I alluded to and at first seemed inclined to deny the charge but when I began to enter on the Subject in a serious manner and to ask him whether he believed there was a Hereafter and a Hell or Heaven to go to he began to be touched. I told him that I was deeply sorry to be under the necessity of parting with him and did it very Reluctantly but the offence was of such a Nature that I could not suffer him to stay any longer and desired him to pack up his things and that I allowed him all his clothes except the last best things. So he got himself ready and when I went to him a second time in the kitchen he cried most bitterly and it affected me very much. I then told him I hoped what had passed would sink deep into his heart and that he would fall down on his knees and pray to his God (whom he had grievously offended) that he might repent of his Wickedness. I then called him into the parlour and spoke to him before Mr Frost and over again repeated with what reluctance I parted with him. He seemed then in an agony of tears. The unmoveable countenance of Frost was affected. The Fellow seemed to aquiesce in what I said and I paid him and he left me overwhelmed with tears. It has relieved our minds much now that he is gone but what to do for another to supply his place at this season of the year is what I cannot guess at. An odd thing happened last night – a Rascally very disagreeable man who has an antipathy to my Clerk Dyer and Phebe who I supposed is to be married to him passed late at night but before we were gone to bed and under the window he called them both the most abusive names he could invent and uttered the most obscene language. The man's name is Joe Hill, one of the worst fellows in the Parish. They never mentioned this to me before we were going to bed. Dyer sleeps here now and goes off every morning (after he has done some matters for me) to assist his father for now George is gone I must have someone to assist till I get another man. Well I was determined this Joe Hill should be punished but said no more for the present.

Wednesday July 4   After breakfast I sent off Dyer to Mr Ruscomb Poole for a Summons for this Rascally Joe Hill and he has brought it and I will see whether or not he can be punished. We went this day to dine with Mr Sealey and met there Mr John Sealy and his wife. He is the Rector of Dodington. We had a good dinner and after I had some talk with Mr John Sealy and agreed to give up the Service of Dodington, not at Michaelmas but at Christmas the end of the year for the Service is becoming unpleasant to me, the Church being out of repairs and admitting wind and rain and I have not a house to go to before I go to Church, being obliged to leave my horse at John Mogg's and to walk afterwards a good way. Mr Sealy agreed and said he would write to the Bishop and say that I was ready to give up Dodington to accommodate him in any arrangement he would make as to the Churches.

Monday July 9   I rode over to Kilve to talk with Mr Mathew on some of the occurencies that have happened in my family. I apologised in the first place for not being able to have them at my house this week as I was obliged to discharge my servant immediately. Then we walked in the garden and we had a long conversation, the servant's crime and its horrid nature. He approved of all that I had done yet was in doubt, on account of the effect it might have on Society, whether I should have him go without prosecution. I answered that as soon as I came to the knowledge of the business I discharged him but (wretch as he was) and Horrid as the *Deed* was I felt disinclined to hang him. Well he returned you have got rid of him, perhaps it is as well. I was obliged to act on the spur of the Moment and lamented much I had no friend near me who had the same feelings as myself with whom I could consult. He said it was exactly the same with himself and all the Country Clergymen. The Country Squires, their Neighbours, look upon the Clergy in general with a jealous eye and often times would rather see them disgraced or scandalized rather than setting things right and to remove from them every aspersion disadvantageous to their character. I came home and found a man waiting to offer his services as Servant. He is of the age of forty but looks fifty at least. Has a shrill weak voice, is bloated in the face and seems wonderfully slow and deliberate but does not speak plain yet he lived 18 years in the place he came from. I fear he will not do.

Wednesday July 11   Porter's wife in the Poorhouse is brought to bed this morning and in a short time afterwards the woman who nurses it brought the child to me to have a name, as they term it in these parts. I answered if the child was ill I was ready to give it a Private Baptism but not otherwise for we were forbidden to do so except in cases of necessity. She thought it was not well, did not eat. Let me see the child. A finer child I never saw. If I was to Christen it before it is brought to Church every parent in the Parish would expect the same and Publick Baptism in the Church would come to Nothing. So she was dismissed and I hear no more of the child.

Saturday July 14   Dyer went off early today with the speckled cow to the bull, which we were glad of having missed the time before. My wife and I walked down to Stowey and I had some talk with Mr Sealy the Rector of Dodington. An account this day in the paper of a Fete given by the Austrian Ambassador in Honour of the Marriage between Buonaparte and the Emperor of Austria's Daughter. As soon as they were all seated in State, a flambeau near Buonaparte fell and the fine gauze hangings took fire and confusion and destruction ensued. However Buonaparte and his Empress moved off uninjured. Two lives of Consequence were lost and many very considerably injured and the apartments were burned to the ground. This seems an ominous solemnisation of a Marriage.

Sunday July 15   This is St Swithin's Day, on which if it rains (according to a vulgar notion) tis supposed it will continue to rain for forty days, and the contrary if it prove fair. It did rain early though it is now a fine day. It was reported that George had returned from Bristol. He had returned again for his clothes and went off afterwards. We had at Dodington this morning Mr Farthing and his family and some others at Church. A woman knealed down fast asleep and was so conspicuous at Church while we were standing up that I was obliged to point to her and a man went and patted her and could scarce awaken her. This was done however without much noise or disturbance and by signs and not Words which is the Best Method of Rebuke in Church

Tuesday July 17   Old George Adams called and begged a cup of drink which I gave him and some bread and cheese and he talked much of growing old, he wants but one year of four score and could not work as he used to. My Poor Old Woman is gone, howsumdever she was a good Old Woman, I shant be long after. I say my Prayers and beg God to forgive me all my sins. Sir, do you think I shall ever meet the Old Woman again? Certainly I do, it is my firm belief those who act well will meet again. But Sir, shall we know one another? Undoubtedly, as well as we do now. The Lord Bless you, I should be glad to meet the Old Woman. The old man went off most joyfully. It rained after this in the afternoon, a good deal of hay must be ruined.

Thursday July 19 I expect a new servant to come today on trial. He came, a man about forty. He understands a horse and gardening but not much waiting at table. I hope he is steady. A short necked, broad backed short fellow with a weak voice and bows to the ground at every word. He lives 18 years at the place he was before, has a respectable look but seems nervous and meek spirited. Miss West dined here, full of complaints of the persons where she lodges as usual. Her income is narrow and the people she is with insulting, tis a hard case. Our new man attempted to wait at table, poor fellow he was wonderfully alarmed but we took no notice and it went off well.

Saturday July 21 I walked to Stowey to change a Bank Bill for cash but no cash to be had and I would not take any Country Bills there being a run on the Banks at this time and I would not part with what is good for what is not.

Monday July 23 Dyer went off early with the cart to Bridgwater with bottles and to return with coal. My new Man Thomas went to the Moors with Molly Weymouth to the hay. We shall carry tomorrow if the weather proves fair. This afternoon my wife and I walked in the garden perceived long streaks in the sky which are commonly called Mare's Tails. These prognosticate in general Rain and accordingly the day did alter. the sky seemed to lowr, the wind whistled, the sun went down dimly and I verily thought there would be rain in the night, but it turned out otherwise. My poor wife seems but indifferent, her leg which at one time appeared almost well alters for the worst and swells which makes her very low. Alas this is the Fate of Man. Old Age and Infirmities must come on if we live, and if we do not then we say that we go off in our Prime, before life itself is half enjoyed. I am myself very tolerable but how long I may continue so in this state only God knows, yet I must expect what Human Nature is subject to.

Thursday July 26 Towards tea time while I was looking through the window who should pass by (to our great surprize) but Margaret, just arrived, first from London and last from Salisbury. Soon after a Post Chaise drove up and out came Mrs Dodwell, Mistress Moore and Miss Dodwell and after mutual Congratulations we sat down and enjoyed ourselves.

Tuesday July 31 I walked down to Stowey, spoke to Mr Francis Poole who said he had paid Shitfield for the newspapers. Dyer went off this day with my cart to Taunton to bring here the Ladies Trunks. Lewis Buonaparte, having abdicated the Throne of Holland makes heavy complaints about his brother Napoleon. No Dyer from Taunton with the Trunks which causes some anxiety but we suppose the Waggon was not arrived.

Wednesday August 1   A good morning and I hope people will be able to do something in the hay. Margaret came into our room betimes and informed us that Dyer was arrived with the Trunks. That it did not come to Taunton before nine at night yesterday and that consequently he travelled all night home and reached this place a quarter after twelve. Finding all gone to bed he put the horse up in the stable and took a nap himself in the pallet, supperless poor fellow and dinnerless. I understand however he had his breakfast this morning and went off to his father's hay early this morning.

Thursday August 2   This is a pleasant morning tho the sun appeared to glisten too much. Thomas has been up at five in the morning planting a row of Celery Plants which was very attentive of him. Indeed he is very fond of the garden which I approve of much. We had company to dinner, Mr and Mrs Sealy and Mr and Mrs Allen. Mr Sealy, pompous as usual, brought with him a prodigious fine melon. They left us after tea.

Saturday August 4   My wife is much alarmed about her leg and Mrs Dodwell having viewed it is so shocked that it made her ill. I am afraid the last medicine has been improperly applied. Someone is to go over the Hill for Mr Ling to see my wife's leg. Ling is the nephew of Mrs Southcomb's Husband and was bred at South Molton under Mr Bryant, consequently in the same mode of practice with Mr Aram Bryant who undertook the cure of my wife's leg. This day concluded in its usual stile.

Wednesday August 8   A little dispute between Phebe and our new servant Thomas. He would not feed the pigs so my wife took him in hand and spoke to him and brought the gentleman to. These are disagreeable things and hard it is that Masters should be plagued with the disputes of the servants about punctillios not worth mentioning. They are not hired for this or that thing, is not the language for me. I hire them for all the work they can do – I am afraid this man drinks. He looks muddled always and is continually running into the cellar.

Thursday August 9   Mr Ling came here before dinner to see my wife's bad leg and he dined but did not stay tea. He seems intelligent in Medical Matters and does not, in my opinion, dislike a glass of wine of two. Before tea came in Mr Sealy and he staid tea. He talked much of a garden wall ninety feet long and ten high that fell down and he seemed much agitated tho he affected not to regard it and launched forth into a considerable pomposity, which he generally does. I was in a hurry to get Thomas off for the newspaper but he ran down to the cellar first. Thomas, Thomas what are you doing said I. Nothing but a cup of ale before I go Sir. I grumbled much, however he returned in a trice as if it were to make amends.

Wednesday August 15 This morning does not promise well, frequent showers and heavy ones. We are to go to Enmore to dinner but I know not what to make of it. To our great surprise instead of a Post Chaise Mr Mower from the George sent over an old coach of the late Mr Guy's which took five of us which I am glad of. My wife and Miss Lewis staid at home, my wife being very poorly with her leg. So Mrs and Miss Dodwell, Miss Moore, Margaret and myself went. We met at Enmore Colonel Polden, Mr Wollen, Mr Ruscomb Poole and the Enmore Family which made up a good party. The Pooles seemed proud to meet Mrs Dodwell and Miss Moore and they were very well and elegantly dressed and notwithstanding the rain we had a very agreeable day. Margaret too was well dressed in a yellow Persian Silk. After tea we entered our vehicle again and got home safe and well and found all right at home.

Friday August 17 Dyer went off early for coal and brought it by eleven and is threshing in the barn. Thomas in the garden and I am about speaking to him about his drinking. He denies it but Phebe is positive. I do not know how matters will end but it is a sad thing just as I am going to take in my Tithe. He might do very well if he could keep off from drinking. On being denied Cyder he drinks water, which I am sorry for.

Saturday August 18 This morning is very fine. After breakfast I found Thomas in the garden. He hummed and hawed and at last got out something about yesterday and drinking. I argued and talked with him and said he supposed it would be uncomfortable to stay longer but that it was false. I shook my head and he went on to be sure if I believed what she said. I answered that she had lived with me many years and moreover there was much the appearance of drinking in his face but that he could go on as others did. He seemed to hesitate and mumble that it would be better to go. If so I replied that I was ready to pay his wages. After this he said something about taking in my Tithe to which I replied that I had paid him so off he went. It is sad to be left at this critical time but he said it was pounds out of his way. The inconveniece is to me and not to you I returned. I sent over to Dyer and he came.

Sunday August 19 Went to Overstowey Church in the morning and my wife joined the other Ladies, which I am glad of. I have been today a little pinched in the bowels but got through the Service very well. Thomas came here in the morning for his razor and Bible.

Monday August 20 From this day to the 26 I have neglected this Diary by some unaccountable thoughtlessness and am therefore to account for that time by memory as well as I can. The week has been very warm and excellent Harvest Weather and I carried my Halsey Cross Wheat and a great deal from Plainsfield. Wednesday we dined at Mr Brice's of Asholt. Mr Brice and all of 'em were very great and bragging and very civil as usual. There was a little girl there, daughter of the important Mr Cruckshanks, Lord Egmont's steward. She danced for us very prettily, had a good deal of the Cruckshank physiognomy which is not very good. My Lyng called here one day in the middle of the week and gave some directions for my wife's leg. Dyer now sleeps here and has been engaged for me every day of the week.

Sunday August 26   This too a fine warm day. Mrs Dodwell complains of a Stricture on her chest. She is a little delicate woman. We had a very full Church at Overstowey and a full Choir of Singers and all went on well. Mr and Mrs Sealey walked in and drank tea and we walked back with them to their house and the young ones went for letters. Mr Sealey is a good tempered man, vain and boastful yet civil tho at bottom in my opinion stingey and selfish. In returning from Stowey Margaret took a tumble from a Stile and hurt herself very much. I was much alarmed and she leaned on my arm all the way home and seemed very poorly. When she got home she had her arm rubbed with brandy. I do not often move out on Sunday and we missed our Reading but has Prayers on our return.

Wednesday August 29   This too is a very warm bright day. Dyer brought home from Farmer White a load of wheat, 21 stitches but he had two horses, one with mine. I worked in the garden a little but it was so hot and the perspiration from my head so very much that I could not stand it long., a proof that the blood flows to my head very much which is the cause of the pains in my face. In the afternoon I attended the reading in the parlour where the others were working and painting. Miss Moore reads to 'em and reads well. She is a sensible woman. Mrs Dodwell has a Boyle on the head which is unpleasant.

Saturday September 1   This is a terrible day for the Partridges yet very little barley is cut so they will have some shelter against their enemies. Dyer came in the afternoon, he did not sleep here the night before as I advised him not to do because he and Phebe being acknowledged Lovers it would be rather awkward for both to sleep by themselves in the same house and might afford some Scandal, we all being at Bridgwater. Dyer came in the afternoon and milked our cows and staid the night as usual.

Sunday September 9   I went into the Sunday School as I generally do and gave a halfpenny to the first comer. There were a great many little ones and they read very tolerably. I rode to Dodington, not many at Church and the tiling not properly mended. Farthing the Churchwarden is a sorry fellow, scarce ever comes to Church, neither were the Whites at our Church, tho formerly very constant. The son is turned Grazier and I fear goes often on Sundays in quest of cattle.

Monday September 10 After breakfast news was brought in that Molly Selleck was dead. I had visited her on Saturday and I did not then expect her to live so long. Poor woman, I fear she has a great deal to answer for, she brought herself to the grave by drinking, used to quarrel with her husband like a Mad Woman and they used to fight so often that many apprehended there would be a murder between them at last. What is worse I fear she brought up her children to pilfering and stealing. However she seemed at last in good temper of mind and I hope God Almighty will have Mercy on her Soul.

Saturday September 15 In the afternoon we had the Funeral of Molly Selleck where there was a great concourse of people, well dressed and respectable. As they neither sent me a Hatband nor Gloves I did not think I had much reason to show much respect to them and did not wear my gown. Ten children followed her to the Grave which had a very melancholy appearance and there were a great many tears shed, more than for many a better woman. For she was a bad mother in many respects, brought 'em up to pilfer and steal, and drinking herself she taught them to do the same. I hope God will have Compassion on her Soul for as a wife she was a sorry companion to her Husband.

Saturday September 29 I sent to Mr Cruckshanks this morning for my Composition for Quantock Woods and Farm and likewise to pay Lord Egmont for my paddocks. But he was gone from home as they said two hours before though Dyer was there before ten o'clock, in short he chose to be out of the way and several persons were waiting for him. I fancy he is hard pressed for money. How can it be otherwise while he swaggers about the country so much and gives such Entertainments and lives in so pompous stile. The whole Family are the most Assuming, presumptious swaggering, expensive and unprincipled people I ever knew. How Lord Egmont shuts his eyes to all this I cannot well conceive. Had Farmer Morle to dine with me today on a Michaelmas Goose and his son in law John Landsey. They paid me some Compositions for Tithe.

Monday October 1 Sent off Dyer early to Squire Cruckshanks. He returned without the money and he is to go off again on Wednesday. So – so Mr Squire I must look to my Tithe sharp. Margaret took a walk in the afternoon as I thought by herself. So seeing some Gentry with dogs &cc coming down the Hill along the Crowcombe Road I thought I would walk to meet her lest such Young Bucks, finding her alone, might say something impertinant to her. After moving one way and tother we at last met and walked home together. These Bucks overtook her at Bincombe but as she took no notice of them nothing was said, besides she was in her own Parish and houses along the side of the road. My wife is still poorly with her leg. Dr Gibbs says it is a Bath Case, so there I suppose we must go, but no great prospect of getting perfectly well. Mrs Mackey dined with us. Poor woman she has spent all her money in a foolish way and is now turned Poettess and publishes sad stuff which will bring neither gain nor credit. She was dressed all in Rings and Trinkets. I rather pity her.

Wednesday October 3 I sent off Dyer early to the great Squire Cruckshanks for my Composition for Quantock Wood and he has now kept till three o'clock. tis strange conduct to keep him so long even if he pays him. The Fair at Bridgwater carries off all the country. Dyer did not return from his errand before eight o'clock. The Great Cruckshanks, after calling for some disbursements said he must go to Taunton and would return in three or four hours if he could stay. He did stay but saw nothing of Mr Cruckshanks any more. This looks in the nature of a swindle, a Jockeyship at least.

Monday October 15 Porter has been uncommonly bad in the Poorhouse, he is raving mad at times. I sent off a letter this evening to Squire Cruckshanks about my Composition for Tithe which he neglects paying me after sending to him three times. It is surprising how this family swagger about the Country and a pity it is that Lord Egmont's eyes were not open to their procedings. Presumptious upstarts they carry themselves high as if they were the Lords of the Country. Two of the sons are most worthless beings, the other no better.

Saturday October 20 To my great surprise this day a Mr Collard called to pay me my Tithe for Quantock and to settle my rent for Lord Egmont's Paddocks. I had sent three times to Squire Cruckshanks for my Composition without effect. At last I sent him a Laconic letter to send me the money here to Overstowey without delay and this produced me payments. Tis strange that a man who swaggers about the country in the manner he does should be so pittiful and shabby.

Sunday October 21 The weather warm but very rainy and unhealthy. My man, Mr Dyer, intends to be married to Miss Phebe but to continue in my service. This news he communicated to me this morning. This evening came in Sally Tutton from Monkton Farley. She has six children and is now big, ready to tumble of the seventh. She came over to see her brothers at Asholt and returns Thursday next.

Sunday October 28   We had but very few at Church this morning. Dyer's Banns were published with our Phebe and he went out of Church before they were published for to be sure he would not be at Church to hear his Banns published. This is a piece of modesty might suit the female very well but I cannot see why it should affect him who stands behind me and is not seen by the Parishioners. He was much more conspicuous in marching out of Church. They are to live with us till Lady Day when we are to have two new servants and then Dyer is to work for us as he used to do, three days in the week. They are good and faithful servants and will do well I hope. They mean to take a house with a few acres of land and have saved money.

Friday November 2   Walked to Stowey to enquire about some little matters at the Post Office. George Paddock opened a box and delivered a book Directed to me from Mrs Mackey and I was to give him a shilling for the carriage. It is a Publication of hers which she denominates – The Scraps of Dame Nature – and the Dame is no other than herself. Of all the Publications I ever read I certainly never met with such Nonsense and in some places quite indelicate. The woman is certainly Mad, but I fear she is poor too so therefore I shall give her something.

Sunday November 4   Dyer and Phebe's Banns were asked today, the second time. Some bread was given away on account of some Turnip Stealers.

Monday November 5   We had Bell Ringing this morning being the Fifth of November. A little Rascal, young Goddin, alarmed the village very much by firing off some Gunpowder, and under my Barton. Dyer chased him for some time but could not overtake him. He had a gun with him but Edward Selleck took it from him. He is a grandson of William Hill and son of Nanny Goodin an old servant of mine and brought up by his grandfather, and ruined by him and turns out to be a mischevious Rascal. News came this day that the Princess Amelia was dead and I understand our Good Old King is much better. I fear it will go hard with him yet trust God Almighty will preserve him to us a little longer.

Wednesday November 7   Dyer went off very early to Taunton and brought home a fine dish of fish by twelve o'clock. About four our Company came, the snug Old Bachelor Mr Jeffrey, Rector of Otterhampton, then came Mr and Mrs St Albyn in their carriage with two servants. Next Mr and Mrs Ruscomb Poole in their Gig and Mr and Mrs Sealey in their Carriage, and their servants filled our house and their carriages our yard. However we did very well for we had Mr Paddock here to wait. The company seemed all to be well pleased with each other and enjoyed themselves much. They staid till about nine when all went off except Mr and Mrs Ruscomb Poole who took a bed here. The snug old Bachelor Mr Jeffrey was obliged to ride a dismal road in the rain which was heavy, but there was a good moon. I had a letter from Mr Northey from Windsor who spoke of the King's Health. He says he will write again when Princess Amalia is buried. We are all to go into Mourning next Sunday.

Monday November 12   Eatly this day my wife went off behind Dyer to Stowgurcy to Mr Davis. On his return his father, brother and sister came and Phebe's father and two sisters and Ann Knight was here and I went to Church and married my servants* Robert Dyer and Phebe and I trust they will be happy in each other and I gave them and their friends a dinner on the occasion and they are to continue with me as servants till Lady next when I hope to be provided with others and if they turn out as faithful and trusty as these have then I shall rejoice. Dyer desired me to Publish the Banns now and they were to be married about Christmas but I answered if the Banns be Published it is best marrying immediately. They took my advice. My wife is to take Phebe wih her to Bath where we mean to go, if it please God, after Christmas and Dyer will stay in the house to take care of things here. After this I and my daughter walked to Stowgurcy leaving the house to the Married People and their friends.

Thursday November 15   Charles Selleck I perceive has erected a sawpit close on the road and in sight of my house, and there will be no passing it with the horse when they are at work. But I will see if I cannot compel him to take it down. A mean drinking fellow and grown impudent since his late acquisition of fortune. I am not very well and have a violent headache.

Sunday November 25   We had not many at first at Prayers but they came afterwards in great numbers with Joany Knight's funeral. I read this day a Prayer on account of our Good King's Illness and was indeed somewhat affected in reading it. Poor Old Man it is his intellect is disordered by the death of his daughter. I feel at his time of life there is no great hope of recovering yet the Prayers of the Whole Nation may do much for I do think that the Prayers of his Creatures are more attended to by the Almighty Creator than is generally noticed.

Friday November 30   The morning clear and has a frosty aspect. I mounted my horse and rode to Stowey and saw the bowing Mr Francis Poole, and as I was going on saw an elegant Barouche by Mr Tom Poole's door and soon came out the puisant man himself and entered into it. I asked him a few questions. He is going to meet Young Acland returned from the Madeiras, a Corpse. He is brought I understand in a pipe of Madeira to preserve him through the voyage, the usual mode they tell me there being no lead coffin to be obtained in the Islands. Mr Acland has now lost six children and only one remains to preserve the Family Name, if God preserve his life too.

Their Wealth is immense but what is wealth alone, it cannot keep them from the Grave. A letter from William today with Latin Verses he shewed up to Mr Stewart and he gives a good account of his Accounts, having gone through Simple Interest and he is beginning Comission.

Tuesday December 4 We had company to dinner, the Divine, Mr John Poole, Mr and Mrs Allen and Mr James Rich. Mr Rich has not dined here except on a Tithe Day these many years. We did not think him quite so well as usual now he is getting old. Mr Poole is very full of the new scheme of Instruction according to Dr Bell's Plan. Lord Egmont supports a School at Enmore and Mr John Poole has taken to it very much.

Monday December 10 This day we were to have dined at Alfoxton with Mr and Mrs St Albyn but the rain was so great and incessant that at two o'clock I was obliged to send over Dyer with a note to excuse ourselves. We were not offered a bed there and tho there was a full moon yet to return late at night did not suit me at all for the road is very dismal and disagreeable. My wife is an invalid and could not think of going tho this is the third Invitation we were obliged to decline.

Wednesday December 12 I walked with Mr John Poole to a School supported by Lord Egmont on Dr Bell's Plan. Mr John Poole attends Dayly to see it go on regularly for the good of the Parish and it is really wonderful to see how expeditiously instruction goes on and it is as easy to teach a hundred as ten. They learn to write, spell and read at the same time. Even children three or four years old learn their letters by writing them on sand tables. In a few months they write, spell and cast accounts with the greatest accuracy and perfection and all this without the least confusion by a word of command like a Band of Soldiers. We staid there till one when they were let out of School and we returned to Mrs Poole's for dinner. Mrs Poole is wonderfully better than she has been. We sat down to cards and I won a large pool of Commerce.

Friday December 14 Mr John Poole shewed me a hole under a bank which covered some drains from the Castle. On this bank were several of the School Children playing a few weeks ago when they fancied they heard a noise below. When running around to explore what it was they saw the head of a black man out of a hole below the bank. At first they started and withdrew and so did the black head, but coming on again a black man came to the mouth of the hole and called out in a stern voice that if they came near him he would kill every one of them on which they all fled but turning round they saw the black man dart over the ground to a thick wood at a little distance and he was never heard of more. It was supposed he was a sailor concealing himself from a Press Gang that were at

Bridgewater. We returned after a tolerable walk, dined and played cards in the evening.

Tuesday December 18 A rainy morning. Notwithstanding the appearance of the day William ventured after breakfast to ride to Bridgewater to dance at the Ball this night, his sister being there. So off he went on Wm Frost's horse and Dyer on my great horse after him. So we two were left by ourselves.

Sunday December 23 We had for Morning Service a tolerable few and good Singing. Rode over to Dodington and the Church filled very well at last tho not one Farthing there except a sister of Mrs Farthing. At Overstowey in the morning I christened two children and Churched two women and at Dodingon I Christened and Churched a child and its mother. I went home to dinner after a tolerable day's work. I am now strictly speaking out of the Curacy of Dodington, having given up on account of the Service and Church being incommodious for all kinds of weather and only serve it once or twice more out of kindness to Mr Sealey.

Saturday December 29 Margaret went with William to Stowey to raffle for a gold necklace of Mrs Mackey but failed in the Prize.

Monday December 31 A PostChaise came to us early this day from Bridgwater and carried us to Mrs Lewis's where we breakfasted. I called on Mr John Sealey and was paid for the Service of Dodington. At Street we heard a good deal of Lucien Bounaparte and his train who passed that way a few days before as the good natured fat landlady of the Inn told us. We passed thro Wells without stopping and got to the Old Down Inn after it was dark. This Inn does not please me so much as it does some people. We were at first shewn into a dull little room but at last were ushered upstairs in a very good room after some apologies. We had very good beds and other accommodation but the waiting was bad and the charges very high. William slept with me and Margaret with her mother.

The Year 1811

Tuesday January 1   This is the first day of the year and it begins briskly for we are up early. A hard frost and strong symptoms of snow. We went off early in order to get to Bath for breakfast and got safe to the White Hart Inn at Bath by ten. After breakfast Margaret and William went out in quest of lodgings and they soon found good ones in Bath Street, No. 13. and there we got ourselves and luggage in a trice and soon found ourselves comfortable there and late at night Phebe came by Coach all safe tho the weather was uncommonly cold and severe. On the road to Bath we passed a Stage Coach overturned compleatly, lying on the road and rather a tremendous appearance, but we understood afterwards no one was injured.

Wednesday January 2   I began to drink the water after taking a little Physick. We sent for Dr Gibbs to see my wife's leg. He says it is nothing but a weakness of the skin and recommends us to send to Baynton* of Bristol, famous for such things. I expected this day Wm Tutton from Monkton Farley with my Rents, but he did not come. Called on Mr Hicks, Curate of Monkton Farley but not at home. The ladies made some calls but they found very few of our friends here at present.

Friday January 4   Hicks called this day and several other persons. William and I went to the Half-price Play in the afternoon and we saw the farce which was our chief object, Valentine and Orion, which pleased me much.

Saturday January 5   This morning Phebe went off with my wife to Bristol to meet Mr Baynton by appointment. Mr Hicks called and was paid for the Service of the Church. At last Wm Tutton appeared and brought the money, to my no small joy. Late in the evening my wife returned from Bristol in good spirits, Baynton undertakes to cure her leg with certainty.

Sunday January 6   We went off in a Postchaise after breakfast for Monkton Farley, the road leading to the village very stoney and the ruts deep, we had nearly been overturned. Got there and went thro the Duty very well. Two of Mr Long's sons were at Church and my wife and Margaret and William in their seat. Bachelor at the Inn very Civil and William and I called at Mr

Long's. He was very civil but not at Church, I know not why for it used to be otherwise. It is certainly a very damp Church. We returned home to Bath a little before 4 but could not go to the Abbey Church in the afternoon.

Friday January 11 The thaw continues very fine and gradual. After drinking my glasses of water and walking about I stepped into an Exhibition Room of Paintings and Fine Art and gave half a crown for William and I, but saw only the Collection of one room and very few Capital Pictures. I think the thing uncommonly dear. In the afternoon William and I went to the play of the Curfew, leaving my wife and Margaret at home for Margaret has got a cold and is unwell. Indeed so have I got a cold for some days past. The Entertainment was – The Forty Thieves, which was very amusing with the aid of its machinery and I believe drew all the children of the place to see it. It kept us late but William and I got home very well.

Saturday January 12 The rain came on in such a manner that I was obliged to send to Mr Hicks to apologise for not going to Monkton Farley tomorrow which I was sorry for as I had undertaken to do, and I was desiring him to do what I declined doing myself for if the weather was too bad for me it might be deemed so for him. But it was his duty to go, mine was Optional.

Sunday January 13 William and I went to Abbey Church. The Service is done very regularly and decently and we had a good Practical Sermon by one Richardson, but I did not much approve of a Prayer of his own composition before the Sermon, which I understand is the practice now. After Service we had an early dinner and about three we carried William to the Coach and off he went to the CharterHouse with a tear or two but no more. There were two ladies with him in the Coach.

Wednesday January 16 Yesterday Margaret went to the Ball with the Mallets and she danced most of the time and had good partners, but her cold increases and almost alarms us and she must give up drinking the waters. I continually drink the waters and walk up and down in the Pump Room and meet and converse with many friends and some strangers. It is a curious place and many odd faces and odd people are to be seen and viewed at one time, with observation better than any place I know. My wife and I dined at Mrs Blagroves and met chiefly a party of Old Maids and Widows, a Berkshire Group, genteel people. Met a young person there, a Miss Pocock, daughter of an old acquaintance of mine, Captain Pocock of Englefield.

Thursday January 24 I went with Margaret to the Play to see Mrs Jordan. Mrs Jourdan acted her part very well and made us laugh much. It was The Country Girl – but the play itself had neither nature nor Morality in it. Mrs Jourdan was grown rather too old and fat for a Country Maid but however she made us laugh but I hate to be pleased with a bad character such as Mrs Jordan has tho she makes me laugh.

Tuesday January 29 After breakfast my wife went off to Bristol to secure lodgings for us and in the afternoon about three my daughter and I went off in the Coach and got safe to our lodgings in an airy situation. The celebrated Mr Baynton came to dress my wife's leg which he in full confidence promises to cure. The man is quick and has abilities.

Saturday February 2 Mr Harford sent his coach with two servants, handsomely dressed, who carried us to his mother's house. We had there a very superb dinner in magnificent stile, every rarity that could be thought of, A Butler out of Livery who waited and a Footman. Mrs Harford the mother is a very Superior Woman. There were two other gentlemen there and two Maiden Aunts, *one* with the remains of great beauty, the other plain, but both civil. The two young boys, pupils of Mr Mathew at Kilve were present and behaved very well. We had a pleasant evening, did not drink much when we went up to tea. There was a remarkable superb silver urn and magnificent cups &cc. Mr Harford entertained us with most excellent drawings and paintings and about nine the coach was ordered and we got safe to our lodgings. Mr Harford is most kind and because I objected to going with him to the Cathedral, it being so distant, he sent to Dr Small the Rector of St Pauls to accomodate us with a seat. I was formerly acquainted with Dr Small and in a polite manner said his seat was at our service.

Sunday February 3 Soon after breakfast Mr Harford and his sons attended and walked with my daughter and self to Church. We filled Dr Small's seat. The Curate, Mr Hunt read the Prayers very well, slow and distinct. It is a handsome Church, new but not handsomely filled, which shocked me. No town abounds with more Sects of Religion than this, they keep unto themselves teachers of every Denomination but whether there is more real Religion and Goodness among them is a doubt to me. I fancy their Religion consists more in Cavils, Quibbles and Enthusiasm than Practice. The common people are more taken with enthusiasms of every kind than solid Reason and fair Argument. Margaret and I went to the Church in the afternoon and found fewer than in the morning. We returned and found Dr Baynton had been dressing my wife's leg. He promised to come in the morning but did not so my wife and Phebe were obliged to stay from Church on his account. He does not keep his word.

Tuesday February 5 I walked out and called on Dr Small. He said he recollected me quite well, not quite so well returned I. He is indeed much altered, his hair from black was become white as snow and his face and whole appearance was old and rather decrepid yet he is by three years younger than I am. We had a good deal of talk of old times when he was Curate of Burfield, near Reading and I Curate of St Mary's Reading. He is Prebendary of Gloucester and Rector of St James in this town, which is now split into two Livings of Considerable Value. A man of ready wit and sociability but not so much a Divine. He has lately lost his wife and is recovering from a fever.

Monday May 20 This is my Birthday and I compleat the 65th year of my age and I cannot say that my feelings are so strong and vigourous as at this time last year. I am grown thinner and weaker and more low and nervous at times. The winter has been a heavy one and the long continuance of wet has made it more so. As to my Moral and Religious Capacities the Principles are the same but the exertions seem to be more languid and feeble. I have not the same Spirit in doing Duty as I used to have but God's Will be done. Some people think I am wonderfully young for my time of life, however I must think of another place where I am gradually advancing to and I pray God whenever that time does arrive that I may be prepared for it. I must turn over a new leaf and exert myself. Who knows I may yet, if it please God, have some days of enjoyment before I enter the Dark Mansion of the Grave. We drank tea this day at Mr Sealey's.

Friday May 24 A good day. My wife and Margaret went over in a Gig to Mrs St Albyn's to pay a lying in visit and I rode over to Asholt and saw Mr Brice very busy in Justice business. I paid my respects to Mr and Mrs Vicars. Returned to Overstowey and then rode to Stowey to bury a corpse.

Sunday May 26 It rained very heavily and I thought it impossible I should be able to do Duty. But the day cleared up and I dressed myself and roused myself and entering the Church got through the Service very well. I must exert myself or I shall get into a very bad way. I went into the Sunday School and heard the children say their Catechism and I found myself considerably better for the exertion and the day turned out to be a tolerably good one.

Saturday June 1 I rode out this day a ride I had not taken for some time. First to Farmer Stone then up the narrow lane towards Quantock along the Ely Green Road. Was attacked by a Stallion towards the upper part of the wood where there was a mare and colt. He came up to me boldly and began to attack my horse and stamped with his forefeet. On which I rode up to him and whippd at his nostrils with my cane till at last he desisted and I got into a field. I saw William Hill and spoke to him about his Grandson breaking the Sunday School window. He said he did not know anything of it but would enquire. After this I sat down to dinner and the day went off in the usual manner.

Monday June 3 Mr Petherbridge the Blacksmith is broke and his goods, what they could lay hold of, taken. Yet it was said he had taken to work again so I sent my horse to him to have his shoes removed and to bring him back. He was not at home but the wife said he would be back in half an hour and my Blockhead John left the horse there. I sent him back immediately to bring the horse home. He did so and I mounted him for a little ride, went to Sealey the Blacksmith who put a few nails in his shoes and will shoe him on Wednesday. In returning I met Mrs Poole on horseback. She told me that the Bailiffs were just come to Petherbridge's and so had my horse been there they would have seizd him.

Friday June 7 I mounted my horse after breakfast to ride to Stowgurcy to my Old Friend Mr Davis. He was at home but engaged to dine with Mr Acland so I could not stay with him long. He was busy papering his Sitting Parlour and Stockham one of the Jurymen on the woman who drowned herself was there. He says she was drunk when she did it, had a quarrel before with her Husband but he was not to blame in this matter nor aware of her intentions. She came into the house, put her cloak and hat on a nail and without saying a word went to the Well and threw herself down. It was forty feet deep and had twenty of water in it. The man went down after her at the Peril of his life, fastened her by a rope to the bucket. She when brought near the summit fell off and he went down again and brought her up by the assistance of men coming from Stowgurcy. He and his wife were large corpulent people and with the water in their clothes weighed little less than five hundred pounds and all this was brought up by the strength of a small rope. Stockham said he would not have attempted the thing for all Mr Acland's Fortune. I and my wife after tea walked to Dyer's to consult about mowing. The evening was not promising and so we deferred it till Monday next.

Sunday June 9 In the afternoon we had a very full Church. They brought a corpse from Spaxton, a pauper, and yet it is astonishing what a number of people attended. The brother, a Palmer, was at the expence which indeed was generous. The Coffin was very handsome indeed. I went through the Service better than usual. I had a Christening and Churching and after I went into the Sunday School and made the children say their Catechism.

Monday June 10 Very early this morning Dyer and Charles Carlisse began mowing my Paddocks and a very prodigious crop it is. They worked hard this day and mowed down both of them before night. Two men mowed

three and a half acres in one day which is great work and there is 6 tun of
hay at least from them. I rode to Stowgurcy to bring here Mr Davis but he
could not come, being engaged. So I returned to my wife to dinner but had
short commons on the presumption that I would dine with Mr Davis.

Thursday June 13 This day doubtful at first. Thermometer 56 but has not
advanced to 60 all summer. Our Apples are entirely destroyed tho the
bloom was great and more trees have been killed this season than I ever
remember. A fine cherry tree full of blossoms and even covered with fruit
this very year yet has been struck with a blight, the fruits all falling off and
the leaves withered and the tree dying. An apricot, very fine and flourishing
ever since I came to this place has been struck in the same manner and is, I
am afraid, dying without any visible cause unless the ground be too
shallow. I have some nectarine trees before the House dying, indeed dead
but this was not entirely this year. I fancy I must get some clay to lay under
the roots of the next trees I plant.

Sunday June 16 We had here the Church very full in the afternoon, several
persons from other Parishes having come on account of the woman that
was lately buried, one of the Palmers and so all the Broom Squires were at
Church and some of them I believe had not been at Church since they were
Christened. One man absolutely kneeled down at the time through
Ignorance of what he was to do.

Monday June 17 A very fine morning. Up and in the hay early. I did not stir
from home this day and we did get the hay in, in very good order as I have
done now for many years past. We gave them a supper and Phebe was here
and Nanny our old Nursery Maid from Monkton Farley, Wm Hill's
daughter. So ended this day but we do not hear very pleasant accounts of our
Bristol Serving Maid, she discovers a levity of behaviour we can by no means
approve of. If so we must send her off which is an unpleasant thing and we
may have difficulty in getting another to supply her place. Indeed servants are
now become so corrupt and profligate that one hardly knows where to get a
good one. My daughter looks pretty well this day but she grows very thin
which I am shocked to see. She is taking a prescription of Dr Gibbs.

Wednesday June 19 Thermometer approaching near to 60 where it has not
been this year before. I was obliged to send John with the horse to the
Blacksmith this morning. In the afternoon I rode to Stowey and delivered
to Mr Paddock a letter directed to Mr Baynton with Bank Notes in it for
the cure of my wife's leg which (by the by) is not perfectly cured and the
sum required is large★, no less than thirty pounds and a multiplicity of
expences besides. My Journey to Bath and Bristol cost above a Hundred
and twenty pounds.

Friday June 21 Tis a cold morning. I am to preach this afternoon before the Female Club Society. There is a high wind too. I went down with my wife after dinner and went to Mr Allen's and there I waited so long I was sick of it. It was past five before we got to Church. Mr Allen does Duty with great difficulty, he has an impediment in his utterance that distresses one. I gave them a Sermon I made for the purpose and which they were much pleased with and Mr Tom Poole paid many Compliments on the occasion. After this we went to the Rose and Crown and drank tea with all the Members who were all females except Mr Ward, Mr Tom Poole, Mr Forbes and myself. The women enjoyed themselves and were very merry and besides tea and bread and butter they had two immense cakes cut into slices and given among them. After this we had a few songs from some of the Females who had good voices and then my wife and I moved off and indeed so did most of the company.

Wednesday June 26 I have been very busy in writing letters and inclosing halves of notes for Mr Baynton for the cure of my wife's leg, if it may be called so for I do not think it is quite well. Mr and Mrs Brice, Mr and Mrs Vicars and Mr and Mrs Allen dined here today. Mr Vicars seems a civil, well behaved man and modest but not very deep in intellect, yet on the whole agreeable. Mrs Vicars is his second wife, he had nine children by the first which he lost. Mrs Vicars is very plain but has a great sensibility about her eye. Justice Brice talked away as usual some truth, a good many lies. On the whole the dinner passed off very well and every one parted in good humour with one another.

Saturday June 29 Mr Frost, our neighbour, is dangerously ill. I called on him but he did not seem inclined to Pray much. By and by came in Mr Tom Poole and Mr Bennet. They think him better than yesterday, he talks of making his Will. – Has done so with the assistance of Mr Tom Poole who spoke to me on the subject. Tom Poole attends regularly as if he was a Physician but Alas poor Tom has had no education that way and the knowledge he has is but ideal and picked up out of the writings of his brother, deceased. Tom's wish is to be thought an Universal Genius which I call an Universal Pretender. However he does a great deal of good in attending poor people and being very generous and charitable to them on occasions. And tho Vanity seems to be the fundamental motive of most of his actions yet we must not judge too hard for the actions themselves are Benevolent and Good. Tom has too much of the Philosophical Cant of the day about him and often talks of Humanity and sheds a tear and prays too but morality and sentimental feelings and latitude and linearity of thoughts on these matters he mostly boasts of insomuch that every Scoundrel who talks smoothly and pretends greatly is sure of his Patronage. I have known him travel far and near to save a man from the Gallows who was the greatest Villain that ever existed, and made use of unjustifiable arguments and said untruths for that purpose. However, God be Praised, he failed.

Wednesday July 3 I took a ride through Stowey and then by the Mines and up the hill under Dowesbury. On the way back got into an intricate wood and almost lost myself but at last got on to the Watchet Road beyond Dodington. Then I turned round and went past the Castle of Comfort where John Mogg's red nose was to be seen a few weeks ago but the poor man is gone and the house is to be lett. The daughter, a girl about fourteen, wishes to take it but alas a Publick House for a girl of fourteen will never do. Wm Frost is very ill and I fear will die.

Friday July 5 I rode to Stowey, bowed to Mr Francis Poole and he to me and gave me a quire of paper and I gave him fourteen Pence. It grew colder in the afternoon and so I did not move further than the garden and I retired to the Study to Think, which is a great treat to me.

Sunday July 14 We had few at Church at first but they came in afterwards, I suppose the clocks did not agree. Harriet has not been in Church for two or three Sundays. People have got an odd notion of her as if there was a levity in her behaviour and looks that indicated something wrong in her tho we have seen nothing of that kind. She is an excellent working Servant, very clean, attentive, sober and honest yet they say foolish and immodest. Immodest in her conversation which induces us at all events to part with her, tis sad. She is very temperate and in no ways extravagant yet hot and resolute if provoked. She is to leave us Tuesday. She is very illiterate yet attends Prayers and Reading and learns all that she hears by Heart. Badly brought up I fear otherwise she would make a good Member of Society.

Tuesday July 16 A tolerable morning. Harriet went off this morning and John carried her box to Stowey. She was very loth to leave us and we were sorry it should be so. My wife told her that she brought all on herself by her imprudent conduct and conversation. She denied all but we had too many Witnesses against her. She shed tears which affected my wife much but it is better now she is gone. The news today is not very good from abroad. His Majesty has had an increase of his disorder, in short his bodily health is very good but his Intellect is much disordered, poor man.

From this time until the beginning of next year Mr Holland's Diaries are missing so we have no way of knowing how they managed without a servant nor how they replaced the unfortunate Harriet.

The Year 1812

Tuesday January 7 John is gone off for coal. I rode the young horse to Stowey and round by Halsey Cross, he went very well. We sold one half bushell of wheat to a poor woman today. I am very sorry I sold so much barley to Mr Ward for the poor would have bought it all up, which would have lengthened the consumption of wheat for at present it is said there is not wheat sufficient for the consumption of the Kingdom.

Thursday January 9 This day rather misty, sour and unpleasant. In the afternoon they brought here to be buried a son of Lewis Brown who died of a Consumption. Every one spoke well of the young man and the mother is inconsolable. They kept him so long before they carried him to the Grave that I was obliged to have a candle to read the Service, the first time I had one since I had the Living of Overstowey. There were some gifts of Charity given to the second poor in the Parish this day.

Monday January 13 This morning was fine, the day rather mild for the time of the year. We had a good deal of bustle about a marriage. Old Savage Ware, past seventy, married to Jane Long, about sixty. Old Ware had lost his teeth and I had hard work to make him pronounce his words right. They were married out of the Poor House but kept their Revelling at Molly Weymouth's of the next door. The day afterwards they marched to a house of Ware's at Tyren. Ware, tho old, is a very laborious hearty workman. His children did not behave well to him and so he married.

Sunday January 19 I had a Christening after Prayers and to my great surprize Sally Pocock who had been a servant of mine and was objected to on account of never having been Baptised offered to stand. I said it could not be for how can you answer for another who have never been Baptized yourself. So Mrs Crook the grandmother of the child stood. I told Sally Pocock that I was ready to Baptize her any time she chose to be so. I was this day much offended by the appearance of Thomas Porter's daughter at Church dressed out in a very gay manner. She has been at Wells before the Justices charged with stealing some articles of apparel and tho the articles could not or would not be sworn to there was no doubt of her guilt.

However she got off and so now triumphs in a most disgusting manner. The father had some Psalms given out for singing, expressive of his case as he foolishly imagined. It has given offence to the whole Parish.

Wednesday January 22 I rode out this day. Saw some of the Broomers making up a new enclosure on the side of the Crowcombe Rode. They were going to plant potatoes. Know you said I that I must have Tithe. We intend it answered they. They told me that the Palmers were sent to jail for stealing wood. Dyer and John are winnowing but we have scarce preserved enough of wheat to keep us to the next Harvest, we must manage accordingly. Sad plague with this Scoundrel Porter at the Poor House. He will not work tho he can earn more than anyone, but he wants the Parish to maintain him in idleness and he plays every kind of prank to impose upon us. I say he must work while he can, or starve.

Friday January 24 We dined this day at Mr Sealy's at Stowey. Met there young Acland, Mr and Mrs Shaundry and Mr and Mrs Sweeten. Mr Shaundry seems to be a man that has been in Life among gay and fashionable people and made away with some patrimony of his own which he has repaired by marrying a person of very considerable fortune whom he carried off (as I understand) from a Boarding School but alas such a poor lifeless uncouth creature as would tempt no one to run away with unless it was for the Fortune, and very few for that. Mr Shaundry is a Clergyman and serves a Curacy for the sake of the House. He does the Duty (they Say) well when he chuses but cares not how seldom. He hunts and shoots and keeps famous Pointers. He does not want Abilities. His Physiognomy is rather Good but he has a wildness about the eyes. We played at cards and I lost seven shillings. We walked home by the light of a good moon and had on the whole a pleasant day.

Sunday January 26 Poor Mrs Morle came to Church with a long train of her children in deep and hansome Mourning. They pay her great respect which I am glad to see. I asked her to walk in and take a glass of wine but they could not stay. Her daughter, lately married, rode before, what in these parts is called riding Gioliphant. I went into the Sunday School after dinner and heard the First Class say their Catechism with Explanation by question and answer.

Monday January 27 Rode out to Plainsfield and spoke to Farmer Stone about this Infamous Girl they have taken into the Parish (Porter). She will corrupt the whole Parish if she continues here, the parents take her in the hopes to make gain of her, and moreover they expect support from the Parish too. I will put a stop to this and Farmer Stone says he has a Summons for her for she does not belong to this Parish. She is the daughter of Villain

Porter's wife by the brother of the husband before marriage. It is grievous to have such things take place under ones nose and yet not be able to stop it. Alas – what will this world come to.

Wednesday February 5 This was a Fast Day to implore Divine Assistance against our Inveterate Enemies. It was a very dark and gloomy day and rainy. We had not many at Church yet considering the day pretty well. I did not move out after Church. No newspaper today, sad complaints of the Bridgewater Post Office.

Saturday February 8 John went for the newspaper and brought it tho it was not brought as it ought to be and the Tuesday's paper was not sent. I suppose Mr Taylor amuses himself with reading or sending them to his friends or off to some Pot House. I must put an end to such practices.

Tuesday February 11 I rode out this day but the young horse seemed very lame and a stiffness in the left front leg and he is uncommonly thin and poor in spight of all I can do. However I rode first to Stowey and then to Plainsfield. The horse continued indifferent and weak but in coming homewards towards the Blacksmith's down he went to the ground and there we lay sprawling. I soon got up and the horse afterwards. This will not do, I cant think what is the matter with him. He certainly is not sound and has a lameness which I never observed before. I was covered with dirt and my wife soon discovered I had been down. I sent in the afternoon to Mr James Rich to inform him what had happened but he was going to bed which he does very early.

Wednesday February 12 I spoke to Mr Rich about the horse and asked him to look at him but he declined this, neither did he say he was ready to take him. I only consider him as taken on trial tho indeed I have kept him some time for I had a man to break him and Mr Rich promised to be somewhat towards the Expence. But the horse is not well, he has the worms I think. I have not paid for him yet neither am I inclined to do so as he has certainly been declining since he came to me tho I have kept him very well, gave him excellent hay and corn. The horse is certainly unsound tho I do not believe Mr Rich was aware of it, yet when he offered the horse to me he said he would take him back. I will do anything that is fair and refer to any two Gentlemen.

Friday February 14 Dyer is here in the barn and a man came from Kilve to fetch my Holly berrys for Mr Harford. I am to go to Mr Sealy to dine and meet the Post Master's Agent from London to regulate the Business and Reprimand the Bridgewater Postmaster. I met at Mr Sealy's this important director of the Posts, Mr Hust, of immense size rather a young man but married and I think he is so fat that he will never live to grow old. He talks much, eats and drinks much and boasts much. He was bred at Winchester School on which he values himself much. He swears not a little and seems to be a man of pretty free principles and manners. However he will regulate our Posts.

Monday February 17 I took my umbrella and walked down to Stowey for letters to the New Post Office, Stanbury's son near Mr Sealy's. I found one from William which was what I expected. Called on Mr Sealy who had not been very well. Opened William's letter and found Mr Sealy had been so kind as to give him seven shillings when last in London. I read this and thanked Mr Sealy. John went off on the young horse with the Society Books to Mr Brice at Asholt. We have had of late a great quantity of rain.

Friday February 21 We had a Vestry in the morning but the key of the Church Door was with Clerk Dyer and so we went in through the Belfry Door. I do not recollect notice being given yet Mr James Rich and Mr Buller and Mr Tom Poole were assembled and they must have information conveyed to them in some way or other. It looked like smuggled business. However I agreed to what was proposed about the roads. As soon as dinner was over I was summoned out to bury an Idiot of the Parish who was nicknamed Squire. He was an old man so he came in and went out of the World no one concerning himself about him. I hope he will meet a better Reception in another World.

Tuesday February 25 I waited for Farmer Dibble to pay me some Tithe but he did not come till the afternoon. I gave him a jug or two of strong beer which raised the Farmer's spirits and he shook hands with me several times. he is about to leave the Parish. He has lived above twenty years in the Parish on a good farm of Lord Egmont's and he is now going to retire to a little Estate of his own.

Tuesday March 3 The new Cooper from Stowey has been here and done some Jobbs. He succeeded a strange old man at Stowey who was in France when the Bastille fell. He was very formal and particular, spoke loud and was deafish and loved a little liquor which his stumpy little Dame used to call him to account for. The Paper full of debates. I really think Perceval an Honest Man and has the real interest of the Country at heart.

Monday March 9 Mrs Frost came here in a plaintive tone begging my horse to go for a midwife for her daughter who is taken in labour. Now this good woman refused her horse for my son riding tho I had given feed and agreed with the husband that he should ride him when he came from school. However I let my horse go. There is little gratitude in these lower people, at least it lasts only for a moment. Mrs Bayley was brought here, a large woman as big as a mountain. Mrs Styling is not yet likely to have a child very soon.

Tuesday March 10   John is gone to Crowcombe to be measured again to know whether his height will do for the Militia for it is suspected that it was not fairly done before when he was exempted. He returned in the afternoon and is found two inches short of measure. In the paper there was a remarkable trial of a man for Blasphamy. He was found guilty but punishment was not pronounced yet. It was indeed horrible to read and I trust the man will be severely Punished. What was published was from that notorious Rascal Thomas Paine. Expelled from England, had in some honour in France till he was obliged to quit that Licentious Country and settle at last in America where this infamous book was unnoticed by the Legislature but, Thank God, the book was soon noticed in England and will be suppressed I presume. The Wretch who printed it here, in his own defence read abstracts out of it, so abominable that the Judge several times declared that he could not sit on the Bench to hear it. There was a most able speach of the Attorney General in defence of Religion and against the Criminal. I rode out on the young horse, he carried me tolerable at first but began to flag after I had rode some time. He is weak and thin still.

Wednesday March 11   John caught young Goddin who frightened his horse and layed on him with a stick. I put John in the Paddock to clean it and walked a little way towards Stowey. On my return John was absent and no one could tell where he was gone. I thought he might have gone to Mr Crosse to offer as he is to leave me. Instead I found he had gone to the Hounds that were hunting a small way off. I took my telescope and could see him very plainly and enjoying himself above two hours. He returned to prepare himself for dinner. I took him to task after dinner and remonstrated on the Heinousness of the Offence. It was not so material now he was to leave but while he continued with me I would make him do his Duty, I am afraid he has often taken the Liberty of trifling or absenting himself when I am away. A downlooking, lazy fellow and very False.

Sunday March 15   I mounted my horse to go to Asholt to do Duty for Mr Brice who is ill with a sore throat. I went through the Duty very well though Apprehensive about my face. They have built a new Singing Gallery where the Singers were all arranged in due order. The Gallery improves the Church very much. Not many at Overstowey Church this afternoon. Mr Buller from Stowey came to say something about Jack Hunt but I do not much approve of Inhabitants of Stowey who serve no Office here to come merely to speak for their own Servants. I was glad when the Service was over being apprehensive about my face.

Friday March 20 I bounced out of bed very early and found it hard snowing and very deep with a drifting wind, the greatest fall I ever knew in one night. The barometer is so low the mark will not follow it. The wind so high and the snow so penetrating that it is driven under the new tiling into the upper Garret and from thence distills drop by drop through the ceiling into our bed chamber a thing I never knew before. Had it happened in the night we should have been in an awkward situation.

Monday March 23 I had the burying of an infant of Mrs Styling this evening when the wind was so powerful and the rain as to almost prevent my standing over the grave. Mr William Tutton and Mr Robert Bachelor came to dinner. We agreed on the taking of the Rectory of Monkton Farley and tomorrow they are to carry the Heads of Agreement to Mr Ruscomb Poole for him to draw out a Lease. Bachelor is to retake my Tithe of Monkton Farley and we settled for seven years to come.

Saturday April 4 At the proper time I walked down to Mr Sealy's and found Mr Verelst and Mr Poole of Shurton, now of Weymouth. Mrs and Miss Sykes came also. We had an agreeable day and Mr Poole was very agreeable and did not rhodomontade as much as he does sometimes. John came for me with a candle and lantern and we got home safe. A note this evening from Miss Brice saying her father was not come home and desiring me to Serve the Church tomorrow. This provoked me for I hate to be called on Saturday evenings in this way and am never master of my own time and can never know what I am to do with certainty, yet this is the way they always serve me.

Sunday April 5 Rode to Asholt and knocking on the door found Mr Brice, dressed like a Great Beau, ready to receive me. He did not seem to have much the matter with him. I did the Duty tolerably till the latter end of the Sermon when my face was troublesome. I called on Mr Brice after Church and told him I would undertake the Church for the next Sunday if he desired me to do so. But in God's Name why should he desire it, he is as able to do the Duty as myself. We are to assist each other when something calls from home or in case of sickness but why should I be called on to do his Duty when he is able to do it himself, it is more than I comprehend. Mr James Rich was not at our Church, neither has he been for several Sundays having some Dropsical complaint. One of our cows calved this day.

Tuesday April 7 Dr Dunning is expected at Mr Rich's and I will endeavour to meet him there. I did so and had some conversation with him about our neighbour, I think they call his complaint Hydropskere. These keen winds are bad for my face and I have considerable inflamation there. Mr Tom Poole recommended a Spunge in water to dash my face, which allayed the pain for a moment.

Saturday April 18 I received a Handsome Print from Mr Northey of Our Good Old King taken from a picture nine years ago. It is a Capital Drawing in full length and very like him. I shall give it a Handsome Frame and take great care of it.

Sunday April 26 We had a Vestry about a man who claims Relief from this Parish. I Churched a woman who did not bring her child to be received at Church and grumbled much about it and at last made her promise to bring the child next Sunday. We received a letter from William who is much agitated about entering into the Fifth Form, as the examination by Russel is peculiarly strict. Harshness will not do for my boy he wants encouragement more than threats. You may sooner drive what is in him out than force it in.

Monday April 27 I was surprised to see women carrying heath from Quantock almost half naked, they generally put all the rags they have on on the occasion as they find the Heath to tear their peticoats. One woman seemed to have nothing but a flannel peticoat on. I could not see what was the matter but while I passed by she sat down and two others put a large bundle of heather on her to cover. I took no notice but went on yet thought they should have been further removed from the side of the road. The day not quite so cold on the Hill as the time before.

Monday August 17 After breakfast William went off on the young horse to his friend, Mr John Poole of Enmore, to get him to look over his holiday task. John walked over to carry his things and bring his horse home. In the afternoon a young person approached the gate so I went up. It was a Young Damsel, Miss Poole, and her mother soon appeared on her donkey. Mrs Richard Poole seems in my opinion in a bad way and if she should die it would be a bad thing for her daughter.

Thursday August 20 John went off early this morning for coal with the old horse. He has not done anything for this long time on account of a strain in his leg but he must work now. William walked to Stowey and brought home the paper. Great Illuminations in London on account of Wellington's Victory and the Prince Regent has made him a Marquess, Wellington of Wellington in Somersetshire. It is supposed that Marmant's Army will never get back to France again, Joseph Buonaparte is prevented from joining him and I trust in God that Genl Hill will give a good account of Soult and then we shall clear the Peninsula of the Vermin.

Sunday August 23   I went into the Sunday School, not many there but a woman in the Workhouse made such a noise with her children and cursed and swore as quite disturbed me. I have sent once before to remonstrate with her, a wicked woman, I think she is mad. I threatened that the Overseer should have her before a Justice of the Peace or that he should deduct some of her Parish Pay if she behaves in that manner any more. We had a good many at Church in the afternoon. After Church I called the Overseer of the Poor to me and pointed out the Feerncomb woman who behaved ill in the Workhouse and he promised to go in to see the place she had broke into the Sunday School.

Tuesday August 25   We dined at Mr Allen's but met no company except Mr Rudd, Miss Ferris's lover and indeed very loving they were, but tho this might be very pleasant to themselves it was not so much so to those who were in the room. Miss Ferris is the sister of Mrs Allen.

Thursday August 27   Dyer is here and threshing out corn which goes off as soon as it can be got ready. I have reduced the price to twelve shilling which gives Universal Joy around. My face has been very bad. We walked to Stowey and I called on Mr Forbes who hummed and hawed about my complaints but could decide nothing nor advise anything but draughts which he knows have no effect at all. Never was such a poor thing in Physick.

Sunday September 13   Before eleven o'clock Mr Sealy's carriage drove up and Mr and Mrs Sealy and John Sealy and Miss Sweeten came in. They have permission to sit in Mr Buller's seat in this Church, they having lost the seat in Stowey Church they used to sit in. The Sealys are delighted with our Church and they were going to compliment me on doing Duty my way. Stop says I, you quit Stowey on account of having no seat there, not a word of any other reason for it. So that we shall have this Family in future at our Church to be sure. Mr Allen has a sad defect in his utterance but he is attentive to his duty and a Good Man.

Monday September 14   Dyer is in the barn threshing wheat for the poor for I have promised to sell to my own Parish at a very reduced price. I charge twelve shillings and old wheat is now at a guinea pr bushell. They come so fast that they are quite troublesome before I can thrash it out. John has spoiled the look of my horse under the notion of trimming his mane. He has absolutely pinched it up by the roots and made it quite bare, the conceited yet ignorant Fool.

Tuesday September 15   My wife's nephew, Mr Tom Ridding, came here a little after four and had beds and dined here. Tom is grown very fat, particularly in the face. He has a large Roman nose like his mother tho not so handsom indeed he is a plainlooking man, very broad and short. His companion, Mr Marrat is like wise short but slender and a very delicate sickly looking man. They could stay but one night and went off the next morning before I was up. Tom is very steady and a man of business, very upright but of no great address and his utterance is bad, but he is not overgiven to talking. I lent Dyer my horse and cart to carry his goods to the new house he has taken where his wife is to lye in.

Thursday September 17 Dyer's wife is brought to bed of a fine boy which prevented his working hard today. Mr Brice called in on his way to Minehead. He is now as usual, full of Business and Rhotomontade.

Friday September 18 We drank tea at Mr Sealy's and met there two Miss Philpot and Miss Sweeten. I met a very extraordinary young lady, she has a very Religious and indeed Enthusiastic turn of mind and exerts herself in a great degree in that direction. At Gloucester she went into the Common Jail and preached to some of the Criminals there and particularly among the Debtors. She made Conversion of one, a Jew and plumes herself very much upon it. She continued in this way for half a year going dayly into the jail in all weathers, Hail, Snow or rain till her Relations interfered as it injured her health standing on bare cold damp stones who was always used to carpets. So at last she declined this Business for a time. She is one of five and twenty children all of whom are provided for and remarkably clever and one brother is married to a daughter of Lord Eldon and is in a fair way to be made a Bishop. She is indeed an interesting young woman, has a great quickness not to say Wildness in her looks, argues very learnedly in the Scriptures and not easily put off her notions. She took to me surprizingly and seemed to give way in some points to what I said. We got talking on one subject or another so long that I had trouble in getting off to walk home with my wife by the light of a fine moon.

Friday September 25 John is gone for coal in spite of rain and Charlotte to the Moors for milking which must be bad for a woman, however she is a good tempered girl and did not grumble. Dyer is come to the barn and he had not been there long before he was called out to drive the sow to the boar for the second time. Our neighbour William Weymouth has been taken dangerously ill and Bennet attends him and I understand has little hopes. Tis wonderful how many have died in this small village within the last twelve months. We used to have not above one or two in the whole Parish die within the year but the case is very different now.

Sunday September 27 Our neighbour Weymouth gets worse. I went to him this night and found him much altered and evidently dying so I read the Recommendatory Prayer. He has lost his eyesight yet knew my voice and said he understood what I read. I desired them to ask what he thought of himself. He replied that he should get better and live for a time longer, but it did not turn out so and he died after three o'clock. A quiet inoffensive man, honest, yet he did not exhibit in his last hours that Pious Sense of Religion which I expected of him.

Tuesday September 29 I sent off Dyer early to Squire Cruckshanks and he returned without his errand. Instead of paying me thirty five pounds for Tithe he demanded twenty one pounds as a deduction for Property Tax, which Tax I have constantly paid for myself and which he never attempted to claim before. I have sent off to Mr Ruscomb Poole to know how I am to proceed against this Accomplished Scoundrel. A dirty, pitiful shift.

Friday October 2 Charlotte went off early to Bridgewater to the Fair and Sally Styling came in to us to do her work. John went off for coal, he is an excellent fellow for this work and generally steady. Charlotte came home from Bridgewater tolerably well but we did not approve of females coming home in the dark for in this case they are often accompanied by their Sweethearts, which is not always Prudent.

Sunday October 4 My face very bad, I could hardly speak and with great difficulty eat my breakfast yet I had two Christenings and two Churchings. I began the Service in pain but got better as I went on. In the meantime this poor man Weymouth was brought to Church in the middle of the Service and such a train of the Club with him as quite overflowed the Church and several persons were obliged to stand out and poor Mrs Forbes after trying about to no purpose was obliged to stand out. I got on at last in the Service and the pains in my face wore away.

Thursday October 8 I rode out to Plainsfield and called on Mrs Morle and poor Young White who is ill, dangerously – a black jaundice. I went in to him and was shocked to see this young man. He was very restless but turned round when he understood that I was there. He did not wish for Prayers, indeed he could not speak to be understood nor indeed attend to anything. A very pretty kind of young woman attended and gave him medicine. She was just going to be married to him and was much affected by the state he was in. Miss North, the young woman who attended to him gave him with a tea spoon a boiled egg. As many as you can said I but if they were raw it would be better. They are almost raw said she. I said to several as I went off that young woman will do him more good than all the Medicines. So I left them and returned to dinner.

Sunday October 11 I should have observed yesterday that the Great Squire Cruckshanks after bilking me of my rent for Quantock Tithe on receiving a laconic letter from me sent over in a hurry on Saturday afternoon to speak with Dyer at Mr Fish's and we thought he would certainly pay me. Not a farthing but impudently orders my servant to attend him at Enmore on Monday next, and all this in high stile as if he had done nothing wrong tho he has made a most impudent attempt to cheat me of twenty guineas. No Sharper in the Kingdom has more tricks than this man yet he is Lord Egmont's Steward and Fac totum.

Monday October 12 Dyer went off today by appointment to Enmore in order to be paid by that great man Squire Cruckshanks, Lord Egmont's steward. But the Squire, as I expected, was off and Mr Collard his under steward had no directions from him to pay anyone, tho the Great Man had promised most faithfully to settle the matter this day. – Alas Lord Egmont.

Monday October 19 Towards twelve I mounted the young horse and my wife rode behind John and off we went to Enmore. We had some rain but got safe. Old Mrs Poole and my friend John Poole were glad to see us. Miss Poole and Charlotte were at home and there was Mrs Richard Poole the widow of Tom Poole's brother, and her daughter Elizabeth Poole a very extraordinary girl of fourteen. She has a thirst for knowledge of every kind. She has made great proficiency in Latin and Greek and is making the same advances in French and Italian. She is now translating Thucidydes and indeed is never idle. At night she takes to Musick in which she excells to a great degree. Mr John Poole her Uncle is her instructor and is as fond of teaching as she is of being taught. After the Musick is over he gives her some difficult questions to solve in Algebra and thus day after day goes on. It is a pity she was not a boy for then such Studies would turn to better account for tis a pity female manners and accomplishments should be less cultivated than these useless studies as they appear to me. Yet she is not impertinent and presuming but timid and submissive to her mother. Her person is tall but her movement not very graceful, she is improved of late in the features of her face yet still not very agreeable. Her person altogether would be much improved if she held herself up and did not poke. I know not where this will end but is not a likely mode to get her well married.

Friday October 23 The Divine went to inspect his School. Several parties had been to see the School he presides over. It is a great expence to him besides trouble. He has published his Plan combining Dr Bell's and Mr Lancester's.

Saturday October 24 John came with the great horse and so after a little preparation we set off for Overstowey taking leave of this Worthy Family and indeed I may say extraordinary as to the abilities and Mental qualifications. We soon got safe to Overstowey but first called on Mr and Mrs

Yorke at Spaxton. Not much in the newspaper except that the Russians are about to make Moscow very unpleasant Winter Quarters for Buonaparte. I pray God it may turn out so and that after the vast Carnage he has made he may find his Grave in that Place and so relieve the World of the Greatest Villain that ever appeared in it.

Sunday October 25   I went into the Sunday School in the morning but not in the afternoon it being so damp and unpleasant. We had a letter from William today, he is in high Spirits being one of the Upper Fellows as they call them. This is our Wedding Day, having been married one and thirty years.

Saturday October 31   Before dinner, Margaret, the long lost sheep came after an absence of six months among her friends and relations in Shropshire and Wales by every one of which she was received with the utmost kindness and pleasure. A more compleat and satisfying visit was never made by anyone before and she returned in perfect health and spirits and with many Valuable Presents from her cousins and relations. She went first in May to Mrs Anstis at Madely where her stay was short as her intended visit was to the Kinastons at Shrewsbury where she stayed a month or two and where the Middletons came to be introduced to her, they are equally related to us with the Kinastons. The Wynnes in Wales and my eldest Brother heard she was in Shrewsbury and the Yorkes in Erddig and they all invited her and the Kinastons to visit them. The Kinastons went off in their own Carriage taking her with them first to Erdigg near Wrexham, a noble edifice of Simon Yorke who married my brother's eldest daughter. She was just brought to bed so they did not stay long. Then to Mr Wynne's of Wedlock who married my brother's youngest daughter, and from thence to Teyrden where my brother lives, in the next Parish. After they had staid at these places they all returned to Erdigg to the Christening where there was great Doings, Balls, Races and Plays and the families of Yorkes, Hollands and Kinastons in their respective carriages made a very splendid appearance. Thence the Kinastons brought Margaret back to Shrewsbury whence Mrs Leighton from Ford took her to see my old friend Mr Leighton who was miserably laid up with the Gout and enquired much after me and his Godson William. After a day or two she returned and was conveyed to Mrs Anstis at Madeley near Ironbridge where she met Miss Susan Poole and they set off for Worcester in the Shrewsbury coach. From Worcester they took a PostChaise for Comberton where her relations the Middletons received her with great kindness and alacrity. Mr and Miss Middleton are brother and sister, he has the Livings of Great and Little Comberton and is a person of Good Fortune and is to have the Ryton Estate after the Kinastons. From Comberton they got to Tewkesbury and from thence took Coach to Bath, saw Mrs Hame, then back to Bristol. Slept at

Mrs King's where they met the Wollens, the Rector of Bridgewater and all came safe to Bridgewater to which place I sent Paddock with his Gig who brought her safe to this place so that a compleater and more satisfactory Expedition was never made by anyone, or more pleasant, more honourable or less expensive.

Tuesday November 3 I tunned my cyder today and put half a pint of Sweet Spirit of Nitre in it which I suppose will stop the fermentation and keep the sweets in. It is the only hogshead I made this year, apples are very dear. I called on Young White. He looks brought down very much yet rides a little about. I endeavoured to persuade him to try the Bath Waters as he has a deal of Bile about him. He complained of a great weakness in one thigh and leg.

Thursday November 5 I was awakened this day by the Ringing of Bells.* Mrs Lewis and her two daughters came here and are to continue for some days.

Friday November 20 I am going to Christen Mr Allen's child and some of the Ladies as well as myself are to dine there. He and Mrs Allen always stand to represent some of their friends but I always ask them who they represent that it may be known they do not stand for themselves.

Saturday November 21 John is gone for four bags of red potatoes to Farmer Dyer for seven shillings pr bag, an immoderate price, especially when there is in the country so large a quantity, which they pit in order to raise the price in the Spring. However perhaps they may be disappointed at last for if all do the same thing they will be overstocked in the Spring and then be obliged to let them go at any rate. The paper contains a dismal account of Buonaparte's Army, the Russians press upon them from every quarter, take their provisions and cannon and kill innumerable quantities of them. Not a word of Buonaparte himself, some think him dead.

Monday November 23 Mrs Lewis and her two amiable daughters are going home, they have spent with us a fortnight and four days and I think that in that time they improved in Health and Spirits. The weather was bad but altogether they enjoyed themselves very much. Dyer is in the barn threshing wheat for the poor who are very clamourous for it, and thankful.

Friday November 27 I rode as far as Mr Davis's at Stowgurcy and there I met Mr Dawes, Mr Davis has been poorly of late but is better now tho still feeble. I staid with him about an hour. Found my wife at home and ready for dinner. Margaret staid with Mrs Sealy and Charlotte went for her in the afternoon. There is, I understand, sad doings at Stowey. Bennet the Apothecary is charged with a connection with another man's wife. In consequence there is rough Musick every night, Horns carried along the streets. If true it is a bad business, if not he ought to clear his Character.

Tuesday December 1   This is the most nasty foggy day we have had this season. Dyer is in the barn and the poor are crouding for pecks of wheat which I sell to them under price. I did not stir out all day. Sad account of Buonaparte's Flight.

Saturday December 5   I rode out and was going on towards Stowgurcy to call on Nurse Symons to come to us for a few days as we are going to Bridgewater. Meeting Tommy Staden on the road he bowed to the ground. Do you know where Nurse Symons Lives? The Lord Love you Reverend Sir she is now at Stowey says Tommy. Tommy is past seventy yet delighted with the name Tommy. The most Whyning Hypocrite in the Universe and most Humble in his address apparently, and the most saucy when affronted. The most dirty fellow I have ever met with, his clothes are all rags and his face covered with snuff. A most fillthy creature indeed. He goes about selling poultry for Farmers.

The Year 1813

Wednesday April 14 A very fine morning and warm. In the afternoon Mr Thomas Rich was buried. A famous Brass Chandelier which he gave the Church was filled with candles and the Church illuminated. The Chandelier looked very handsome and beautiful and Mr Thomas Rich was buried under it. The Church was crouded beyond measure and they stood on the tops of the seats which I did not observe otherwise I would have made them sit down, but we had no noise or accident. So ends the earthly Career of this man from whom the World received neither much good or bad. He had it in his power to do much good but he had neither the Head, Heart or Education to set about it.

Thursday April 15 I rode up the Hill with Luke with the cart to shew the way to Dyer who was cutting wood in the Custom Wood. I met Old John French on the road, hard at work tho 83. He gave me strange accounts of the Quantock Hills formerly. He said there were several Bulls and Cows running wild there formerly and that when the cows calved they generally hid among the bushes and if found by anyone they pared their feet that they could not walk far and so when they got fat they laid hold of them and killed them. Dyer and Luke brought home half a hundred of wood with the old horse.

Sunday April 18 This is Easter Day. We had our Church very full as all the Pall Bearers were there and others so I gave them a suitable Sermon composed for the purpose and as it was the day of the Resurrection of Our Blessed Lord I connected the Circumstances as a matter of Comfort to us all that we should rise again. It seems the Sermon took very well and was much spoken of. Mr James Rich was at Church and the Sacrament.

Tuesday April 20 Mr Rich cannot dine with us today on account of his brother's death, neither can Mr Tom Poole as his brotherin law Mr King is with him. Mr Beadon Buller promised to dine with us but did not come and this he has done for several years. I fear he is a Shabby, dirty little fellow at bottom or he is poor or something of that kind. We had however a full meeting, Farmer Fish and Mr Sully dined here for the first time. Old

Charles Selleck dined here too at the age of 83. They all behaved with great decency and were well satisfied and went off in good time. So ended this day. My Cow calved this day.

Saturday April 24 A letter from William today, he has been Confirmed. Miss Ferris* that was is married and become Mrs Rudd. Mrs Allen sent the children yesterday to us with a large piece of Bride Cake. Dyer brought my wine safe from Bridgewater, unfortunately he lost a one Pound Note of his own but my change was safe and right. He was so disturbed that he walked back to Bridgewater to Mrs Dean the China Woman to enquire whether he had dropped it there. Tis lost and not to be discovered.

Monday May 3 Farmer Rich came and took away our last calf, a Bull calf. He intends to keep him. Our cattle are so covetted and admired that we for these twenty years past never fatted or sold to be fatted above one. Mr Sealy had the other, a cow calf and we have now a most beautiful yearling heifer which would sell very well if we would part with her. Luke went for coal this morning. Mr and Mrs Allen called and brought with them a Captain Ferris, brother to Mrs Allen. He commanded a Frigate and got into a French Port and was haled by a Battery. He answered in French and passed on and afterwards cut out one or two vessels and got safe before it was discovered who he was, but received a discharge or two from the Battery on his return. I think it was Alicante, a Spanish Port then in the Occupation of the French.

Sunday May 9 This turned out a very good day. I went into the Sunday School, heard the children say and explain their Catechism. Grace Chidgey the Mistress to my great surprize brought a son of hers and placed him in the Upper Class who were saying to me, a short squat shrimpy cub with a large white face, rough with the marks of small pox, and without a neck at all. It seemed like a large block fastened between two shoulders. He was very like the Old Clerk his Grandfather. I was very surprised she pushed him there without my calling for him but there he stood rolling his large eyes like a large owl and grinning at everyone. The boy was not a fool but I did not perceive that he could say anything better than other children but Mammy was wondrous proud of the Cub. From the Sunday School I came to the house and read the Morning Service to my Family.

Tuesday May 11 Luke went off early this morning for coal and a droll kind of trick he played on us for he carried the key of the garden gate in his pocket so that we were kind of prisoners in our own house as there was no coming in but through the Back Yard and Door. Had any strangers come we should have cut a ridiculous figure.

Wednesday May 12   Ruscomb Poole came here to breakfast and on business in his magnificent Gig. He looked over my papers and drew a sketch of a Will. Towards twelve and one the rain began. Mr Ruscomb Poole went to Stowey before me and I followed to dine at the Globe being the Book Club Dinner. It thundered before I could get to Stowey and by the time I got to the Inn it poured down most violently. I sat by myself in the long room and heard several most tremendous crashes and saw great flashes of lightning. By and by in came Justice Brice and we dined nine in number. Mr Tom Poole looked ill having had a touch of the gout. I bought a book or two and had my horse brought by Luke and so I rode home, but the evening cold and wet. The weather affected me much.

Wednesday May 19   I called on Mr Rich and had some chat with him. He had a good deal of unaccounted money with Mr Charter which rather disturbs him. Luke went off early for coal with money to pay for three loads. We all went to dine at Mr Sealy's and there we met Mr and Mrs Allen and Old John Sealy the Rector of Dodington. He married late in life and indeed was a perfect old Batchelor before he married and thus marriage did not cure him but he remains a mulish particular old man at this time. His wife is a good deal younger than he is but she is not very good tempered and capricious and has a multitude of complaints about her, but she was not at Stowey with him. We returned about dusk.

Thursday May 20   This is my Birthday and I compleat my 67 years and God only knows how many more days I have to live to see. However I thank God I have settled my affairs and given full instructions for my Will to provide for all emergencies as well as I can forsee and leave the rest to Providence. Therefore my mind is at ease and I am in a certain degree prepared for all Events and I trust God will enable me to finish my career at least in a manner conformable to my progress hitherto, if I do not continue to improve further in Piety and Virtue. In point of health I think I am stronger and better than I was two years ago when I came from Bristol yet my face is at times troublesome and painful. My Family, I thank God, are all in a comfortable state of health and my wife walks about as well as ever and the state of my wordly affairs afford a prospect certainly more cheerful than gloomy and tho there is no great degree of Affluence and Luxury, my expectations with regard to this Life and the Next are both good and comfortable.

Saturday May 22   Still rain and unpleasant. I have just sent off Luke with the sow to the boar, but it rains and will continue so I fear. Luke has returned and the day tolerable, the sow would not take the boar. Edward Selleck called in and explained matters about the Tithe.

Thursday May 27 Mrs Crosse from Bridgewater dined with us this day and brought a little boy with her. They are in lodgings at Paddock's, the boy being not well. She is an open-hearted, good tempered woman and very amusing in her conversation and must have been handsome formerly. The paper brought the information (to my great surprize and Joy) that the Catholick Bill was lost in the House by a Majority of four, so now it is rejected. There may be some disturbances in Ireland but the Disturbances would have been worse if the Bill had passed in favour of the Catholicks. Abbot the Speaker of the House, in a most excellent speech described the total consequences of Admitting them to the House of Commons. He was ready to give the Catholicks free scope in the Navy and Army but as to the Legislature, he could not permit them to legislate for Protestants. So the Bill was thrown out entirely.

Thursday June 3 A very fine morning after the rain and thunder yesterday. My wife and daughter went off to Enmore to breakfast and about twelve I followed. We met at Enmore Mr and Mrs Anstis from Shropshire with five children and two servants. Old Mrs Poole was very well for her age, in her eightieth year. The Divine gets fat, has been building and is very busy about his School. We spent a very agreeable day there. Margaret soon after dinner went off to Bridgewater in Paddock's Gig, who returned again to carry my wife home and so after ten we went off together.

Saturday June 5 I sent off my man with a cart for the Iron Register Box from Stowey. I called at Sealy's and found Mrs Sealy still poorly. Old Mrs Chester stood with Old John Sealy like a Queen looking down the town as if it belonged to her. John Sealy picked up some news which, if true, would have alarmed us much. It was told him that Allen's boy died suddenly. On enquiry it was very true that Allen's boy died, but not our Allen but Allen the Methodist Preacher. I took a ride on Quantock after this. They are very busy in Church placing some boards around the Altar to keep the damp from the Communicants.

Sunday June 6 This is WhitSunday and we have a Sacrament at Church. Was tolerably full but not many staid tho I have had the place round the Communion Table made very comfortable.

Monday June 7 The Bell rang for Prayers but no one came but Mr James Rich and he did not think it was worthwhile to begin for it was not a Congregation.

Friday June 18 Paddock came about ten and I set off in his Gig with a greatcoat and a large blue cloak and my face guarded with a net, and I really stood in need of this warmth. I left the haymakers to my wife's care and she too was to walk in Procession at Stowey and to drink tea at the Female Club Society. We had a Sermon at Bridgewater but no Charge from the Archdeacon. We all signed an Address and Thanks to the Speaker of the House of Commons and the Majority who threw out the Catholick Bill – and likewise we signed an address to the High Sherriff requesting him not to call a meeting of the County in consequence of an application to him from a Mr Hunt to summon the Freeholders to Address the Princess of Wales on account of the Calumny against her Character by Sir John Douglas and Lady Douglas because Seditious Persons have made a handle of the Business to raise disturbances in the Kingdom. The Clergy and their Archdeacon this day were very unanimous in their proceedings and Political Sentiments. We had a very good dinner. The Archdeacon is grown old and feeble and is, I understand, past fourscore. When I got home I found all things well and the hay perfectly secured and the haymakers filled with Mutton and Pudding.

Saturday June 19 I sent off Dyer with a cart to Bridgewater for some china which is brought from Shropshire by water to Bridgewater. He brought it safe and we much approve of it. I called on Mr Allen and told him that I was commissioned by the Clergy to propose his being a Secretary to an Auxilliary Society to that for Promoting Christian Knowledge in the Deanery. He did not seem to object to it. There must be a Meeting on the Occasion.

Wednesday June 23 Is omitted by mistake tho I have no doubt but the Events that took place are entered among other days.

Friday June 25 We expect Mr John Poole and his sister Mrs Anstis to meet his sisters Charlotte and Susan. They have just come in a Gig. We asked Mr Tom Poole but I expect he is not come from London. We had a comfortable meeting, almost like one family for I have known them all from children. The Divine and I after dinner had a Tete au Tete and he enjoyed himself wonderfully. He is a very solid young man and has distinguished himself lately very much in conducting National Schools. They left about dusk because Mrs Anstis was obliged to go to suckle her child.

Sunday July 4 I gave notice that Prayers would be next Sunday in the morning in order to bring us alternate with Asholt. I went into the Sunday School and made them read in the Testament. The Post came down from London with Laurels. I had a letter from William which gave the particulars of the great Victory of Marquis Wellington in Spain on the 21 of June at Vitoria. The Lord Wellington was saluted on the Field of Battle – Duke da Victoria. 151 Cannon taken from the Enemy, 461 wagons loaded with all manner of stores, and treasures. We lost 500 killed and 3000 wounded, the loss of the enemy immense and not yet ascertained. They are fled to Pamplona and the last gun taken from them. Lord Wellington is in active pursuit and within forty miles from France where there is utmost consternation.

Friday July 9 I and Nephew Dodwell rode down to Stowgurcy. I endeavoured to get a Broom Squire's horse for him but they were so bad I mounted him on the great blind horse. Mr Davis was glad to see us and Mr Dawes dined there and Mrs Dawes made tea. In the afternoon we moved into the Church which is very fine, newly fitted up by the Chamber of Bristol who have the Great Tithes. There are some famous Saxon Arches there. After tea and spending an agreeable day there we mounted our horses and got home well pleased with our expedition.

Monday July 12 I took my nephew to Enmore. On our return we met Dr Dunning who endeavoured to speak to us but we passed by so sudden that he had no opportunity to say much but how do you do. When I got home I found he had been with Mr James Rich who has had a stroke of the Palsey. I immediately went to him and found him upstairs with his mouth distorted and he talked continually and loud and seemingly in a Passion and perfectly aware of what was the matter with him and sometimes he cried, but he recovered himself much while I was with him, so I left him.

Tuesday July 13 I called on Mr James Rich and found there Mr Coles of Cannington. Mr Rich was considerably better and I talked along time with him. He seemed restless but is taking Medicines. After this I walked to Stowey.

Wednesday July 14 I rode up Quantock almost to Crowcombe. Met Old John French on the road, a shrewd old man past fourscore. He asked much about Mr Rich's illness. Has he made a Will says everyone. I hope he will says Old John or people will curse him in his Grave. When I rode on I met crackbrained wicked Bill Hill. He said Mr Cary had given him a shilling for working on the road. But this is like a sow with one ear said I, you only have one side of it. Oh Sir returned he I intends to make the other side, I will make a good road of it. So I returned back the way I came and had no rain. In the afternoon we had company to tea, Mrs Bordes and her two sons, Mrs and Miss Monteath and soon after came Mr and Mrs Allen so there was long and spirited chat kept up but Mrs Monteath's clack was the loudest. A short strong-featured Scotch woman with a brogue to a great degree. Her daughter was young and of a good figure.

Friday July 16 We had at one part of this day one of the most tremendous rain storms that has been known for these many years past. It carried off some part of Mr Mathew's garden wall and some sheds or outhouses of Mr Govett and Mr Sealy who called on Mr Acland was obliged to stay the night. I have had a letter from my friend Leighton who speaks feelingly of his illness and suffering in the Gout and Gravel, if he has not got the Stone. He seems to think he shall not see his next birth in November. I hope he will not prove a true Prophet.

Friday July 23 Rode to Stowgurcy. Mr Davis was tolerable. Poor Dawes has lost his only child, I called on him and he seemed much obliged to me. I intended to return but it began to rain as I was going to take out my horse so I was obliged to stay and take pot luck. We sat chatting till coffee and tea and I had a pleasant evening to return.

Sunday July 25 In the afternoon I went into the Sunday School and found few there, they were gone, I suppose, to Ely Green to the Revel for it is Whort Sunday as they call it for on this day the Parishioners see their friends and give them Whortleberry Pies so that they come to Church with black mouths. I do not much object to these kinds of enjoyments among the lower people as it keeps them in Spirits and is a great comfort and Refreshment to them for their dayly labours. But I would feign keep them from Sunday Revelling tho if I hear no great noise I do not make much enquiry about them.

Saturday July 31 Luke off early for coal but had a misfortune with the cart and horse. Carried off on the shafts a part of Captain Blake's paling before his house, close to the road. Luke said the damage was trifling but I found it otherwise for after dinner a tall straight young man with a Military Air and a famous horse rang at my gate. I went up to him and found it was no one I was acquainted with. He asked for Mr Holland. I bowed to him. I am come he said about a servant of yours. Yes I answered I know and begged him to walk in and so we talked the matter over and seemed to imply great neglect in my servant. I called the servant in who argued that the horse was stung by something and flew from him against the paling. I asked him what he supposed the expence would be to set the matter right. Two guincas at least returned he. Two guineas answered I he told me five shillings. Well Sir said I, I am very sorry for it and will send down a carpenter who will rectify the matter be it what it will. So after some more conversation he left me with great civility saying that he did not wish to put me to more expence than was necessary and so we bowed to each other and on the whole he behaved very much like a gentleman. We called on the Sealy's. There was Mr Best that Apostate from the Protestant Religion very civil to me but, poor fellow, the man is bewildered in the head.

Thursday August 5 Our servant Charlotte is taken ill with a Rheumatick Fever I think. A strong healthy young woman she used to be but now she can scarce walk. It will be a calamitous business if the poor girl should be unable to get her bread. It sinks her very low and she cries all day but we must try to do something for her.

Friday August 6 We expect company to dine here today and we have a cook come from Stowgurcy to dress the meat but Charlotte is very poorly indeed and we have sent to Mr Forbes who has sent her something to take. Our Company came, Mr and Mrs Sealy, Mr and Mrs Best and Mr Verelst. Mr Best is an extraordinary man, bred to the Established Church he entered Orders and preached and Officiated in this Church for a year or two and then turned Roman Catholick and left our Church, married a daughter of Mr Sealy and converted her to a Roman Catholick. When he came to settle here some years ago I would not visit because he turned Apostate from our Church. I said I did not want to have acquaintance with such a man. Some blamed me for this but I satisfied myself to my own mind, behaved civil to him when we met, met him on his visit to his father in law who behaved to me at that time insolently, which I shall not soon forget. He has since been more attentive to me than usual and I have asked the Bests to dine with me as Mr Sealy's Visitants but I have still kept to my point and have no intercourse with him. They say he is a Scholar and very clever but I see not much of that. A poor bewildered, wrong-headed man no great acquisition to the Catholicks nor loss to us. He has a wife, a poor creature and both as plain as plain can be, and he is almost blind. Blind I should say in body and Mind too. We had a good day and all went off very well.

Tuesday August 10 I rode out and towards dinner time Edward Dodwell returned from Devonshire in George Paddock's Gig. He seems much improved in health by his journey. Mrs Lewis and her daughters are still with us so Dodwell will be a fine companion for the Nymphs as he is so delicate in his make and helth and cannot walk far, but is cheerful and has a good deal of Chit Chat for the ladies.

Wednesday August 25 This is a very fine morning. Notice to carry Tithe wheat from Mr White. It was brought but unfit for carriage. I scarce know what to make of this young man, he is never satisfied with any agreement and seems inclined to cheat if he knew how. He gave me notice to pay Tithe in Kind which I accepted, but he has set forth no Tithe and he has contrived to have neither wool nor lamb and now he pretends that I agreed again because I said I would not be hard on him. I do not like such Shuffling. William did not return from Bridgwater but sent a note to say that he wished to go to the Town Hall to hear Speeches about the Bible Society. Now tho I do not disprove of his curiosity on such occasions yet as I ordered him to return without fail with the Mail Gig I am much displeased that he durst disobey me. Young people should be taught to have a command over themselves and not to give way to every solicitation to break their promises on the injunctions they have received.

Thursday September 2 My son and daughter rode to Asholt, Margaret on the little Poney which with great persuasion we got her to ride. William on my horse and Luke on foot after them so she was well guarded. Luke carried Books to Mr Brice. My wife and I drank Coffee with Colonel Bordes and brought to Margaret a letter from Miss Kinaston.

Saturday September 4 A letter from Mrs Hinds of great consequence. It contained an abstract from Dr Hall's letter, the present Dean of Christ Church, containing a promise of a Studentship for my son as soon as he can arrange matters for the purpose. He says he cannot tell exactly when he shall be able to appoint him but advises me to enter him as a Commoner and on the suggestion of the College being full and a difficulty in procuring Rooms he assures me he will take care that he shall have rooms whenever he comes. So he is sure of the Patronage of the Dean and Studentships are in fact Fellowships and succeed to Livings, which are many and valuable and all this I have gained through my Valuable and Zealous friend Mrs Hind, and not only this but his appointment to the Charter House was through the same Channel. Mrs Hind was the first mover and her cousin Mrs Wyndham took it up so warmly that she prevailed on Mr Wyndham to give my son the first turn he had and indeed the only Appointment he made during his life. Mrs Hind's maiden name was Loveday, Mrs Wyndham's Forrest, and I knew them very early in life when I was Curate at St Mary's at Reading. God be Praised, it is a very fortunate connection both for my son as well as for myself.

Sunday September 5 Prayers in the morning, not many at Church and the two principal Singers not at Church. We were obliged to send the Clerk to Kilve in the afternoon to enquire about a servant for we are much distressed since Charlotte has been ill and gone home. We have an old servant who is married and supplies her place at present but she cannot stay much longer and Charlotte is unable to return and we have promised to take her back and no one will come for a few weeks unless she is hired for the year so we are in a bad case.

Tuesday September 7 We are brewing this morning and Phebe is here and Dyer is in the barn. Not much news in the paper yet there is an account of the Macedonian, frigate, being retaken from the Americans by the Tenedos, Captain Parker, and likewise it is mentioned that the President, Commodore Rogers, is taken. I pray God it may prove true for the Rascally

Americans seduce our men and then fight us with our own men. They are the most perfidious Boasting Cowardly Men in the Universe.

Saturday September 11 William and I rode to Asholt for Mr Brice has been sending over for me to assist him. I saw him, he looks poorly, a little cold I think, but I think he is as able to do Duty as I am. I promised to assist him tomorrow if it does not rain.

Sunday September 12 This was a fine morning. I rode over to Asholt according to my Promise. I went through the Service famously and had many compliments on my looks and the manner I did Duty. The Old Clerk of Asholt is dead, the little man who used to beat time on another's shoulder and to squeak out the Psalms in a curious manner.

Tuesday September 14 I finished a letter to Mrs Hinds thanking her for her extraordinary exertions to gain William a promise of a Studentship at Christ Church. Then rode off with William to Spaxton to call on Mr Yorke and dine there. After tea I received a letter from Colonel Leighton who guards Lucien Buonaparte, informing me of the death of my much loved and much valued friend Mr Leighton his father. Oh, this is a heavy stroke for me, where shall I meet such another. He was a man of very great and Noble Abilities, a perfect master of Antient as well as modern Languages. Our acquaintance begun in Reading where I was Curate and lasted till Death. He was Godfather to my son William. He suffered much from Gout and Gravel and other complaints. He suffered much and is now Happy.

Thursday September 16 In the afternoon William moved out to meet his Cousins and Margaret. They came rather late, Hatton Dodwell looked rather old, indeed all three seemed much fatigued tho the journey was only from Bath. Susan Dodwell looked thin and Henry pale but Margaret looked very well.

Monday September 20 Up early, a very fine morning. William went off early by the Mail Gig to Bridgewater and on the Mail to Bath. He was in good Spirits which gave me pleasure. Carrying corn today and a good deal of bustle about one thing or another. My daughter, nephew and niece are gone to Stowey after dinner and Woolcot the maid servant is gone to the Fair at Stowey. So my wife, my niece Hatton Dodwell and I are left at home by ourselves. Dyer and Luke gone for more Tithe.

Sunday September 26 Service in the afternoon, a very full Congregation. The Poor, I understand, were very saucy and impudent. Corn is fallen very considerably and so the Overseers endeavoured to lessen their pay, as indeed they ought to do, for the Poor Rates are increasing annually and will ruin the Nation if not attended to.

Tuesday September 28 To our great surprize our old servant Charlotte came here today in hopes of being able to keep her place but alas I fear not, she is too weak. From a healthy girl crippled and brought down low, I pity her.

Wednesday September 29 Some of my Parishioners dined with me to pay their Compositions and at the same time I sent to the great man Mr Cruchshanks and to my great surprize Dyer brought me the money, tho he has doubled my rent to Lord Egmont. I do not think Lord Egmont knows anything of the matter, it is enormously high for, without dressing, the land is poor. This upstart man I do not like, he is nothing but presumption and arrogance and I do not think him quite upright in his dealings. This Greatness will have a fall some day or other.

Saturday October 2 Poor Charlotte went off early this day being unable to keep her place. Poor Girl she went off reluctantly and it is a great distress to us for we might have hired one or two good servants yet still kept our place open for her, and now we are absolutely without a servant and expect some friends in a day or two, Phoebe, a married woman, is with us but she has two children, a sad inconvenience.

Monday October 4 Luke went off early to Bridgewater Fair and I gave him a Holiday. Dyer is in the barn. Francis Hill came in this day and I paid him this day fifteen shillings for painting the gates. A young woman offered herself as a servant but I fear she is too sickly for our place. Luke returned before nine as he promised.

Tuesday October 5 I rode to Stowgurcy, saw Mr Davis but not Mr Dawes. I did not dine with Mr Davis, his servant had hurt her arm in returning from Bridgewater Fair, the cart being overset. About dusk Mrs Dodwell, Miss Moore her sister, and Ann Dodwell, niece to the last and daughter to the first, drove up to the gate and came to us. They will stay with us for a few days and then return to London. They all looked fat and well and highly pleased with their journey to Mrs Southcombe where they have been for ten weeks past.

Wednesday October 6 Called at various places in my Parish about Tithes, and took apples and pears at Halsey Cross. Young White overtook me and said he was going to call me about Tithe beans, wished to buy them. I said I had partly promised them. He said he ought to have the first offer. I said I did not understand that. He intimated that his Conduct had been fair. I replied that that was not clear to me, he had no lamb or wool for me on a farm which used to abound in both. He mumbled something in a very insolent manner, said I had agreed with him. For what sum I replied. He could not name it. I only said I did not mean to be harder with him than any other person. Yes you did, you agreed with me continued he insolently. Tis False said I angrily. Yes you did continued he. How dare you utter such a Falsehood to my face. This I uttered in a stern manner which silenced him a little tho he rode by my side as far as my house and so we parted.

Sunday October 17　I had a letter this day from William at Charter House in which he sends me a neat Epigram of his own written on a boy at School who had on an immense waistcoat. Mr Russel the Headmaster laughed at it most heartily: William read it to the Sixth Form and it was shewn to the other Masters. William says that the Stipend from the Charter House will be henceforth extended from sixty to eighty pounds pr Ann for the first four years at University and from eighty to £100 pr Ann for four years afterwards, a Noble Foundation.

Monday October 18　As I was getting up I saw a flight of swallows fly about for a short time but they soon retired. This is a nest of youngsters (I conclude) and will not travel far this year. After breakfast our good friends and relations left us and they will spend the night at Mrs Lewis's at Bridgewater and set off tomorrow towards London from whence they have been absent many months. I never saw them all in better health and they are all very sensible agreeable people.

Thursday October 21　I rode out this day thro Stowey and then up the Hill. Thomas Palmer, a Broomer, was unwilling to pay his Tithe from land inclosed on Quantock, but he has now paid so as I passed I called to him – Now you begin to pay your Tithe you'll have a good crop and prosper. He smiled and said he hoped he would. An elderly woman in the field said I do not grudge it at all for you be a Good Kind of Gentleman. In my return I met Mr Lyng who has been to see my wife. He says matters are going on well with my wife's boil but there is still a speck which must be either burnt or cut out.It has continued long.

Monday October 25　Dyer is here in the barn threshing and I am busy taking Tithe potatoes. A woman offered her service in the afternoon but we expect Charlotte again tomorrow. This is our Wedding Day and we have been Married 32 years.

Wednesday October 27　In the afternoon who should come in but our old servant Charlotte who looks tolerably and is able to go about and I think will take to her place again.

Thursday October 28   Dyer and Luke have gone to take up potatoes. I rode out towards Davis at Halsey Cross. His is a poor crop, I wonder at it. Sent again in the afternoon to Tithe what he has taken up, found little more than a bag. The man speaks fair, but I suspect him strongly. Mr Lyng says my wife's back is getting better very fast. They have got a strange notion hereabouts that it is something very bad. Tis no such thing, a small inoffensive humour which nevertheless now it is open ought to be eradicated. Margaret has been very active and dressed it every day uncommonly well, but it is hard to keep her at home for such a thing as that and for so long.

Monday November 1   Old Colonel Landsey, as they call him, came to me with a basket of apples for which I gave him a shilling. I asked him what his age is, he told me 85 and he walks many miles in a day. Tis suprizing that this man should be alive so long for twenty years I remember that he used to be sadly afflicted with the Gravel and Rheumatism. He is a shrewd old man and I must have some talk with him again in the Kitchin.

Sunday November 7   This day sourish. I found few in the Sunday School in the morning, most of the children have got Scarlet Fever and it runs through the Parish and through Stowey yet few die here. We had a Serenade from the Young Singers this day but I did not think they performed well, hardly perfect.

Monday November 8   Dyer is here carrying out the dung, the day gets worse. Herrings in great plenty this year, we turned off a woman just now who offered them for 6 pence pr dozen, we wanted them for fourpence. Mr Lyng was here and cut out the root of the small tumour in my wife's back which has put us all in Spirits. He says we may now allow it to heal up immediately. It was a hard substance about as large as a pea.

Thursday November 11   Dyer thrashed out my wheat what was in the barn and a man is to come to see it to buy it. I kept it for a long time for the Poor but they did not come for it for now wheat is low they are become saucy and as discontented as ever. If corn is high they complain with reason, if low they complain without reason and are more riotous when there is plenty than scarcity. The man of Castle Hill has seen my wheat and gives eleven shillings pr bushell. As things are and Estates rented Farmers cannot afford it much lower.

Wednesday November 17   After breakfast at Mrs Lewis's I walked about the town, met Mr Ruscomb Poole and went to his Office. While we were there it Thundered and the third Clap was so near that we both started up and ran to Mrs Poole. She is in the Family Way but was not so alarmed as we anticipated. We guessed it must have done some harm. It struck the Steeple at Bridgewater and has injured it much. The Church at Weston is damaged very materially.

Saturday November 20   A tolerable morning. After breakfast I mounted my horse. Tho I paid the Ostler well he did not take care of my horse, he said the horse would not drink but I suspect that he gave him no water. He could hardly move and I could not get him on but when I came to water he drank very well and revived. Got safe home and found all things well and the house clean.

Sunday November 28   Dyer brought me a letter, not from William as I expected but from Mr Hickes my Curate at Monkton Farley, rather unpleasant as he is going to quit Farley. Luke was obliged to go after dinner with the Sow to the Bore which provoked me much.

Monday December 20   We had a fine pig killed this day. I rode out and called on some sick people. I found one woman deranged after child bearing. I privately Baptized the child this day. Sarah Selleck I wished to talk to and she promised to come to me for that purpose as she is desirous of being Baptized before she is brought to bed, being an Anabaptist. She lived with us for a year or two and we did not chuse to keep her on account of her not being Baptized. Her children have been Baptized. My face has been poorly for some time.

Friday December 24   We had a great many of our Poor Parishioners to whom we distributed some wheat. After breakfast Mr Dawes walked with me to the Church and he went up the Tower. The poor woman is still in the same mad state, and Sarah Selleck who was to be Christened is brought to bed so that she cannot now be Christened.

Tuesday December 28   A hard frost with thick fog. A boy brought ten shillings here from Mr Tom Poole, the remainder of money lodged in my hands by him for distribution to the Poor. William is now at Enmore with his friend Mr John Poole and is to return tomorrow.

Friday December 31   This was the last day of the year, still a hard frost. Mr and Mrs Mathew, Mr and Mrs Sealy and Mr John Poole dined with us.

The Year 1814

Thursday January 6   After breakfast at Mr Dawes's I called on Mr Davis and he wished me to dine with him but I could not stay. I never heard a man talk so calm and resigned as Mr Davis did about his Death. He said he went to the Sacrament to Church for the last time, he said he had settled all his wordly affairs and was quite prepared and easy. I shook him by the hand and said that was the state of mind I wished to be in myself when the time came, as come it must some day or other. So I left him, he is four or five years older than I am. So I mounted my horse to ride home. My wife, Margaret and William walked through the snow having first furnished themselves with worsted stockings about their legs so we all got safe home.

Friday January 7   This was a hard frost. Thermometer* has been about thirty or under for many days and the barometer high. My wife has been busy this evening preparing William for his journey to the Charter House tomorrow.

Saturday January 8   A hard frost still and gloomy which has made us somewhat alarmed about William's intended journey to London. His sister is to go with him as far as Bath to Mrs Hume where she is to have a Dentist for her teeth which troubled her much of late. George Paddock came over with his Gig about twelve and about one William and his sister were off for Bridgewater to Mrs Lewis's.

Wednesday January 12   More snow fell in the night, it is uncommonly deep. No Mail last night at Bridgewater and none this morning. No tidings from William, indeed there could be none for no Mail has arrived. Dyer and Luke very busy in shovelling off snow. I have been busy with a Thanksgiving Sermon for tomorrow.

Thursday January 13   A very clear keen frosty morning. The snow lies deep, I scarce ever remember deeper. The Bells rang merrily, I gave something for the purpose. It is the Thanksgiving Day appointed by Government for a series of Victories over the Enemy Buonaparte. Very few at Church. I am sorry for it but many are drawn to Bridgewater where there are great doings and moreover it is Market Day. I gave them a new Sermon and took some pains in making it and the few that came to Church were uncommonly attentive. After Prayers my wife and I walked to Stowey and with some difficulty for the path through the fields was so narrow and so deep that I am astonished how my wife got on. My nail presses into my toe, otherwise I should walk very well for I feel in good spirits and health. I shall not send for the paper till tomorrow.

Friday January 14 It threatens snow, freezes hard beyond measure. Mr Balch was carried this day from St Hadry to Bridgewater to be buried and buried he has been all his life. I never saw him but once. His intellects were narrow, his health very bad, scarce ever stirred out of his house where he lived many years with a sister that now survives. Poor Creature we can say nothing of him but that he lived and died. Luke brought me with the newspaper two letters, one from William from the Charter House and one from Margaret at Bath. Margaret has had two teeth drawn and the others rectified.

Sunday January 16 We had more by far at the Church than I expected for I scarce know how the women could come but it was Payday for the Poor and that brought some. Mr Rich has not been at Church, I fear he is not well, I must call on him. The frost being so severe we cannot get Barm for baking so that we are obliged to buy bread dear and sell wheat to the Poor cheap. I hope this will not continue, people do not care to brew this frosty weather which causes this scarcity of Barm.

Monday January 17 We have got Barm at last and are busy baking. I walked over to call on Mr Rich today. While I was there Tom Poole sneaked in He staid there some time, some business between them I suppose. Tom has insinuated himself into Mr Rich's confidence in a manner I do not much approve of. He is a selfish vain artful man and has got the direction of all his affairs now. My wife at night played Chess with me before a good fire.

Thursday January 20 The frost very severe. I do not remember such a deep fall of snow tho they say there was one about forty years ago. We invited the people of the Poor House to our gates and gave them a whole pot full of Broth, made out of pease and Meat Bones and Onions which they are very glad of. The times now begin to be hard for the Poor for they cannot work or pick up wood. I think a collection should be made and something distributed but I cannot get out to rouse the Churchwardens to do something for them. I do not think that our neighbour Mr Rich does anything tho his wealth is so great tis sad indeed. I think I shall give him a hint that way.

Friday January 21 It freezes hard but the sky is clear and we have a brilliant sun. All the trees and shrubs glisten and the hedges display the same splendour. The path made through the snow to a Certain House in the Garden is as slippery as Glass and I more than once had nearly fallen in passing along notwithstanding the caution I took.

Saturday January 22 I set Dyer and the Sexton to make a path through the Churchyard to the Church and hard work it was. I sent Luke to Stowey after dinner, the Postman come but no Mails arrived at Bridgewater, three Mails missing, no letters can either go or be received. I know not what will become of the Poor, no work for them,. I sent yesterday my Letter of Notification to the Bishop of Salisbury of claiming an Exemption from Residence at Monkton Farley. I put this down as a memorandum in case my letter should not be received in this perilous state of Posts and the Mail.

Sunday January 23 Still a very hard frost. Very few at Church, the women could not come from a distance but what is surprising is we had none of our neighbours in particular just around us. We had one newspaper at last but not the Saturday one, and a letter from Margaret at Bath. She has caught a cold in her teeth and face but wishes to come home very much. Several ill hereabouts with Inflamation and Mortifications. I thank God my wife and I are tolerable though I complain much of my toes and the nails of them so that I cannot walk as I wish to do. I think the shoes press too much on them. Our coal gets low and there is none to be got at Bridgwater or Combych.

Friday February 4 Rode out to the sick family at Pepril, poor Mrs Rich the mother is almost worn out. Her eldest son lay in a room by himself in a wretched state, I was almost stiffled when I entered. It was a small room and close, I think he has a putrid fever. The doctors said he was better than he had been. I read Prayers by him and left the Book with the mother, giving her directions what to do, then went into the next room which was very large and comfortable. In this there was a boy in bed whose leg was so bad they feared it would Mortify and a young girl who had been ill standing by the fire. There was another girl in bed, I did not see her. They are a very fine family and brought up very well with rather scanty means and the parents much to be pittied.

Saturday February 12 Mr Forbes called in to see my toes and nails but he could not see much the matter with them tho I am unable to walk they are so pinched. I called on Mr James Rich and found him very poorly tho they told me he was better. They will wear him out with their Physick. I chatted with him some time and prayed by him and then left him to go to dinner. Mrs Way who is his nearest Relative is with him and attentive to him. I fear she has a little of the Methodistical Cant about her.,

Sunday February 13 Many at Church because we have bread given away, a fine for stealing wood. Our Singers were not a choice band, neither Farmer Fish nor Morle were there. The Richs of Peperill are still very bad and more taken ill since I was there. It certainly must be a bad putrid fever otherwise it would not take 'em one after another. It is indeed a Melancholy House.

Monday February 14 I sent Dyer and Luke for some Poplar Trees to plant in the Churchyard to cover the Poorhouse. We got some in, hope to finish tomorrow. After dark the Richs of Peperel sent for more Brandy. I gave them a bottle before and a bottle of wine and now a good part of a bottle, they will break me down at this rate. My pens are so bad I cannot go on.*

Monday February 21 A very hard frost, thermometer under 30. Dyer here but the frost so severe could do nothing in the garden. I have covered my early potatoes with litter to secure them. I rode out this day thro Stowey and towards the Castle of Comfort but soon returned being desired to call on Mr Rich and pray by him, which I did. Paid Myster Forbes Bill which he made as much as he could for he is a terrible man for a Bill.

Tuesday March 1 I had invited Mr Humphreys to come here this day to celebrate the first of March with me, he being a Welshman. But he was afraid of the weather. He is Curate of Crowcombe over the Hill and a very respectable man. Poor Davis of Stowgurcy who used to celebrate this day with me by wearing a leek and dining with me cannot move from his home now being so infirm. The weather altered and we had hail and snow and the ground was white before night. This appeared sad at this time of year and after so severe a winter.

Friday March 4 A hard frost. Having made many attempts to go to see my friend Mr Davis I this day rode over to Stowcurcy. I dined with Mr Davis and had every thing very neat and clean about him. The two girls about keep him very comfortable. He seemed tolerable but feeble, particularly in his walk. I staid to five and then came home. I sat myself with great pleasure before a good fire, drank my tea and amused myself by looking at my wife and daughter playing chess.

Thursday March 10 Mr Verelst and Mr Dawes called here, they were sent for by the Bishop to take out Licences for their Curacies so I signed their Testimonials. Then I rode with them as far as Plainsfield to make enquiries about a poor boy who was brought before the Bath Society for Distressed Poor. It is James Porter a runaway apprentice from Mr White, a sad wicked boy. Mr Verelst and Mr Dawes went on to Mr Brice. The papers this evening speak of Lord Wellington having crossed the Adour with 100,000 men. Buonaparte and the Allies are still fighting with alternate success.

Saturday March 12   A man rung at the Gate this morning, it was a labourer of Mr Allen. He told us that Mrs Allen was dead, she was brought to bed on Tuesday and it was thought she was doing well but she died this day about seven in the morning. It was like a thunder clap to all of us. She has left poor Mr Allen with seven children, the eldest not above eight years old. Our house was confounded with the news and so was the town of Stowey. She was much beloved there. An Excellent wife of very agreeable manners, scarce a dry eye in the town of Stowey. My wife and I were unhinged all day. I walked to Stowey, called on the Bordes and even on Tom Poole. Poor Allen like a Statue, walks silent up and down the room and every now and then bursts into tears. The papers were brought but no news of Lord Wellington.

Saturday March 19   I went down to Stowey to bury Mrs Allen, found there Mr Mathew and Captain Ferris*, Mr Tom Poole and Mr Bennet. We had all Hatband and Scarfs and tho a private it was a very decent Funeral. None of the family except Captain Ferris attended. The Poor Children, ignorant of their loss all appeared at the window to see us move on as if it was a fine sight. Blucher's success confirmed in the paper today.

Sunday March 20   There were Prayers in the morning and a tolerable congregation. We had the Stowey Singers. In the afternoon I walked to Stowey to do the Duty there and the pains in my face came on so severely that I had great difficulty in getting on. The whole congregation seemed to feel for me yet I persevered and got to the end, very well. After this I walked to Mr Sealy's and met my wife there to drink tea. It is the first time for these many years we have drunk tea out and we would not have done so now had I not done the afternoon Duty at Stowey. We walked home and were in time enough to have the Servants in for Reading &cc.

Friday March 25   I rode out and between Mr Crosse's and Mr Washer's I was stopped by some young Bullocks who stood across the road affrighted by a carpet which hung over a hedge into the road. I called out and Mrs Crosse came and I told her the man's distress and my own, so she called out her maid servant who let me into the yard and carried off the carpet to the no small exultation of the man who was driving the Bullocks. After this called on Mr Allen and Mrs Ferris, they were tolerable. Captain Ferris was just gone off to Bath. In the evening my wife and I attacked each other at Chess and I am generally Victorious.

Sunday April 3 I had a letter from William this afternoon. He complains of the Head Master neglecting the Upper Form to introduce Dr Bell's new System of Teaching. I do not much approve of William's discontented fault finding disposition and shall give him a Lecture on the occasion.

Monday April 4 Dyer came here in the afternoon with a dismal tale. The cow and calf which he bought at Taunton on Saturday, do not belong to each other and so now he is to go to Bishop Lidiart Fair tomorrow to try to pass them off again for the cow has no milk and must be fatted off.

Thursday April 7 Early this morning Charlotte came up with a grin on her face and told us the cow had a very fine calf, a cow calf.

Sunday April 10 Easter Day, a very fine day. A very full Church and a tolerable number at the Sacrament, we had new faces which looks well. We had a burial, a labouring man who died of an inflamation in the leg. It is a disorder that lately showed itself in the village and is infectious. It begun in Mr Rich of Peperel's family. There is now one son a cripple and the eldest has been some time adying. The Wilkins caught it from the Richs by nursing, it begins in the foot or leg and soon turns to a gangrene. The man had several children who attended him to the Grave.

Monday April 11 Heard firing last night and there is a rumour that Buonaparte is taken. Our Bells began to ring early after breakfast. It is said that he surrendered to the Allies who informed him that he might retire to a small island in the mediterranean, Elba by name, about 10 miles in length and 3 in breadth. I had Prayers in the afternoon to take in the Farmers who were coming to settle Parish matters. They retired to my house where we signed and I gave them a Jug of Strong Beer.

Tuesday April 12 We went off in a Post Chaise to Bridgwater where we stayed till Saturday the sixteenth. Great rejoicing on Wednesday evening. We got a position in a room on the Cornhill where we could see the Bonfire and Squibs and Rockets thrown. In a narrow passage we had a Squib thrown amongst us and Margaret's gown was burnt and when we got upstairs a Squib with a stone was thrown through the window and the broken glass flew to Mr John Symes face. Buonaparte at last finishes his Career of Wickedness like a Poor Cowardly Scoundrel in the Hand of Providence. On the sixteenth there was a meeting of the Mayor and Corporation to form an Address to the Prince Regent, I was present and among others appointed to the committee to draw up the address, which was done.

Now we have the longest gap of all in Mr Holland's story for his books numbered 82 to 84 are missing, i.e. April 12 1814 – October 12 1815. What his thoughts were on the return of Buonaparte and his final defeat at Waterloo we shall never know. His friend and Churchwarden Mr James Rich was buried on April 22 1815 and Mr Davis of Stowgurcy. By October 1815 William was at Oxford undoubtedly to the joy of his father.

The Year 1815

Thursday October 12   A tolerable good day and my wife and I walked to Stowey. Had two letters, one from Margaret to my wife and the other from Mrs Hume to Margaret. William went off yesterday to Bath and is at Oxford I trust now tho we have not heard from him yet. Luke went for coal today.

Saturday October 14   Luke is gone for coal. My wife and I walked to Stowey but were obliged to borrow an umbrella to come home and even notwithstanding this my wife was so wetted was obliged to change her shoes and stockings.

Sunday October 22   We had a letter from William last night, he is in borrowed Rooms but is not at all alarmed about having some as he is sure of coming in by Rotation. He seems to speak cheerfully and in Spirits. Our Church in the afternoon was full but we had none of our Chief Singers, none of the Morles except Betty. They are become a divided Family and are dispassing, who used to be constant at Church when the Old Man was alive. Very few of the Methodistical Riches, sad this.

Tuesday October 24   Before dusk in the afternoon a Chaise came to the gate and soon after Mrs Southcombe and her maid appeared. They walked over the Downfield and Mrs Southcombe does this to prevent fits at her first arrival, which she had been subject to. But now the bustle and perspiration of a walk takes them off – she escaped this time. She found out the Method by being compelled to walk by a drunken driver some years ago and she finds it has answered ever since. She seems surprizingly well and is going on towards London and Windsor and makes us another visit on her return.

Wednesday October 25   We have breakfasted but Mrs Southcomb is not yet come down being up yesterday about three in the morning and travelled all day. She needs rest. I rode out and called on little Allen and he dined here and staid till nine. Margaret was expected from Bridgwater but did not come. This is our Wedding Day, we have been married 35 years. Morle came in and paid me some Tithe.

Thursday October 26 A fine pleasant morning. Dyer is gone with the heifer to the Bull and Luke gone with a note to Mr Jeffrey, Grace, Mrs Southcomb's maid is gone to Stowey where my wife and I are to go soon. We found our daughter at Stowey, just arrived from Bridgwater and this is the first day she came home from her journey to Wales. Mr Lyng dined with us this day but was obliged to return over the Hill in the Dark.

Saturday October 28 Margaret walked to Stowey to return to her Station at Mr Edward Sealy's as Bride's Maid. I sent off Dyer to Bridgwater for goods for Margaret's room and they arrived safe without damage. Margaret's Room is now become the best in the house.

Tuesday October 31 Mrs Southcombe and her Maid, Grace, went off early this morning for Bristol and is to proceed from thence to London and afterwards to various places and will finish her visit to us again five months hence. She is an extraordinary person, immures in a lonely house, sees little company and goes out nowhere except on these excursions which she takes once in two or three years and then enjoys herself as if she had lived all her time in the World. She has a good income which she has obtained partly by good management. In her own neighbourhood she is highly respected by the Gentry and adored by the Poor. Dyer is gone off to take Tithe potatoes and Luke follows with the cart. They brought a number of the best Red Potatoes which will serve my purpose for the year.

Wednesday November 1 Luke went off early this morning for coal. I asked Mr Sealy to come and eat some Tithe Pie with us but he declined. I returned and my wife and I sat down to one of Margaret's pigs. I liked the pig but wished the sow to Jericho, a great immense thing of the Indian kind. I do think pigs the nastiest animals that can be kept as they are continually dunging as they walk along.

Sunday November 5 The Bells rang early this morning being the fifth of November, but our Prayers are in the afternoon in their due course so the Thanksgiving Service was passed over and there is no appropriate Service for the afternoon. As this Service has been and is to continue it should be altered and the Prayers made more general and those Prayers (many of them) more expressive of the Circumstances of the time omitted. We had a good many at Church, among them Mr Edmund Rich of Crosse with two of his sons and some strangers of his acquaintance. Indeed I had spoken to him a day or two before about his non appearance at Church but he is, it seems, a Methodist, an ignorant illiterate man tho he is now come into some Property, I fear I shall have trouble with them for they have not yet said anything to me on the subject of Tithe but I shall try gentleness with him and see what that will do.

Monday November 6 Called on Rich that lived at Ely Green but now at Landsey's old house. He told me a sad story of the Baker that married Crook's daughter being sent to Jail. He was arrested I understand by Reed the partner of Parsons the Lawyer, and Parsons is coming to take up the matter. Parsons is the owner of an Estate at Plainsfield and I fear Parsons is at the bottom of this matter for he wants the house the poor man lives in and indeed all the Cottages that way. He is a sad paltry fellow, buys everything and pays nothing, a bad way of going on.

Thursday November 9 I rode first to Stowey and had a pound of Ginger-bread Nuts from Mrs Landsey, sallied forth to Plainsfield and called on Mrs Morle and Pray by her. She seems poor and low but in no immediate danger. Then I called on Colonel Landsey, as they call him. He is eighty eight, complains that he is poor and low and well he may be for he takes a quarter of a pound of Brimstone and Jollep and some other Drug, enough to kill a horse. He takes too much says the woman that attends him. Indeed he does answered I.

Friday November 10 It is the day fixed for the sale of Squire Cruckshank's property the Scoundrel who has taken in half the Country.

Thursday November 16 Four of my daughter's pigs were sold and carried off this day by Thomas Porter who lives near Ely Green, a soft sly, smooth spoken man, industrious and very attentive to his own interest but he was liberal in one respect for he commended the pigs at the best in the Parish when he purchased them. On which I ordered him a cup of drink for his fair dealings. Pigs are now very cheap.

Friday November 24 We walked to Stowey to meet Mr and Mrs Hole and some other company but no one came but Mr Hole, which was awkward. Mr Hole is come to these parts from Devonshire to serve three Churches, Dodington, Holford and Kilton making a good Curacy of the whole*. A strong healthy man with a good deal of the Devonshire Brogue. He has not a large family and is at lodgings at Paddock's till he can get into the Parsonage House at Holford.

Sunday December 3 Prayers in the afternoon, we had a Christening, Burial and Churching. A child died suddenly in the Workhouse. I wish the Apothecary to examine the corpse. I spoke to the woman at the Grave who was crying so violently that she lamented the child but had more reason to lament herself for the violence she shewed a day or two before and the Horrid Oaths she swore. The Riches of Cross were at Church but Farmer Fish has mist several Sundays, I shall speak to him at the first opportunity.

Monday December 11 A fine morning, we are preparing to walk to Enmore, the frost very severe. We did walk there, calling first at Mr Yorke's and sat there chatting a small time. The nephew, Mr Coombs walked with my wife and I putting us on our way through Mr Jeffrey's Lawn and Lord Egmont's Park so we got to Mrs Poole's safe and well and not fatigued considering I was in my 70th year and my wife in her 66th. Old Mrs Poole seemed very well in her 83rd year. They were glad to see us and we found ourselves At Home. Mr John Poole and I took a walk or two but tho I was in spirits yet was I so Costive and uneasy in my Stomach and Bowels that I was obliged to take a good dose of Salts after many other things before. This brought me Right again.

Monday December 18 A good deal of snow fell in the night. Mr Carew from Crowcombe called, he was going to Bridgwater for his son whom he expects from Oxford, I likewise expect mine tomorrow. If he should arrive at Bridgwater with his he will bring him home. They are to have a famous Ball at Crowcombe where William and Margaret are invited. Mr Carew says 45 persons promised to come which with their own Family will make a large number. My wife and Margaret walked to Stowey to see the new married couple Mr and Mrs Edward Sealy. My face has been very painful and troublesome all this day.

Wednesday December 20 This is a sourish day with frequent showers. We are very busy in getting our children to go over to Crowcombe to the Grand Ball this night. The evening seemed somewhat more favourable so we had Paddock's New Gig and William drove his sister and Luke walked by the side to bring home the Gig as they are to stay the night.

Friday December 29 Towards twelve o'clock William and I called on Dr Wollen and I went with him to the meeting of the Select Committee of the Society for Promoting Christian Knowledge. William I left among the Miss Wollens who laid hold of him as soon as he came in. In the afternoon we had a famous Ball where children were admitted, the Christmas Ball. My wife and I and two children went with Mr and Mrs Edward Sealy. It was indeed a very good Ball. There my wife and I saw our children both dance at the same time and they made a good figure. It was very late before we returned and our young ones staid behind.

Sunday December 31 A good day still. I was late this morning not having recovered the fatigue of the Ball. I did not dance but sitting up does not agree with me. In the afternoon we had a full Church. The day ended as usual.

The Year 1816

Monday January 1　A New year, 1816, commenced and it was ushered in by Ringing of Bells as usual. William went off early this day to Bridgwater and Enmore. The Year has been eventful and Victorious to Great Britain and she now enjoys real Peace everywhere throughout her extended Dominions, a Peace founded on Justice and Honour and Religion and she is universally acknowledged to be the First Empire in the World. But her former Colonies in America, tho now at Peace with her are still full of Envy and Malice against her and ready to join in any scheme for her destruction, tho she has been their Saviour, evidently from the Dominion of Buonaparte who has now a strong party among them. I am now entering into a New Year and find myself in tolerable health and not much impaired since last year. My complaint in the face still continues tho at present it is not very violent and I have some hopes of relief from the Tincture of Phetony Root which my friend Stowell of South Molton lately prescribed for me after experiencing himself an absolute cure of the same complaint by means of this root.

Wednesday January 3　We had a Parish Meeting about the roads which were presented by Mr Carew they say, tho his name was not mentioned in the Presentation. We agreed to take Mr Ruscombe Poole's opinion on the occasion.

Thursday January 4　I mounted my horse and rode up the Hill, Crowcombe way to observe the road presented. I thought the road tolerable and might have been rectified without Presentation. They said they had no notice before of this presentation but I fear they had, which they neglected often times. This day William kept close to his studies. We all dined together this day. Luke gone for the paper and letters to Stowey.

Monday January 8　This was an uncomfortable rainy day. William close to his studies most of the day and we did not stir out. I was much alarmed by sheep breaking into the Paddock and I had no one nigh to turn them out. For some time I turned them out but they were soon in again. I turned out of the house too an Impudent Sailor, begging. An impudent Fellow.

Tuesday January 16 We have very stormy weather with snow and sleet but William went off this day for Bath and Oxford. Margaret is still at home with us. I have not been very well for some days being very Costive and Puffed up so that I scarce know what to do with myself.

Tuesday January 23 My wife and Margaret walked to Stowy but I had taken some Salts and could not go out except backwards and forwards in the garden with Luke. I have been of late so Costive I know not what to do. A man came to see my cow and I hope he has done her some good but I am always apprehensive of such people, they are so ignorant tho they pretend to have much knowlege.

Thursday January 25 Margaret went off to Bridgwater by Enmore on my double horse being disappointed in a coach and Paddock's Gig and she was obliged to go being engaged to Mrs Ruscomb Poole for Friday's Ball, Mr Ruscombe Poole being one of the Stewards. I am still very dissatisfied with the state of my Stomach and Bowels, being uncommonly Costive and full of Wind. Forbes gave me some Pills and I have taken various things but nothing gains a Passage which alarms me much. Yet I sleep well and have an appetite to my food, only my stomach and bowels feel uneasy and extended.

Friday January 26 This day very gloomy and misty, worse than yesterday. My Stomach still full and extended tho I have took Castor Oil this morning. I scarce know what to do I have so little opinion of Forbes as an Apothecary. If it please God my wife and I will go to Bridgwater on Monday next to Mrs Lewis where we shall meet with some advice to be depended on.

Wednesday February 14 The weather frosty with a deep snow. We have in the neighbourhood discovered a whole nest of Thieves and Housebreakers, five or six of whom have been sent to Jail. In short we have a very bad neighbourhood and I do not think it very safe to live among them but put my trust in Providence for the Protection of myself and House.

Friday February 16 The snow and frost almost compleatly gone. Dyer is here and has been almost every day this winter. Most of the Farmers have lowered the wages of their servants. I have not lowered mine yet so Master Dyer clings to me and ekes out his work as much as he can. He was out in the Moors today which he might have finished long ago.

Wednesday February 21 Dyer is here and finished planting some part of the seeds. I have planted too some early potatoes. I rode out and called at the house of the man who had his face hurt by the explosion of gunpowder at the quarry just by. He came to the door, he is covered in scars. I hope Sir, I shall not lose my eye. I hope not indeed but the eye tho weak itself has strong bones around to defend it and those scars will soon wear off. As I passed along I saw Jack Hunt in his garden working, the son of Old Ben Hunt. Well you are building a town here and enclosing a whole farm. Why Sir it is better than sitting by the fire all day. It is so, and I love to see industry but why do you not let this hedge grow high and prune down that before you to view the fine prospect. Ah that is Mr Buller's hedge and I can see twelve Parish Churches from my door. After this I moved along.

Wednesday February 28 A tolerable fine morning. Dyer and Luke gone to the Hill to cut wood. This day Col Bordes is to be buried at Stowey. He died the 23rd. His burial is as private as possible for he did not dye in affluence. God rest his Soul for his sufferings have been great, a Gentleman-like man of some Observation, of the Old School of the Military Line. He had many anecdotes and had seen a great deal of Life in the Military Line and had served in the East Indies. A burial today, Jane Japp aged 89.

Friday March 1 Dry with something of a frost. This being the first of March I used to wear a Leek in my hat and had other Welshmen and Mr Davis to dine with me, but they are all gone and I do not chuse to distinguish myself now that I am old and alone. Dyer and Luke gone again to the Hill for wood.

Sunday March 3 There was but a poor attendance at Church this morning but it did fill at last. Mr John Symes and Mrs Tracey were at Church in Mr Buller's seat. Some say they are married but dare not own it because in that Mrs Tracy would lose part of her fortune. Be that as it may the situation they appear in at present is not very respectable. None of the Riches of Crosse were at Church except one young man but they go constantly to the Meeting at Stowey and seduce as many as they can from my Parish to follow them. Poor, Ignorant, Illiterate people who scarce know what they are about. There is a sad collection of girls from the Silk House* in this Parish who attend these Meetings and sad work there is, I am told, amongst the young men and them. These Methodists preach Salvation through Faith in Christ without Repentance from Sin and I Preach Repentance from Sin and then Salvation through Christ. No wonder that the first takes with disorderly people more than the last for if they may be saved without forsaking their Sins tis an easy thing to say they have Faith, but it is not an easy thing to forsake their Sins.

Monday March 4 The Glass is low, I mean the Barometer. I ventured out but before I could take my round I got finely soused and my wife who walked to Stowey got her dressing too. The Rectorial House, under the

Chamber of Bristol is undergoing a thorough repair and the front taking down. The Lessee who is coming to live in is a Rank Methodist, but a wicked fellow, keeps a woman in the house under his wife's nose. The wife is just lay'n in and this woman is going to do so, yet this man is a saint. This is Faith without works with a Vengeance.

Saturday March 23 I did not stir out for the weather does not suit me at all. I am not much better that I have been for my face very spasmodic and a complaint in my bowels at the same time. No news in the paper only that the Property Tax is taken off and part of the Malt Tax. I shall discontinue the London paper from this time.

Monday March 25 I married a couple this day and then moved off to Plainsfield to administer the Sacrament to poor Mrs Morle who is in a very weak way and I fancy going off the Stage after her husband. I have observed when man and wife have lived together for a long time they always follow each other in a very short time to another world. She was far gone in dropsy and five daughters around her who all received the Sacrament with her. It was indeed a most comfortable sight. One of them was in Service and came to see her mother on her way to Lady Byron her Mistress. Another daughter was Mrs Shepherd, married in the neighbourhood.

Wednesday March 27 Dyer does not work here at present having taken a task on the road. Luke returned early this morning from his sister's wedding at Broomfield. From this time to April 4th I have neglected my Diary again which I do now too frequently, growing older and more indolent, yet I can state the most remarkable circumstances within the time from one omission to the other.

Thursday April 4 My wife and daughter are gone over the Hill to call on the Carew's. I have taken Ware, who was hurt so much a few days ago in the Quarry to run up a dry wall for me against the Terrace in the garden. We have been very uneasy this day when we found no letter from my son as I have sent him some days ago a draft for thirty pounds which he has not acknowledged and I have sent him a letter to express our surprize at not hearing from him. He is so punctual and exact in general that we are astonished at the circumstances and conjecture itself is at a loss what to conclude.

Friday April 5 I have the man still at the Ha Ha wall and Luke has been digging in the garden. At night I received a letter from William expressing himself as much concerned about our alarm but that he had sent a letter by a young Collegian by the name of Warry who was coming to Somersetshire for his Easter Holidays. Now this letter we have not received and there is a small parcel with an Oxford Calendar with it. But letters of consequence should never be sent by private hands for the Post is more expeditious and safe and William says he will never do so again. There was no difficulty in negotiating the draft, all is perfectly well and we easy. No news in the paper, I do not now take the London paper, only the Bath and North Wales Gazette.

Friday April 12 Good Friday. We went to Church and had a tolerable congregation. I gave them a Sermon which was much attended to. An odd circumstance happened this day. A servant came and (as I thought) Mr Forbes begged that his carriage might stand in my Barton. I said yes and to my surprize found no one but Mrs Forbes there. We do not visit her nor chuse to visit tho Mr Forbes is my Apothecary. Twas a bold push. She went into Church but did not sit in the same seat as my family. Nothing material after this.

Wednesday April 17 A fine open mild morning. I rode out and called on many of my Old and Poor Parishioners and I found out at last Old George Adams at the end of a long lane in Cockercombe. He is 86 and came out at last, weak and with a long beard. I gave him some of the Sacrament Money. God Bless you said he I have no one but you and Madam to look after me. I answered you have your own family, son and daughter. He shook his head and replied, looking steadfast at me, they are best off who can help themselves. Then I called on the Old Colonel as they call him. He is 87 if not eight. He has got two houses so I did not give him any money but he may have something to eat and drink if he sends for it. He has been a shrewd old man in his day. Then I called on Rich who lately lived at Ely Green, he kept a Publick House, got rich by it and took a little himself so that he and his wife look dropsical and blodded but he was a relation of the late Mr Rich of Crosse who gave him a little eastate so now he means to live soberly and moderately and repent of his sins as he told me. I enquired of the health of both of them and had some Parish news of him and understood the Whites are coming to Plainsfield again. After speaking a word to one or two others I returned home and Mrs Sealy came in to drink tea. We had a brewing this morning, Mr Luke managed the whole business.

Friday April 19 I have had of late frequent bleedings of the nose and I walked down to Stowy to consult Mr Forbes on the occasion but he was not to be found.

Saturday April 20 Still bleeding of the nose and I have preserved some of the blood today to shew it to Mr Forbes. He came over and on view declared it to be salutary. Dyer went off to Bridgwater early for wine to Mr Chubb. He had money with him to discharge last year's Bill and is to bring a fresh cargo back. After dinner Edward Dodwell came here in Paddock's Gig. He is weak and poorly yet better than I thought he was. He is to stay here a few days, having drunk the Bath Water. I saw some swallows this day, the first time this year.

Friday April 26 My Farmers dined with me and were very merry and brought their payments handsomely except Tom Poole who is very Backward, not because he wants money but because he does not chuse to part with it. This man will be found out some day or other, a vain selfish superficial fellow. I had a note this day to attend poor Mrs Field's Funeral. I must be at Eddington on Wednesday next, a mild inoffensive Religious woman. By her death a large Fortune comes to her daughter, Miss Fields, a lively spirited sprightly young woman, short in Stature but Great in Soul.

Sunday April 28 William has got possession of his Rooms at ChristChurch and thinks the thirds reasonable considering how extravagant his Predecessor had been in the furniture. I am to send him a draft for forty pounds tomorrow or next. We all go to Bridgwater tomorrow that I may be ready to attend at Eddington by eleven o'clock.

Wednesday May 1 Not a very pleasant day. My friend John Poole came to Bridgwater in his new Gig with a head to it and took me to Eddington. As we passed the flat beyond Bridgwater towards the hills or rising ground leading to Piper's Hill he made his Observations. There along that side of the Hills the manners of the people are quite different from what they are the other side of Bridgwater, for all of this flat was once the sea. We have proof of it in seashells in abundance and of the very same kind you find on the shore around Stirt Point and in the Channel. The language of the people and their customs are very different. The flat spades begin on that ridge, no shovels to be found, nay they cut their [turf?] in a different manner, a proof that a sea seperated the two countries. We got to Eddingon in good time, many Clergy there, we attended in our Gowns. Mr Taylor and myself as Pall Bearers lead the way then Mr Hobbs and Mr Ruscombe Poole and last Dr Wollen and Mr Jacob. John Poole and Mr Jeremy walked together and John Poole did the Duty very well and distinct. All was conducted with great order and decency. We had something to eat and the Divine carried me back to Bridgwater, with my Hatband and Scarf. I went off immediately from Mrs Lewis's to dine with Mr Edward Sealy where we met the Miss Wollens and our own party.

Friday May 3 We set off this morning on our way to return to Overstowey, passed first through Enmore. Saw poor Mrs Anstis very weak indeed. She has had a miscarriage and she will not be able to leave Enmore for some time.

Monday May 20 I am now continually neglecting my diary and then cannot remember what happened in the meantime. This is my Birthday when I compleat my 70th year, a great age. I am thankful God Almighty has been pleased to continue me to my family to this time and if He vouchsafes a few more years to me I hope I shall prove not unmindful of the Blessing but dedicate them to His Service In health I do not think I am in worse state than I have been for the last five years, indeed I grow fatter and in many respects Stouter but whether this may make an improvement in health is more than I can tell. In moral Goodness and Piety I really think I do improve and shall do I trust with the assistance of God's Grace. From this time till first of June I have been a delinquient with regard to my diary, not being very well with a severe cold. I am still troubled with wind in my stomach and know not whether I shall ever get the better of it or not but must submit to whatever affliction God is pleased to send me. Mrs Southcombe and her maid Grace returned from Stowgumber in Paddock's Gig. They are tolerably well.

Wednesday June 5 I do not recall much of this day. We have had cutting winds for many days past which is bad for the trees and fruit. I did not ride out on account of the cutting weather and my cold has not left me and I am uncommonly Costive.

Thursday June 6 I did not ride on account of the wind but challenged my wife to a long walk. We set off and first I called on a woman at Marsh Mill, Mrs Robinson, wife of the Clerk of the Silk Mill in this Parish who is in a decline. She is a Cheshire woman and so is her husband a Cheshire man. They are modest and well behaved people. I remonstrated with her on not coming to Church. She answered that she would come if she got well, they said they were Church people and would certainly attend Church but that they were as yet Strangers and knew not where to go. I observed that they would find places if they would try.

Tuesday June 11 Mrs Southcombe had a Chaise from Dunster to take her and her maid home to South Molton, or rather to Honiton House, from whence she has been absent eight months. These visits she makes every five years tho she comes to us or we visit her yearly. She is a person of great Resolution and Exertion, of firm Principle and unaffected Piety. She enjoys half the Manor of Honiton which she had by Marriage from the Southcombes and has improved that Manor to them to the greatest degree, and indeed has saved the family (I may say) otherwise they would have come to ruin. Her Income now, by her management is ample and she desposes of it in the most liberal manner among her friends and relations and the Poor in general. She is very fond of my wife, her sister, and spends more time and offner with us than at any other place. I had a letter from William this day which very satisfactorily exculpates him from some imprudencies that had been suggested to me.

Sunday June 16 We had not so many at the Sunday School as we usually do. Lord Egmont's Donation of five pounds to support the Sunday School fails us I fear through the Rascality of Squire Cruckshanks for tho there is scarce a doubt but that Lord Egmont is charged annually for the sum yet to the Masters of the School it is not paid. There is now about a year and a half due. If Cruckshank charges Lord Egmont with the sum then it is Robbery in him not to pay it to the Masters, or if he suppresses the sum entirely without his Lordships Authority then it is an abominable thing.

Sunday June 23 We had a good many at Church. Four of the Richs of Crosse came, but very late indeed. I happened to have a Sermon against Illiterate and Unqualified Persons setting up for Preachers without Commision or Authority and brought some Home observations and Quotations from the Scriptures against such persons. I suppose they were not well pleased, I mean the Riches, but others were delighted with what I said and I thought it my Duty to let my Parishioners know my Sentiments on the occasion for the Riches are doing all they can to support the cause of Methodism.

Tuesday July 2 This turned out a very wet day and bad for the hay. I had a letter from William who is at Bristol with his Cousin and intend to be with us Thursday. He is still very full of passing an Examination at the Schools at Oxford. I saw Mr Allen and the great Tom Poole.

Tuesday July 9 A better day than we have had of late. I walked with my son to Stowey and we called on Mr Allen and had a long chat and on our return called on Mr Sealy. There we met Mr Jacobs of Woolavington and two young boys with him, one his son. Mr Jacobs came to Stowey to enter two little boys of his at the School of Stowey* on the Enmore Plan. A very improper thing in my opinion to mix Gentlemen's children with all kinds as they do in that School, where if they come on a little faster yet must they learn and see many things they ought not to do. Which must of course give them a touch of the Tincture of the Vulgarity of the Common.

Monday July 15 Luke went off for coal this morning. William and I ventured out for a little walk towards the New Canal*. Before we had gone far we were obliged to shelter ourselves under a tree with an umbrella. At last we marched on, it growing fairer. I saw two men mowing in a field and called on them to remember it was St Swithin's Day. They shook their heads and said it was bad for the hay.

Tuesday July 30   A very fine day. My wife, son and daughter are all gone to Bridgwater to see the Races and a Ball, my wife and daughter in Paddock's Gig and William on horseback. Dyer I had with me instead of Luke who went off to Bridgwater to see the Races and to bring back William's horse for William stays for the Ball. In the meantime I walked down to Stowey to dine with Mr Allen. Found him, the Governess and four children at table very decently. After dinner they left us and Mr Allen made tea for me in the afternoon. So I called for letters at the Post Office and walked home and found Luke returned from the Races with my horse. He gave little account of the Races but was very full of the Single Stick Play which he admired very much.

Sunday August 4   Prayers in the afternoon. Few in the Sunday School, all gone gathering Hurtleberries. All the children are now out every day gathering Hurtleberries for families provide for their clothing in this way.

Tuesday August 6   Young Richard Symes wished to prevail on William to go with him on a little voyage in the Bristol Channel to Tenby and Swansea for a day or two. Symes was ordered for his health. I did not approve for why should my son throw away money on such a useless expedition where no pleasure was to be gained and some danger might be endured. It rained so hard Symes took a bed here but his horse was such a Vicious one as I never wish to see again here. His mare kicked my Stall to pieces and my horse too so that I scarce know what the consequences may be, and not content with this when put into another Stable his mare tore to pieces the best Halter I had.

Sunday September 1   Not many in the Sunday School but very many at Church. We had a burial, Old George Adams. He was eighty five and for some years past had dinner from me and some drink and sometimes more but now, poor old man, he is gone. I have now to account from this day to the thirteenth of the month, almost a fortnight. I have not omitted my diary for so long before but William being now at home occupies my Study and even the Parlour with books, drawing or his flute that I cannot sit down to my Diary as I used to do. Properly speaking we have had no summer for we scarce have been a week without a fire. I have this very day a fire in the Parlour.

Tuesday September 17   My horse went off this day for the first load of Tithe Wheat and brought two which I soon threshed and I hope to have bread from it in a short time. This is the latest beginning of wheat Harvest I ever remember. Mr Allen called on me this morning.

Monday September 30   William is still with us and we three dined together. Govat, another Methodistical man is come into the Rectorial House, who has a lease of the Great Tithe under the Chamber of Bristol. He has got a woman with him by whom he has had a child and is parted from his wife. This is Faith assuredly without Good Works with a Vengeance. Their Doctrines lead to these enormities.

Sunday October 6 I forgot mentioning that our neighbour Charles Selleck was carried to the Grave on Friday last and a numerous train of relatives followed. No less than 10 children, some of them young and not able to provide for themselves. This Day, Sunday, was better than the days before. Service in the morning and I preached a Sermon to them on a Future State to which they were attentive.

Monday October 28 Luke went off early for coal and all of us walked to Stowey. Dyer threshed some wheat this day but it is grown and I am afraid people must eat a good deal of grown corn this year for the old corn is gone and the new is generally in this way, moreover wheat is high. I called on Verrier to tell him to put some tiling on my house up.

Tuesday October 29 We have a great brewing which lasts two days. Luke is become a famous brewer and manages very well. Dyer took down some bags of apples and two women gathered them in, a good crop but small.

Sunday November 3 Prayers in the morning. We had a very tolerable Congregation and good singing. Young Rich of Crosse was with the Singers and they say he has a good voice. The Hero of Waterloo was at Church with his medal and I spoke to him before them all as I came from Church. He is my old Clerk's son. They say he gives a good account of things. We had a tolerable appearance at the Sunday School.

Tuesday November 12 The wind continues yet the ground becomes dry. The tiling of the Church most discomposed. Dyer and Luke are today busy about the Cyder, we have made above a Hogshead of cyder from my own Paddock. The apples are small this year and do not ripen well. A bad crop of potatoes. Margaret is poorly and my lumbago is better but not gone off yet. Betty walked to Stowey under her umbrella to get something to take for the cold.

Thursday November 21 This is a fine open day. We are about tunning our cyder. My wife and I walked to Stowey and met Mr Allen, his Governess and most of his children. Some of his girls are getting very tall. What he will do with them when they have to be introduced in the world I scarce know for they are all girls save one.

Friday November 22 This was a fine sharp day. We were to dine at Mr Sealy's at five o'clock so we had Hartnell's Chaise to carry us, with Lamps. We did not meet with so many there as were expected which I am not surprized at as there was no moon. Yet we had in the end a large party, Old Mr Sealy and his wife, Mr Edward Sealy and his wife and Mr John Jeffreys and ourselves. Then after dinner came in Mrs Strong, six young gentlemen from Mr Strong's preparing for the University and two or three of the Knights. We had a man with three of his children who gave us a most extraordinary Concert. The youngest child was not above six years old and blew the French Horn and his brother about nine or ten who played on the fiddle. It is astonishing how well and with what accuracy they played. The man's wife is now brought to bed at Taunton of her seventh child. They are all Musical and take to it very early. I have observed that Musick has little to do with Intellect in general but depends mostly on ear and it is thus that children before their understanding arrives in any degree of perfection yet become proficient in Musick and even Idiots, and certainly Madmen, sometimes excel in Singing and Musick. We staid till nine and then moved for Overstowey and by the assistance of our lamps got safe to Overstowey before eleven.

Saturday November 30 We had a bustle at the Poorhouse, Justice Tom Poole being there and the Parish Officers. Many of the Poor were in a sad condition and cleanliness much wanted. The times are growing very hard and corn rising and no work to be found and they were clamorous, but several were found to sell the things they were given by the Parish. These were threatened and orders were given to burn rags and to procure new things and the walls were to be Whitewahsed and I have proposed to go in with the Officers of the Parish once a month to see that everything goes on right. Indeed things were so bad that I did not care to go very near any of them. I do not much approve of these Poor Houses where everyone is independent of the others, there should be a Governor.

Sunday December 1 In the afternoon I went into the Sunday School. I had promised a girl a Common Prayer Book last Sunday as she read and said her Catechism very well but Esther Selleck called me on Saturday and gave such a Character of the girl as made me hold my hand and gave her a severe reprimand for her conduct at the School. She hid her eyes and face and burst into tears, but she is an artful Hussy and I am afraid will come to no good.

Friday December 13 A most showery day yet in the afternoon we ventured out to dine at the Sealys and there we met Mr and Mrs St Albyn, Captain and Mrs and Miss Cumberland. Mr John and Mr George Sealy and two Miss Sweetens so we made up a full party. The Captain is in the Navy and would have been an Admiral had the War lasted. He is a fashionable man and of a good Character and is married to a woman of family. He has nine children and is lately come to this neighbourhood.

Thursday December 18   Dyer is here but he threshes for the straw so he is not paid in money this day. I sent off Luke with the great horse to meet William at Bridgwater in his road from Oxford to this place. He came in just as we sat down to dinner, we had a full chat about various things.

Saturday December 21   William and Margaret walked over to Alfoxen to call on Mr and Mrs St Albyn. My wife and I walked over to Plainsfield to call on several old persons. First on Old Landsey who is 88 and was very glad to see me and gave him something to comfort him and promised a little gin to put in his tea in the morning to drive out the wind. We next went to Mrs Morle who was very weak and lay on the settle before the fire with her daughter attending her. She too was very glad to see us and shook hands with me. We spoke to Rich, formerly of Ely Green. He was lame and looked padded in the face. We returned to dinner where William and his sister found us.

Wednesday December 25   This is Christmas Day, we had Singing as usual in the morning. A tolerable many at Church in the morning, there was a Sacrament. Rich and his wife, of Crosse, were there but to my great surprize just before I began Rich got up, left his seat and quitted the Church. I am not yet certain of his reason but suppose it was on account of Washer with whom Rich has had a quarrel lately. For when he perceived that Washer staid to the Sacrament he got up and left his wife to go to the Sacrament. I shall speak to them both on the Subject, it was very improper. Washer is constant to the Church but Rich attends the Meeting at Stowey.

Thursday December 26   A very rainy morning. Dyer keeps Holiday today. Luke gone to Stowey, William busy with his Algebra. Mr John Poole and his sister came to stay till Saturday. The weather so bad we could not get anyone to meet them. William and Mr John Poole amused themselves in various matters, Musick, Algebra and Oxford conversation. When it held up a little they sallied forth in quest of some Geological Discoveries.

Tuesday December 31   William rode over to Crowcombe to apologise to the Carews for his having disappointed them twice. He returned and had some thought of going to Taunton to the Ashen Faggot Ball but could not accomplish this. Then he called on Mr Allen and rode with him to dine with Mr Dawes where they had been before invited. He returned a little after tea.

The Year 1817

Wednesday January 1   The New Year begins as the Old one went out, but I hope it will not end like the Old for the last has been the most wet year I ever remember and most deficient in crops. As to myself I feel in as good Health as I have been for these few years past and as good as I can expect. May the same continue, improvements in that way cannot be much expected.

Friday January 3   William was called by his friend Dick Symes to go out ahunting and Old Woodhouse with them. So I lent him my horse, a little aprehensive about him as he had never before been out a Fox Hunting. But he returned to dinner in high Spirits having had good sport, having been in at the Earthing of the Fox. It was a Bag Fox. Margaret has been poorly for some days past.

Thursday January 23   Lately the Mason alarmed us with an account of the chimney being in a very dangerous state so bad that I was fearful that it would not wait till he could take it down. When he got up and his boys and they stood the wind and weather very high as it was and seemingly finished it. But Lo! on trial the chimney was found to smoak most violently and filled the whole house. So yesterday I sent my cart down for more bricks and at the chimney they went again.

Saturday January 25   The mason has just finished the chimney and is about the Oven.

Sunday February 2   A fine morning and mild. We have a new Monument put up to the Memory of Mr James Rich who lately dyed leaving a large Fortune behind, the Residue of which, no less than twenty thousand pounds was divided among two hundred of his Relations. The monument is very elegant and the Inscription modest and plain, merely accounting his Benefactions. I sent to Mr Sealy to come to this Church when he could have an opportunity of viewing and admiring it. He did so and his son Henry from Liverpool dined with us. The Church of course was very full and Mr and Mrs John Sealy came in the view the Monument after Church but they did not dine with us.

Monday February 3   My wife and Margaret called on Mrs Morle who is in the last stage of a Dropsy. Alas poor woman she suffers much and it is to be hoped that God Almighty will release her soon from all her pains. They are still busy in the Churchyard about Mr Rich's Tombstones, which are repairing.

Friday February 7   Met Mr Allen and he gives sad account of Mr Hole, Curate at Holford. He is ruined for life, lost a cause for a sum of money he was bound for which he thought was paid, but the Bond was not delivered up, so that he has the money and the Lawsuit to pay, it is a knock up for life. His wife an excellent woman, one son failed in the farming line. He has nothing but a Curacy to live on but is going to be turned out of that, Buckstone is coming down to take to the Living of Holford so, poor man, misfortunes multiply upon him. I am very sorry for all this, especially as he is a Clergyman. Dyer in the Paddock brushing the dung. Mr James Rich's Tombstones for his Ancestors is new done with Iron Railings and painted and looks very magnificent and the Churchyard begins to recover itself.

Friday February 14   We had a consultation this afternoon about the distribution of Mr James Rich's interest of five hundred pounds to the Second Poor of the Parish. Mr Tom Poole and the two Churchwardens and the Overseers of the Poor attended at my house in the evening when we marked out those that were to receive it.

Sunday February 16   Prayers in the afternoon. A good many children in the Sunday School. A vast Concourse of people collected themselves to come to Church. After Church the distribution was made, the Church was crouded. Stowey singers occupied the Singing Gallery. I went through the Service with great ease. Then those that were called for pay passed from the body of the Church into the Chancel and received not more than twenty shillings and not less than ten shillings each, then went off through the Chancel Door. When that was over they that remained in the Body of the Church and received nothing were inclined to be clamerous, but were soon silenced and at last I got to the Font and Christened three children. Mr Edward Sealy dined and slept here this night.

Wednesday February 26   Poor Mrs Morle of Plainsfield was buried. Poor woman she died of a Dropsy and suffered much and lingered long. A few years ago I buried her husband who died in great pain from a Mortification in his Great Toe. We must alas all go in due time yet if it would please God to permit us to depart without great suffering it would be a desireable thing.

Saturday March 1   This day came in like a Lion, very rainy and windy. I did not stir out, neither did I wear a Leek as usual on this day, my old Welsh Acquaintances are gone.

Monday March 10 We have continual ringing of our Bell at the Gate, the Poor being in continual want of something or other, either Medicine or corn for food. And so life goes on.

Thursday March 13 This is a most pleasant morning, everything in the garden flourishes, the birds sing and twitter and revive the thoughts of Spring. Mrs Sealy called this morning and a Miss Pine, a sensible Old Maid, an old acquaintance of Mrs Sealy. She is a Genteel, agreeable Woman. We had a letter from my Brother in Law Henry Dodwell who writes in High Spirits and seemingly in good health at the age of seventy four. I was so pleased with his facetiousness that I answered it immediately. Luke worked in the garden and I amused myself by walking about and looking at him.

Sunday March 23 Service in the morning and not one of the Methodistical Richs. They never miss a Meeting at Stowey, no nor that Methodist Govett who keeps a Strumpet in his house and her sister and brother and is parted from his wife. But the woman he keeps came tho she concealed herself in such a manner as I could not see her face. Margaret is soon going to London to her Aunt Mrs Dodwell.

Monday March 24 I have resolved with my wife to go to every person or house in the Parish to remonstrate with the inhabitants about their neglect of the Publick Worship of the Church and so we went off this day and had conversation with many of them and made them sensible of their Duty and they promised fairly. A little higher up the Quantock Hill I found Old Savage Ware and his wife, he dying. He is past fourscore and has been a hardworking man. This is his second wife, they formerly lived in the Poorhouse. He scarcely knows what Religion means, he lead in his younger days a reprobate kind of life, a mixture of Immorality, Irreligion and Oddity. He lay in his bed in a miserable hut with pieces of linen wrapt round his head and much flushed as if in a fever. He is dying said I. Yes to be sure answered his wife. He spoke at last – Have you seen my flowers? I will go to see them, he has always been fond of gardening and what he pursued all his lifetime continued till death for he died next day. A few Polyanthas he had but not worth the anxiety of mind during his last moments.

Tuesday March 25 My wife and I went to some persons at Adscombe. One man I went to was a fierce looking man. He lives with his brother's wife and has many very fine children by her. The brother is at Botany Bay. This man has been for some years returned from hence. I could not marry him because I knew the case yet it is better he was married than to live in this uncomfortable way. Lady Day and we had a Vestry in the afternoon to chuse Overseers of the Poor.

Monday April 7 Margaret has got safe to London and Little Allen of Stowey is to go there for a few days to see his friends. But the real great change at Stowey is the Sealy family. The old people have given up house keeping at Stowey and gone to France. Mr Henry who came from Liverpool is in a decline and his brother in law Dr Gibbs declared it to be an Atrophy. He advised him and likewise his sister, Mrs Gibbs, who has been for some time in a bad way to go immediately to France, the South of France. The air of that place might recover both of them but nothing else would do. So the mother Mrs Sealy would go off with them at the age of seventy five or six, and they are now both safe in France. Things are packing up at Stowey, servants discharged and in a day or two Mr Sealy will join them, in France where they are to continue at least for a twelvemonth, a serious thing for persons of their age so that I look upon it as an entire breakup. How many may ever return I cannot tell but it seems to me to be a sad expedition. So many people are gone from this Kingdom to France to spend their Fortunes there that they talk of laying a Tax on them of forty per cent, for surely in this time of General Distress tis base that people should draw their resources from hence to enrich Foreigners instead of contributing to the support of their own Country. However the Sealys do not leave us on this Principle.

Sunday May 4 Service in the morning and as Mr Allen had no Service at Stowey being gone to London to see his friends we had many from Stowey at our Church, Mrs Francis Poole and her daughter and many strangers that I did not know. I still have the Gout and hobble but my wife says I did the Duty as well as ever I did. I did not go to the Sunday School today because it was too damp and cold for my gouty foot.

Tuesday May 6 A fine day in the usual manner and milder than it has been. No signs of rain and every thing dying in the gardens except potatoes. My Gout still continues and declines slowly, of course I do not walk further than the garden. The painter from Stowey has been here and painted the outward Gate Green and the skirting boards along the passage and stairs a Chocolate colour.

Wednesday May 14 I have been able to draw on my own shoe on my foot today and I intend to go to the Book Club to dine at Stowey. The day turned out very wet and I could not venture to walk to Stowey but had my horse and Luke walked by the side. It thundered as I went but I got safe at last. I met there my friends John and Ruscombe Poole and the great Mr Tom Poole, my friend Mr Mathew who is going to republish his Sermon, The silent Mr Bennet, the laughing and obliging Mr Ward, John Brice the speaker of strange Boasting Stories and the bowing Mr Francis Poole with his red pimpled face. We had a good dinner, were very friendly and elected a new member. The evening became perfectly mild and pleasant and I returned home in good time and safe.

Monday May 19 Somerville came about the paper for my daughter's bedchamber. My wife and I walked as far as Stone's to Ealy Green and brought him over to rectify the frame for the canvass in Margaret's room against the damp wall.

Tuesday May 20 This is my Birthday and I am arrived at the 71st year of my age. How many returns of this day I may see God only knows. Yet I trust I shall always be prepared to go whenever He is pleased to call me. At present I feel myself tolerable in Health and so is my wife, who is not four years younger than myself, and she has prepared a dinner for the occasion and Mr Allen and Mr George Sealy is to dine here. We had a good dinner and a good agreeable day of it and pleasant chat. We sent to Bridgwater for a Salmon which the Postman brought this morning, a very fine one and a good part we had for dinner.

Wednesday May 21 The weather rather cold and we have a fire every day. Luke told me a sad calamity this day, tho he heard of it last night from Mr Allen's Servant. He said that Mr Yorke, the Rector of Spaxton fell down dead as he and his wife attended a house on fire at the Village. A vein burst in his head and he was quite dead in half an hour's time. He was hopeful of two valuable Livings of his own which he wished to sell on his wife's account, being unprovided for. He is not yet buried, a dull heavy man but Charitable and well disposed. May God give his Soul Rest.

Wednesday June 4 Mrs Southcombe and her Maid Grace set out for South Molton in Devonshire in a Dunster Chaise precisely at seven and she is to be at South Molton to drink tea in her house of Honiton precisely at five in the afternoon and fresh horses are waiting at Dunster to take her on in a south Molton Chaise to carry her to her journey's end. She will dine in the Carriage while the horses are baiting. While she was with us she did not move out but once or twice into the garden and she was at Church and the Sacrament, but before she left this place she left many Donations to the Poor &cc. She seemed to enjoy herself and is much attached to her sister my wife Tho very peculiar is a very good companion and liberal to the greatest degree.

Tuesday June 10 I attended the Visitation having a new Archdeacon, Mr Trevelyan. Mr Coney preached, his voice was strong so that I heard every word. His Sermon tolerable tho in the old Stile, but his manner affected. A son of Sir John Trevelyan, bred a soldier, the Archdeacon gave us a good Charge and well delivered. Not much of a learned man but a good regular

Divine and much beloved by everyone, we passed a good day with him. Our dinner at the George was not well dressed.

Sunday June 22 The weather very sultry, thermometer 71, higher than I ever remember it. This day I finished a letter to the Duke of Somerset in answer to a very kind message which he sent to me by Mr Thos Poole in the Committee Room of the House of Lords, Mr Poole being called there to appear before them to give information about the state of the Poor in the West of England. Our correspondence had ceased for twelve years* past and is now likely to rivive again but it was not sought by me.

Wednesday June. 25 Carlisse who mowed with Dyer, Luke and the late Clerk's daughter a steady Old Virgin and her niece finished the business of the hay but the Old Soldier was taken up and carried to Stowey on the charge of having secreted a Bank Note of Five Pounds from the box of Mrs Marsh. He was detained and in fear of being committed to Jail. His wife called here and begged me to go down to be his Friend. I did not think highly of Mrs Marsh, she brought on the Charge, but I promised nothing.

Thursday June 26 On seeing Farmer Stone and others go to Stowey about this business of the Soldier I thought I'd go down. Mr Acland and Mr Tom Poole received me with great civility and they were glad I came. They said they would read over to me the whole examination, they were much prejudiced against the Soldier. I said I doubted the Accuser more than the person accused. She was, I fear, a bad woman. However there was only suspicion at most, at last I doubted there was a Bank Note as she described in the box. Phebe our old servant was sent for, and Mrs Marsh an old woman of 84, was contradicted in various things that the Justices thought it much better to discharge the man than proceed on such imperfect evidence. So the matter concluded and I think to the satisfaction of every one.

Monday June 30 A good day and mowing and haymaking went on very well. I walked to Stowey and met Mr Forbes. He is going to quit Stowey and is introducing a young man to succeed him, a Mr Rymer, but I think he is too young for me. I shall apply to Bennet. Met Mr Tom Poole and I went in and chatted with him some time.

Wednesday July 9 A very good day for the hay and I believe a great deal will be carried and they that neglect such fine weather deserve to have their hay spoiled. Washer is carrying his and Farmer Stone is mowing. I received a letter, very kind, from the Duke of Somerset and I carry it to the Great Tom Poole to deliver the message of thanks from His Grace to him, in carrying down his message to me. Mr Tom was pleased and snapped at the compliment and said he would make no difficulty of calling on the Duke when he went to London. I smiled but said not a word.

Sunday July 13 Prayers in the morning. I had a marriage early this day, one of the name of Long and Rich's daughter of the White Horse. a handsome couple. We had not so many at the Church as I expected, none of the Riches of Crosse tho a daughter of his was Bridesmaid, being a cousin of the Rich that married Long. Few at the Sunday School. Being whortlebury time they absent themselves on Sundays.

Saturday July 19 They were working about my hay and will I believe get it in. Sad uproar about my cows, they broke into Weymouth's garden. The making of the hedge lies with him. I offered to pay the damage and said I was not obliged to do so. He scrupled. I told him, let a Justice decide. I was ready to pay anything reasonable but insisted on their making up the hedge. The cows broke in again but did little damage and I have satisfied the Old Woman.

Friday August 15 It was rather a good day and we all dined at Mr Edward Sealy's, a large party with Mrs Dodwell and her sister Miss Moore and her daughter Anne Dodwell. A little after dinner who should surprize us but Old Mr Sealy from France and soon after Mrs Sealy, we were all astonished. They had a very tempestuous passage but seemed in good spirits and all the party are at Weymouth where they will stay a few days. When they arrive they will give Life to this part of the World.

Saturday August 23 William rode over to Bridgwater to Mr Gill for another Lecture on the Algebra and is now returned and the horse carried him well. I have just sent off my horse to Halsey Cross for the first load of Tithe Wheat. The wheat this year I understand is very fine.

Sunday August 24 Prayers in the morning, the Church tolerably full but not so much as in the afternoon. I have of late had so much pain and spasms in my face that I cannot write with the ease and comfort that I used to do, for keeping my attention to one point and bending my head to write brings on the Spasms in my face. From this time to Saturday 31st I have omitted my Diary and the weather has been rainy and uncomfortable. On the 26th Mrs Dodwell and Miss Moore and Anne Dodwell left us for South Molton to Mrs Southcombe. They had bad roads but got there safe.

Friday September 5 This too is a fine day. The Bells ring merrily this morning. On enquiry I find John Morle married a Miss Rollins of Stowgurcy. I am glad of it and he secceeds his father in the Farm at

Plainsfield Court House where the famous Admiral Blake was born. I have now seen the Old People all out and the youngest son come in. All of them are very respectably settled. William went to Mr Gill and found that the problem in Algebra which had perplexed him so much and given him so much uneasiness was not to be found out owing to some misstatement. I believe the horse will go for one load of wheat this afternoon.

Tuesday September 16 A misty morning, no rain yet no corn carried. William rode over to Mr Dawes but is to return and then go to Stowey to dine with Mr Allen. This morning he took a Brisk Dose of Salts and before he rode out he was busy with some Greek Plays. In short, he is not one moment at rest.

Thursday September 18 In the afternoon we went to dine with the Celebrated Mr Tom Poole, it being Stowey Fair. Met there his sister in law Mrs Richard Poole and niece Miss Poole and an odd genius a Mr Coleridge*, I think a son of a Mr Coleridge who distinguished himself some time ago as a writer. He is scarce five foot high and broad shouldered, a short neck, jet black hair and eyebrows, wild eyes and a voice more peculiar still. Very strong at first and then with an odd turn into a Squeak. He has been boasting that he contested the prize with Boone, my son's friend and school fellow at the Charter House, and narrowly mist it, not without strong insinuations that he ought to have carried it off from Boone. He is very proud of shewing these verses of his and I have a Copy now by me. There is in fact no competition in the case, there could have been no competition about them or doubt in anyones mind which to prefer, Boone has so decidedly the advantage. Coleridge's Verses are very harsh and inharmonious in themselves. Four good lines I believe I could pick out in them, the rest were either unintelligible or unpoetic. He has no Judgment, no appropriate ideas for poetry no language or Conception of Images for Similes nor any proper mode of Comparison for their introduction. He compared the Sinews of the strong armed Hercules to the round pebbles of a Rivulet clear. Need I say more.

Sunday October 5 Prayers in the morning, the Congregation full but very few at the Sacrament this day which astonished me which was administered to fewer than I ever remember since I have been Vicar of this Parish so that I must ride round to speak to them. Few at the Sunday School for I have discharged the woman and retained only the Clerk.

Wednesday October 8 William rode off to Bridgwater for a Draft on a Banker to carry with him to Oxford, for he goes next week. My wife and I walked to Stowey. Dyer is busy in the barn threshing wheat which is carried off as soon as he can get it ready. Wheat is fallen in price and many are pressing to purchase it.

Friday October 10 My wife and I went off in the Minehead Machine and were let out at Putsham. We dined and slept at Mr Mathew's at Kilve. We met there none but their own family which is numerous. I got hold of the Christian Observer and his criticism of Mr Mathew's Sermon. I think the quotations he makes from Mr Mathew's Sermon shew the futility of the criticism. Mr Mathew will not deign to give it an answer.

Tuesday October 14 William is preparing for Oxford but first goes to Taunton to the Ball at night and thence off again in the morning in the coach for Bath and from thence to Oxford. He went off about two in Paddock's Gig.

Sunday October 19 This day far from good, I mean dry tho rain was wanted. Not so many at Church as I expected. Neither the Morles, the Riches nor many of the Stones. There are more Meeting Houses and Preachers at Stowey and encouraged by Rich of our Parish, a bad fellow and false and shallow. He does a great deal of harm. Few at the Sunday School.

Monday October 20 I rode out and spoke to several of my Parishioners and went through Stowey and called on Mr Allen. Mr Tom Poole was not at home but Mr Ward met me and said he would pay me the Tithe of Quantock Wood and Farm which I took, 35 pounds in all. Mr Rymer and his wife came in while I was writing out a receipt to whom I was once more introduced and Mrs Ward was present, very elegantly dressed.

Wednesday October 29 I rode to Stowey to a famous meeting about Savings Banks. Went to Mr Tom Poole's and there met Mr Acland Snr and Junior, Councellor Trip and Mr John Poole of Enmore. We all went from Mr Tom Poole's to the large room in the Rose and Crown and there met a large concourse of people. Sir Samuel Hood proposed Mr Peregrine Acland for the chair and indeed he performed the Office very well. Then Mr Acland Senior began and spoke tolerably at first but at last he used so much teutology and mumbled that I could not understand. I got up once or twice and made Observations that were approved of and so did Mr John Poole and Mr John Jeffreys. Mr Mathew and Tom Poole contended for some time about a matter of no manner of Consequence. At last they came to the point and a Donation was made. I think they have already about a hundred and ten pounds. I received a letter from William and found there a Bitter Pill. He is got safe to Oxford and carried his money safe but not taking out his Bill sowed up in his waistcoat his Washerwoman caught hold of it and the Bank Bills were washed into Atoms. William in a doleful plight wrote to me. I have sent him a draft for 15 pounds and desired the fragments of his Bills that we may see what can be done, and that as nothing could be offered as an excuse for his negligence I should say nothing on the occasion.

Sunday November 16 Prayers in the morning and the Church decently filled but none of the Riches of Crosse. The whole of the Kingdon is now in Gloom and Sorrow on account of the Death of Our Most Excellent Princess Charlotte who died in bed of a young Prince. Alas in the bloom of youth with every expectation of Health, Glory and Happiness before her. I never remember so universal a sorrow before. I preached on the subject of Death and noticed it in my Sermon which seemed to have a great effect on everyone. There were a great many this day at the Sunday School.

Wednesday November 19 Sent Luke on my horse to Cannington at first and then he and Betty went to Stowey Church where there were great doings on account of Princess Charlotte's Burial, which took place at 7 o'clock in the afternoon, when the Service was read at Stowey and a Sermon preached. We had no orders for Service from the Higher Powers but the Sunday before I noticed her death very particularly and preached a Sermon on Mortality, and on this very day the Princess was buried the Bell Tolled for an hour by my orders.

Tuesday December 2 A very stormy day. My daughter and Miss Lewis walked to Stowey to see Mrs Edward Sealy where they dined and staid tea. They walked home at last, Luke going before with a candle and lantern and he brought me a letter from Dr Hall Dean of ChChurch Oxford informing me that he would do the utmost in his power to get my son elected a Student of Ch Ch and regretting much that he had not done so sooner.

Monday December 8 A sad accident happened this day at Stowey. Verrier's grandson a little boy that lived with his grandfather in carrying a knife to cut leather from Clitson the Shoemaker to his father, a Currier in Stowey, in running through the street with it in the dark stumbled over some loose stones and fell on the blade of the knife which ran into his neck and killed him on the spot. This has affected the grandfather very much, an industrious mason at Stowey of some note.

Tuesday December 16 This is a thoroughly wet day. It is a joyous day for we had a letter from William informing us that he is a Student Designatus of Christ Church and that the Dean had told him that he should give him a Studentship on Christmas Day next when he would put on his Student Gown, and therefore he stays at Oxford till then and whence he sets off the next day for Overstowey.

Friday December 19 Mr Allen past by and enquired after my son. He cannot come down before he is invested in his new promotion on Christmas Day. Now I expected Congratulations on this occasion instead he slightly observed Then he has got his Scholarship. He is made a Student returned I sharply, a Studentship, to all intents and purposes a Fellowship for he can take Offices in the College and succeeds to Livings and it is the Genteelest thing for a young man throughout the University. A little Paultry envious snarling young man, without Preferment himself and yet he cannot bear to hear of such for others. And William he pretends to be fond of. Went to see a strange object at Mr Bennet's. A woman who has neither arms nor legs yet capable with her stumps and mouth of drawing portraits &cc to great perfection. Her parents are poor and lamented much that such an object would be a burden on them but a painter took her and she learned to do things in the perfect manner she does and earns a surprizing quantity of money and maintains the people about her as well as herself. She spoke very well and sensibly.

Sunday December 21 Luke went off early this day to meet his family to prepare for the Funeral of his father who is now dead. He returned about nine. I was obliged to send off Dyer to Mr Bennet for Quaicum Pills for my Rheumatick complaint in my Hip which was violent.

Thursday December 25 We had our kitchen full of guests, old Servants &cc and among others the Hero of Waterloo with a Medal, my old Clerk's son. We had a Sacrament this day and many attended and the Congregation at Church was full. I should have observed that many Poor attended for their Donation of wheat. We gave away two bushells which as it sells now at Thirteen shillings a Bushell amounts to something.

Saturday December 27 My hip still painful at times and my face much so, so there must be something to give a check to our present exultations, no perfect happiness in Life. My children have had a letter from Mrs Yorke congratulating us on my son's advancement to a Studentship but notwithstanding my face pains me. Well so that perfect happiness is obtained at last in another World I must be content with this mixture while here below.

Monday December 29 A very severe frost. We expect a good round party here this day but my teeth ache most sadly. They came, Young Carew and his sister, Mr and Mrs Sealy, Mr Tom Poole amd his niece Miss Elizabeth Poole and Mr Allen. We spent an agreeable day and everyone well pleased.

Tom Poole great and pompous as usual, Miss Carew rather laughing at Miss Elizabeth Poole on account of her learning and tendency to Methodism. Carew seems much improved and is become steady and more manly. Mr Tom Poole and Mr Allen left us in the afternoon but the Carews and Miss Elizabeth staid with us.

Tuesday December 30 All up early this day as the Carews were to be off for Taunton to see a Proceession of FreeMasons and they prevailed on my son to accompany them. William returned about dusk and gave us a full account of things.

Wednesday December 31 I received a letter from the Duke of Somerset pressing me to come to him at Bradley, which still I must decline as from the frequent pains I have in my face and the advance of age I do not feel myself equal to the Society of large company and large houses tho my general health is surprizing for my years. The Duke was of Christ Church and has a large family three sons and four daughters.

The Year 1818

Saturday January 3   William is gone off to Stowey in hopes of recovering a Bank Bill which by mistake was washed in the lining of his waistcoat at Oxford where it had been sewn and crumbled to rags. From this time to the 4th February I am to account for the omissions in my Diary for the pains in my face, company and visits to Bridgwater.

Tuesday February 3   The snow continues yet it turned out tolerable and Margaret was able to go behind Luke to Stowey to go on in Mr Sealy's PostChaise to Bridgwater where she is to remain some time, and now we are only myself and my wife. This day we had Pancakes for dinner and a roast pig so that if we can but get some coal we shall do very well this sharp weather.

Wednesday February 4   Ash Wednesday – I would have had Prayers today if I could have got a Congregation but it is difficult to get one in the country. When the Pooles lived here and the Riches were alive we could do something but now there is nothing but canting and singing Psalms and breaking through every Rule of Good Morals. The Methodist Govett who has kept a woman in the house and Bastard with her has now sent her off again somewhere to bring him another Bastard I suppose. But I can do nothing with him, yet he constantly attends some Methodist Meeting or other. Mr Harvy the new Clergyman of Fiddington returned my visit.

Friday February 13   This day being fine and mild my horse was employed in carrying Gravel for the walks which I have enlarged and made broader which gives a very magnificent appearance to the Garden. This is William's Birthday when he arrives at his one and twentieth year so we rejoiced among ourselves and gave a dinner and holiday to the servants.

Sunday February 15   The Church very full but not one of the Riches. They have made themselves despicable now in quitting the Meeting House they frequented and attending the nonsense of the Preachers in Private Houses. I never knew Methodism make a better man of anyone. If they find him in Sin they continue him in the same course and only substitute Hypocricy and Cant instead of real Holiness.

Sunday February 22 This is a great day for the Parish, 25 pounds the interest of £500 to be given away to the Second Poor of the Parish according to Mr James Rich's Will. Accordingly Mr Tom Poole and his nephew came in. Service in the morning yet the Church was filled and all went off without noise or tumult as had before concerted at my house. I was surprized when we came out of the Church to find the ground white with a deep snow and falling fast.

Thursday March 12 This is a great and important day for the Ball at Crowcombe. About four o'clock a very elegant Chaise appeared and good horses but rather before his time. My daughter did not move off before five to be at Mr Carew's at six, the Company were to make their appearance at nine but she had to dress. Luke rode on the Barouche with the driver and my daughter permitted Mrs Waddon the Mantlemaker to ride with her as far as the Lodge where she got out and walked to the House where she was Serviceable to some of the Company. There were most magnificent doings at the house and a very large Appearance of Ladies and Gentlemen, Sir Alexander Hood, Sir – Sykes, Mr Tynt and a variety of all the neighbouring Gentry with the most Fashionable Ladies dressed uncommonly well and the Supper was most Magnificent indeed, served up with the greatest Elegance and Taste and they continued the Dance until the morning to usher in the Birthday of Young Carew for whose Honour the whole was performed. As soon as the morning commenced the Bells set off aringing to announce the day and infuse new vigour into the Company and the Dance continued till six.

Friday March 13 On this day young Carew completed his one and twentieth year just one month after William and Luke was sent for my daughter who brought her home in the afternoon. She gave us a full account for there was an Ox roasted whole, girls running races for Ribbands, men in bags competing for prizes and Old Women racing for snuff and tobacco, besides a compleat entertainment for the Tennants and Farmers and a dance at night and moreover a Grand Dinner for the Gentlemen. Neither my wife nor I attended because we could not have a bed, neither could we sit up all night. Most of the Company were obliged to return in the morning after the Ball.

Tuesday March 24 From this day to the 30th I have been confined by the Gout. I got Mr Bennet to call and he soon determined that it was and that it showed great strength of constitution at my time of life and probably would do me much good. On Friday 27th I ventured to bury a corpse and stood on the ground in the Churchyard which was not the thing but I had a shoe with a cork soul so that might protect me. On Saturday a little girl was to be buried and as it rained my wife asked Mr Allen to call and bury the corpse. He did and then drank tea with us.

Sunday March 29 As it was dry I hobbled to Church which was very full with Relatives of the persons buried, and I had a Christening and a Churching. Before I could get out of Church it rained and I paused, what to do? At last the Clerk and Luke carried me to the House in an armed chair.

Wednesday April 1 I do not recollect more of this day than that nothing happened in the April Fool* way and I am still hobbling with my gout and my face continues painful.

Wednesday April 8 My Gout being got under and my shoe being drawn on my wife and I walked to Stowey. First we met Mr Allen and his little boy. Then we saw Mr Sealy going into his house so we went in and staid a while. Mr Sealy lent me a little Pamphlet about the Tic Doloureux in my face, a cure being just found out for it, but I do not like the circumstances of its Operation. It is Baledonna, the Tincture, but I suppose more will be found in it by and by as it is a very new discovery. As soon as we got home the rain began so we made good use of our time while it continued fair.

Thursday April 9 My wife was very busy indoors with Betty and they wiped and cleaned every book and made it very neat and clean. A very tedious business and it had not been done before these two years past tho my wife used to have cleaned off dust &cc every year. Govett who lives in the Rectory sent to borrow a Willy full of coal. Tho the man is a Methodist and is separated from his wife and keeps a woman in the house and I have no intercourse with him yet I did not chuse to refuse him such a thing and so let him have it. He must have a tolerable good opinion of my Liberality to venture to ask me such a favour, seeing that we do not speak to each other.

Wednesday April 15 Yesterday Dyer and Luke compleated the hundred of wood from the Hill which they begun on Monday. My wife and I walked to Esther Selleck's and I read part of a pamphlet just come out about the Tic Doloureux in my face which proposed an entire cure for it. She says she will try anything that promises a cure but I do not chuse to administer the Pills without a Medical Person with me as there are some objections to the operation of them. Dyer went about inviting the farmers, the dinner next Wednesday.

Monday April 27 I received a very kind letter from my old friend the Duke of Somerset saying that he would be glad to give my son a Chaplaincy when he is able to take it and wear a Scarf*, and his Grace moreover says that he now has a Vacancy in Reserve but desires to be reminded again when my son comes of age to wear a Scarf.

Sunday May 3 Walking before the door before the Service I heard a great noise and quarrelling just at the hatch Gate of the Church yard. Being somewhat displeased at this I walked out and found it to be no less a person than Thomas Mogg the Shoemaker, politician, orator, physician and I know not what else. With beard unshaven, clothing not very clean or free from rents, and face unwashed, he was extending his fist towards a son of poor Thomas Porter, bellowing out that lad to leave his Church where his father and grandfather and family always came. Well said I on Sunday and before the Churchyard Gate. Yes Sir he replied I know it is a Sunday and if it was not for that I would give it thee says he, again pushing out a Huge Fat Fist. So added I you give him occasion to speak by your violence and I too must act against you and so at last I sent him off and then turned round to the boy who it seems had called the great Thomas Mogg a Child of the Devil. You too are wrong, not only to use such expressions but because you desert your Parish Church to go to follow Idle Pretenders who preach their Nonsense to lead astray the Parishioners from their Legal and Natural Pastors.

Tuesday May 19 Mr Allen called here in his Gig and carried me to Bridgwater to the Visitation. We had a very good Sermon by Mr Ruddock and well delivered. It was the Bishop's Visitation and the Chancellor, his son, represented him tho Mr Trevilion the Archdeacon was with him. We had a tolerable dinner but our numbers were not many. Mr Gordin, young Lutterel and young Harvey did not dine with us which gave great offence – Puppies –.

Thursay May 21 My wife, Mrs Southcombe and her servant Grace went off this morning in Hartknell's Chaise for Southampton to see their sister Mrs Ridding who is old and has been ill and declining for some time and has suffered much with her family, two of her daughters having been in a bad way for many years. It will, I fear, be the last time the sisters will meet in this world again tho I trust they will assuredly meet in the next as they are all three most excellent women.

Friday May 22 In the afternoon Margaret and I walked to Stowey and drank tea at the Sealys where Mrs Best is. Mr Best is gone to France to look out a place of aboad for his family for a few years. He was in Holy Orders and in the Church of England and Oh Shame, after preaching and doing Duty for half a year he left the Pure, Sublime Service of the Church of England for the Tawdry Bloated and Overceremonious Worship of the

Church of Rome, the Scarlet Whore. He pretends from full conviction but I say from a disordered turn of the brain, and he has converted, or rather perverted, his wife too. He holds our Ordination as invalid and so becomes a Layman. Alas poor man I fear he must answer seriously for this some day or other.

Saturday May 30 Yesterday about 2 o'clock my wife and Mrs Southcombe returned in Health and Safety from Southampton where they saw their sister and most of the inhabitants of Southampton were rejoiced to see them. I have Mr Bennet to see me who has resolved to get the better of this troublesome costiveness which disorders me so much.

Wednesday June 17 This day brought us, I thank God, some rain which has made the garden rejoice and has saved the barley. Dyer came with the intention to thatch the hay rick but could not touch it in the rain and I set him and Charles Carlisse on clearing the Necessary which has been very offensive for some time past. I have been for some days very poorly in the ancle of my left foot. It is very sore and I cannot bear much wait on it. It swells a little but is not much enflamed, whether it is Gout or Rheumatism I cannot yet tell. It plagues me much however and I am not able to move further than the garden.

Friday June 26 I am still limping and my ancle very painful. William keeps close to his studies and I fear does not take enough exercise. Young Buller* from Stowey called this day and chatted some time. He is much improved and has taken a degree at Cambridge and is endeavouring a Fellowship there.

Monday June 29 Dyer, my Clerk, went off very early this morning to vote for the Old Members at Ilchester and there was a large party with him, Mr Tom Poole commanded them. We had a large party to dine with us. Old Mrs Poole of Enmore came with her children and grandchildren, viz Mrs Poole aged 84, Miss Poole, Mr John Poole, Mr and Mrs Anstis and a son and daughter of Mrs Anstis. She had several Pensioners among the Poor to flock round to whom she gave something handsome and they loaded her with Blessings and Congratulations. We had a very good dinner and everyone in high spirits.

Tuesday June 30 I walked over this morning to Dyer who was returned from Ilchester and was mowing his fields. He said the Old Members were high on the Poll above Lethbridge and vast numbers poured in from Bath every day. He voted as directed. I now understand Lethbridge has given up. He has the pleasure of throwing away 7000 pounds for nothing and putting the other members to the expence of 5000 pounds apiece,* and all for his caprice.

Thursday July 2 A great number went off this morning to Exeter to vote for Sir Thomas Acland. Lord Ebrington is first on the Poll and Mr Bastard is likely to be thrown out. Miss Lewis seems very well after taking an Emetic. My foot seems better and Mr Bennet attributes it to the tightness of my gaiters but I fear is not entirely so.

Friday July 3 Sir Thomas Acland has given up the Poll at Exeter which I am very sorry for as Lord Ebrington his opponent is a very violent man and a great Democrat. I never heard of more Riots than there have been this Election, there is a desperate spirit among the Lower People at this time but I trust a better kind of people will rouse themselves and quell them.

Sunday July 5 William has been looking over his Divinity and he and I had a good deal of conversation on the subject and I perceive that he has considered things deeply and accurately and I trust he will make a good Divine.

Friday July 10 From this time to the second of August I have neglected my Diary being far from well for some time past tho now tolerably recovered. On Tuesday 14th my wife and self and daughter went over to Bridgwater leaving William behind at his studies. We staid till Saturday and I was ill all the time and shrunk very much in appearance. The weather was uncommonly sultry.

Wednesday August 5 More intolerably hot than ever. I have not been able to stir beyond the garden. I know not what to do about the garden stuff. It is become a famine in this respect that I never knew before.

Sunday August 16 Still the same uniform dry weather. Potatoes have nothing under them, the grass burnt up and all things in the garden burnt up. The harvest goes on very well and most of the wheat got in. William is not very well and gets thin. Some think he wears himself out by studying.

Sunday September 6 After the rain yesterday the ground moist and well soaked and cabbages seem to pluck up their heads and look green as if they meant to grow. The verdure of the grass too seems to come. I had a letter this day from my son now in Oxford.

Tuesday September 8 I dined this day at Mr Thomas Poole's and met the Dean of Wells and Bishop of Gloucester. Stowey is a Peculiar of his as Dean of Wells and tomorrow he is to preach at the Church, a very good well meaning man, perfectly a gentleman in his manners but too easy and lets himself down in running about to preach in Country Churches and everywhere if he can. Too much encourages Sectaries of all kinds and I fear ordains Methodistical or Evangelical people as they are called, and in short improper persons for the Ministry. John Poole was of the company and Dr Ridoubt, Beden Buller and his son as relations of the Bishop of this Diocese, and myself. I could not stay very long after dinner being not very well in my Bowells, neither was I able to go next day to hear his Lordship.

Monday September 14 Became dry with a brisk wind so that I had my Tithe all in and gave a supper on the occasion.

Saturday September 19 I do not recollect anything about this day for it is now the 26th. I have suffered considerably through costiveness and was obliged to send for Mr Bennet who relieved me at last but I must guard against it in future. We have heard from Margaret who is now in Ilfracombe and not very well and from William who is at Oxford and finds it an agreeable place in Vacation time. I have been very busy all this week with my apples and have made one Hogshead of cyder and am collecting for another and I have had in hoards of keeping apples. My Barley sells at the enormous price of eight shillings a Bushell and the Poor are eager for it.

Monday September 28 Busy in making up apples for the second hogshead of Cyder. Farmers Morle and Squib dined here today, paid their Tithes and soaked themselves with Brandy and water.

Sunday October 11 This was a tolerable morning. Prayers in the morning and a Sacrament. I had much Duty this day, a Christening and a Churching after the Sacrament but I was determined to do it on a Sunday to induce the Parishioners to bring their Children to Church on Holidays for they begin to think it is Genteeler to have the Service for them in particular on a week day and the Methodists will not come on Holidays merely because our Liturgy requires it and because by so doing they think to lessen the Solemnity of our Baptism in order to favour the notion of an After Call as they term it.

Saturday October 17 Last night I took a large dose of Rhubarb and worked it off this morning. Mr Atherston called and I was well then but the dose continued working afterwards to such a degree that I began to find myself faint and went on the bed. It was too great a dose.

Sunday October 18 Service at two for the Winter season for the afternoon. Tho I had been worked by my dose the day before yet I was able to go through the Duty of this day very well.

Monday October 19 Luke went for coals. My wife walked to Stowey and brought a letter from my noble Friend the Duke of Somerset. He writes sensibly and kindly and we are now deeply engaged in the Science of

Physiognomy. Luke returned with the coal and brought some celery plants from Cannington and we put them down immediately.

Tuesday October 20 Busy brewing. The weather muggy and rainy. Mr Atherston made me a vist this day too.

This last entry takes Mr Holland to the bottom of the last page and it is certain that there must have been at least one more book before he died the following April, for he continued active and made his last entry in the Parish Register only a week before his end.

Clearing Up

The last record of a Marriage celebrated by Mr Holland was on February 17 1819, and on April 9 1819 the Baptism of Thomas Major of Marsh Mills son of the Miller. The final entry dealing with Mr Holland records his death on April 17 1819 at the age of 72. His burial service was conducted by his friend John Brice the Rector of Asholt. How John must have enjoyed being able to have the last word.

Mrs Holland moved to Bath with Margaret and was there in 1831. Margaret never married and died in Shrewsbury in January 1861. She was interred at her brother's Church.

'My son' William was Ordained and became Rector of Cold Norton, Essex February 12 1824 and held the Living until his death December 1 1867, aged 70. In 1827 he rebuilt his Rectory and in 1855 since his Church had fallen into serious disorder it was pulled down and rebuilt at the expense of the Rector, William Holland, former Scholar of the Charter House in whose gift was the Living. Both his marriages were childless, his first wife, Mary Brown from Welbourn in Lincolnshire was only 37 when she died in 1840. His Second Wife was Matilda Bullock, daughter of the Rector of Radwinter, Essex. She survived until December 12 1905 when she was 90.

The Dodwell Connection*

William Holland's wife Mary was the second daughter of Rev. Dr William Dodwell, Archdeacon of Berkshire and a Canon of Salisbury Cathedral.* He also held simultaneously the Livings of three Berkshire Parishes, Shottesbrooke, White Waltham and Bucklebury. He was the son of Dr Henry Dodwell, sometime Camden Professor of History at Oxford, which Chair he was obliged to vacate, being a Non-Juror on the Accession of William and Mary. William is reputed to have remarked 'Professor Dodwell has set his heart on being a martyr and I have set mine on disapppointing him.'

Of Mary's brothers and sisters we meet Revd Henry, Vicar of Maidenhead who also held the Livings of Harlaxton and Colsterworth in Lincolnshire. His children were Hatton, Henry, George and William by his first wife and Edward, Susan and Anna by the second. Brother Arthur held only two Livings, Bishops Canning near Devizes and one of the Salisbury Churches, and was also Prebendary of Brecknock. Mr Robert Dodwell of Doctors Commons had died in 1793 but we read of his widow and her sister Miss Moore and daughter Anne. Elizabeth Ann the eldest sister married Thomas Ridding of Southampton and was the mother of Thomas, Henry, Mary and Elizabeth. The other sister Margaret, a childless widow at this time, had married into the Southcombe family of Rose Ash in Devon, a remarkable family who through eight generations provided the Rector of that Parish up to 1948.

Two ledger slabs in Shottesbrooke Church are of interest.

Here lieth the Learned and Pious Henry DODWELL MA Sometime Fellow of Trinity Colledge near Dublin Cambden Profefsor of Hiftory in Oxon Born at Dublin Oct MDCXLI Dyed at Shottefbrooke the VII of June MDCCXI Anno AEt LXX Here lieth also his Relict Mrs Anna Dodwell who died April 2 1750 aged 81.

Here lie the remains of SUSANNA, wife of Revd HENRY DODWELL of Maidenhead, Berkshire who died on the 16th December 1821 aged 70 years.

Also the Before mentioned Revd HENRY DODWELL Who departed this life May 15th 1826 in his 84th year.

WILLIAM DODWELL DD Archdeacon of Berkshire and Rector of this Parish, Father of the above Henry Dodwell and the Second son of the Learned and Pious HENRY DODWELL WHOSE remains lie in the adjoining grave was buried in the Cathedral Church of Salisbury.

Some Correspondence

Copy of a letter from the Duke of Somerset to Mr Holland

Plymouth Dock,
September 7th 1799

My Dear Sir,

I was never more astonished than at receiving your letter which I shall keep as a great curiosity. You have exactly described the character of the last profile I sent you, though it is universally thought to convey no meaning. It is true that 'intense thought, & collected firmness and resolution form the general characteristick; that the erect posture denotes dignity of mind, that the nose bespeaks quick investigation, & the closed lips not only firmness but secrecy.' No man but you can however read these qualities in that countenance. Common observers say it is the face of a simpleton. In sending you the likeness I meant to take you by surprise, & to prove to you *that sense appears under a masque.* You have not only discovered the abilities, but the professional habits. You might well say that he is a statesman, for it is the profile of Pitt himself.

After this proof of your proficiency in Physiognomy, it would be ridiculous to dispute with you about the principles of that science. I must of course allow that the mental powers can be discovered in the countenance, for you can discover them where nobody else ever could. That the talents are particularly conspicuous in moments of thought & reflection, must be still more obvious; and I only wish you could see Pitt in those moments when his eloquence electrifies our legislative body & he appears as the great spring of our political machine. If you can discover his character in a mere outline, drawn from memory more than eighteen months after sight, what might you not see in his eyes and motion; what might you not hear in his emphasis?

I do not think the Clergy are by any means generally profligate, very far from it, but there are in this part of England many profligate characters in the Church. I am at a loss to conjecture what the reason may be but it is observed that throughout England & Wales, the further the Clergy are removed from the Metropolis the less attentive they are to the preservation of their characters. This is the general rule; there are exceptions of course.

I send you another profile &
am Sir
your most obdt Sert
Somerset.

From the Duke of Somerset, and Holland's draft reply.

Bradley House, Jan 12 1800.

My Dear Sir,

I send you enclosed a profile of a boy eleven years old & request you to send me the character directed to me in Upper Grosvenor Street London, for which place I shall set out on Tuesday Morning & will send you some Birthday Faces. I have not had time to write to Mr Leighton for a long while. His letters require some thought, which it is impossible to bestow upon them in the hurry of business or the dissipation of much company. I have just shewn those letters of his which relate to the Welsh language to Mr Meyrick my old Schoolmaster who is a Welshman and has not forgotten his native language. He perfectly agreed with the Philosopher of Shrewsbury & seemed to admire the acumen which appeared in all his remarks. You was very right as to the last head I sent you; it was that of a negro belonging to the Band of my late regiment.

I remain Dear Sir
your most obedt Servant
Somerset.

Draft of reply

This boy in my opinion does not promise great things. the general cast of features seems sullen and sulky, nothing open cheerful & ingenuous in the face and posture of the head. There will be character in the nose by and by when it rises more which will not be I suppose till the boy is fifteen for that is the age when the nose fixes into form and when the character of the man begins to take a determined byass. The chin of the boy retreats, I should suppose him fearful. His mouth pouts like a spoild child but has no resolution or firmness in it at present. The nose (I am sorry to say) has a good deal of ill nature in it. The forehead has rather a melancholy appearance, it swells in the wrong place comes forward at the upper part rather than at the eyebrows, yet the head rounds very well behind so that there may be dormant intellect in it, which possibly may come to application some time or other.

From the Duke of Somerset.

Farley House July 15, 1800

My Dear Sir,

I received your congratulations on my marriage with much satisfaction because I believe them to be sincere, never having found you a man of much compliment nor apt to make studied speeches. I was married in London in Gros" Place & we went immediately afterwards to Belvidere, a seat of Lord Eardling's which he lent us for a few days. We came to this place yesterday senight and intend staying here chiefly for about a month till some repairs are finished at Bradley.

Sunday Mr Monkhouse dined with us, after preaching to us in the afternoon. I don't much like his way of reading, not being accustomed to the North Country pronunciation. But that does not signify; it does as well for the people. He has more to say than I should have expected from his appearance.

I should be glad if you could send Coles the Clock Maker to Bradley to put his Clock right. He may be a Democrat but that I shall not mind so long as his clock goes by the old calendar.

My wife joins me in Compl" to you and Mrs Holland & I remain Dear Sir
your most obed" Sert
Somerset.

(on a separate scrap of paper)
PS My mother is at Bradley, but is going soon to London.

Mrs Holland writes to Miss Mary Brown (Post marked January 21 1831)

Bath January 21 1830.

My Dear Miss Mary Brown

Excuse the feelings of a Mother if you should dislike any thing that I say as you must suppose my son is as dear to me as you are to your Father. I understand from him that the Idea of filling up the Drawing Room is not given up and that Mr Brown has full confidence in him that he will not spend too much in the Carriage or Furniture of the Room. Certainly Mr Brown will have reason to blame him if he exceeds his Income, but then he must not be led into Expences he feels that he cannot afford, especially in these times when the value of Property appears to be going back. No doubt to have the use of the room will be a great advantage when you can afford to furnish it and if my Son and you find you can do it by degrees I shall be very glad of it but at present I suppose you can neither of you estimate very exactly what your Household expences will be, until they are assertained and the different sums paid off. I think it will be highly Imprudent to enter into further expences except the Carriage and Horse being convinced that his Respectability would be diminished by his incurring expenses he is not sure he could afford. My son says Mr Brown proposes two hundred more from your Fortune but that does not seem at all to enable you to have more money to spend as I understand it will but barely cover the expences of the Marriage Settlement and the Money Matters with your Father.

My Son's being in debt at all was in consequence of the heavy and unforeseen expences incurrd by his Premises, Road &c in a new Place which too generally exceeds the Calculations of most People who embark in such an undertaking – No one could have conducted himself at College with higher credit both in Money Matters & in all other respects, and this debt has preyed on his mind so much that as you are greatly attached to him I am sure you would not for the World have him run the risque of suffering so again, but had things turned out as he expected his debt would have been settled long ago. I am now nearly 81 years of age & it would hurt me extremely to go out of the World and leave him in debt. My son has a good Library of Books for a young man, well off in Silver. I divided what I had as soon as I came to Lodgings, when the House was furnished I gave him fifty pounds for some handsome Chairs. I am sorry it is not in power to do so now. I am much obliged to Mr Brown for his kind Wish that my Son should pay his debt off to us and sincerely hope he may not be under the necessity of accepting Mr Brown's offer of lending him a hundred pounds, as I much disapprove of borrowing Money. When you look at my writing I hope you will consider my age as an apology. My daughter in general writes my letters for me, I have great comfort in her living with me, & you both at Cold Norton can add greatly to my happiness at the end of my Life if I can have good accounts from you there. I am rather of an anxious turn for the only two Children I have left out of seven. It is rather awkward writing to a person that I have not seen. I hope and trust that I may have the gratification of seeing my Son and you happily settled at Norton, a Blessing to one another.

I must now conclude with every good wish
attending you, believe me to be
Most Sincerely Yours,
Mary Holland.

Kind regards to your whole Family.
My Daughter desires her love
We asked Mr James Wilson
to dine with us today but
unfortunately he was engaged.

Notes

1799

October 23: This is Sara, wife of T.S. Coleridge. The Coleridges lived in Nether Stowey (Stowey to Mr Holland) from winter 1796/7 until July 1800. Coleridge used to preach at Taunton Unitarian Chapel, hence Holland's dislike. Mr Tom Poole the tanner was their friend and local benefactor, he had also helped the Wordsworths obtain the tenancy of Alfoxden. Poole's Memorial in Stowey Church differs greatly from Mr Holland's opinion.

October 25: Convention of Alkmar, October 18 1799. The Duke of York to leave the Netherlands following the failure of British and Russian Expedition, August – October.

October 28: All Parish Clerks are 'Amen' or 'Mr Amen' to Holland. The Overstowey Clerk who also worked as a day labourer was at this time William Perrott.

November 12: Mr Barbay (Barbé?) French Priest displaced by the Revolution.

November 14: See the note on the Dodwell Connection.

November 24: One of the succession of Curates at Stowey whose Living was held by Dr Langford, Canon of Windsor. He is only reported by Holland to be in the area on one occasion, August 16 1800.

December 3: See also June 4 1807.

December 8: Harriet Palmer, an infant.

December 10: Lavater, Swiss authority on Physiognomy was another correspondent of the Duke of Somerset. Parson Woodford the Norfolk Diarist purchased a copy of Lavater's Book – October 16 1799.

1800

January 29: William Lewis of Cannington had been Curate for Holland 1792–1799 and was also responsible for Holford at this time.

February 13: Children died at Monkton Farley in 1795. William Dodwell born April 17 1787. Mary December 8 1788. Thomas September 20 1790, John 1793.

March 8: John Brice, Patron of the Living of Aisholt became Rector there after the death of Rev Reeks. Friend of Coleridge.

April 26: Richard Graves, 1715–1804. Rector of Claverton 1749–1804. A Bath Character, said never to have been absent from his Church for a month at a time. His marriage to Lucy, beautiful but uneducated, offended everyone and cost his Fellowship of All Souls. Sent his wife to London to acquire good manners and needful knowledge.

August 22: Mary Lovelace.

October 9: Possibly Nogheaded. The written 'W' and 'N' are so similar I would settle for either.

October 15: Younger sister of Mrs Holland, widow of brother of Rector of Rose Ash, Devon, whose family provided eight generations of Rectors from 1675–1948.

October 19: John Chidgey married Hannah Rowdley, by Banns. No record of Christening on this day.

November 30: Edward Adolphus, 11th Duke 1775–1855. Eton and Christ Church, Oxon. Succeeded father 1793. FRS 1797, F Soc Antiquarians 1816, Linnean Soc 1820, Vice Pres Zoological Soc. 1826–31. KG 1837.

1801
December 17: The discovery of the 'Polden Hoard' in 1803 leads one to infer that some 'exploration' was underway for several years.
December 25: Leather leggings.

1802
January 3: William Bishop. An example of frequent disagreements with the Parish Register which gives January 8. It appears Holland entered the Registers only once weekly, mostly Friday or Sunday, and dated events for these days.
August 9: Anna Maria, widow of the tenth Duke. She lived in the Manor House at Monkton Farley. It is said, that according to her Will, she was buried 20 feet each way from the extreme SE corner of the Churchyard, 15 feet down.
August 23: Son of the Clerk of Aisholt.
September 10: William Davis of this Parish married Mary Patrick of Nether Stowey, by Licence.

1803
March 13: Buried James and Betty May
March 17: Mary, daughter and heiress of Holland's eldest brother John.
April 7: Caradock Butler, Vicar of Over Stowey 1691–1713
April 19: Mr Cobley, friend from earlier days, later Rector of Cheddar.
September 9: Rev Wollen was Rector of Bridgewater but lived mostly in Stowey.

1804
In one of the missing books under March 10 there would be an entry noting that Rev William Lewis was brought from Cannington and buried here. The Hollands continue their friendship with Mrs Lewis, frequently exchanging visits.
April 1: Mary, Robert, William and Charlotte the children of Wm and Mary E Edbrooke.

1805
February 6: This is the Horse at Cherhill. The other horse referred to is the one at Westbury. It is strange that there is no mention of Silbury Hill which they must have passed as they traversed the present A4.
March 6: Mrs Holland did not go with her husband to dine with the Duke and Duchess. – 'Though my wife was asked by the Duke yet as the Duchess sent no message my wife thought it best not to go, not wishing to intrude' – 'The Duchess said but little and I fear was displeased.' Contact between the Duke and Mr Holland did not resume until 1817.
August 19: Henry Singleton 1766–1839. Portrait painter of some distinction. R.A. Silver Medal 1784. Gold 1788.
August 25: Abraham and Isaac, sons of William and Betty Shallice, born August 1. These are the only twins noted in the twenty years of the Diary.

1806
December 31: Buried Thomas and Esther Selleck. Their mother is the Esther Selleck who had been Margaret's nursemaid.

1807
December 20: Rural Dean, Rev Parsons, Rector of Gothurst.

1808
January 11: William Windham 1750–1810. Secretary of State for War 1794–1802 and 1806–1807.
January 11: This friend of William later became Vicar of Overstowey.
June 30: John Couch was buried, killed by the Mill.
August 23: William Perrot buried, Late Parish Clerk.

December 11: From Parish Register:– Ann Palmer the Bastard of William Hill and Sarah Palmer, born October 27. Lavinia Hill the Bastard of George Adams and Elizabeth Hill, born October 25.

December 14: This is the first reference to Robert Dyer who had lately become Parish Clerk and was following the old Mr Amen in working as a day labourer for Holland. Later developments suggest he was the Servant who deserted his Master, as is detailed on November 23 1807. He was still remembered in the Parish in 1900.

1809

November 16: Joan Walford, buried August 30 1778, was murdered the year before Holland received the living of Overstowey.

December 30: When Holland later records the Baptism of these children he notes them as the base born son and daughter of —. This is his mildest term of censure. Another girl produces over the years offspring base born, Illegitimate and finally, Bastard.

1810

April 25: See also note December 11, 1808.

April 28: John Olman, widower of Box, married by Licence Susanna White spinster of this Parish. Holland does not enlarge on the behaviour with the Ring.

June 24: Thomas Milward, Vicar 1777–1779.

November 12: Robert Dyer married Phebe Symons. Witnesses John Dyere and Sarah Coxe. Both ladies made their mark.

1811

January 2: Baynton of Bristol, Surgeon and Medical Author. Noted for discoveries in the treatment of Ulcers and Wounds. 1797 wrote 'Descriptive account of a New Method of Treating Ulcers of the Leg.'

June 19: Present day values of the order £600 and £2500.

1812

November 5: Thanksgiving for the Discovery of Guy Fawkes. The Service was appointed by Act of Parliament and was based on the form of normal Morning Service. Holland had no Services except on Sunday or Holy Days. See also November 5 1815.

1813

April 24: Sister to Mrs Allen.

1814

January 7: Thermometer mounted in the Study.

February 14: The writing has become very thick and blotted. Next morning he continues with fine nibs.

March 19: Brother of Mrs Allen.

1815

November 24: By the end of the century each of these Parishes had its own Priest.

1816

March 3: Part of Marsh Mills.

July 9: School started largely by the efforts of Tom Poole.

July 15: New Canal – water supply to the Silk Mill.

1817

June 22: See note March 6, 1805.

September 18: Hartley Coleridge son of that Hoyden who appeared on October 23 1799. Tom Poole had maintained contact with the Coleridge family and this was certainly not the first visit.

1818
April 1: This is the only time he mentions April Fools' Day.
April 27: Old enough to be Ordained.
June 26: Vicar of Overstowey 1820–1856.
June 30: At 1983 values this would be of the order £250,000 for the Seat.

Dodwell Connection. An account of his election is given in 'A Parson in the Vale of the White Horse' – published by Alan Sutton. Pages 64–67.

An Historical Note on the Diaries

The existing forty-five books are now in the possession of Major C. F. Johnston of Newbury. His paternal grandfather was a nephew of Mrs Matilda Holland (née Bullock), the widow of the Reverend William Holland the son of the diarist. It appears that the diaries passed to Mr Johnston at Matilda's death in December 1905, for his son, C. E. Johnston, did some work with the present incomplete set in 1906 and 1907. Following this they were lost and unknown for many years until the present owner discovered them when winding up his mother's estate and clearing the proverbial attic.

Why only half the books were preserved is a mystery. One cannot think that Mrs Holland divided the set between her son and daughter as she did her silver when she 'came to Lodgings' (page 305), for the selection is much too random. It would appear rather that the present forty-five survived by being missed during a clearing operation and not by any deliberate act of conservation on the part of the Hollands. While there is a possibility that the missing books may yet come to light, this must be considered to be extremely unlikely.